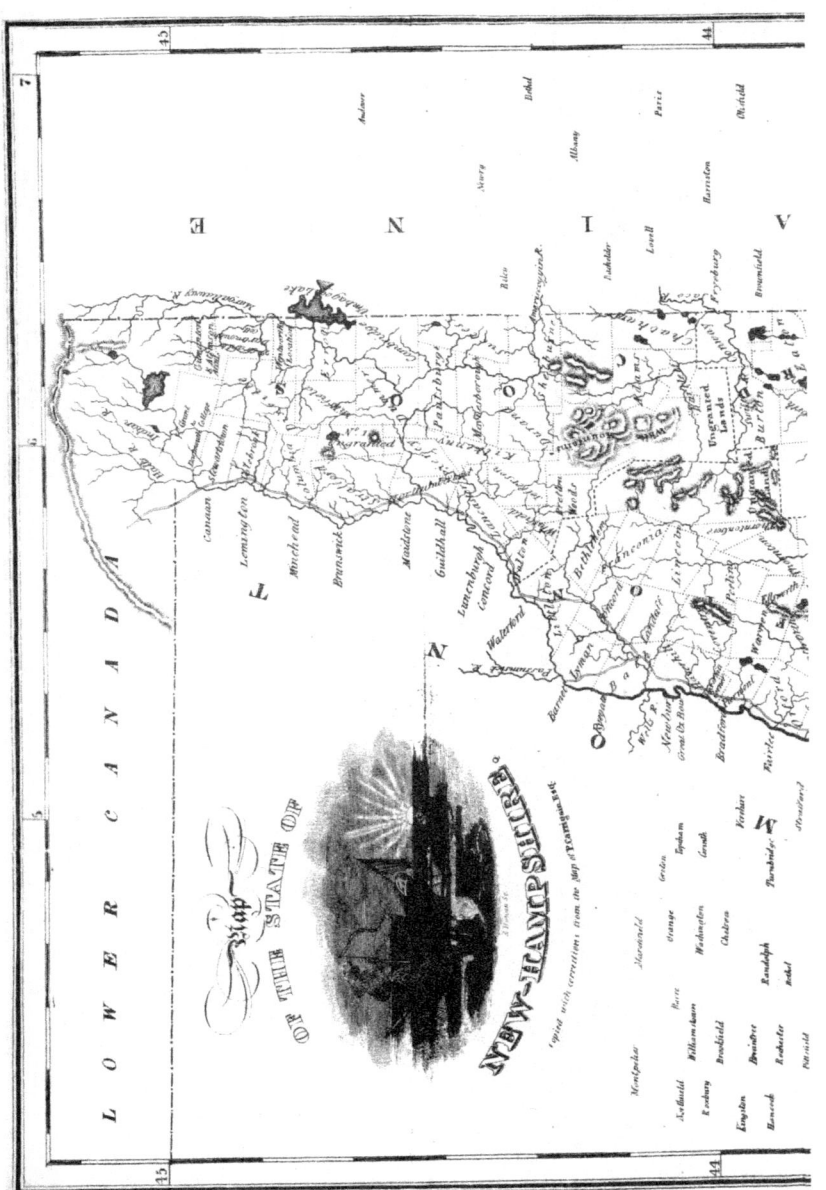

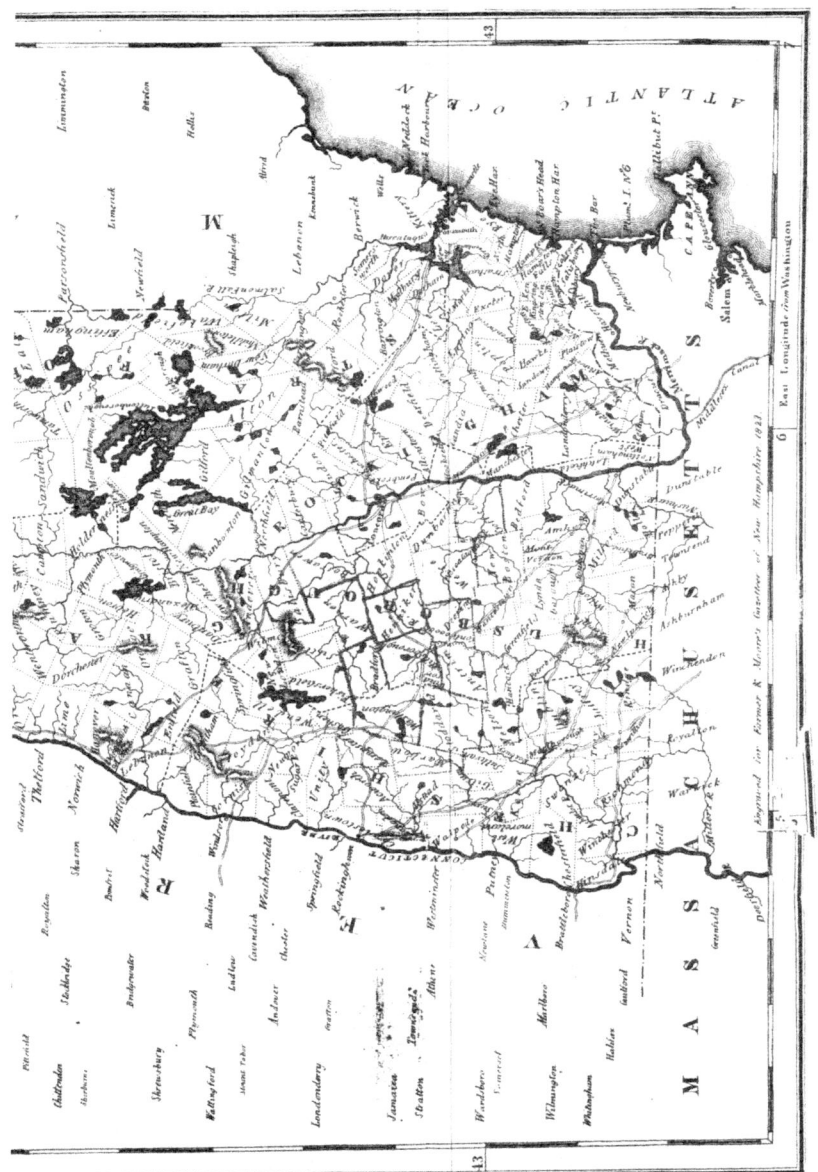

A
GAZETTEER
OF THE
STATE OF NEW-HAMPSHIRE

John Farmer
and Jacob B. Moore

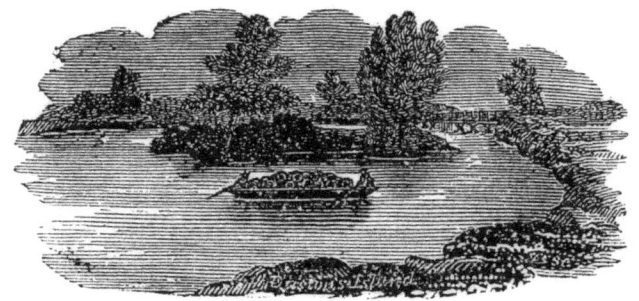

EMBELLISHED WITH AN ACCURATE MAP
OF THE STATE, AND SEVERAL OTHER
ENGRAVINGS BY ABEL BOWEN

HERITAGE BOOKS
2013

HERITAGE BOOKS
AN IMPRINT OF HERITAGE BOOKS, INC.

Books, CDs, and more—Worldwide

For our listing of thousands of titles see our website
at
www.HeritageBooks.com

A Facsimile Reprint
Published 2013 by
HERITAGE BOOKS, INC.
Publishing Division
5810 Ruatan Street
Berwyn Heights, Md. 20740

Copyright © 1997 Heritage Books, Inc.

NEW-HAMPSHIRE DISTRICT, TO WIT:
District Clerk's Office.

L. S. BE it remembered, that on the sixth day of May, A. D. 1823, and in the forty-seventh year of the Independence of the United States of America, JOHN FARMER and JACOB BAILEY MOORE, of the said district, have deposited in this office the title of a book, the right whereof they claim as authors, in the words following, to wit: "A Gazetteer of the State of New-Hampshire. By John Farmer and Jacob B. Moore. Embellished with an accurate Map of the State, and several other engravings: by Abel Bowen." In conformity to the act of the Congress of the United States, entitled "An act for the encouragement of learning, by securing the copies of maps, charts, and books, to the authors and proprietors of such copies, during the times therein mentioned;" and also, to an act, entitled, "An act supplementary to an act, entitled an act for the encouragement of learning by securing the copies of maps, charts, and books, to the authors and proprietors of such copies, during the times therein mentioned, and extending the benefits thereof to the arts of designing, engraving and etching historical and other prints."

WILLIAM CLAGGETT, *Clerk of the District of New-Hampshire.*
A true copy of record;—
Attest, WILLIAM CLAGGETT, *Clerk.*

Originally published by Jacob B. Moore, Concord: 1823

— Publisher's Notice —
In reprints such as this, it is often not possible to remove blemishes from the original. We feel the contents of this book warrant its reissue despite these blemishes and hope you will agree and read it with pleasure.

International Standard Book Numbers
Paperbound: 978-0-7884-0808-3
Clothbound: 978-0-7884-6800-1

PREFACE.

THE citizens of New-Hampshire are now presented with a new GAZETTEER of the State, compiled from original and authentic materials, and embracing the following subjects :

I. A general view of the State of New-Hampshire, comprehending the boundaries and area ; divisions ; face of the country ; soil and productions ; climate ; health and longevity ; mountains ; lakes and rivers ; canals ; turnpikes and bridges ; geology and mineralogy ; government and laws ; revenue and expenses ; militia ; population ; manufactures and commerce ; literary institutions ; education ; manners and customs ; religion ; societies ; banks ; state-house ; penitentiary ; curiosities ; Indians, and history.

II. A general view of the Counties, topographical and historical ; with statistical tables, exhibiting the number of meeting-houses, school-houses, taverns, stores, mills, factories, &c., in each.

III. A general description of Towns, and of all the mountains, lakes, ponds, rivers, &c., comprehending 1. A concise description of the several towns in the State, in relation to their boundaries, divisions, mountains, lakes, ponds, &c. 2. The early history of each town ; names of the first settlers, and what were their hardships and adventures ; instances of longevity, or of great mortality ; and short biographical notices of the most distinguished and useful men. 3. A concise notice of the formation of the first churches in the several towns ; the names of those who have been successively ordained as ministers, and the time of their settlement, removal or death. Also, notices of permanent charitable and other institutions, literary societies, &c.

It is unnecessary to offer an apology to the public for the appearance of a work, the utility of which, if well executed, no one will question. We rather claim indulgence, that so long a period has elapsed, since we first announced our intended publication. To have completed it at an earlier period, was originally our intention ; and it was not until several months of diligent inquiry had passed, that we understood the difficulty of the task in which we had engaged. Though in many cases, we have had prompt and able assistance, the difficulty of procuring the necessary information in others, has caused no inconsiderable anxiety and delay. Few men are intimately acquainted with the early history of their own towns—the generation active in the first settlements having passed away, and little pains being taken to preserve their history. Fewer still have the leisure or patience necessary to pore over musty records or ancient files, for the gratification of their curiosity, or the mere chance of finding perhaps some single fact, buried like the diamond in a mass of rubbish. While, on the one hand, our anxiety increased to finish the work, and be rid of its labor ; we felt, on the other, a strong obligation to retain it in our hands, until we could give it at least a tolerable degree of accuracy. The book is at length completed. And embracing, as it does, a great variety of information, we cannot but hope it may be useful to the public. To escape errors entirely, was impossible ; but we trust their number and magnitude will be found as small as the nature of such an undertaking will permit. In our biographical notices, it was our intention to present facts, rather than estimates of character. Many worthy and eminent persons we may not have noticed ; and our excuse must be the want of necessary information. In the several statistical tables, we have conformed to the latest returns received. The population at the present time is in some instances given ; but more generally that of 1820. Distances are generally given from the centre of the towns, or from the principal village. They are stated from the most correct information we could obtain. When the distance is said to be from Concord, the seat of government is intended. The names of clergymen now in office are printed in italics. At the close of the work will be found some additional facts, relating to the several towns, which came to our knowledge after the book had been put to press ; and also some corrections. In the appendix is given a table of population at different periods, and also a list of the former names of the several towns.

In the prosecution of our labors, we have been much indebted to the obliging attentions of SAMUEL SPARHAWK, Esq., the Secretary of State ; to the Hon. WILLIAM PLUMER, Hon. SAMUEL BELL, Prof. JAMES F. DANA, Gen. JOSEPH LOW, ADINO N. BRACKETT, Esq. and others. We would gladly tender our acknowledgments to our numerous correspondents individually ; but trust that a sufficient reason for the omission will be seen in the fact, that we have written, received and consulted more than a thousand letters and communications. We lay claim to no merit, other than that of patience and an unwearied effort to be correct. How far we have succeeded in our labors, and whether we shall receive an adequate reward, will appear, when the public shall have had time to examine, and shall feel disposed to patronize the work.

GENERAL VIEW

OF THE

State of New-Hampshire.

COMPREHENDING

BOUNDARIES AND AREA; DIVISIONS; FACE OF THE COUNTRY, SOIL AND PRODUCTIONS; CLIMATE; HEALTH AND LONGEVITY; MOUNTAINS; LAKES AND RIVERS; CANALS; TURNPIKES AND BRIDGES; GEOLOGY AND MINERALOGY; GOVERNMENT AND LAWS; REVENUE AND EXPENSES; MILITIA; POPULATION; MANUFACTURES AND COMMERCE; LITERARY INSTITUTIONS; EDUCATION; MANNERS AND CUSTOMS; RELIGION; SOCIETIES; BANKS; STATE-HOUSE; PENITENTIARY; CURIOSITIES; INDIANS; HISTORY.

BOUNDARIES AND AREA.—The state of New-Hampshire is situated between 42°, 41′, and 45°, 11′, north latitude; and between 70°, 40′, and 72°, 28′, longitude west from Greenwich. Its extreme length from north to south is 168 miles—its greatest width, 90 miles. North of lat. 43°, the state decreases in width, and at the northern extremity is only 19 miles wide. This state is bounded N. on the highlands between Lower Canada and the United States; W. by the western bank of Connecticut river, from its northerly source to the south point of Hinsdale, below the entrance of Ashuelot river; S. by Massachusetts; E. by the Atlantic, a distance of eighteen miles, and by the state of Maine. This territory comprises an area of 9,491 square miles, or 6,074,240 acres, including about 110,000 acres of water.

DIVISIONS.—The state is divided into six counties, and two hundred seventeen towns, beside several locations and grants; and the public lands.

STATISTICAL TABLE.

COUNTIES.	No. Twns	POPULATION.				SEATS OF JUSTICE.
		1790.	1800.	1810.	1820.	
Rockingham..	45	43,169	45,427	50,175	55,246	*Concord, Exeter.*
Strafford.......	31	23,742	32,878	41,595	51,117	*Dover, Gilford.*
Hillsborough..	42	32,871	43,899	49,249	53,884	*Amherst, Hopk'n.*
Cheshire........	37	28,772	38,825	40,988	45,376	*Keene, Charlestn.*
Grafton.........	37	12,449	20,171	28,462	32,989	*Haverhill, Plymo.*
Coos.............	25	882	2,658	3,991	5,549	*Lancaster.*
Total,	217	141,885	183,858	214,460	244,161	

FACE OF THE COUNTRY, SOIL AND PRODUCTIONS.—The whole extent of our sea-coast is but eighteen miles, from the S. E. corner of the town of Seabrook to the mouth of the Pascataqua. The shore is in most places a sandy beach, bordered by salt-marshes. For the distance of 20 or 30 miles back from the sea, the country is generally level, occasionally diversified with hills and valleys. Beyond this, the hills increase in size and number, and in many parts of the state swell into lofty mountains, particularly in the north, and along the heights between the Merrimack and Connecticut. The highest summits between these two rivers, are, the *Monadnock*, in Dublin; *Sunapee* mountain, in Fishersfield; *Kearsarge*, in Warner; *Carr's* mountain, in Ellsworth and Warren, and the *Mooschillock*, or *Mooshelock*, in Coventry. But the highest mountains in the state, and the most elevated on this side the Mississippi, are the *White Mountains.* The scenery about these mountains, and other numerous elevations—the lakes, cascades, &c. are exceedingly beautiful; and the classic author of the state map has very properly styled it "the Switzerland of America."

The SOIL of New Hampshire is generally fertile, presenting in different sections all the varieties common to New-England. The best lands are undoubtedly those on the borders of our larger rivers, which being frequently covered by the waters, are enriched by the sediment left when they subside. Our wide spreading hills, being of a rocky, moist and warm soil, afford the greenest pasturage and support immense numbers of cattle and sheep. Barrens in any extent are unknown, and with the exception of the wild and unexplored regions of the north, the state is very generally capable of cultivation.

The great pursuit of the inhabitants is, and must continue to be agriculture;* and in this art, improvements are constantly making. The introduction of gypsum, or plaister of Paris, the establishment and active exertions of agricultural societies, and the increased zeal of all professions to promote the interests of the farmer, upon whom all ultimately depend—are circumstances highly favorable. Every opening which is made in our forests, displays for the use of man a soil that richly rewards cultivation. Maize, wheat, rye, oats, barley, flax, &c. are the common products; and vast quantities of pork, beef, mutton, poultry, butter and cheese are annually exported. Hemp has in some instances been successfully cultivated, and, it is believed, might be made a source of great profit to the farmer. The quantities raised of different productions on the acre are various. On the intervals which border our rivers, wheat often yields 20 or 30 bushels, though from 15 to 20 is considered a good crop. Indian corn will average 30 or 40 bushels to the acre, and potatoes from 200 to 300. Instances of extraordinary crops, however, prove that with due cultivation our soil may in general be made to yield in far greater profusion.

Of FRUIT we have a variety. No country in the world produces more abundant crops of apples, and our cider, by proper management, may be made of the first quality. Peaches, and other fruit requiring a warm climate, do not flourish here; but pears, plums, cherries, and various excellent wild fruits grow in abundance. Prunes of fine flavor are found in the neighborhood of Lancaster. Our gardens, though less attention is paid to them than taste or usefulness would seem to require, still furnish a long list of fruits and vegetables that grow in abundance and in great variety.

The Botany of New-Hampshire should of itself form the subject of a volume. Our native forest trees are lofty and luxuriant. No country produces better timber, and vast quantities are annually exported. This state was originally an entire forest—the mountainous regions covered with a thick growth of oak, maple, beech, walnut, hemlock, fir, white pine, &c.; the plains and valleys with the elm, cherry, ash, poplar, hornbeam, birch, sumach, locust, and many others. Of the pine we have several varieties. The white pine is perhaps the noblest tree in the world: its stem, though sometimes of the height of 260 feet, is perfectly straight, and crowned with a beautiful tuft of green. It sometimes

---

* The number engaged in agriculture in New-Hampshire, in 1820, was 52,384; in commerce, 1,068; in manufactures, 8,699.

exceeds six feet in diameter.* The pitch pine, which also grows to a great height, is a beautiful tree. The hemlock is often a tree of great height and size. The fir and other species of pine grow to a more moderate height. Of the oak, elm, birch, maple, &c. we have varieties.— The *hard*, or *rock* maple, is the *sugar* maple of this region, and grows to a great height, yielding a sap which makes the finest sugar. The *red* and *white* maple also yield sugar, but in less quantities than the hard.

Of wild plants and roots valuable for culinary and medicinal purposes, we have a great variety. The ginseng, so much esteemed by the Chinese, and long supposed to be found only in China and Tartary, is found in abundance and of good quality. The buck bean grows in Peterborough and some other places; the true *uva ursi*, or bear's whortle-berry, and *cornus sericea*, or large flowering dogwood, at Kingston and in other parts. Lobelia, henbane, cicuta, &c. are common in various parts of the state.

CLIMATE, &c.—The climate varies in temperature from a range of the thermometer of 15° below the zero of Fahrenheit to 95° above it. The mercury rarely descends to 20° below 0, except in an unusually cold winter. In the month of February, 1818, during several days, it sunk from 20 to 30° below 0, and once, on the 11th, at 7, A. M. it descended to 32°. In several winters since, in different parts of the state, it has been noticed at 20° below 0. The highest degree which has been noticed for the last seventeen years, was in July, 1811, when the mercury was at 98°; and in July, 1820, when it stood at 100°. Such instances very rarely occur. The air of New-Hampshire is pure and salubrious. During the winter months, the prevailing wind is generally from the N. W., the coldness of which has been attributed to various causes.— European philosophers have supposed the cold of our N. W. winds to proceed *from the great lakes*, which lie in the interior of North-America. But since it has been fully known that the great lakes lie westward of the true N. W. point, this opinion has been exploded. A second cause to which the coldness of these winds has been attributed is, *a chain of high mountains running from S. W. to N. E.* in Canada and New-Britain, at a great distance beyond the St. Lawrence. A third opinion is that of the venerable Dr. Holyoke, of Salem, who supposes that *the numerous evergreens in this country* are the source of the peculiar cold

---

* " Anno 1736, near Merrimack river, a little above Dunstable, was cut a white pine, straight and sound, 7 feet 8 inches in diameter at the butt end."
Douglass, vol. ii. p. 53.

which it experiences. A fourth opinion is, that the coldness of these winds proceeds from the *forested state of the country.* The late President Dwight entertained an opinion different from all those we have mentioned, viz. that the winds which generate the peculiar cold of this country *descend, in most cases, from the superior regions of the atmosphere.** The N. W. wind rarely brings snow, but when it does, the degree of cold is increased. The deepest snows fall with a N. E. wind, and storms from that quarter are most violent and of longest duration. On the mountains, the snow falls earlier and remains later than in the low grounds. On those elevated summits, the winds have greater force in driving the snow into the long and deep gullies of the mountains, where it is so consolidated, as not to be dissolved by the vernal sun.— Spots of snow are seen on the south sides of mountains as late as May, and on the highest till July. A S. E. storm is often as violent, but commonly shorter, than one from the N. E. If it begin with snow, it soon changes to rain. A brisk wind from the W. or S. W. with snow or rain, sometimes happens, but its duration is very short. Squalls of this kind are common in March.

One of the greatest inconveniences suffered by the inhabitants of our country, is derived from the frequent changes in the state of the atmosphere. At Portsmouth, in January, 1810, the change of temperature in about 24 hours was 44° of Fahrenheit. In other places it was equally great. Similar changes, which are disagreeable and cannot but be injurious to health, are frequent, though not in the same degree. Changes from wet to dry, and from dry to wet, are at times unpleasant, and probably unhealthy. There is no month in the year which is not sometimes very pleasant, and sometimes disagreeable. In a series of years, our most pleasant months are June, September and October. Often the first two, and not unfrequently the first three weeks in September are, however, very warm. From the 20th of September to the 20th of October, the weather is delightful. The temperature is mild, the air is sweet, and the sky singularly bright and beautiful. This is the period denominated the Indian Summer. Some persons will think June to be a more pleasant month than either September or October. In June, there are usually a few days of intense heat. In all other respects, except the brilliancy and beauty of the heavens, this month must be confessed to have the su-

---

* See Dwight's Travels, vol. i. page 65.

periority over those last mentioned. The progress of vegetation is wonderful; and it seems as if the creative hand was, in the literal sense, renewing its original plastic efforts, to adorn the world with richness and splendor. All things are alive and gay. "The little hills rejoice on every side. The pastures are clothed with flocks. The valleys are also covered with corn, and shout for joy." Health at the same time prevails in a peculiar degree. The Spring is often chilled by easterly winds and rendered uncomfortable by rains. The Winter is the season for enjoyment to the active part of the community.

The number of fair days in a year compared with the cloudy, is as 3 to 1. We have had but few meteorological journals kept and published in this state. For several years past they have become more frequent, and it is hoped, that from the increasing attention to the subject, comparative results of the weather will become more numerous and exact. [For further remarks on this subject, the reader is referred to Belknap's Hist. N. H. and Dwight's Travels in New-England, &c.]

HEALTH AND LONGEVITY.—New-Hampshire may be justly considered a healthy section of our country. Epidemics have seldom spread throughout the state. The most memorable were the *cynanche maligna*, or putrid sore throat, which first made its appearance at Kingston, in May, 1735, and the *petechial*, or spotted fever, which appeared in different places in 1811 and several succeeding years. The healthiness of this state may, in a general manner, be estimated from the increase of its inhabitants, and from the great number of instances of longevity which it has furnished. We have only room to notice those instances where persons have attained their hundredth year, or have lived, or exceeded a complete century. These, so far as practicable, will be given in chronological order.

Instances of longevity in New-Hampshire, with the places of residence and the time when each person died, and their ages.

1732	William Perkins, of New-Market,	116
1736	John Buss, of Durham,	108
1739	James Wilson, of Chester,	100
1754	William Scoby, of Londonderry,	110
1754	James Shirley, of Chester,	105
1765	Elizabeth Hight, of Newington,	100
1772	Howard Henderson, of Dover,	100
1775	William Craige, of Chester,	100
1775	Mrs. Craige, (his wife) of Chester,	100
1775	Mrs. Lear, of Portsmouth,	103
1775	Mrs. Mayo, of Portsmouth,	106
1787	Robert Macklin, of Wakefield,	115

1789	Mrs. Ulrick, of Hollis,	104
1790	Mrs. Hayley, of Exeter,	101
1791	Jacob Green, of Hanover,	100
1791	Widow Davis,	102
1791	James Shirley, of Chester,	100
1793	James Wilson, of Chester,	100
1800	Sarah Newmarch, of Portsmouth,	101
1800	Thomas Wason, of Chester,	100
1801	Ezekiel Leathers, of Durham,	100
1802	Abednego Leathers, of Durham,	101
1805	Hannah Lovejoy, of Amherst,	102
1808	Martha Chesmore, of Dunbarton,	101
1808	Daniel Davis, of Allenstown,	105
1808	Margaret Bacon,	101
1808	Mrs. M'Clench, of Merrimack,	100
1808	Martha Porter, of Lebanon,	100
1808	Catherine Sherburne, of Conway,	101
1809	Joshua Foss, of Barrington,	100
1810	Catharine Sanborn, of Saubornton,	100
1810	Mrs. Hixon. of Portsmouth,	100
1810	Tabitha Bohonnon, of Salisbury,	101
1811	Mrs. M'Intire, of Goffstown,	106
1811	Ezra Deolph, of Hopkinton,	102
1811	Mary Bean, of Sutton,	100
1811	Nathan Blake, of Keene,	100
1811	Benjamin Conner, of Exeter,	100
1812	James Atwood, of Pelham,	100
1813	Joanna Hixon, of Newington,	105
1813	Mary Davidson, of Goffstown,	100
1815	Anna Leavitt, of Hampton,	100
1815	Sarah Morse, of Salem,	100
1815	John Shaw, of Holderness,	101
1815	John Crocker, of Richmond,	100
1816	Elizabeth Richards, of Newington,	101
1816	Phebe Dow, of Seabrook,	101
1816	Zene, (a negro) of Nottingham,	101
1817	Elizabeth Darling, of Portsmouth,	102
1817	Elizabeth Pitman, of Epsom,	100
1817	Abigail Craig, of Rumney,	105
1817	Mrs. Bunker, of Barnstead,	105
1817	Mary Fernald, of Portsmouth,	100
1818	Hannah Foss, of Gilmanton,	103
1818	Dorcas Rowe, of Meredith,	100
1818	Dye, (of Indian descent) of Exeter,	105
1818	Corydon, (a negro) of Exeter,	100
1819	Eleanor Pike, of Meredith,	101
1819	Jacob Davis, of Sutton,	105
1819	William Prescott, of Gilford,	102
1820	Dorothy Creighton, of Epping,	101
1820	Samuel Downs, of Somersworth,	100

1820	Mrs. Cilley, of Poplin,	101
1821	Jonathan Foster, of Mason,	101
1821	Joanna Aplin, of Keene,	100
1821	Jane M'Lellan, of Wentworth,	100
1821	Mrs. Godfrey, of Deerfield,	101
1821	Mary Smith, of Salem,	101
1822	Reuben Abbot, of Concord,	100
1822	Thomas Walker, of Sutton,	103

Of uncertain date.

Mr. Lovewell, of Dunstable, (father to Col. Zaccheus Lovewell, mentioned in Belknap's Hist. N. H. vol. ii. page 233) aged	120
Mrs. Belknap, of Atkinson,	107
Mrs. Tucker, of Rye,	100
Mrs. Beals, of Keene,	101
Mrs. Parker, of Chesterfield,	103
Mrs. Welch, of Rumney,	100

Besides the preceding list of aged persons who have deceased, there are still living in this state the following persons over 100 years of age : *Tryphena Stiles*, of Somersworth, 101 ; *Sarah Kelley*, of New-Hampton, 103 ; *Mrs. Bailey*, of Chesterfield, 101 ; *Mary Barnard*, of Amherst, 101 ; and the venerable *Samuel Welch*, of Bow, in his 113th year.

The annual average number of deaths in New-Hampshire, is estimated at about 3000. This number has been obtained by taking the mean annual average of a number of towns in different parts of the state for a series of years, and making a comparison, by the rule of proportion, between those towns and the other towns in the state.

MOUNTAINS.—The mountains of New-Hampshire, particularly in the north part of the state, furnish a rich profusion of the sublime and beautiful. They are the highest on this side of Mexico, and are not exceeded in wildness and grandeur by the mountains of Europe. 'Tis true our majestic hills are not yet adorned with classical recollections, like the Pays de Vaud, or the pass of St. Bernard, still we have the infinitely varied landscape of forest-covered hills, woods, groves, orchards, villas, and all that can charm in the magnificence of nature. Those who cannot have an opportunity to visit the Cordilleras, or Mont-Blanche, or other towering hills of the old and new world, may here gratify their taste and curiosity by ascending the White Mountains. Here, although they can see no " blue Rhone" rushing or meandering at their feet, they may behold the majestic Connecticut rolling along the valley—the Merrimack streaming from the bowels of the mountain—and the Saco tumbling down its sides.

The first range of hills in this state is about 30 miles from the sea, ex-

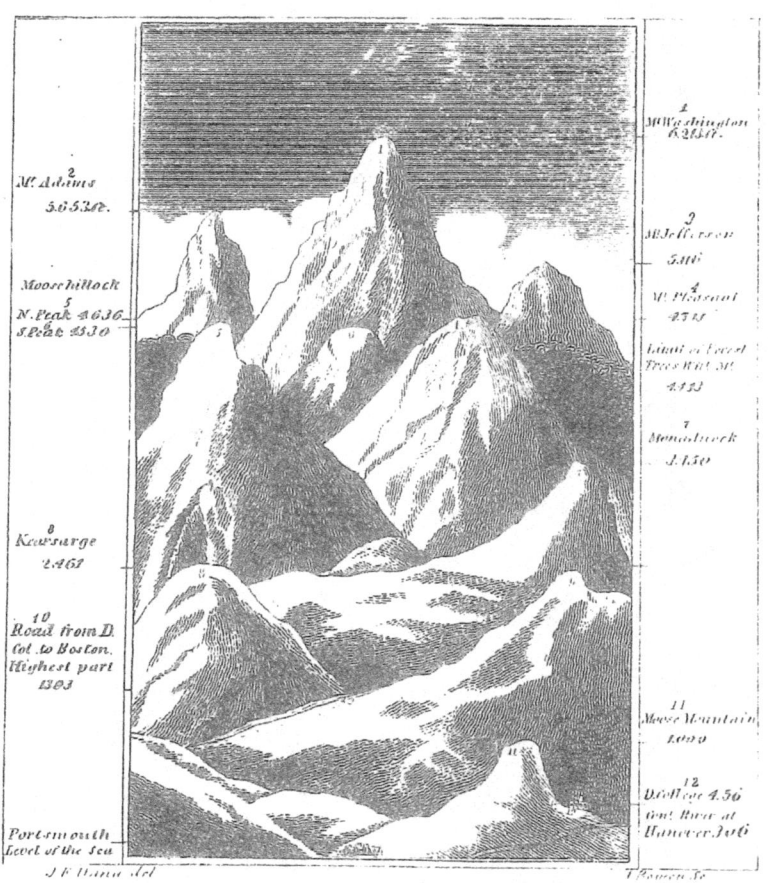

COMPARATIVE VIEW

Of the Heights of Mountains &c. in N. Hampshire.

tending through Rochester, Nottingham, &c. and of no great height. Further back, Moose and Ossipee mountains appear, of higher elevation. The White Mountain range extends from the western part of the state, between the waters of the Connecticut and Merrimack, N. by E. till beyond the sources of the Pemigewasset, and thence N. E. by N. towards the sources of the Ameriscoggin. The Sunapee and Monadnock mountains are parts of the grand chain. For a particular description of these mountains, see articles under their respective heads. There are several ranges of mountains north of Lancaster, extending from the neighborhood of Connecticut river, in a right angled direction to its course. The first is Little Moosehillock, beginning in Northumberland and running east toward the north limit of the White Mountains. The second is called the Peaks, and commences in Stratford. The third range lies north of Stratford. The fourth is the range of Preston hills, in Columbia. There are no other mountains in New-England which run in the same direction.

The plate annexed will afford a very correct view of the comparative heights of our principal mountains. Their altitudes have been ascertained with much accuracy by means of the barometer and thermometer. The heights of Mounts Washington, Adams, Jefferson and Pleasant, the Moosehillock and Kearsarge, by Capt. PARTRIDGE; the Monadnock, Moose mountain, &c. by Dr. DANA; and the limit of forest trees on the mountains, by Dr. BIGELOW.

LAKES AND RIVERS.—The largest body of water in New-Hampshire is *Winnepisiogee* lake. It is of very unequal width, varying from 1 to 8 miles, and is 22 miles in length, from S. E. to N. W. Beside this lake, are *Squam, Ossipee, Newfound, Sunapee* and *Spafford's* lakes, and lake *Connecticut*, in the extreme north part of the state. A part of *Umbagog* lake lies within this state, and its waters are discharged into the Ameriscoggin, which passes within a short distance of the lake. Five of the largest rivers in New-England have their principal sources in this state—the *Connecticut, Merrimack, Ameriscoggin, Saco* and *Pascataqua*.* There are numerous other considerable streams watering the various parts of the state—all which are noticed under the proper heads.

---

* In using this word in the following work, we shall follow the orthography of Dr. Belknap. In our most ancient records, it is written *Pascataquack*, but was most commonly pronounced *Pascatawa*. With the aboriginals, the last syllable probably had a strong aspirate, as *Pascataquah*.

CANALS.—Twenty canal companies have been incorporated in this state since the year 1776—some of which, however, were never organized, and others never went into effectual operation. The canals on the Connecticut river are three: at Bellows-Falls, opposite Walpole; at Waterqueechy, opposite Plainfield, and at White river, in Lebanon.— The expense of these works was about $36,000. The canals which unite the waters of the Merrimack with those of Boston harbor, were originated by public spirited individuals as early as 1789. From Boston a water communication has been opened by the Middlesex canal, thro' twenty locks, a distance of twenty-seven miles, to the Merrimack river at the bend in Chelmsford,—at the cost of $520,000; thence the Merrimack was made boatable, by works at Wicassee falls in Massachusetts, at the expense of $14,000; through the Union locks and canals, over seven falls in the river, at the cost of $50,000; thence over Amoskeag falls, forty-five feet perpendicular height, thirty miles from the head of the canal, at the cost of $50,000; thence over Hooksett falls, sixteen feet height, at the cost of $17,000; thence through Bow canal, twenty-five feet height, at the expense of $21,000, to the upper landing in Concord, eighty-five miles from Boston:—the whole cost amounting to $627,000. The communication which these great works have opened, is annually becoming more important to the country.

In 1811, a charter was granted, which has since been renewed, empowering a company of individuals to cut a canal and lock all the falls between the Winnepisiogee lake, and the Cocheco branch of the Pascataqua, below the landing in Dover. The distance is twenty-seven miles. The waters of the lake are 452 feet above the level of the Pascataqua—and the fall would require fifty-three locks. The expense would not probably exceed $300,000. The opening of this canal, if it should hereafter be effected, will extend to more than fourteen hundred square miles of territory, bordering on the lake and rivers, the benefits of a boat navigation to Portsmouth. The communication might be made to extend still further, beyond the lake to within three or four miles of the Pemigewasset river; and even beyond this, through Plymouth, as far as Wentworth, if not into the Connecticut. The great advantages which would result from the accomplishment of this object, will, it is hoped, hereafter induce more successful efforts. The immense quantities of fine timber on the borders of the lake and its numerous islands, would offer facilities in the building of vessels of war unequalled in the United States. And, in connection with the safe and commodious harbor at Portsmouth, the opening of the canal would seem to be an object meriting the attention of the national government.

A company has also been incorporated for the purpose of continuing the great works on the Merrimack, and as a connection with others contemplated to extend to the Winnepisiogee lake in that direction. Independent of this connection, however, the utility of the design is unquestionable—as it would greatly facilitate the trade of the interior with the capital of New-England. But the expense of the work will probably defeat the enterprize, unless the aid of government is afforded.

The canal long talked of between the Merrimack and Connecticut rivers, through Sunapee lake, has been found to be impracticable. A survey was made in 1816, and the fall each way from the lake to these rivers was found to be more than 800 feet, much greater than that of the Languedoc canal, the largest in Europe. The expense of the locks and canals would probably exceed two millions of dollars.

TURNPIKES AND BRIDGES.—There have been created by the authority of this state fifty-three turnpike corporations, of which the following are the principal:

The *New-Hampshire Turnpike Road*, incorporated June, 1796—from Pascataqua bridge, Durham, Lee, Barrington, Nottingham, Northwood, Epsom, Chichester, Concord, to Merrimack river—distance 36 miles.

The *Second N. H. Turnpike Road*, incorporated Dec. 26, 1799—from Claremont, Unity, Lempster, Washington, corner of Windsor, of Hillsborough and of Antrim, Deering, Francestown, corner of Lyndeborough and New-Boston, Mont-Vernon, Amherst—distance 50 miles—cost $80,000.

The *Third Turnpike Road in New-Hampshire*, incorporated Dec. 27, 1799—from Bellows-Falls in Walpole, Westmoreland, Surry, Keene, Marlborough, Jaffrey, New-Ipswich, Ashby, Ms. in a direction toward Boston—distance 50 miles—cost $50,000.

The *Fourth N. H. Turnpike Road*, incorporated Dec. 1800—from Connecticut river, Lebanon, Enfield, corner of Grafton, Springfield, Wilmot, Andover, Salisbury, Boscawen, to Merrimack river—distance 40 miles.

The *Branch Road and Bridge Company*—incorporated June 16, 1802—from Keene, corner of Swanzey, Marlborough, to north line of Fitzwilliam—distance 7 miles 195 rods—cost $7,510.

The *Fifth N. H. Turnpike Road*.

The *Sixth N. H. Turnpike Road and Bridge Company*—incorporated June 16, 1802—from Brattleborough, Vt. bridge over Connecticut river, Hinsdale, Winchester, to Massachusetts line at Warwick—cost $16,000.

NEW-HAMPSHIRE GAZETTEER.

Proprietors Dover Turnpike Road—incorporated Dec. 21, 1803—from Dover, Somersworth, to Berwick, Me.—distance 4 1-2 miles.

Coos Turnpike Road—incorporated Dec. 29, 1803—from Haverhill, Piermont, Warren—distance 12 miles—cost $15,074.

Orford Turnpike Road—incorporated Dec. 27, 1803.

The *Tenth N. H. Turnpike Road*—incorporated Dec. 28, 1803—from west line of Bartlett, Nash and Sawyer's and Hart's Locations, through the notch of the White Hills—distance 20 miles—expense $40,000.

The *Charlestown Turnpike Road*—incorporated Dec. 27, 1803—from Charlestown, Acworth, to Second N. H. Turnpike in Lempster—distance 12 miles.

The *Mayhew Turnpike Road*—incorporated Dec. 29, 1803—from New-Chester, Bristol, Hebron, corner of Plymouth, toward Haverhill—distance 17 miles.

The *Chester Turnpike Road*—incorporated June 12, 1804—from Pembroke, Allenstown, Candia, to Chester—distance 14 miles.

The *Londonderry Turnpike Road*—incorporated June, 1804—from Concord, Bow, Hooksett, Chester, Londonderry, corner of Windham, Salem, to line of Massachusetts—distance 35 miles.

Grafton Turnpike Road—incorporated June 21, 1804—from Orford, Lime, corner of Hanover, Canaan, Orange, Grafton, Danbury, New-Chester, to the Fourth N. H. Turnpike in Andover—distance 35 miles.

The *Jefferson Turnpike Road*—incorporated Dec. 11, 1804—from Lancaster, Jefferson, Bretton-Woods, to the Tenth N. H. Turnpike—distance 14 miles—cost $18,400.

The *Croydon Turnpike Road*—incorporated June 21, 1804—from Lebanon, corner of Plainfield, Grantham, Croydon, Newport, Lempster, to Second N. H. Turnpike in Washington—distance 34 miles—expense $35,948.

The *Cheshire Turnpike Road*—incorporated Dec. 13, 1804—from Charlestown, Langdon, part of Walpole, Alstead, Surry, to Third N. H. Turnpike in Keene—distance 24 miles—cost $19,610.

The *Ashuelot Turnpike Road*—incorporated June 18, 1807—from the Sixth N. H. Turnpike in Winchester, Richmond, Fitzwilliam-Village—distance 15 miles.

Rindge Turnpike Road—incorporated June 12, 1807—from Branch Turnpike in Fitzwilliam, through Rindge, to line of Massachusetts, at corner of New-Ipswich—distance 4 miles.

The *Cornish Turnpike Road*—incorporated Dec. 9, 1808—from Cornish Bridge to Croydon Turnpike in Newport—distance 11 miles.

Hampton Causeway Turnpike Corporation—incorporated Dec. 23, 1808, in Hampton—distance 1 3-4 miles—cost $14.173 66.

The *Fitzwilliam Village Turnpike Road*— incorporated Dec. 9, 1809—from village in Fitzwilliam to line of Massachusetts—distance 4 1-2 miles.

Londonderry Branch Turnpike Road—from Hooksett, Bow, to Hopkinton—distance 11 miles.

The *Sanbornton Turnpike Road*—from Sanbornton to New-Hampton—distance 10 miles.

There have been fifty-nine BRIDGE companies incorporated within this state, some of which have been broken up, and their bridges removed. The following are the principal bridges in the state:

Brattleborough Bridge, built in 1804, over Connecticut river, between Hinsdale and Brattleborough, Vt.—expense $16,000, with 16 miles road by same corporation.

Westmoreland Bridge, over Connecticut river, from Westmoreland to Putney, Vt.—430 feet length, 24 feet width—cost $9,160.

Walpole Village Bridge, over Connecticut river, from Walpole to Westminster, Vt.—540 feet length, 28 feet width—cost $5,852.

Bellows-Falls Bridge, built in 1797, over Connecticut river, from Walpole to Rockingham, Vt., 180 feet length, 27 feet width.

Cheshire Bridge, over Connecticut river, from Charlestown to Springfield, Vt.

Cornish Bridge, over Connecticut river, from Cornish to Windsor, Vt.

White-River Bridge, over Connecticut river, from Lebanon to Hartland, Vt.

Hanover Bridge, over Connecticut river, from Hanover to Norwich, Vt.

Orford Bridge, built in 1802, over Connecticut river, from Orford to Fairlee, Vt.—cost $6,500.

Bedell's Bridge, built in 1804, over Connecticut river, from Haverhill to Newbury, Vt.—cost $3,800.

Haverhill Bridge, over Connecticut river, from Haverhill to Newbury, Vt.

Lancaster Bridge, over Connecticut river, from Lancaster to Guildhall, Vt.

Northumberland Bridge, over Connecticut river, from Northumberland to Maidstone, Vt.

Hooksett Bridge, over Merrimack river, in Hooksett.

Concord Bridge, over the Merrimack river, in Concord.

Federal Bridge, over the same river, in Concord.

Boscawen Bridge, over the Merrimack river, between Boscawen and Concord.

Canterbury Bridge, over Merrimack river, from Boscawen to Canterbury.

Republican Bridge, over Pemigewasset river, from Salisbury to Sanbornton.

New-Chester Union Bridge, over Pemigewasset river, from New-Chester to Sanbornton.

Pemigewasset Bridge, over Pemigewasset river, from Bristol to New-Hampton.

Stratham & New-Market Bridge, over Exeter river, from Stratham to New-Market.

Pascataqua Bridge, built 1793, over Pascataqua river, from Newington to Durham—2600 feet in length, 40 feet wide—cost $65,401.

New-Castle Bridge, from Portsmouth to New-Castle, built in 1821—2370 feet long, 20 feet wide—cost $7000.

Portsmouth Bridge, over the Pascataqua, from Portsmouth to Ham's Island, 500 feet, and from thence over the main channel to Kittery, Me. 1650 feet, width 40 feet—cost $40,000.

GEOLOGY AND MINERALOGY.—The tract of country embraced within the bounds of the state of New-Hampshire, is rough, broken and uneven, and is decidedly of *primitive* formation. The high ridge of mountains which divides the branches of the Merrimack and Connecticut from each other, has a N. E. and S. W. direction; it is composed of the older primitive rocks. Granite predominates at the northern and more elevated part of the ridge, while mica slate appears more abundantly at the southern portions, where it forms the Grand Monadnock and several other very elevated eminences. Mica slate is the predominant rock in this chain; but throughout its whole extent granite appears in various places, and frequently, as at Hillsborough, Andover, Wilmot, &c. It has a coarse porphyritic structure; the imbedded grains of feldspar are large, but very seldom in twin crystals. Porphyritic granite occurs also in boulders and in rolled masses in many places eastward of this ridge. A beautiful fine grained granite occurs in many parts of the state, both *in situ* and in boulders and rolled masses; particularly at Concord, Boscawen, Hopkinton, &c. This also probably constitutes the bald rugged peak in the vicinity of Hooksett falls. This granite affords an admirable building stone; large quantities are used in the vicinity of the rocks and are transported to Boston for various architectural purposes. The Capitol and State-Prison at Concord are built of this rock.—It derives its superiority over the granite of many other countries from the circumstance that it contains no sulphuret of iron, which, by the action of atmospheric agents, produces an iron-rust stain, which destroys the beauty of the material.

Eastward of this great ridge, mica slate, gneiss and greenstone are found; but with the more particular geological features we are unacquainted.

A remarkable alluvial formation, which may with propriety be called the *Merrimack Alluvion*, is worthy of notice : through this formation the river Merrimack passes, and by it, is embraced all those sandy plains which are covered with pine and black timber, in the neighborhood of the river. The towns of Boscawen, Concord, Pembroke, Bow, Bedford, Amherst, Merrimack, Hollis, Dunstable, &c. in this state, are formed in part or entirely of this alluvion ; and it also extends through Tyngsborough, Chelmsford, to West-Cambridge, Cambridge, Boston and Waltham in Massachusetts, on the one hand ; and on the other side it follows the course of the river, embracing large tracts of land on each side, quite to the ocean. Its extent from Concord towards Maine is not known, but probably the town of Wells is also included in this formation. Rocks in some places break through this alluvial deposite, but they form no very elevated hills. In passing from Concord eastward to Portsmouth, we find the following succession of rocks :—Granite four miles from Concord ; gneiss, 11 miles ; mica slate, 14 miles ; granite, 15 miles ; then gneiss, and lastly greenstone. The direction of the strata nearly N. E. and S. W.

Steatite, or *soapstone*, is found at Francestown and Orford, where it is quarried and wrought into covings, jams, &c. of fire places, and is also employed for other useful and ornamental purposes. It occurs at both these places in beds. Mica slate is found both above and below it.

Primitive limestone is found in beds in some parts of the ridge : it occurs at Orford, also at Hanover, where it is stratified with mica slate ; at Concord, (Grafton co.) and Meredith.—These quarries furnish excellent lime for various purposes.

It is a commonly received opinion, that mountainous districts are uniformly rich in minerals and metals; but actual observation teaches us that this opinion is to be received with some limitation. Primitive mountains usually abound in metallic ores, and metalliferous minerals ; and the rocks which give the geological features to this state, viz. granite, gneiss, mica slate, &c. usually contain ores of gold, silver, copper, lead, tin, iron, &c. Copper and iron are the only metals hitherto found in sufficient quantities to justify the erection of works for smelting ; yet from the fact, that the primitive rocks are more metalliferous than others, we should be induced, at every opportunity, to examine our grounds and farms for other metals ; not, however, in a secret, mysterious manner, with chimerical notions about the existence of precious ores, but with good and honest hearts, willing not only to benefit ourselves, but our state and country. But to return from this digression. Metallic veins in primitive rocks do not sometimes excel a few hundred fathoms in length, and are usually very narrow ; and from the facts already known respecting the New-Hampshire hills and mountains, we are not authorized to affirm that they afford a rich treat for the mineralogist or geologist: they may, perhaps, hereafter afford a productive source of revenue and profit to the state.

Specimens of *pyritous copper*, found at Franconia, have been recently examined; which cannot be distinguished from the celebrated ore wrought at Anglesea. It is said to exist in *large quantities*, and promises to become a source of profit to the state. It is from this kind of ore that almost all the copper used in commerce and the arts is procured.

A vein of *sulphuret of lead*, or *galena*, has been explored in Lebanon, but does not afford sufficient quantities to defray the expense of smelting at the present price of labor and lead. Galena is also found at Orford, of fine texture. See Orford.

A small mass, containing a large proportion of *native silver*, has been found near Portsmouth ; and small quantities of *horn silver* occur in the same mass. Diligent investigation has not yet discovered any more of this valuable metal.

A rich iron ore is found at Franconia.—It is a magnetic ore, called by mineralogists *magnetic oxide of iron*. It yields from 60 to 75 per cent. At Franconia it is wrought, and affords the *mottled* or *grey cast iron :* it would probably make excellent cannon. Some other ores of iron are also found in this state. The *iron pyrites* are found in many places.— Their fine golden yellow color has frequently led persons to suppose that they were gold. Such persons may be convinced that they are not gold, by reducing them to powder, and throwing it on a red hot iron : a strong smell of brimstone is immediately perceived, and its peculiar blue flame may often be noticed. The *brown hematite* iron ore is found in Chesterfield.—From this ore, a very good kind of steel may be manufactured at a small expense. *Ochrey oxide of iron* is found in Jaffrey on the Monadnock. *Carbonate of iron* in small quantity has been found in Hanover. At Lebanon, a vein of iron ore has been found, which appears to be composed of the magnetic oxide, mixed with the pyrites.

The substance called *Plumbago*, or *black lead*, is found in several places in New-Hampshire. The most abundant locality is Bristol. It appears to be of that valuable kind which is employed for making pencils, and might be used in the manufacture of crucibles and melting pots. It is equal to the celebrated Burrowdale ore, and has been recently discovered. At Sutton it is also found, and of a quality adapted to the manufacture of crucibles and anti-attrition paste.

In addition to the above, it may be useful to mention the following localities.

Granular Limestone—Orford, Hanover; it is used for the various purposes for which lime is employed. It is stratified with mica slate.

Fetid Limestone—Orford; of a greyish white, distinctly crystallized. (*Silliman.*)

Sienite—Hanover, in small quantity; also at Charlestown. (*Hall.*)

Staurotide, fine specimens, crystallized in primitive form—Franconia; near Bellows-Falls, in argillite. (*Hall.*) In mica slate, large crystals, at Chesterfield. (*Allen.*)

Quartz, very abundant, both crystallized and amorphous. At Amherst is a large quantity of white opaque quartz, which may be found very useful in porcelain pottery. A manufactory of this kind was not many years since commenced near Boston, and relinquished for want of this material. The Amherst quartz is within eight or ten miles of the Merrimack, and might have been easily carried in boats almost into the kilns of the manufactory.

Milky quartz—Andover, near the mountain, amorphous, and easily broken.

Rose quartz--Mount Washington.

Ferruginous quartz—Gilmanton, red and yellow, in beautiful crystals —also at Francestown.

Hornstone—Burton and Gilmanton.

Mica—Grafton and Walpole, very fine; Gilmanton, good specimens; and at Alstead, in very large plates.

Schorl—Gilmanton, radiating on quartz, and darting through it in all directions; Lime, very beautiful, imbedded in white semi-transparent quartz; also at Chichester. *Indicolite*, at Hinsdale, large crystals, in feldspar and quartz. (*Allen.*)

Feldspar, abundant—Burton, Gilmanton, Tamworth, &c. Some specimens approach nearly to adularia.

Beryl, is found in small quantities at New-Ipswich; also on the White Hills.

Garnet, very abundant in this state—the finest specimens, approaching the precious garnet, at Hanover. Common garnet, Monadnock.—

Amorphous and in imperfect crystals, very elegant, at Franconia iron mine.

Epidote—Franconia, in the iron mine, in light yellow acicular crystals; at Portsmouth, in a porphyritic hornblende; at Exeter, in beautiful groups of radiating crystals; at Gilmanton; at Bedford. (*Woodbury.*)

Tremolite—Gilmanton; Chester, near the Devil's den, bladed and abundant.

Hornblende—Hanover, Exeter; superb specimens are found at Franconia; at Bedford. (*Woodbury.*)

Steatite—Orford, Francestown.

Manganese, tuberous and mammillary, investing granite—Northwood.

Magnetic iron, dodecædral crystals—Amherst.

Fluate of Lime—near the gap of the White Mountains, (*Gibbs.*) At Westmoreland, light green. (*Hall.*)

Asbestus—Franconia.

Amethyst—White Hills, a few rods S. E. from the Notch, in crystals; Hampton-Falls, in rolled pieces. (*Cleaveland.*)

Jasper—Gilmanton, and White Hills, near the Notch, of a reddish color. (*Gibbs.*)

Basanite—North-Hampton, in scattered fragments. (*Cleaveland.*)

Macle—Bellows-Falls, Croydon, Charlestown, in argillite. (*Hall.*)

Yellow Ochre—New-Boston, Jaffrey, Rindge, Mason, Salisbury, Gilmanton.

Alum—Bath. *Emery*—Lyman and Lancaster.

Sulphate of iron, or *Copperas*—Gilmanton, Brentwood, Hopkinton, Plymouth and Rindge.

Cyanite—Charlestown, abundant, of a dark blue color, imbedded in quartz. (*Hall.*)

Pinite—Near Bellows-Falls, in light grey cylindrical crystals, of 1-6 to 1-4 inch diameter, and sometimes 2 inches long. (*Hall.*)

Kaolin, or *porcelain-clay*—New-Ipswich.

Zoisite—Westmoreland.

Mineral Springs.—Of springs thus denominated, we have a number, though of no very great celebrity. The most noted are those at Amherst, Milford, Jaffrey, Unity, Hanover, Concord, (Grafton co.) Lebanon, Littleton, Meredith, Moultonborough and Wolfborough. Each of these has its visitors; and the waters of all have proved highly beneficial in some complaints. The mineral spring at Milford is not impregnated with any foreign substances to so great a degree as to render it a *hard water*; but like rain water and river water, *washes well*, and is a pure good water. The spring at Amherst contains a minute portion of hepatic air, or sulphuretted hydrogene. The spring at Lebanon contains a minute portion of sulphuretted hydrogene and of iron. The spring at Concord contains the same ingredients, together with a minute portion of muriate of soda. Jaffrey spring contains a small portion of carbonate of iron. None of these springs, however, are, strictly speaking, entitled to the name of *mineral springs*---their waters may be used in domestic economy.

GOVERNMENT AND LAWS.—New-Hampshire has a written constitution, which was established by a convention of the people in 1792. It is founded upon the broad principles of rational liberty, and guarantees at once the safety of the state and the personal rights of the citizen.— No person can be restrained in his freedom, until by crime he cuts off the obligation of society to protect him; unless it be a matter of his own choice or sufferance. The supreme executive power of this state is vested in the Governor and Council. The Governor is annually elected by the people: or, if there be no choice by the people, the Legislature chooses from the two highest candidates. The Council consists of five persons, chosen by the people. The Senate consists of twelve members, who are chosen by the people, in districts. Every town containing 150 rateable polls sends one representative, and for every additional 300 polls, is entitled to another. The annual election is holden on the second Tuesday of March. The following extracts from the constitution will sufficiently explain the nature and powers of our government:

Of the Governor and Council.—Every bill or resolve of the General Court, shall, before it become a law, be presented to the Governor; if he approve, he shall sign it; if not, return it, with his objections, to that house where it originated, who shall reconsider it, &c.

All judicial officers, the Attorney General, Solicitors, all Sheriffs, Coroners, Registers of Probate, and all officers of the Navy and Militia, shall be nominated and appointed by the Governor and Council.

The power of pardoning offences, except such as persons may be convicted of before the Senate, by impeachment of the House, shall be in the Governor, by and with the consent of the Council.

No officer duly commissioned to command in the militia shall be removed from office but by the address of both houses to the Governor, or trial by court martial.

No moneys shall be issued out of the Treasury of this State and disposed of (except such sums as may be appropriated for the redemption of bills of credit, treasurer's notes, or payment of interest arising thereon) but by warrant under the hand of the Governor by and with the advice and consent of the Council.

Of the Senate.—The Senate shall consist of twelve members, who shall hold their office for one year from the first Wednesday of June next ensuing their election.

The Senate shall be final judges of the elections, returns and qualifications of their own members, as pointed out in the Constitution.

The Senate shall have power to adjourn themselves, provided such adjournment do not exceed two days at a time.

The Senate shall be a court, with full power and authority to hear, and determine, all impeachments made by the House of Representatives against any officer of the State, for bribery, corruption, mal-practice or mal-administration in office, with full power to issue summons, on compulsory process for convening witnesses before them: but previous to the trial of any such impeachment, the members of the Senate shall be sworn truly and impartially to try and determine the charge in question, according to evidence.

Of the House of Representatives.—The House of Representatives shall be the grand inquest of the State, and all impeachments made by them, shall be heard and tried by the Senate.

All money bills shall originate in the House of Representatives; but the Senate may propose to concur with amendments, as on other bills.

The House of Representatives shall have power to adjourn themselves, but no longer than two days at a time.

No member of the Legislature shall be arrested or held to bail on mesne process, during his going to, returning from, or attending upon the Court.

The laws of this state, and the proceedings of the legislature, are by the constitution required to be published, and are annually distributed to the several towns for the information of the people.

The federal constitution was ratified by this state on the 21st of June, 1788, by a majority of eleven in the convention.

FUNDS, REVENUE, TAXES AND EXPENSES.—The productive and unproductive funds of the state, invested in U. S. funded stock, bank stock and other securities, amount to $151,360 86. From these sources an annual revenue is realized to the state, amounting to $8,110 07.

Funds of the State.

Seven per cent. stock of the United States,	17,605 00
Deferred six per cent. stock of do.	3,689 61
Three per cent. stock of do.	95,134 45
Fifty shares of stock in N. H. Bank, at present unproductive,	25,000 00
Bond executed by Treasurer of Dartmouth University, unproductive,	4,000 00
Notes for consideration money of lands sold by Treasurer,	931 80
	$151,360 86

Revenue.

The annual revenue of the state may be estimated at $8,110 07, derived from the following sources:

Interest on seven per cent. stock of the United States,	1,232 35
Reimbursement of principal and interest on deferred six per cent. stock of the U. S.	3,967 79
Interest on three per cent. stock of the U. S.	2,854 03
Interest on notes for consideration money of lands sold,	55 90
	$8,110 07

Moneys received into the Treasury during the political year ending June 4, 1822.

For taxes outstanding prior to the year 1821, $2,696 43; state tax of 1821, 30,000; for rents of rooms of medical building at Hanover, 18 92; principal and interest of notes given for lands sold, 1,145 16; for reimbursement of principal and interest on stock in U. S. funds, 8,054 17; for loans from banks, 17,000; for fines of militia exempts, 16 00;—making in all $58,930 68. Or, exclusive of loans to defray the expenses of the government, $41,930 68.

During the year above mentioned, there were paid out of the Treasury, for money borrowed, and to meet the current and ordinary demands on the government, sums amounting in the whole to $51,891 03:—exhibiting the following state of the Treasury on the 4th day of June, 1822.

Balance remaining in the Treasury, June 4, 1821,	4,765 44
Amount received into the Treasury during the year ending June 4, 1822,	58,930 68
	63,696 12
Deduct disbursements during the year,	51,891 03
Balance in the Treasury,	$11,805 09

Estimate of the expenses of government for the political year ending June 4, 1823.

Salaries of the officers of government, viz. governor, 1200; secretary, 300; treasurer, 600; attorney-general, 800; adjutant-general, 400; warden state prison, 800; justices superior court, 3800; for compensation to members and officers of the legislature, including incidental expenses of the session, 16,145 75; allowance to courts-martial, brigade inspectors and for military commissions, 1100; for adjutant general's department, 2234; compensation to commissary general, 190 98; sheriffs' accounts, 50 00; for printing, stationary and postage, 1250; encouragement of agriculture, 250; for educating deaf and dumb children, 1000; bounties on wild cats, 190; expenses of enquiry into the official conduct of Hon. Edward Evans, 263 72; contingencies, say 600. To which if the principal and interest of debts due banks be added, amounting—if payment can be made from the proceeds of the state tax as soon as the first of Feb. 1823—to 11,450; and also certain unexpended balances of appropriations for agricultural purposes, and for education of deaf and dumb children, amounting to $385,—there will be presented an aggregate amount of $43,009 45, for the expenses and disbursements of government, for the political year ending June 4, 1823.

Literary Fund.—This fund, which was established by an act of the legislature, passed June 29, 1821, for the purpose of endowing "a college for instruction in the higher branches of science and literature," consists of the proceeds of a tax of one half of one per cent. on the amount of the capital stock of the several banking corporations in this state. The aggregate amount of the tax for the last year was $4,770 37. This sum has been converted into United States' six per cent. stock of 1815.

MILITIA.—In New-Hampshire, the militia is composed of every able-bodied white male citizen, between the ages of 18 and 45, except those exempted by law, among whom to the honor of the state, are those whose religious scruples render them averse to war. The militia of this state is divided by law into three divisions, six brigades and thirty-nine regiments. Each division is commanded by a major-general who is allowed one division-inspector with the rank of colonel, and two aids with the rank of major. Each brigade has one brigadier-general, who is allowed one brigade inspector and one brigade quartermaster with the rank of major, and one aid with the rank of captain. To each brigade, there is a judge advocate. Each regiment is commanded by one colonel, one lieutenant-colonel and one major. The regimental staff consists of an adjutant, quartermaster, paymaster, surgeon, surgeon's mate and chaplain, who are commissioned by the governor, one quarter-master-sergeant, one sergeant major, one drum major and one fife major, who are appointed by the colonel or commandant of the regiment. Companies of infantry consist of one captain, one lieutenant and one ensign, four sergeants, four corporals, one drummer, one fifer and sixty four rank and file. Companies of light infantry or grenadiers, of which two are allowed to each regiment, consist of forty eight rank and file. Companies of artillery consist of one captain, two lieutenants, four sergeants, four corporals, six gunners, six bombardiers, two drivers, one drummer, one fifer and sixteen matrosses. The cavalry consists of one captain, two lieutenants, one cornet, four sergeants, four corporals, two musicians, one farrier, one saddler, and fifty privates.

The last annual return of the adjutant general furnishes the following abstract of the numbers of the militia, and of the arms and accoutrements. *General officers and Staff.*—Three major generals, 3 division inspectors, 6 aids-de-camp ; 6 brigadier generals, 4 brigade inspectors, 6 brigade quartermasters, 6 aids-de-camp and 4 judge advocates. *Field and Staff.*—35 colonels, 35 lieutenant-colonels, 36 majors, 37 adjutants,

38 quartermasters, 37 paymasters, 38 surgeons, 32 surgeons' mates, 32 chaplains, 37 sergeant majors, 35 quartermaster sergeants, 37 drum-majors and 38 fife-majors. *Cavalry.*—41 companies, 40 captains, 74 lieutenants, 38 cornets, 144 sergeants. 84 corporals, 81 musicians, 1450 privates. *Artillery.*—38 companies, 35 captains, 74 lieutenants, 141 sergeants, 91 corporals, 99 musicians, 979 privates. *Infantry, light infantry and grenadiers.*—376 companies, 359 captains, 340 lieutenants, 336 ensigns, 1270 sergeants, 518 corporals, 1043 musicians, 21,124 privates. *Riflemen.*—8 companies, 8 captains, 8 lieutenants, 8 ensigns, 30 sergeants, 18 corporals, 31 musicians, 287 privates.

Arms and Accoutrements.

Cavalry.—1449 swords, 1446 sword scabbards and belts, 2905 pistols, 1658 holsters, 1499 saddles and bridles, 1486 mail pillions, 1375 valises, 1491 cartridge boxes and belts, 1468 pairs of boots, 1468 pairs of spurs, 35 trumpets and bugles, 22 colors. *Artillery.*—1137 swords, 28 pieces of brass ordnance, 1 piece of iron do, 53 drums and fifes, 22 colours, &c. &c. *Infantry, &c.*—16,369 muskets, 15,967 bayonets, 16,104 iron ramrods, 16,019 cartridge boxes and belts, 31,157 spare flints, 15,883 priming wires and brushes, 15,323 knapsacks, 15,414 canteens, 345 drums, 287 fifes. *Riflemen.*—83 rifles, 51 powder horns, 83 pouches, 63 knapsacks, 40 canteens, 6 drums, 4 fifes. *Books, Colors, &c.*—35 regimental colors, 1123 infantry regulations, 418 militia laws, 127 roll books, 308 orderly books.

POPULATION.—The earliest enumeration which we find of the inhabitants of this state, was a partial one, made in 1680, when the province contained only the towns of Portsmouth, Dover, Exeter and Hampton. There were then " between two and three hundred *voters.*" Though no accurate survey was made until 1767, it has been estimated that the population amounted to 30,000 in the year 1749.

TABLE I. *Showing the progressive population since 1749.*

1749.	1767.	1775.	1790.	1800.	1810.	1820.
30,000	52,880	82,200	141,885	183,858	214,460	244,161

TABLE II. *Exhibiting the average increase in different periods.*

	No. Yrs.	Daily inc.	Yearly inc.	Total increa.	Remarks.
From 1749 to 1767.	18	3.4	1271	22,880	The annual incr. for the last 71 yrs. is 3016 :—daily incr. during the same period, about 8.
" 1767 to 1775,	8	10.0	3652	29,320	
" 1775 to 1790,	15	10.9	3979	59,685	
" 1790 to 1800,	10	11.4	4197	41,973	
" 1800 to 1810,	10	8.4	3060	30,602	
" 1810 to 1820,	10	8.1	2970	29,701	

The rapid increase of population between the years 1767 and 1800, was owing in part to adventitious causes. After the peace of 1763, emigrations became frequent from the neighboring states into the new townships of New-Hampshire, and many also removed from the older settlements to the new, under encouragements from government or the proprietors of the lands. In 1790, the population of the Union was principally confined to the Atlantic states; those west of the Alleghany mountains containing scarcely 100,000 inhabitants. Since that period the tide of emigration has set strongly to the west; great states have arisen beyond the mountains, a great proportion of whose inhabitants were from New-England. New-Hampshire has furnished her full share of adventurers; and the increase of her inhabitants has been proportionably less, within the last thirty years.

From the returns of the census for the year 1820, it appears that there were in this state,

	Under 10 years.	From 10 to 16.	16 to 26.	26 to 45	45 & upw'ds.
Males,	35.466	19,672	22,703	22,956	18,413
Females,	34,599	18,899	24,806	25,797	19,925

The excess of *females* in our population is 4,816. There are 786 free persons of color in this state; but the footstep of a slave does not pollute our soil.

TABLE III. *Shewing the proportion of Sexes at different periods; and of black and white population in 1820.*

[N. B. In this table is included the whole of New-England, that the reader may at a glance see the proportion of the different states.]

STATES.	No. of females to 100 males.				Proportion—1820.	
	1790.	1800.	1810.	1820.	Blacks.	Whites.
New-Hampshire	98.90	100.52	101.44	104.05	0.32	99.68
Maine	95.39	96.27	97.15	99.36	0.31	99.69
Massachusetts	104.07	102.92	102.53	104.83	1.28	98.72
Connecticut	102.19	101.92	101.92	104.26	2.89	97.11
Rhode-Island	102.66	105.46	104.83	106.53	4.34	95.66
Vermont	90.48	94.01	97.48	100.20	0.39	99.61

The population of this state is 26 to a square mile. That of Massachusetts is 74; of Maine, 9; Connecticut, 55; Rhode-Island, 53; and Vermont, 22. New-Hampshire was in 1790, in point of population, the tenth state in the Union; at the second census, in 1800, the 11th; at the third, in 1810, the 14th; and at the last census, the 15th.

MANUFACTURES AND COMMERCE.—New-Hampshire is emphatically an agricultural state. Manufactures and commerce engross the attention of a comparatively small portion of its citizens. Young as we are in the arts, it has not yet become our interest to abandon the cultivation of the soil, for the purpose of creating extensive manufactories,—in which must be required large capitals, and a patience and automaton constancy to which we are unused,—while the rewards are uncertain and feeble. In the departments of *domestic* or *household manufactures*, our citizens already excel, and it is pleasing to observe an increasing emulation. To be independent, we must manufacture for ourselves. The earth is bountiful; and by suitable attention we may gather from its bosom what will not only feed our mouths, but clothe our bodies. We shall perhaps be unable to give a very accurate view of the manufactures of this state; but the following facts will enable the reader to judge of their variety and extent. We manufacture comparatively little, for exportation: most of our products are required at home. In 1810, we had twelve manufacturing establishments, with 5,956 spindles.—Those at Dover, Peterborough and Pembroke were the principal. The quantity of cloth annually manufactured at those establishments, is not accurately stated; but the number of yards of various kinds of cloth manufactured in the whole state, in families, factories, &c. in 1810, according to the returns, was as follows:

	Yards.
Cotton goods,	516,985
Mixed, cotton, &c.	930,978
Flaxen,	1,030,320
Blended unnamed stuffs,	112,540
Woollen,	900,273
Tow,	723,089
	4,274,185

There were, at this time, for cotton, wool, &c. in the state, 20,670 looms; 109 carding machines, which carded 478,000 lbs. per annum; 135 fulling mills, which fulled 497,500 yards of cloth. Of the article *hats*, we manufactured in that year 36,700 of wool, and 17,160 of fur, in value $106,500. In 1810, there were 236 tanneries, in which were tanned of hides, skins, &c. 853,890—worth $250,000. In 19 oil-mills, were made 20,560 gallons linseed oil. Distilleries, 18: gallons distilled from grain, fruit, &c. 135,950. At the iron furnaces in this state, five in number, were made 1120 tons bar iron—worth $150,000. Of nails, in 14 factories, were made 203,840 lbs. Trip-hammers, 42. Paper mills,

6—amount of paper manufactured not known. The total value of our manufactures in 1810, excluding doubtful items, was $5,225,045.

The manufactures of this state have gradually increased since 1810. During the war with Great-Britain, which shut out for a season the flood of foreign goods which had long poured in upon the country, they were indeed more flourishing than at any former period in our history; but this prosperity was temporary, and subsided when the cause was removed. A gradual increase of manufactures will and ought to continue, as the wants of the people are augmented, and their solicitude for these establishments increases. There are at the present time in this state, 28 cotton, and 18 woollen factories; 307 carding machines; 256 fulling mills; 22 distilleries; 20 oil mills; 193 bark mills; 304 tanneries; 54 trip-hammers, and 12 paper mills. In Mason there is a starch manufactory—and in several towns have been erected circular saw clapboard machines, which from their great perfection promise extensive usefulness.

The staple commodities of this state, are lumber, provisions, horses, neat cattle, pot and pearl ashes, flax-seed, &c. These are exported in great quantities annually. But in estimating the *commerce* of this state, it should be recollected, that New-Hampshire lies in the bosom of Massachusetts and Maine, with only one port and a narrow strip of sea-coast. The exports from the north part of the state are necessarily to the markets in Maine, while a great portion of those from the middle and southern parts, is carried to Newburyport, Boston or Hartford.—The most valuable intercourse of the state is thus cut off by nature from her only port: and it is therefore impossible to ascertain the amount annually exported from the state. The following statement will afford a view of the *commerce of Portsmouth.*

The average value of imports from foreign countries in the
five years ending June 30, 1822, is $455,637
The average value of exports to foreign countries
for the same period in articles of the growth or manufacture of the United States, is . . . 235,059
Foreign articles, ... 110,748
————$345,807

The tonnage of vessels registered for foreign trade
on the 30th June, 1817, was . . . 26,042 *tons.*
Enrolled and licensed for the coasting and fishing
trade, including only those above 20 tons, 5,233
Total amount tonnage, June 30, 1817, ————31,275
June 30, 1818—Registered tonnage . . . 16,974
Enrolled do. . . . 5,516
————22,490

DARTMOUTH COLLEGE, HANOVER.

June 30, 1819—Registered,	17,162	
Enrolled,	5,911	
		23,073
June 30, 1820—Registered,	16,586	
Enrolled,	5,959	
		22,545
June 30, 1821—Registered,	17,604	
Enrolled,	5,778	
		23,382
June 30, 1822—Registered,	17,086	
Enrolled,	6,592	
		23,678

A large number of vessels which had been laid up during the late war, were either lost, sold out of the district, or broken up and their registers surrendered subsequent to the 30th June, 1817, which accounts for the great difference between the tonnage of that and the following years. Since 1818, the tonnage has been kept up, by building new vessels to supply the place of those worn out or sold, which will amount on an average to from 1500 to 2000 tons. From sixty to seventy licensed vessels, of from 20 to 75 tons each, and about 550 men, exclusive of those in boats and smaller vessels, are employed during the fishing season, or from about the first of March to the latter part of November, in the bank and mackerel fisheries. These vessels take from 38,000 to 45,000 quintals of cod and pollock fish, and on an average above 6,000 barrels of mackerel. The market is also abundantly supplied by boats and smaller vessels with fresh fish of various kinds, of which no estimate can be made. More than three-fifths of the registered tonnage of this port is employed in the carrying trade—taking cargoes from southern ports to Europe, from whence they return in the latter part of summer and autumn, with salt, iron, coals, and other heavy and bulky articles, which are sold here as cheap as in any part of the United States. The earnings or freight of these vessels make up the difference between the value of the exports and imports. Of the value of the coasting trade, no accurate account can be given. It is however on the increase—is carried on in both registered and enrolled vessels, and forms a very valuable part of the commerce of this port.

LITERARY INSTITUTIONS.—Dartmouth College, in the township of Hanover, is the only literary institution in this state which exercises the functions of a college. It derives its name from the Rt. Hon. William Legge, LL. D. F. R. S. Earl of Dartmouth, one of its early and principal benefactors. It was founded by Rev. Eleazar Wheelock, D. D. a pious and benevolent clergyman of Connecticut. It originated from the establishment of a school for the instruction of Indian youth at Stockbridge, Mass. to which the name of 'Moor's School' was given, from Mr. Joshua Moor, of Mansfield, Conn. whose liberal donations justly entitled it to receive his name. After this school had been in operation a few years, it was found that the public benefits of the institution might be greatly increased by erecting it into a college and locating it in a more favorable situation. Accordingly, a royal charter was obtained by Dr. Wheelock, from John Wentworth, the provincial governor of N. Hampshire, on the 13th of December, 1769, and the township of Hanover was selected for the site of the new institution. In September, the next year, Dr. Wheelock with his family removed to this place, where there were only twenty families living in as many log huts. Their first accommodations were but mean. They built log houses, which they occupied till better edifices could be prepared. In 1771, the first commencement was holden, and degrees were conferred on Levi Frisbie, Samuel Gray, Sylvanus Ripley and John Wheelock. In 1779, on the 24th of April, Pres. Wheelock died, and was succeeded by his second son, Col. John Wheelock, at that time in the army of the United States. When peace between this country and England was restored, Pres. J. Wheelock made a successful visit to England, as well as to other parts of Europe, in the cause of the institution, and received several valuable donations. In 1786, a new college building, 150 feet by 50, three stories high, was erected: in 1790, a college chapel: in 1791, the commons hall, and in 1810, the medical institution building. In 1815, an open rupture occurred between president Wheelock and a majority of the trustees.— Difficulties had existed for several years. President Wheelock appealed to the legislature, who appointed a committee to repair to Hanover, hear the parties, and make report at the next session. Soon after the examination closed, the trustees removed Dr. Wheelock from the presidency, and appointed Rev. Francis Brown, of North-Yarmouth, in his room. At the next session of the legislature, in 1816, an act was passed, entitled "An act to amend the charter and enlarge and improve the corporation of Dartmouth College." By this act, the number of trustees was increased, a board of overseers was appointed, and the College was changed to a University. The old trustees resisted this act, declaring it unconstitutional—and, although deprived of the college building, philosophical apparatus, &c. continued instruction, as usual, in private buildings, and appealed to the judiciary. In 1817, the cause was decided in favor of the University, and the constitutionality of the laws, by the superior court of New-Hampshire. The cause was then carried before the supreme court of the United States at Washington, who, on the 2d February 1819, reversed the whole proceedings, declaring the act of the state establishing a university unconstitutional and void. In July, 1820, Pres. Brown died, and was succeeded, the same year, by Rev. Daniel Dana, D. D. of Newburyport, Ms. who resigned the presidency in 1821. In 1822, Rev. Bennet Tyler, of Southbury, Conn. succeeded the Rev. Dr. Dana in the office of President.

The immediate instruction and government of the college is entrusted to the president, professors and tutors. From the first commencement, in 1771, to the present time, 1341 have proceeded bachelors of arts, of whom 332 have been settled in the ministry. The whole number on whom degrees have been conferred, is 1784. For admission into the Freshman class, it is required that the candidates be well versed in the grammar of the English, Latin and Greek languages, in Virgil, Cicero's Select Orations, Sallust, the Greek Testament, Dalzel's Collectanea Græca Minora, Latin and Greek Prosody, Arithmetic, Ancient and Modern Geography, and that he be able accurately to translate English into Latin. The course of instruction and study for undergraduates in this seminary is as follows.

For Freshmen.—Livy, 5 books—Horace's Odes—Cicero de Oratore, 2 books—in Dalzel's Collect. Græca Majora, Herodotus, Xenophon's History, Homer, Hesiod, Œlianus, Polyenus and Theophrastus—Adam's Roman Antiquities—Tytler's Ancient History—Walker's Rhetorical Grammar—Review of Geography and Arithmetic—Algebra.

Sophomores.—Horace finished—De Oratore finished—in Majora, Thucydides, Plato, Isocrates, Æschines, Demosthenes, Xenophon's Philosophy, Dionysius, Longinus, Aristotle—Excerpta Latina—Tytler's Modern History—Hedge's Elements of Logic—Blair's Rhetoric, 2 vols.—Euclid's Elements of Geometry—Trigonometry—Mensuration of Heights and Distances, Superficies and Solids—Surveying—Navigation—Guaging and Dialling.

Juniors.—Tacitus, 5 books—Majora finished—Conic Sections—Chemistry—Enfield's Natural Philosophy and Astronomy—Paley's Natural Theology— Paley's Moral and Political Philosophy.

Seniors.—Locke's Essay on the Human Understanding—Edwards on the Will—Stewart's Philosophy of the Human Mind, 2 vols.—Burlemaqui on Natural and Political Law—Paley's Evidences of the Christian Religion—Butler's Analogy of Religion to the Constitution and Course of Nature—the Federalist.

The Medical Department in this institution is respectable and extremely useful. It was established in 1798. For the lectures on Anatomy, the professor is furnished with valuable preparations, and in the Chemical department there is a well furnished laboratory. The chemical and philosophical apparatus is new, well chosen, and sufficiently extensive for all important purposes. The college library contains 5000 volumes: the libraries of the two societies, composed of the students, contain 6000 volumes. The lectures on Anatomy and Surgery, Chemistry and Materia Medica, and the Theory and Practice of Physic, commence early in the fall and continue three months. The productive funds of the college amount to 50,000 dollars: the annual income from the funds and tuition, to about $6000, and the annual expenditures to something less than $6000. There are also funds to a considerable amount, not at present productive. The demands of the college, after making a liberal allowance for probable losses, fall short of the debts by about $2900.

Moor's Charity School is connected with the college, having the same trustees and president. Its annual revenue is from 400 to 600 dollars.

Academies.--The academies which have been incorporated in this state are as follow: viz. Phillip's Exeter Academy, incorporated April 3, 1781. New-Ipswich Academy, June 18, 1789. Chesterfield Academy, January 12, 1790. Charlestown Academy, February 16, 1791. Atkinson Academy, February 17, 1791. Aurean Academy at Amherst, Feb. 17, 1791. Haverhill Academy, Feb. 11, 1794. Gilmanton Academy, June 20, 1794. Franklin Academy, at Dover, Dec. 28, 1805. Portsmouth Academy, Dec. 9, 1808. Salisbury Academical Association, Dec. 10, 1808. Lancaster Academy, Dec. 10, 1808. Hampton Proprietary School, June 16, 1810. Union Academy at Plainfield, June 16, 1813. Pinkerton Academy at Londonderry, June 15, 1814. Durham Academy, June 25, 1817. New-Market Wesleyan Academy, June 23, 1818. Pembroke Academy, June 25, 1818. Effingham Union Academy, June 18, 1819. Francestown Academy, June 24, 1819. Alstead Academy, July 1, 1820. Gilford Academy, June 20, 1820. Newport Academy, June 24, 1819. Sanbornton Academy, Dec. 22, 1820. New-Hampton Academy June 27, 1821. Hillsborough Academy, June 29, 1821. Several of these exist only in name. Those which are in successful operation will be hereafter noticed.

EDUCATION.--Whatever of literary character the people of our country claim, arises from early education and the habits it creates. Though less splendid in name, it is more useful in practice than that of foreign nations. The existence of schools, in which are grounded the first principles of learning, may be traced to an early period in our history. The old laws of this state required every town of one hundred families to keep a grammar school; by which was meant a school in which the learned languages should be taught, and youth might be prepared for admission to a university. The same preceptor was obliged to teach reading, writing and arithmetic; unless the town were of sufficient ability to keep two or more schools, one of which was called a grammar school by way of distinction. When there were but few towns, much better care was taken to observe the ancient law concerning schools, than after the settlements were multiplied. But there was never uniform attention paid to this important subject throughout the state, until the law of 1805, empowering towns to divide into school districts and authorizing districts to build and repair school houses. Since that period, these primary sources of instruction, in the benefits of which the children of all classes of our citizens may equally participate, have acquired a higher character; but still in many towns, there is great room for improvement, especially in the selection of well qualified instructors, and in the use of suitable books of elementary instruction.

For the support of district schools, a certain part, or the whole of the year, the selectmen of the different places in this state are required to assess annually, the inhabitants, according to their polls and rateable estate, together with the improved and unimproved lands and buildings of non-residents, in a sum to be computed at the rate of ninety dollars for every one dollar of their proportion for public taxes for the time being, and so for a greater or less sum. The amount of the assessments, when collected, are required to be appropriated to the sole purpose of keeping an English school, or schools, within the places for which the sums shall be assessed, for teaching the various sounds and powers of the letters in the English language, reading, writing, English grammar, arithmetic, geography, and such other branches of education as it may be necessary to teach in an English school. The purchase of necessary wood or fuel for such schools is to be included. No person is deemed qualified to instruct any district school, without first procuring a certificate from some able and respectable teacher, or learned minister of the gospel, preceptor of an academy, or president, professor, or tutor of a college, that such person is qualified to teach such school. The law also requires a certificate from the selectmen, or minister of the place where the person resides, furnishing evidence that the person sustains a good moral character; and this, with the other certificate, must be presented to the selectmen, or visiting committee of the place where the school is to be kept, previous to the commencement of such school. Each town is required to appoint three or more suitable persons to visit and inspect the schools annually in their respective towns, at suitable times, and in a manner most conducive to the progress of literature, morality and religion. In case of failure to appoint such persons, the duty of inspecting schools devolves upon the selectmen. School books are by law exempted from attachment. The number of school districts in this state amounts to 1698; and the number of school houses to 1560. The number of scholars instructed in these districts cannot be less than 50,000.

MANNERS AND CUSTOMS.—The habits of the people of this state are similar to those of New-England generally. Descendants principally of the same ancestors, they inherit alike the same feelings and traits of character ; and may be distinguished from inhabitants of other sections of our vast country, by their hardihood in danger and patience in suffering, as well as by their sobriety and hospitality. It is, perhaps, fortunate for our country, that its settlers were from England, and that religious persecution laid the foundation of our empire and liberties. Had we been colonies of France or Spain, the lands would have been divided between the nobles and ecclesiastics ; and the very soil we tread upon, like the island of Montreal, might have been the property of a convent—and we the slaves of its inmates. The firmness of spirit which braved the terrors of Indian warfare, and afterwards, of the revolution—still exists and animates our countrymen ; and among all classes, you will observe that their chiefest pride and boast is their *independence*. Among the virtues of the people, industry and frugality are conspicuous. Though few are very wealthy, all are comfortable, and a greater portion in easy circumstances. The doors of the citizen are never closed against the decent looking traveller ; nor are the wretched often left to suffer. No man ever perished here for want of food or raiment. Public and private charities are every where bestowed : the number of charitable institutions, and the amount annually distributed by them, are by no means disproportioned to the wealth of the state. Whatever opinion the foreigner may form from the roughness of our exterior, which, like that of our country, is certainly apparent ; he will find hospitality to inhabit every dwelling, from the mansions of the rich, to the scattered cottages among our mountains.*

RELIGION.—The Constitution declares that " every individual has a natural and unalienable right to worship God according to the dictates of his own conscience and reason ; and no subject shall be hurt, molest-

---

* For the employments, diversions, &c. of the people, see *Belknap's N. H. vol. iii. 191.*

ed, or restrained, in his person, liberty or estate for worshipping God in the manner and season most agreeable to the dictates of his own conscience, or for his religious profession, sentiments or persuasion : provided he doth not disturb the public peace, or disturb others in their religious worship." In order to promote " the institution of the public worship of the Deity, and of public instruction in morality and religion," the legislature is empowered " to authorize, from time to time, the several towns, parishes, bodies corporate or religious societies, within this state, to make adequate provision, at their own expense, for the support and maintenance of public Protestant teachers of piety, religion and morality." All religious communities have the exclusive right of electing their public teachers, and of contracting with them for their support and maintenance ; and no person of any particular religious sect or denomination, is compelled to contribute towards supporting teachers of a different sect or persuasion. "And every denomination of christians demeaning themselves quietly, and as good subjects of the state, shall be equally under the protection of the law. And no subordination of any one sect or denomination to another, shall ever be established by law." In July, 1819, the memorable act called the Toleration Law passed the Legislature. This acts provides that no person shall be compelled to join or support, or be classed with, or associated to any congregation, church or religious society, without his express consent first had and obtained. And any person who shall choose to separate himself from any society or association formed under said act, to which he may belong, may, by leaving a written notice with the clerk of such society, be exempted from any future expenses which may be incurred by said society or association.

The various religious denominations in this state are Congregationalists, Episcopalians, Quakers, Presbyterians, Calvinistic Baptists, Sandemanians, Freewill Baptists, Methodists, Universalists and Shakers. These we have endeavored to enumerate in the order of time in which they appeared in New-Hampshire. The *Congregationalists* are the most numerous. The first settlers of Dover and Exeter adopted the congregational form of worship. In those places, were the first churches of this denomination organized. In the year 1700, there existed only five churches ; in 1748, there were 30 ; and the present number may be estimated at about 160, though some of them are very small, and several have become nearly extinct. The present number of communicants is from 11,000 to 12,000. The *Episcopalians* were here at an early peried. Prior to 1638, an Episcopal church or chapel was erected at Portsmouth, and Rev. Richard Gibson was the first minister, who remained till 1642. A few *Quakers* were here at an early period, and a society was formed at Seabrook in the year 1701. The *Calvinistic Baptists* are the second denomination in point of numbers. The first church was formed at Newtown in 1755. In 1780, there existed in this state 19 churches. The *Presbyterians* who were first established here were a colony of Scotch emigrants, who settled Londonderry in 1719. The *Freewill Baptists* are a numerous class of christians. The first church of this denomination was founded at New-Durham, in 1780, by Elder Benjamin Randall. This denomination was recognized as a distinct sect by an act of the Legislature, Dec. 7, 1804. The *Methodists* were recognized by law as a distinct religious sect June 15, 1807. The *Sandemanians* are the followers of Mr. Robert Sandeman, who came to this country in 1764. There is but one society, which is at Portsmouth. The *Universalists* were recognized as a distinct religious sect June 13, 1805. The first society of this denomination was formed at Portsmouth as early as 1781. The *Shakers*, of which there are two communities, one at Canterbury, the other at Enfield, first appeared in this state in 1782.

SOCIETIES.—The New-Hampshire Medical Society was incorporated Feb. 16, 1791. It was formed for the purpose of diffusing a knowledge of medical science in this state, and for discouraging empiricism and quackery by preventing all unqualified persons from practising Medicine and Surgery. The society consists of three grades of members, viz. Honorary Members, Fellows, and Associates. The two first belong to the general society. The Associates belong to the District Societies, of which there are six, the Eastern, Centre, Western, Strafford, Southern and Grafton Districts. A person must have been in practice two years before he can be elected an Associate. An Associate is at all times eligible to the office of a Fellow. The number of persons named in the act of incorporation was 19, all of whom were constituted Fellows. The number of Fellows who have been elected and accepted, since the society went into operation, is 148. The present number is 114. The number of Honorary Members who have been elected is 26. From Feb. 28, 1794, to Feb. 26, 1822, one hundred and two candidates were examined and approbated by the Censors of the society for the practice of Physic and Surgery. The annual meeting is holden at Concord on the Tuesday preceding the first Wednesday in June. Nine Fellows constitute a quorum to transact business. At this meeting, the officers, consisting of a President, Vice-President, two Counsellors and two Censors from each district, a Secretary, Librarian, the Library Committee, Committee of Correspondence and two Delegates to attend the Medical Examinations at Dartmouth College, are chosen.

There are six Agricultural Societies, one in each county. That in Rockingham was incorporated in 1814; in Cheshire, 1816; those in Strafford, Hillsborough and Grafton in 1818; and in Coos, 1819. Considerable benefit has accrued from these institutions to the agricultural interest. Meetings for Cattle Shows and the exhibition of domestic manufactures are annually holden, and are very generally attended. The distribution of premiums serves to create a spirit of competition among the members of the society, which cannot but be useful in promoting the interests of two of the most important branches of national wealth and prosperity, those of agriculture and manufactures. For a few years, the patronage of the Legislature was extended to these institutions, each of which, excepting Coos, received grants of about $400 in aid of their funds. It is much to be regretted, that one branch of the Legislature at the last session, withdrew their fostering patronage from an object deserving so much encouragement. On the 19th of December, 1820, a Board of Agriculture was incorporated. It consists of six delegates, one to be chosen by ballot from each of the county agricultural societies within this state, who meet annually at Concord on the 2d Wednesday in June. In 1821, the Legislature granted $250 to be appropriated by the Board, in defraying the necessary expenses of procuring and preparing materials for the publication of a pamphlet, to contain such reports and returns from the county societies, and such essays relative to agricultural improvements as the Board may think will conduce to the advancement of agriculture. A similar grant for the same purposes was made at the last session of the Legislature.

There are, in this state, many religious and charitable institutions, of which the mere enumeration would extend this article to a disproportionate length. The most prominent only can be noticed. The New-Hampshire Bible Society was organized in June, 1812. Its object is to supply the destitute with Bibles, either gratuitously, or at reduced prices. It has upwards of 700 members, who are required to pay annually two dollars each, and may receive one bible, or three dollars and receive two bibles. It became auxilary to the American Bible Society in Sept. 1816, to which it has remitted $3216 for bibles, and $1231 97 as donations. The New-Hampshire Missionary Society was instituted in Sept. 1801, and is designed to furnish preaching and religious instruction to destitute churches in this state. The amount of its funds is above $3000. The Rockingham, Hillsborough, Cheshire and Grafton Bible and Charitable Societies are each of them useful institutions, and are extending their benefits to objects within their respective limits.

There are 35 Musical Societies, which have had no small influence in collecting and introducing into practice the best productions on music; in acquiring and diffusing a correct taste for psalmody; and in contributing a large share towards the enjoyment of the pleasures of sacred harmony.

The Grand Lodge of New-Hampshire was constituted July 8, 1789.— Under its jurisdiction, there are 37 Masonic Lodges, several of which have been incorporated. A Grand Royal Arch Chapter was instituted in 1820, and there are six subordinate Chapters, viz. St. Andrews at Hanover, established Jan. 27, 1807; Trinity at Hopkinton, Feb. 16, 1807; Washington at Portsmouth, Nov. 1815; Cheshire, at Keene, May 4, 1816; Franklin, at Bath, July 10, 1820; and Webb at Claremont, July 11, 1821.

There have been incorporated in this state 31 academical associations, 169 social libraries, 117 religious societies and congregations, and 56 societies of various denominations not classed.

BANKS.—There are in this state ten banking institutions in operation, and two others, one at Amherst and the other at Claremont, incorporated in June, 1822, which have not yet gone into operation.

Names of Banks.	Where located.	Incorporated.	Charters expire.	Capital.
New-Hampshire,	Portsmouth,	Jan. 3, 1792.	Jan. 3, 1842.	200,000
N. H. Union,	do.	June 18, 1802.	July 1, 1822.	200,000
Portsmouth,	do.	June 11, 1803.	July 1, 1823.	200,000
Rockingham,	do.	Nov. 5, 1813.	Jan. 1, 1834.	200,000
Strafford,	Dover,	June 11 1803.	July 4, 1823.	150,000
Exeter,	Exeter,	Dec. 19,1803.	Jan. 1, 1824.	200,000
Coos,	Haverhill,	Dec. 24 1803.	Jan. 1, 1824.	100,000
Cheshire,	Keene,	Dec. 24, 1803.	March 1, 1824.	150,000
Concord, (Upper) Concord, (Lower)	Concord,	June 18, 1806.	July 1, 1826.	200,000

Both the Concord Banks issue bills under and claim the same charter. The New-Hampshire Union, Portsmouth, Strafford, Coos and Cheshire Banks were re-incorporated, with certain restrictions and limitations, June 28, 1821, for the further term of twenty years. The name of the oos Bank was altered to Grafton Bank, and all bills issued after the firs

NEW HAMPSHIRE STATE HOUSE, CONCORD.

of January, 1822, were to assume that name. These banking institutions are subject to a tax of one half of one per cent. on the amount which shall, on the second Wednesday of June annually, constitute the actual stock of said banks. The object of this tax is to raise a fund to be pledged and appropriated to the endowment or support of a college for instruction in the higher branches of science and literature in this state, to be applied in such way and manner as the legislature shall hereafter direct. ☞ The sums noted in the preceding table, as the capital of our banks, are their *allowed capital*, and not the amount actually paid in. —*See Literary Fund, p.* 26.

THE STATE HOUSE.—This beautiful edifice is situate in Concord in the county of Rockingham, upon a gently inclined plane between main and state streets, and has two regular fronts, east and west. The centre of the building is fifty feet in front by fifty-seven in depth; the wings are each thirty-eight feet in front by forty-nine in depth; the whole making a parallelogram of one hundred and twenty-six feet in length by forty-nine in width, with the addition of a projection in the centre of each front of four feet. It is two stories above the basement, which rises five feet above the surface of the ground: the first story is nineteen feet; the second eighteen feet in the wings and thirty-one in the centre. The roofs of the wings are levelled at the outer ends and rise ten feet against the body of the centre; the roof of the centre rises thirteen feet, presenting gable ends in front; from the middle of which, the cupola rises, eighteen feet square, to the height of fifteen feet above the ridge; thence in an octangular form, thirteen feet in diameter, seventeen feet, and is covered with a roof in the form of an inverted acorn rising to the height of nine feet, and surmounted with a gilt ball, thirty-three inches in diameter, on which stands an eagle six and a half feet in height, with its wings partially expanded. Each front has in its lower story three doors and six windows, and in its upper story, nine windows with a semi-elliptical window in each gable end: four windows in the south, and two in the north end. The outside walls of the building are of granite stone, hammered, and built in a plain style—the only ornament being a Tuscan frontispiece of stone work at each central front door. The roof and cupola are of wooden materials. The roof is ornamented with a coving appropriate to the Doric order, and a balustrade upon the wings. The square part of the cupola is ornamented with twelve Ionic columns, three at each corner, placed in a triangular position, with an appropriate coving and balustrade. The octangular part has one Ionic column at each corner, surmounted with an urn.

In the second story of the centre is the Representatives' chamber, with an arched ceiling rising thirty feet from the floor, elegantly finished with stucco-work. The north wing contains the Senate chamber, eighteen feet in height, with a beautiful ceiling of plaistering, ornamented with stucco-work, supported by four Ionic columns and an equal number of pilasters. This room, for its neatness and elegance of finishing, is not perhaps inferior to any in the United States. In the south wing are contained the Council chamber and anti-chamber, both of which are finished in a handsome style. In the same wing, in the lower story, which is divided into two parts, are the Secretary's and Treasurer's offices, over which is a suite of committee rooms. In the north wing under the Senate chamber is a spacious room intended for public hearings before committees of the legislature. This room is also conveniently arranged and is sufficiently commodious for the accommodation of the Superior Court, when holding a law term. Under the Representatives' chamber is an open area, in which are eight Doric columns, supporting the flooring above. This area, with the adjacent passages in the wings, cooled by the current of fresh air passing through the spacious doors and windows opening into them, affords, in the warm month of June, a delightful retreat to legislators, when fatigued by long attention to their arduous duties, or heated by the ardor of debate, above stairs; and it is by no means an uncommon case to see them availing themselves of the benefits of this pleasant retirement.

The lot on which the State House stands contains something more than two acres, enclosed on its sides with a solid wall of hammered stone about five feet high; the front fences are of stone posts and sills and iron castings, with gates of the same material.

The expenses of building this house, including the fences, the lot of ground whereon it stands and the furniture of the house, amounted to nearly eighty-two thousand dollars. The amount drawn from the treasury of the state in pursuance of sundry appropriations for that purpose, was $67,372 44
Labor done at the State Prison, as appears from the charges on the books there, amounted to the sum of $10,455 16
The lot of land whereon the house stands, the stone for the house, and drawing the same, all which was given by a few patriotic individuals of Concord, amounted to 4,000 00

$81,827 60

In the construction of this building with its appendages, including the fencing of the lot, there were required 37,000 feet of hammered stone. The facings of the walls and partitions of the basement, which are coarsely hammered, may be estimated at 4,800 square feet; the walls of the house, door posts, threshholds, window sills, &c. which are finely hammered, at 16,200 feet; steps, flagging, walks, &c. at 6000 feet, and 10,000 feet for the fences. In addition to these quantities, there were required 7,000 cubic feet of rough stone for the foundation of the building, and 5,000 feet for the foundation of the fence. There were also required 630 thousand bricks, 840 casks of lime, 12 tons of plaister, 7 tons of soap-stone, 7 tons iron, 4,000 pounds of steel, 8,000 bushels of coal, 500 thousand feet of lumber, two and a half tons of lead, 2000 feet of glass, one thousand dollars value of oil and paints, and five hundred dollars value of nails.

STATE PRISON.—The state prison or penitentiary is a handsome building, situated in Concord, three stories high, built entirely of granite. It is 70 feet in length, 36 feet wide, the walls of which are three feet in thickness. It contains in all 36 cells, the dimensions of which are 8 feet by 9, with the exception of six in the upper story for the accommodation of the sick, &c. which are 10 by 17. The yard is enclosed by a faced wall of 259 feet by 192, fourteen feet high, surmounted by a range of pickets ten feet in length. Connected with the prison, is a house for the accommodation of the warden, his family, guards, &c. built also of granite, four stories high exclusive of the basement, and is 49 feet by 22. The officers, &c. of this institution are a warden, physician, chaplain, deputy-warden, four guards, two overseers of the work-shops – the whole of whom receive their pay directly from the proceeds of the prison, with the exception of the warden, whose salary, $800, is drawn from the treasury. The governor and council for the time being constitute the board of directors or visitors. The convicts are employed in stone-cutting, coopering, smithing, shoe-making, weaving and tailoring. The prison was erected in 1812; and cost with the appurtenances about $37,000—since which time between $4000 and $5000 have been drawn from the treasury to defray the expense of additional buildings. The first commitment to this penitentiary was in November, 1812—since which period, 199 have been confined, four of whom were females, 19 foreigners. Of these, 24 were sentenced for horse-stealing; for counterfeiting and forgery, 30; assault, &c. 8; manslaughter, 3; perjury, 1; arson, 4;

burglary, 3; stealing, 126. The greatest number confined at any one time, 74—present number, 56.

Previous to the establishment of our state prison, there were eight offences, that by a law of the state subjected the offender to capital punishment; but in that year they were reduced to two—treason and wilful murder.* If this benevolent change in our laws has not diminished, it has not increased, the number of crimes. The expenses of our state prison have greatly diminished since the alterations made in the management of its affairs, and the introduction of a new system—the appointment of a new warden, and placing the institution under the immediate control of the governor and council. The police of the prison is rigid and salutary. The convicts are dressed in uniform, and comfortably fed. The sexes are kept apart. Great care is bestowed by the officers of the institution upon their morals—in the hope of reforming the offender, and fitting him to respect and observe those laws, for the violation of which he is condemned to suffer.

In the year ending May 31, 1818, the expenses of this institution exceeded the profits of the labor of convicts, &c. in the sum of $4235 61. In June of that year, the legislature deemed it necessary to alter the internal system of the penitentiary; and appointed new officers to manage its concerns. For the year ending May 31, 1819, the whole expense of the prison exceeded the profits in the sum of $862 72. In the year ending May 31, 1820—$345 45. In the year ending May 31, 1821—$232 89. During the year ending May 31, 1822, there was a net gain over the expense of $392 50. The sums drawn from the treasury for the support of the prison, since 1817, are as follow:

For the year ending May 31, 1818,	7000 00
May 31, 1819,	3152 34
May 31, 1820,	2100 00
May 31, 1821,	963 00
May 31, 1822,	1000 00

And it is confidently expected that no further aid from the treasury will be necessary for the support of the prison for a number of years, unless some unforeseen accident should change the aspect of its affairs.

CURIOSITIES.—As these will be described at some length in the course of this work, the reader is referred to the heads under which they

---

* The crimes formerly punishable with death, were—treason, murder, rape, sodomy, burglary, arson, robbery, and one species of forgery. Fines and imprisonment, the lash and the pillory, were also bestowed, with unsparing severity, on minor offences. The two latter modes of punishment are now entirely abolished.

are noticed. See Amoskeag Falls, Atkinson, Barrington, Bellows Falls, Chester, Durham, Franconia, Hampton, Ossipee, Sanbornton, White Mountains.

INDIANS.—Whatever relates to the aboriginals of our country, those early proprietors of the soil which we inherit, must be interesting to posterity. The lands which we cultivate, the forests, the rivers and mountains around us, once swarmed with a distinct race of the human family. They, whose character was once so lofty and independent, are hardly seen among us, and if seen, are seen " begging the price of their perdition." They, who might have exterminated the Europeans on their arrival, have themselves become exterminated, and most of their memorials have perished with them. It is much to be regretted, that so little has been preserved respecting the Indians of New-Hampshire; but there have been causes for this omission in recording their history which could not easily have been removed. " In the first place, the horror proceeding from the cruelties of their warfare forbade the calmness of investigation. As long as they were formidable, curiosity was overpowered by terror; and there was neither leisure nor inclination, to contemplate their character as a portion of the human family, while the glare of conflagration reddened the midnight sky, and the yells of the savage, mingled with the shrieks of the butchered victims, rode as portentous messengers, on every gale. But that state of things has ceased to exist. The white men in America have become too numerous to fear any longer the effects of savage barbarity, such as assailed the early inhabitants of our state, and carried terror to the stoutest heart." A spirit of sympathy should now be excited for this unfortunate race of beings. Pity for those that remain should fill our breasts.

" Indulge, our native land, indulge the tear,
" That steals impassioned o'er a nation's doom ;
" To us each twig from Adam's stock is dear,
" And tears of sorrow deck an Indian's tomb."

The Indians who formerly inhabited New-Hampshire may be considered under five separate divisions: viz. 1. Those tribes residing on Pascatequa river and its branches. 2. The various tribes on the Merrimack and its tributary streams. 3. The Ossipee Indians on Lake Ossipee and the Pequacketts on Saco river, in the N. E. part of the state. 4. The Indians on Connecticut river. 5. The Coos Indians.

When the first settlers arrived, they found on Squamscot river, in the vicinity of Exeter, a tribe under Wahangnonawitt, as their sagamore;

on Cocheco river around Dover, lived the Newichwannocks, having a sagamore, named Rowls, and on the Pascataqua were the Pascataqua tribe. All these tribes and several others, as far east as Kennebeck river, were generally called by the *generic* name of Abenaquies. On Merrimack river, there were numerous collections of Indians; as we have reason to suppose from the relics which are annually found on its borders. In the summer of 1821, parts of three skeletons were found on this river, at Bedford, in the county of Hillsborough. One of them appeared to be interred in a sitting posture, and all their heads lay towards the south. During the present year, there was found in the garden of Mr. James Riddle of Merrimack, a skeleton supposed to be that of an Indian, which had probably been interred more than eighty years. The Penacook tribe, which lived in the vicinity of Concord, was the most considerable in numbers and importance of any tribe which lived in this state on Merrimack river. In 1629, Passaconaway was their grand sachem, who lived till the year 1660, and who ever remained friendly to the English, and at his death, strictly enjoined his son and successor, Wonalanset, to maintain peace with his English neighbors. Around the falls at Amoskeag, have been discovered many traces of Indians, and here probably was one of their best fishing grounds. The Ossipee and Pequackett Indians at the time the first settlers of this state arrived, probably amounted to nearly 800 souls. On Connecticut river, there were doubtless many tribes, but we are lost in darkness and perplexity when we attempt to name them or point out their individual residence. The history of the Coos Indians is involved in the same obscurity. The Indians, inhabiting this state, several times suffered from the Mohawks, a fierce and savage race living in the county of Montgomery in the state of New-York. Some of the small tribes were nearly exterminated by their ferocity and savage barbarity. They were more cruel to the eastern Indians than the eastern Indians were to the Europeans. The Indians in this state inhabited those regions where the means of subsistence could be the most easily obtained. It was observed by the earliest inhabitants of this country, that they were most numerous on the banks of large rivers, where their wants were, in a great measure, supplied by the abundance of fish, which, at former periods, those streams produced. In the gradual diminution and final extinction of the aboriginals of New-Hampshire, we have a melancholy specimen of what has happened in like manner to all the Indian tribes, who once inhabited the territory of New-England, except a few feeble remnants in the south part of Massachusetts and some in Connecticut; and of hundreds of other powerful tribes, once spread over the settled parts of our country. And such will be the inevitable destiny of all Indians now mingled among our white population, if a radical change in our treatment of them, be not adopted. The *monuments and relics of the Indians* in this state have been accurately described by Dr. Belknap in the 3d vol. of his Hist. of N. H. page 63, to which we refer the reader.

HISTORY.—New-Hampshire was discovered by Capt. John Smith, an English navigator, in 1614. The name was given to it by Capt. John Mason, the original patentee. In the earliest grant made to Mason and Gorges in 1622, it is styled *Laconia*, and in some of our earliest histories it is called *Capt. Mason's Patent* and *Pascataqua*. The first settlements were made at Dover and Portsmouth in the year 1623. The first settlers, of whom the principal were Edward Hilton, William Hilton, and David Thompson, were sent from England by the original proprietors of Laconia, to found a plantation on Pascataqua river; to cultivate the vine, discover mines, carry on the fisheries and trade with the natives. The two Hiltons, with their associates, settled at Dover neck, about seven miles from Portsmouth. Thompson, with his company, set down nearer the harbor. In 1629, Rev. John Wheelwright purchased of several Sachems the country between the Merrimack and Pascataqua, from the ocean a far back as the town of Amherst; about fifty miles. In 1638, Mr. Wheelwright, with a small company from Braintree, commenced the settlement of Exeter; and the same year the town of Hampton was settled. These were the first towns settled in New-Hampshire. The inhabitants of these places met with many difficulties in their progress. Their land was granted over, and over again, in successive patents; and with different patentees, they had many perplexing disputes. The climate was more severe, and their soil less fruitful, than that of Massachusetts and Connecticut. In the beginning of their plantations, they were more divided in their principles, and less harmonious in their measures, than the people of those colonies. At the same time, they had no stable government, of sufficient vigor to discourage dissentions. They were, also, not a little perplexed with loose Ministers, and Magistrates; such as generally withdraw from regular, well principled society, to indulge their mischievous dispositions, and establish their influence in more imperfect communities. In 1641, all these settlements, by a voluntary act, submitted to Massachusetts, and were comprehended in the county of Norfolk, which extended from the Merrimack to the Pascataqua. The government of Great Britain, for many years, paid them but little attention. At length in 1679, a new government was established, and New-Hampshire was made a royal province by commission from Charles II. The commission was brought to Portsmouth by Edward Randolph, January 1, 1680; but it was received with great reluctance by those persons nominated in it to the Presidency and Council. The first General Assembly met at Portsmouth, on the 16th of March following, in which Portsmouth, Dover, Hampton and Exeter were the only towns represented.—In 1686, a change took place, and all New-England was entrusted to a President and Council. After the imprisonment of Andros, the union with Massachusetts was revived in 1689, but in 1692, the old separate government was established. From 1699 to 1702, it was united with Massachusetts and New-York, and from 1702 to 1741, with Massachusetts. In 1741, the boundary lines were established by royal authority, by which New-Hampshire received from Massachusetts a tract of country, of fourteen miles in breadth, and above fifty in length, more than the former had ever claimed. The same year, Benning Wentworth was appointed Governor and continued in office until 1767, when he was superseded by John Wentworth, who continued in office till the revolution. A temporary government was established in 1776, to continue during the war with Great Britain. It consisted of a house of representatives, and a council of twelve, with the addition of an executive committee to act in the recess of the legislature. The number of this committee varied from six to sixteen. The president of the council was also president of the executive committee. The Hon. Mesheck Weare filled this responsible office throughout the war. A new constitution was established in 1784; and this being altered and amended in 1792, is the permanent constitution of the state. We conceive it unnecessary to introduce more of the history of New-Hampshire into this general view, especially when we are in possession of such an invaluable history as that of the Rev. Dr. Belknap.

General View of the Counties.

ROCKINGHAM COUNTY.

The county of Rockingham is situated between 42° 41' and 43° 27' N. latitude. It is bounded N. and N. E. by Strafford county; E. by the Atlantic, from the mouth of the Pascataqua to the line of Massachusetts; S. by Mass.; W. by the county of Hillsborough. Its length is about 50 miles; its breadth, from the S. W. corner of Pelham to Portsmouth, is 36 miles. It is of a triangular shape, being no more than 6 miles wide at the N. W. part. It comprises an area of 661,646 acres, or 1,034 square miles nearly. There are no remarkable elevations in this county: the surface, however, is uneven, and in the N. part, from the higher eminences, affords fine views of the surrounding country. The highest points are, Saddleback mountain in Northwood and Deerfield, Fort, in Epsom, Catamount in Pittsfield, and Bean's hill in Northfield. The Winnepisiogee river washes the N. boundary of this county, falling into the Merrimack at the N. W. corner. From thence the Merrimack forms the western line to the town of Concord, where it receives the waters of the Contoocook from the county of Hillsborough. Meandering through Concord, it enriches some fine tracts of interval land, and receives the waters of the Soucook at the S. E. corner of the town. The Suncook joins the Merrimack at the S. corner of Pembroke. The Lamprey, Exeter, Beaver and Spiggot rivers water the E. and S. E. parts of the county. The largest collection of water is the Great Bay, between Newington and New-Market, and connecting with the Pascataqua. Massabesick pond lies principally in Chester, and is picturesque from its numerous islands and the surrounding elevations. The other principal ponds are, Island pond in Hampstead, Great and Country ponds in Kingston, Pleasant pond in Deerfield, Turkey, Long and Turtle ponds in Concord. The soil of the county of Rockingham, having been longer under cultivation than that of any other county, is very fertile; and agricultural pursuits are here crowned with much success. The number of persons engaged in agriculture, in 1820, was 10,522; in commerce, 609; in manufactures, 1,973. Portsmouth has the only sea-port,

50 NEW-HAMPSHIRE GAZETTEER.

and is the largest town in the state. Exeter is an ancient town, and a place of much business. Concord is the seat of the state government, and is a flourishing town. Exeter and Concord are the seats of justice. The population of this county in 1775, was 37,463; 43.169 in 1790; 45,427 in 1800; 50,175 in 1810: the population in 1820 was 55,246, or 53.4 to the square mile.

STATISTICAL TABLE.

Towns.	Meeting-houses.	School districts.	School houses.	Taverns.	Stores.	Saw-mills.	Grain-mills.	Clothing mills.	Carding machines.	Bark mills.	Tanneries.
Allenstown	1	4	4	2		5	2				
Atkinson	1	6	3	2	2	3	1				1
Bow	1	8	8	3		5	2	1	1	1	1
Brentwood	3		4		3	5	5	3	4	1	4
Candia	2	12	12	1	5	5	6	2	1		
Canterbury	3	9	8	3	4	4	3	1	1	2	2
Chester	2	16	16	7	8	18	10	1	1		4
Chichester	1	6	6	4	3	5	2	1	2		
Concord	2	20	20	11	20	6	7	4	3	2	7
Deerfield	2	11	11	8	6	10	8	2	3	4	6
East Kingston	1	4	4		1	2	4	1	1		
Epping	3	8	8	5	7	5	3	1	1		
Epsom	1	6	6	6	4	6	7	3	3	4	
Exeter	3	6	6	8	19	4	5	1	1	1	
Greenland	1	4	4	2	3	1	4	1			
Hampstead	1	8	6	4	2	2	2	1	2	1	1
Hampton	2	4	4	3	4	3	5				2
Hampton Falls	2	3	3	2	2	2	2	1	1		1
Hawke	1	3	3			2	1				
Kensington	2		3	1	3	2	1				1
Kingston	1	5	5	6	5	4	5			2	2
Londonderry	2	18	18	4	8	10	8	2	2	1	
Loudon	2	9	9	3	8	6	6	2	2	3	3
New-Castle	1	1	1	3	1		1				
Newington	1	1	2	2			1				
New-Market	2	6	6	4	10	2	3	1	1	1	
Newtown	1	2	2	1	1	1					
Northfield	1	8	8		2	5		2	3		4
North-Hampton	1	3	3	1	1	3	4				
Northwood	2	8	2	2	6	8	3	2			4
Nottingham	1	8	8	4	1	7	4	1	1		
Pelham	2	5	5		4	3	3	1	1		1
Pembroke	2	8	8	3	11	6	5	3	1		4

Towns.	Meeting-houses.	School districts.	School houses.	Taverns.	Stores.	Saw-mills.	Grain-mills.	Clothing mills.	Carding machines.	Bank mills.	Tanneries.
Pittsfield	2	9	9	2	3	7	5	2	2	3	3
Plaistow	1	4	4	3	4	1	2			1	1
Poplin	1	3	3	1	1	3	3	1	1		3
Portsmouth	7		9	7	280		4		1	12	12
Raymond	1	8	8			4	3	1	1		4
Rye	2	2	2	2	2	3	4				
Salem	2	3	3	3	4	3	4	2	3		
Sandown	1	3	4			4	2	1	2		3
Seabrook	3	3	3			3	3			5	
South-Hampton	1	4	4	2	3	1	1		1		
Stratham	2	4	4	1	1	2	3	1	1	5	6
Windham	1	7	6		1	2	1	1			1
45 towns	78	276	281	127	453	188	156	47	48	49	81

Besides the above, there are 4 distilleries, 3 woollen and 5 cotton factories, 4 oil mills, and 6 paper mills, four at Pembroke, one in Northfield and one at Exeter. There are nine printing establishments in this county, four at Concord, two at Exeter, and three at Portsmouth. Four of these are newspaper offices, from which about 5600 papers are issued weekly. There are seven incorporated academies in this county, several of which are well endowed. That at Exeter is one of the best institutions of the kind in the country. The first settlements in New-Hampshire were made at Dover, Portsmouth, Exeter and Hampton. The first settlement at Portsmouth commenced in the year 1623. Until the formation of counties in 1771, all the courts were holden and all public business transacted at Portsmouth. On the 19th of March in that year this county was formed, and named by Gov. Wentworth, in honor of Charles Watson Wentworth, K. G. F. R. S. Marquis of Rockingham. On the 16th of June 1791, the divisional lines were defined and established by the new government of the state.

STRAFFORD COUNTY.

This county is situated between 43° 03′ and 44° 02′ N. latitude; bounded N. by the county of Coos, E. by the state of Maine, S. and S. W by Rockingham, W. by the Pemigewasset river, which separates it from parts of the counties of Grafton and Hillsborough, and N. W. by Grafton county. It is 63 miles in length, from the mouth of Lamprey river to the N. line of Burton; 33 miles wide at the centre. Its shape, like that of all the other counties, is irregular. It contains an area of 861,171 acres, being 1345 1-2 square miles. This county, which extends to the neighborhood of the White Mountains, has several considerable mountains within its limits. Chocorua, in Burton, Sandwich mountain in the same range, Ossipee and Effingham mountains, Gunstock mountain in Gilford, Moose, in Brookfield and Middleton, and other heights along the ridge denominated Blue Hills, are the most elevated. Red Hill in Moultonborough has a commanding elevation, and has long attracted visitors. Below, the waters of the Winnepisiogee lie open to the eye, and its numerous islands and bays present a fine appearance. This lake is much the largest body of water in the state, being 22 miles long, and varying from one to eight miles in width. Sullivan, or Squam lake, lies partly in this county, and is 6 miles in length and nearly 5 in width. Ossipee lake is also in this county. Great bay, Long bay and Merrymeeting bay, are connected with the Winnepisiogee lake. Smith's pond, in Wolfborough, Sixmile, in Eaton, Merrymeeting, in New-Durham, and Lovewell's, in Wakefield, are the principal ponds. The larger rivers are the Pascataqua, Salmon-Fall, Cochecho, Saco and Swift rivers. The soil of Strafford county, though presenting a great variety, is generally good. Our lands are generally hard of cultivation, but the patient laborer finds an ample reward for his industry. Persons in this county engaged in agriculture in 1820, were 10,284; in manufactures, 1,538; and in commerce, 9.

STATISTICAL TABLE.

Towns.	Meeting-houses.	School districts.	School houses.	Taverns.	Stores.	Saw-mills.	Grain-mills.	Clothing mills.	Carding machines.	Bark mills.	Tanneries.
Alton	3	20	14	1	5	11	5	1	1	3	3
Barnstead	3	11	11	3	10	7	5	2	3		
Barrington	1	10	7	1	3	4	4	1	1		2
Brookfield	1	4	4			4	1			1	2

NEW-HAMPSHIRE GAZETTEER.

Towns.	Meeting-houses.	School districts.	School houses.	Taverns.	Stores.	Saw-mills.	Grain-mills.	Clothing mills.	Carding machines.	Bark mills.	Tanneries.
Burton		4	3			2	4				
Centre-Harbor	1		2	2	1	2	1			1	1
Conway	2	12	6	3	4	4	5	2	2		
Dover	2	10	8	5	30	2	4	5	4	7	7
Durham	1	8	8	4	12	4	5	2	1	4	4
Eaton	1	9	6	2	1	7	6	1	1		
Effingham	2	10	8	2	6	4	5	1	1	4	4
Farmington	1	12	11	1	4	4	6	1			4
Gilmanton	6	24	24	6	12	11	18	4	3	6	
Gilford	2	10	10	1	5	5	4	1	1	5	
Lee	2	7	7	2	3	7	6	1	1	3	5
Madbury	1	4	4			2	1				1
Meredith	3	15	15	3	10	6	3	4	6	2	2
Middleton	1	3	3	2	2	1	2			1	
Moultonborough	1	9	9	2	1	5	5	1	1	1	1
Milton	1	7	7	5	5	5	4	1	2		1
New-Durham											
New-Hampton	3	12	12	2	2	8	4	2	2	3	
Ossipee	2	17	11	2	8	7	7	1	1		3
Rochester	3	16	14	2	10	5	5	2	3		2
Sanbornton	3	19	18	3	8	15	24	5	8	10	10
Sandwich	3	11	10	1	3	6	6	3	3	3	3
Somersworth	1	6	6	1	2	3	3				
Strafford	1	14	12	1	4	5	4				
Tamworth	1	11	9	3	4	5	5	2	1	2	2
Tuftonborough	1	7	6	3	5	4	5	2	2		1
Wakefield	2	10	9	2	10	7	10	2	4		5
Wolfborough	1	9	8	2	4	4	3	1	1	1	2
32 Towns,	56	321	282	67	174	166	170	48	53	57	65

There are in this county 7 woollen and 8 cotton factories. Two or three of the latter are not constantly in operation. Those at Dover, however, are extensive and profitable. There are 8 oil mills, 4 distilleries, and a paper-mill, the latter at Gilford. There is one printing office, at Dover. The academies at Gilmanton, Effingham, Sanbornton and New-Hampton are incorporated and respectable institutions. There is also an academy at Dover and at Gilford. The first settlement in any part of the State was made at Dover by Edward and William Hilton, from London, in 1623. During the same year, a settlement commenced at Portsmouth. *See Gen. View, p.* 47. The county of Strafford was

F

constituted March 19, 1771. The counties being named after the friends of Gov. Wentworth, Strafford was probably named in honor of William Wentworth, the Earl of Strafford. The population in 1775, was 12,513; in 1790, 23,742; in 1800, 32,614; in 1810, 41,595; and in 1820, 51,117. Population to a square mile, 37.9.

HILLSBOROUGH COUNTY.

Hillsborough county is situated between 42° 41′ and 43° 32′ N. latitude. Its greatest length is 52 miles; its greatest breadth, from the E. line of Manchester to the W. line of Hancock, is 32 miles; and its least breadth, from the W. line of New-London to Pemigewasset river, is about 15 miles. It contains 1245 square miles, or 796,800 acres. It has Grafton county on the N., Rockingham on the E., the state of Massachusetts on the S., and Cheshire county on the W. The surface of this county is generally uneven, though there are but few lofty mountains. The Kearsarge and Ragged mountains in the N. part are the highest elevations, and from their summits, there is an extensive prospect. Lyndeborough mountain in the township of Lyndeborough, Sunapee mountain in Fishersfield, the Unconoonock in Goffstown, Crotched in Francestown and Society-Land, are of considerable altitude. These will be noticed under the towns in which they are situated. This section of New-Hampshire is well watered. The noble and majestic Merrimack has a course of more than 20 miles in this county. In Boscawen, it receives the Contoocook, a river of considerable length and importance, watering several towns in the west part of the county. At Dunstable, the Nashua, a beautiful stream from Massachusetts, discharges its waters into the Merrimack. Between the mouths of these rivers, the Souhegan and Piscataquog, streams of much value and consequence to the manufacturing interests, discharge themselves into the Merrimack; the former in the township of Merrimack; the latter in Bedford. Part of two large collections of water denominated lakes are situated in this county. The southern part of lake Sunapee is in the N. W. part of the township of Fishersfield; and the W. part of lake Massabesick is on the E. boundary of Manchester. Besides these, there are numerous ponds interspersed through the whole extent of territory. Some of the largest of these are Chance pond in Andover, Pleasant pond in New-London, Todd's pond in Fishersfield, Gregg's pond in Antrim, Pleasant pond in Francestown, Babboosuck pond in Amherst, and Potanipo in Brookline. There

NEW-HAMPSHIRE GAZETTEER. 55

are several mineral springs which have been found serviceable in cutaneous affections, but no one has yet acquired general celebrity. Minerals have been found in various places, but not in great abundance. The manufactures in this county in 1810, were as follows, viz. 56 tanneries, at which 6150 hides and 12,000 skins were tanned ; 2 distilleries, producing 5000 gallons of spirit ; 1 paper-mill, making $12,000 worth of paper ; 38 fulling mills, fulling 126,500 yds. of cloth, and dressing 90,000 yds. of thin cloths ; 10 shearing machines ; 35 carding machines, carding 158,000 lbs. of wool ; 2 oil mills, producing 6000 gallons of oil ; 5 nail cutting machines, making 10 tons of nails ; 6 trip-hammers ; 16 hatters, making 4000 fur and 6000 wool hats ; 5490 looms, weaving 1, 158,160 yds. of cloth. All these were produced annually.—This county possesses many advantages for manufacturing establishments, and it is gratifying to find that many of its citizens are turning their attention to this branch of national and individual wealth.

STATISTICAL TABLE.

Towns.	Meeting-houses.	School districts.	School houses.	Taverns.	Stores.	Saw-mills.	Grain-mills.	Clothing mills.	Carding machines.	Bark mills.	Tanneries.
Amherst	1	12	9	4	4	4	3	1		1	1
Andover	2	15	12	3	4	5	3	2	2	1	3
Antrim	1	10	8	2	2	7	6	2	2	2	3
Bedford	2	10	10	3	7	8	6	1	1		2
Boscawen	2	15	15	9	6	17	5	4	5		5
Bradford	1	7	7	1	4	3	3	1		2	2
Brookline	1	3	3	2	3	6	4	1		1	1
Deering	1	10	10	2	2	2	2	1	1		2
Dunbarton	1	8	7	4	5	6	2			1	1
Dunstable	1	9	9	6	5	3	3	1	1	2	3
Fishersfield	1	8	7	1	2	3	2		1		
Francestown	1	10	9	3	6	6	5	2	2		4
Goffstown	2	11	11	4	6	17	8	3	2		2
Greenfield	1	9	9	1	2	3	1	1			2
Hancock	1	9	8	2	3	6	6	1	1		2
Henniker	3	10	10	3	5	7	6	2	4	3	3
Hillsborough	1	13	13	6	7	8	5	3	3	3	6
Hollis	1	13	12	2	4	6	5	1	1		1
Hooksett		5	5	5		4					
Hopkinton	3	17	16	3	7	5	5	2	2	6	6
Lyndeborough	1	10	9	2	2	4	3	1			2

NEW-HAMPSHIRE GAZETTEER.

Towns.	Meeting-houses.	School districts.	School houses.	Taverns.	Stores.	Saw-mills.	Grain-mills.	Clothing mills.	Carding machines.	Bark mills.	Tanneries.
Litchfield	1	3	3	1		4	2		1		
Manchester	1	7	4	2	2	7	4				
Mason	1	10	10	1	3	5	4	1	2		1
Merrimack	1	9	9	5	5	8	5	2	2		2
Milford	2	7	7		3	12	4	2	2		1
Mont-Vernon	1	4	4	1	3	2	1				1
New-Boston	2	16	14	1	3	25	6	2	2	1	2
New-Ipswich	2	9	9	3	4	4	3		3	1	1
New-London	1	8	8		3	4	3	2	2		2
Nottingham-West	2	10	10	1	3	4	4	2	1		
Peterborough	2	6	6	1	6	4	3	2	1	1	1
Salisbury	3	13	13	3	8	10	5	3	3	2	6
Sharon		3	2		1	2	1				
Society-Land	1	3	1								
Sutton	2	10	9		2	8	3	3	1	3	3
Temple	1	6	6		2	4	4	1	1		1
Warner	2	17	15	2	4	6	4	2	2	2	2
Weare	4	24	23		9	11	9	3	3	1	8
Wilmot	1	8	7	1	1	5	3				
Wilton	2	9	9	1	1	5	5	2	2	2	3
Windsor		3	2	1		2	1	1			
42 Towns,	60	399	370	92	149	256	157	58	56	35	85

Besides the preceding mills, factories, &c. there are 2 paper mills, one at Warner, the other at Peterborough; 11 cotton factories, 7 woollen factories; 10 trip-hammers; a number of distilleries and oil mills; a starch manufactory, which manufactures between 4000 and 5000 bushels of potatoes into the useful article of starch.—There is one printing establishment at Amherst, which issues weekly more than 1000 papers. There are five incorporated academies in this county, three of which are in operation. That at New-Ipswich is highly respectable, and has funds. Those at Francestown and Hillsborough have been in operation but a short time. Hillsborough has 42 townships, 34 post-offices, sends 44 members to the General Court. The Superior Court and Court of Sessions are holden alternately at Amherst and Hopkinton. The first permanent settlement of this county was made at Dunstable, then considered as belonging to Massachusetts, a few years before the war with King Phllip in 1675. It was constituted a county by an act of the General Assembly of the province, on the 19th of March, 1771. Its name is supposed to be derived from *Wills Hills*, the Earl of Hillsborough, who was one of the privy council of George III., and whose residence was at Hillsborough, in the county of Down in Ireland. The population in 1775, was 15,986; in 1790, 32,871; in 1800, 43,899; in 1810, 49,249, and in 1820, 53,884. The population to a square mile is 43.2. The number of persons engaged in agriculture, 13,197; in commerce, 238; and in manufactures, 2,400.

CHESHIRE COUNTY.

Cheshire, the western county in this state, extends from lat. 42° 43′ to 43° 36′ N. Its length is 54 miles; its greatest breadth 26 miles; and its least breadth 15. It is bounded N. by the county of Grafton, E. by Hillsborough, S. by the state of Massachusetts and W. by Vermont. It contains 802,638 acres, or a little more than 1254 square miles. Throughout the whole extent on the west, this county is watered by the Connecticut, the western bank of which forms the boundary between New-Hampshire and Vermont. Ashuelot and Sugar rivers are considerable streams, and are tributary to Connecticut river. The former has its source from a pond in Washington, and after receiving two branches in Keene and Swanzey, and several smaller streams in Winchester, empties into Connecticut river at Hinsdale. Sugar river issues from the west side of Lake Sunapee; passes through Newport and Claremont, where it unites with the Connecticut. Lake Sunapee and Spafford's Lake are considerable collections of water. The former is in the N. E. part of the county, lying principally in Wendell. Spafford's Lake, of about eight miles in circumference, is situated in Chesterfield. There is a pleasant island in this lake containing about eight acres. The Grand Monadnock in Dublin and Jaffrey is the highest mountain, its altitude having been repeatedly found to be more than 3000 feet above the level of the sea. Croydon mountains in the townships of Croydon and Grantham, are the next most considerable elevations. Bellows Falls in Connecticut river, in Walpole, have been regarded as one of the greatest natural curiosities in this county.

A variety of soil is found in this county. Much of it is very good, and particularly the intervals on Connecticut river. In nineteen towns, containing 371,243 acres and 22,958 inhabitants, the agricultural products in 1820, were 406,900 lbs. of butter, 660,500 lbs. of cheese, 1,480,-

500 lbs. of beef, 1,761,500 lbs. of pork, 110,200 lbs. of flax, 10,333 barrels of cider, and 27 tons of pearl ashes.

STATISTICAL TABLE.

Towns.	Meeting-houses.	School districts.	School houses.	Taverns.	Stores.	Saw-mills.	Grain-mills.	Clothing mills.	Carding machines.	Bark mills.	Tanneries.
Acworth	2	12	12	0	3	5	1	2		1	2
Alstead	3	14	14	2	3	5	3	1	2		2
Charlestown	2	11	11	6	5	6	3	1	1		4
Chesterfield	1	14	13	4	5	9	3	3	2	1	3
Claremont	3	15	14	7	7	6	4	4	3	2	4
Cornish	3	12	12	2	3	10	5	3	3		1
Croydon	1	8	7	1	3	2	2	2	1		2
Dublin	2	10	10	1	3	8	7	2	1	1	1
Fitzwilliam	1	12	12	2	2	4	2	1	1	1	1
Gilsum	1	5	5	1		2	2	1	1		
Goshen	1	3	3	2	1	4	1	1	0	1	
Grantham		12	12	1		3	2	1	1		
Hinsdale	2	6	6	4	1	4	1	1	1		2
Jaffrey	1	12	12	2	4	3	3	2	2	2	2
Keene	2	12	12	6	8	9	4	2	1		1
Langdon	1	7	6	1	2	5	1	1	1		
Lempster	1	7	7	3	2	5	3	1	1	1	1
Marlborough	1	6	5	3	3	4	2	3	1	2	2
Marlow	1	6	6	2	3	4	3	1	1	1	2
Nelson	1	8	8		1	3	4	2	1		
Newport	3	14	14	4	4	9	3	3	1	2	2
Plainfield	2	12	12	5	5	3	2	3	3	3	3
Richmond	2	12	12	2	3	4	5	1	2	1	3
Rindge	1	12	12	3	3	2	2	1			3
Roxbury	1	3	3			2	1				
Springfield	1	13	11	1	3	5	3	1		1	1
Stoddard	1	8	8	1	2	3	3				
Surry	1	4	4	3	2	2	1	1	1		1
Sullivan	1	6	6	1	1	2	2				
Swanzey	2	13	13	2	3	9	4	3	3		1
Troy	1	7	6	1	1	3	2	1	1		
Unity	3	12	10	2		5	3	2	1	1	1
Walpole	1	13	12	6	6	3	4	3	3	2	3
Washington	1	8	7	2	3	6	4	1	2		1
Wendell		7	5	1	1	4	3	2	2		
Westmoreland	3	12	12	1	3	6	6	2	1	1	2
Winchester	2	15	13	5	5	10	4	2	2		1
37 Towns,	56	363	347	90	104	179	108	61	46	24	53

There are, besides the preceding, 5 cotton factories, several woollen factories, 5 oil mills, 1 paper mill, several distilleries and furnaces, and 20 trip-hammers. There is one printing press at Keene, which issues a weekly paper, and has in connection with it a large bookselling establishment. There are five incorporated academies, of which Union Academy at Plainfield, has funds to the amount of 40,000 dollars. Several of them are in a flourishing condition. The number of persons engaged in agriculture in 1820, was 7,968; in commerce, 82; in manufactures, 1,620. Cheshire has 37 towns, 29 post-offices, sends 38 members to the General Court. The Superior Court and Court of Sessions are holden alternately at Keene and Charlestown. The earliest settlement in this county was made about the year 1682 at Hinsdale, then a part of Northfield, and under the government of Massachusetts. The county was formed March 19, 1771, and it probably received its name from Cheshire, one of the western counties in England. Population in 1775, 10,252; in 1790, 28,772; in 1800, 38,825; in 1810, 40,988, and in 1820, 45,376. Population to the square mile, 36.2.

GRAFTON COUNTY.

Grafton county extends from lat. 43° 27' to 44° 22' N. It is 58 miles in length, and its greatest breadth is 30 miles. It contains 828,623 acres, besides a large tract of ungranted land. It is bounded N. by the county of Coos, E. by Strafford, S. by Hillsborough and W. by the state of Vermont. Grafton is watered by Connecticut river, on which are several pleasant and flourishing towns; by Pemigewasset, Lower Amonoosuck rivers, and by many smaller streams which will be hereafter noticed. Squam and Newfound lakes are the largest collections of water. The former, of which a considerable part lies in Strafford county, has been much celebrated for its picturesque beauties. Its numerous angular projections, the variety of its islands covered with wood, and the vicinity of lofty mountains, render it an object peculiarly interesting. There are numerous elevations which come under the name of mountains. Those of the most importance are Gardner's in Lyman, Peaked in Bethlehem, Moosehillock in Coventry, Cushman's and the Blue mount in Peeling, Carr's in Warren and Ellsworth, Moose in Hanover, Cardigan in Orange, and some others which will be described under the respective towns.

The soil of this county is very much diversified. A large portion of it is mountainous and hilly, but this circumstance does not prevent its productiveness. It presents fine tracts for pasturage, a large proportion of arable land, and on the rivers, extensive and fertile intervals.

STATISTICAL TABLE.

Towns.	Meeting-houses.	School districts.	School houses.	Taverns.	Stores.	Saw mills.	Grain mills.	Clothing mills.	Carding machines.	Bark mills.	Tanneries.
Alexandria	1	7	6	1	1	4	2	1			1
Bath	1	11	10	2	7	7	3	2	3	1	2
Bethlehem	2	5	4	2	2	1	1		1		
Bridgewater	2	9	7			6	2	1	1		1
Bristol	1	8	7	1	2	3	2	1	1	1	4
Campton	1	10	9		1	5	3	2	1	1	1
Canaan	1	14	12	4	2	6	4	2	2		2
Concord	2	8	7	3	2	5	2	1	1	1	1
Coventry		3	3	1		1					
Danbury		7	4	2		2	2	1			
Dorchester	1	8	6	2	1	4	2	1	1		
Ellsworth		2	2			1	1				
Enfield	2	12	12	2	5	7	4	2	2	4	4
Franconia		3	3	3	1	2	1				
Grafton	2	10	7	4	1	5	7	1	1	1	1
Groton	1	9	6	2	1	4	3	1	1	1	1
Hanover	3	12	12	4	7	5	1	2	1	3	
Haverhill	2	9	9	5	9	12	4	1	1	2	1
Hebron	1	7	7	2	2	2	1	1		1	1
Holderness	2	12	6	1	1	5	3	1	2	1	2
Landaff	1	6	6	1	2	3	1				
Lebanon	1	16	16	9	6	7	4	5	6	1	3
Lime	2	14	12	9	4	11	4	3	2	2	
Lincoln											
Littleton	1	11	8	4	2	4	2	2	2		1
Lyman	3	7	7	1	1	5	3	1	1	1	2
New Chester	2	14	10	2	3	5	2	1	2	1	1
Orange		3	2	1							
Orford	3	12	10	3	3	7	2	2	2	2	2
Peeling		3	3	2		2	3	1	1		
Piermont	1	8	8	2	2	3	3	1	1		1
Plymouth	1	9	8	1	5	5	2			1	3
Rumney	1	11	7	5	5	5	2				3
Thornton	2	10	8	3	1	3	3	1	1	1	2
Warren	1	7	7	2	1	2	1	1	1	1	2
Wentworth	1	6	6	2	4	6	4	3	3	1	1
36 Towns,	45	306	257	87	85	154	86	42	41	28	43

There are in this county 2 cotton factories, 2 paper mills, 3 oil mills, 2 distilleries and six trip-hammers. There are two printing establishments, one at Haverhill, the other at Enfield. From the former issues a weekly paper; from the other a religious magazine, devoted to the dissemination of Freewill Baptist sentiments. In this county, are two incorporated academies, Holmes Plymouth Academy and Haverhill Academy. It contains 36 townships, 26 post-offices, sends 30 representatives, and with the county of Coos, two senators to the General Court. The number of persons engaged in agriculture in 1820, was 8,653; in manufactures, 1,097; and in commerce, 118. The number of rateable polls that year was 5764; the valuation $126 11. The sessions of the Superior Court and of the Court of Sessions are held alternately at Haverhill and Plymouth. The first settlement in this county was made at Lebanon, and this was the first settlement on Connecticut river north of Charlestown. It was constituted a county, March 19, 1771, and received its name in honor of Augustus Henry Fitzroy, Duke of Grafton. Population in 1775, 3597; in 1790, 12,449; in 1800, 20,171; in 1810, 28,462; and in 1820, 32,989. Population to a square mile, 25.7.

COOS COUNTY.

Coos is the largest county in the state, and within its limits are situated the greater part of the ungranted lands—most of which, being very mountainous, cannot be cultivated, and will probably never be settled. This county extends from latitude 43° 58' to the extreme north part of the state—being 76 miles in length, and having a mean width of about 20 miles. The area of this county is estimated to contain 1600 square miles, or, in round numbers, 1,000,000 of acres. It is bounded N. by Lower Canada, E. by Maine, S. by the county of Strafford, W. by Grafton county and the state of Vermont. Besides the stupendous pile of the White Mountains, which distinguishes this county, there are several other mountains of no inconsiderable height. Those in Shelburne, Adams and Chatham, on the east of the White Mountains, are bold and abrupt. The Peaks and Bowback mountains in Stratford; the elevations in Dixville, Columbia and Kilkenny; Pilot and Mill mountains in Piercy; Cape Horn in Northumberland, and Pondcherry, S. W. of Jefferson, are all of considerable magnitude, and partake of the grandeur of the White Hills. A particular account of these wonders of nature will be given under their appropriate heads. In the neighborhood of high mountains are generally found the sources of our greater rivers. Three of the principal rivers of New-England, the Connecticut, Ameriscoggin and Saco, take their rise in this county. There are numerous other streams which become tributary to these rivers, the principal of which are the Mohawk, Amonoosuck, Israel's and John's rivers. The Margallaway, after receiving the waters of Dead and Diamond rivers, unites with the Ameriscoggin, near Umbagog lake. This lake lies principally in Maine. Lake Connecticut is situated N. of the 45° of latitude, and is a source of the Connecticut river. The largest pond in this county lies N. of Lake Connecticut, and is connected with it by an outlet. There are several small ponds, which will be noticed under the towns where they are situated. A great portion of this county yet lies uncultivated, and large tracts will probably never be settled. If the husbandman cannot behold wide-spreading cultivated hills and extensive plains—the lover of nature may here behold her seated in gorgeous splendor and beauty. There are, however, extensive tracts of fine interval and upland, and the soil in the vale of the Connecticut is very rich and fruitful. Persons engaged in agriculture in 1820, 1,760 ; manufactures, 71 ; commerce, 12.

STATISTICAL TABLE.

Towns.	Meeting-houses.	School districts.	School-houses.	Taverns.	Stores.	Saw-mills.	Grain-mills.	Clothing mills.	Carding machines.	Bark mills.	Tanneries.
Adams	1	6	5			1	2				
Bartlett		4	4	2	2	3	1				
Bretton-Woods											
Cambridge											
Chatham	1	3	3			1	3	1	1		
Columbia		6	2		1	2	2				1
Colebrook		6	2	1	2	4	2	1	1		2
College Grant											
Dixville											
Dummer											
Dalton		2	2	2	1	2	2	1	1		
Durand											
Erroll											
Hale's Location											
Hart's Location											
Jefferson		2	2	1		1					
Kilkenny											

NEW-HAMPSHIRE GAZETTEER. 63

Towns.	Meeting houses.	School districts.	School houses.	Taverns.	Stores.	Saw mills.	Grain mills.	Clothing mills.	Carding machines.	Bark mills.	Tanneries.
Lancaster	1	8	4	1	4	2	4	2	3		
Maynesborough											
Millsfield											
Northumberland	1	3	3			1	1	1	1		
Nash & Sawyer's Loc.											
Paulsburgh											
Public Lands											
Piercy						1	1				
Stratford	1	5	5	2							
Shelburne					2		1	2			
Stewartstown		5	4								
Success											
Warner's Patent											
Whitefield		3	3			2	1				
Winslow's Location											
25 Towns,	5	47	34	11	10	21	20	6	7		3

There is a woollen factory at Colebrook, 2 distilleries at Adams and 2 at Colebrook. Lancaster is the principal town in the county, and there the courts are holden. The first settlement was made in 1763 at Lancaster. The county was formed by an act of the legislature Dec. 24, 1803. Coos* is the Indian name applied to the Connecticut in the vicinity of Lancaster, and was adopted as the name of the county. The population in 1775, was 227; in 1790, 882; in 1800, 2658; in 1810, 3991; and in 1820, 5,549. Population to a square mile, 3.4.

---

*This word signifies *crooked*, and was pronounced by the Indians as if containing but one syllable.

COMPARATIVE VIEWS.

(A.)

Counties.	Area in acres.	Towns.	P.O.	Repr.	Settled.	Incorp.
Rockingham,	661,646	45	31	48	1623	1771
Strafford,	861,171	32	31	36	1623	1771
Hillsborough,	796,800	42	34	44	1675	1771
Cheshire,	802,638	37	29	38	1682	1771
Grafton,	828,623	36	26	30		1771
Coos,	1,000,000	25	6	6	1763	1803

(B.)

	Population.			Persons engaged in		
Counties.	In 1775.	In 1820.	Increase.	Agricul.	Comm.	Manuf.
Rockingham,	37,463	55,246	17,783	10,522	609	1,973
Strafford,	12,513	51,117	38,604	10,284	9	1,538
Hillsborough,	15,986	53,884	37,898	13,197	238	2,400
Cheshire,	10,252	45,376	35,124	7,968	82	1,620
Grafton,	3,597	32,989	29,392	8,653	118	1,097
Coos,	227	5,549	5,322	1,760	12	71

(C.)

	Factories.		Mills.			
Counties.	Cotton.	Woollen.	Paper.	Oil.	Cloth.	Card.mac.
Rockingham,	5	3	6	4		
Strafford,	8	7	1	8	47	48
Hillsborough	11	7	2			
Cheshire,	5		1	5	57	56
Grafton,	2		2	3	61	46
Coos,		1			42	41
					6	7

General Description of Towns,

TOPOGRAPHICAL AND HISTORICAL.

AND OF ALL THE MOUNTAINS, LAKES, PONDS, RIVERS, ETC.

ARRANGED ALPHABETICALLY.

A.

ACWORTH, a post township in Cheshire county, in lat. 43° 13′ N.[*] is bounded N. by Unity, E. by Lempster, S. by Marlow and Alstead, and W. by Langdon and Charlestown. It contains an area of 24,846 acres. It is 50 miles from Concord, 87 from Portsmouth and 93 from Boston. Cold river, affording a number of good mill seats, is the only stream of any note. It rises from Cold pond in the N. E. part of the town, which extends nearly a mile on the line between Acworth and Unity. This pond is from 60 to 100 rods in width. Mitchell's pond is about 120 rods in length and 80 rods in width. This town is chiefly agricultural in its pursuits, having few advantages for manufacturing, excepting such articles as are needed for its own consumption. The agricultural products in 1820 were, 26,000 lbs. of butter, 40,000 lbs. of cheese, 120,000 lbs. of beef, 100,000 lbs. of pork, 15,000 lbs. of flax, 700 barrels of cider and 8 tons of pearl ashes. The soil is generally good. Few towns are more distinguished for raising flax. The soil seems peculiarly adapted to the raising this article, which is wrought by some of the inhabitants into the finest of linen, equal to any imported from Colerain in Ireland. Beef is, perhaps, the staple commodity. Charlestown turnpike passes through nearly the centre of this place. This town was granted Sept. 19, 1766, to Col. Samson Stoddard and 64 others. It was settled in 1768 by William Keyes, Samuel Harper and John Rogers, with their families. The settlement increased but slowly, and it was not until 1771, that there was a sufficient number of inhabitants to require the usual civil regulations of a town. In 1772, it contained 14 houses. A congregational church, consisting of 18 members, was organized March 12, 1773. The first minister was Rev. Thomas Archibald, who was settled Nov. 11, 1789 ; and dismissed June 14, 1794. Rev. John Kimball succeeded, and was ordained in June, 1797 ; dismissed May 4, 1813. Rev. *Phinehas Cooke* was ordained in September, 1814. A baptist church was formed Nov. 9, 1809 ; but has no settled minister. The spotted fever appeared in this town Feb. 28, 1812, and from that time to May 13, there occurred 58 deaths, of which 53 were by the fever. Population in 1820, 1479.

[*] As the whole State of New-Hampshire is situated in *North* latitude, the repetition of this Initial will be omitted.

ADAMS, a town in Coos county, situated on the E. side of the White Mountains, in lat. 44° 9′, is bounded E. by Chatham, N. by unlocated lands, S. by Bartlett, and contains 31,968 acres of land and water. The surface of the town is uneven, and in some parts rocky; but the soil is rich and productive. It is watered principally by the two branches of Ellis's river, passing from the N. and uniting on the S. border near Spruce mountain. The principal elevations are called Black, Baldface and Thorn mountains. Benjamin Copp was the first settler: he moved into Adams in 1779, and with his family buffeted the terrors of the wilderness 14 years, before any other person settled there. The town was incorporated Dec. 4, 1800. A free-will baptist church was formed here in 1803; *Daniel Elkins* settled as their pastor in 1809; and their present number consists of about 50. Population 363.

ALEXANDRIA, a township in Grafton county, in lat. 43° 36′, is bounded N. by Orange and Hebron, E. by Bristol, S. by New-Chester, and W. by Danbury, containing about 20,800 acres. Its N. E. corner extends to Hebron line and includes a part of Newfound lake. It is 9 miles from Bristol village, 30 miles from Concord and 72 from Portsmouth. Alexandria is watered by Smith's river, passing through the S. part, and by Fowler's river, through the N. part of the town. On these rivers and several other smaller streams, are about 2000 acres of interval land, of which the natural growth is hemlock, pine, maple, butternut and elm. The soil of the interval is excellent for producing flax, potatoes and grass. In other parts of the town, it is favorable for wheat and maize. The swells of land are generally moist. The highest and mountainous parts abound in ledges. This town was granted March 13, 1767, to Joseph Butterfield, jun. and others. It was incorporated Nov. 23, 1782. Its first settlement was made in Dec. 1769, by Jonathan Corliss, John M. Corliss and William Corliss. In Feb. 1821, its territorial limits were lessened by annexing a considerable tract to New-Chester according to an act of the legislature, passed Dec. 21, 1820. A congregational church was formed about the year 1788, and Rev. Enoch Whipple was settled in July, the same year. He was dismissed in 1794. There are three religious societies in this town, no one of which has a settled minister. Population in 1820, 707.

ALLENSTOWN, a township in Rockingham county, is in lat. 43° 8′, bounded W. by the river Suncook, N. by Epsom, E. by Deerfield, and S. by Hooksett; distant from Concord, 11 miles, from Boston, 58, from Portsmouth, 38. It contains about 12,225 acres of land, generally of an ordinary quality, though there are some fine farms. The town is principally covered with a growth of oak and pine timber; and great quantities of lumber are annually taken down the river to Boston, &c. Allenstown is well watered, though no large stream passes through it. Great Bear brook furnishes the principal mill-seats. Catamount hill is the highest land in town. On this hill are found large quantities of fine granite, which is used in building. At the E. end of this hill is a precipice of 70 feet nearly perpendicular, at the foot of which is a cavern of some extent, inclining upwards. The first settlers of the tract called *Allens-Town* (after the name of the purchaser of Mason's claim) were John Wolcutt, Andrew Smith, Daniel Evans, Robert Buntin and others. In 1748, while at work on the western bank of the Merrimack river, opposite the mouth of the Suncook, in company with James Carr, Mr. Buntin and his son, ten years of age, were surprised by a party of Indians. Carr attempted to escape, and was shot down. Buntin and his son, making no resistance, were not harmed; but taken through the wilderness to Canada, and sold to a French trader at Montreal—with whom they remained about eleven months, escaped, and fortunately reached home in safety. Andrew, the son, continued on his father's farm until the commencement of the revolution, when, entering the service of his country, he died in her defence at White-Plains, Oct. 28, 1776. There is no settled minister in Allenstown; their meeting-house is open to all religious sects, and they occasionally have preaching. There is also a town-house. Population, 433.

ALSTEAD, a post township in Cheshire county, in lat. 43° 6', is bounded N. by Acworth and Langdon, E. by Marlow, S. by Gilsum and Surry, and W. by Walpole and Langdon. It is 12 miles S. E. from Charlestown, 14 N. from Keene, and 50 W. from Concord. It contains 24,756 acres. This town is well watered by small streams. Cold river passes through the N. W. part; and some of the branches of Ashuelot river have their sources in this town. There are a number of ponds, the principal of which is Warren's pond;—length 250 rods, breadth 150. Perch and pickerel are here caught in great abundance. The soil is strong and productive, and the farms generally well cultivated. There are two meeting-houses and an academy in the centre of the town, and one meeting-house in the east parish. The academy was incorporated July 1, 1820. It has no funds, but the patronage and encouragement it has received are flattering, and induce a hope that it may continue to be useful, and to deserve public favor. There are 14 school districts, in which schools are kept about half the year, and sometimes more. Four persons from this town have received a public education. There are two libraries, one incorporated in 1798, containing 127 volumes; the other in 1804, having 121 volumes. Besides the mills, &c. in the statistical table under Cheshire county, there is one paper mill, one gun factory, and a large establishment for the manufacture of boots and shoes, in which from 10 to 15 workmen are constantly employed. The sales for the last 9 years, have amounted to $6000 annually. Alstead was originally called Newton, and was granted by charter, August 6, 1763, to Samuel Chase and 69 other proprietors. In 1771, there were 25 families, besides 10 single men that were cultivating their lands, and 9 others who partially resided there. The first congregational church was gathered in 1777. Rev. Jacob Mann was ordained in Feb. 1782; dismissed in May, 1789. Rev. Samuel Mead was ordained June 15, 1791; dismissed April 28, 1797. Rev. Seth S. Arnold was ordained Jan. 17, 1817. To this church and society, was left in 1817, by Mrs. Shepard, widow of Gen. Shepard, a legacy of $1000; and, in 1819, by Major Samuel Hutchinson, a legacy of $1000, the interest of which sums is to be appropriated towards the support of an ordained minister of the congregational order, in said society, forever, provided there shall be such a minister so ordained ; otherwise for the benefit of the school in the district of the old meeting-house. The second congregational church was formed in the east parish, Nov. 20, 1788. Rev. *Levi Lankton* was ordained Sept. 3, 1789. The baptist church was formed Dec. 18, 1790, and Rev. *Jeremiah Higbee* was ordained May 28, 1794. There have been special attentions to religion in these churches in 1788, 1798, 1808, 1815 and 1819. There is a small universalist society formed in May, 1820, of citizens in this town and its vicinity. The average number of deaths for 15 years past, excepting 1812 and 1814, has been about 20. In those years, the spotted fever prevailed and swept off 90 persons. General AMOS SHEPARD, who was for many years a member of the General Court of this state, and President of the Senate 7 years, from 1797 to 1804, resided in this town, and was one of its principal inhabitants from 1777 to the time of his death, Jan. 1, 1812. By his persevering industry, his economy and correctness in business, and at the same time, by a rigid adherence to uprightness and integrity in his dealings with his fellow men, he acquired a handsome fortune, and was in many things, a pattern worthy of imitation. Population 1611.

ALTON, post township, Strafford county, in lat. 43° 28', 22 miles from Concord, and 25 from Dover, is bounded N. by Winnepisiogee lake and bay, N. E. by Wolfeborough, E. by New-Durham, S. by Barnstead, W. by Gilmanton and Gilford ; and has an area of 23,843 acres. The town is rough and uneven ; the soil hard and rocky, but productive when well cultivated. The growth of wood is chiefly oak, beech, maple and pine. The principal elevation is called Mount-Major. There is also a large swell of land called Prospect-Hill, affording fine grazing almost to its summit, from which in a clear sky the ocean is visible. Merrymeeting bay extends S. about 1800 rods into this town, where it receives the waters of Merrymeeting river. Half-moon pond, between Alton and Barnstead, is 300 rods long and 150 wide. This town was originally called *New-Durham Gore*—was owned by the Masonian proprietors—settled in 1770, by Jacob Chamberlain and others. It was incorporated Jan. 15, 1796, and named by one of the proprietors after Alton, a market-town, in Southamptonshire, Eng. A freewill baptist church was formed here in 1805 ; and Elder *John Page* ordained in 1811. Pop. 2058.

AMERISCOGGIN, or ANDROSCOGGIN, river, has its sources N. of lat. 45°, and enters this state near the S. E. corner of the second grant to Dartmouth College. Its most northerly branch is the Margallaway river which receives the waters of Dead and Diamond rivers, and unites with those flowing from Umbagog lake, about a mile distant from its outlet. From this junction, the confluent stream pursues a southerly course till it approaches near the White Mountains, where it receives several considerable tributaries, and passes into Maine N. of Mount Moriah. It there bends to the E. and S. E. ; in which course, through a fertile country it passes near the sea-coast, and turning N. runs over the falls at Brunswick, a few miles from Bowdoin College, into Merrymeeting Bay, forming a junction with the Kennebeck, 20 miles from the sea.

AMHERST, a post township and one of the seats of justice in Hillsborough county, is situated on Souhegan river, in lat. 42° 51′; bounded N. by New-Boston and Bedford, E. by Bedford and Merrimack, S. by Hollis, and W. by Milford and Mont-Vernon. It contains by the survey made in 1805, an area of 22,435 acres. It is 28 miles from Concord, about the same distance from Hopkinton, 47 from Boston, 40 from Keene, 60 from Windsor, and 485 from the city of Washington. This town is watered by Souhegan river, of which the most considerable branch originates in Ashburnham, Ms. It is a considerable and very important stream, and in its course to the Merrimack river from this town, affords some of the finest water privileges in the county. It has two bridges over it in Amherst, and one at Milford near the line between these towns. Babboosuck, Little Babboosuck and Jo English ponds are the largest collections of water. The first, 1 1-2 mile in length, and of various breadth, lies in the N. E. part of this town and in Merrimack. From its N. E. extremity issues Babboosuck brook, which takes a N. E. course towards the town of Merrimack. Little Babboosuck is W. from the other and connected with it. Jo English pond is in the N. part of the town and in New-Boston. A stream issues from it which runs into the Babboosuck. Stearns' pond is in the south part of the town. The soil is rather unequal. In some parts, and particularly on Souhegan river, it is of an excellent quality, producing abundant crops. In other parts, on the hills elevated above the village, the soil is of a good quality, and several valuable farms are found under good cultivation. There is a pleasant village, containing a meeting house, court house, jail, school house, two taverns, five stores and 58 dwelling houses. The public buildings, and 42 of the dwelling houses are situated on a plain, extending about 1-2 mile N. and S. and the same distance E. and W. There is a spacious common between the two principal rows of houses, which is often used for public purposes. S. W. of the turnpike road leading from the village to Mont-Vernon, are valuable meadows. On Souhegan river, is a considerable portion of good interval. This town affords no curiosities. No minerals of consequence have been found except iron ore, which more than forty years since, was wrought to some advantage. There is what is termed a mineral spring, about 1 1-2 miles E. of the meeting house. The water has been found useful in rheumatic complaints, and in scrofulous and scorbutic habits; for poisons by ivy, dog-wood, &c. The geological character of the town has been represented to us as follows: The compact part is situated on an alluvion. This deposition consists principally of silicious sand, which occurs in many places of a beautiful greyish white color. This variety resembles very much that formed on the sea shore, and is used for the same domestic purposes. Argill enters into the composition of the soil, but the proportion is too small to give it much firmness. Water filters through it very soon, and consequently it is generally very dry. Large rolled masses of granite, quartz and sometimes greenstone are scattered over the surface of this deposition, and in some places so abundant as to resemble an ill paved street. The surrounding hills are primitive. They are composed of granite and quartz. Their ascent is generally easy, but in some places present mural precipices. A printing press, the first in the county, was established here about 1795, by Nathaniel Coverly. A weekly newspaper, called the "Amherst Journal and New-Hampshire Advertiser," commenced Jan. 16, 1795, and discontinued in January the next year. The "Village Messenger" commenced Jan. 6, 1796; discontinued Dec. 5, 1801. The "Farmer's Cabinet" succeeded Nov. 11, 1802, and is still continued. The "Hillsborough Telegraph" commenced Jan. 1, 1820; discontinued July 13, 1822. There is a social library, incorporated June 20, 1797, having a small collection of books. The Aurean Academy, instituted here in 1790, and incorporated Feb. 17, 1791, flourished about ten years. There is a public school generally every year. The aggregate number of scholars who have attended since 1807, is about 500. In the winter of 1817-18, there were instructed in the several district schools, 527 pupils, of whom 105 were taught arithmetic, and 86 the elements of English grammar. The number of deaths from Jan. 1, 1805, for the ensuing 15 years, was 343, of which the aggregate amount of ages was 10,512, and the mean average age, 30 years. Nearly one half lived to the age of 25 years or upwards, and a sixth part to 70 or more years. Two persons have lived beyond one hundred years. This town was granted in 1733, by Massachusetts, to those persons living and the heirs of those not living, who were officers and soldiers in the Narraganset war of 1675. It was called *Narraganset No.* 3, and afterwards *Souhegan-West.* The number of proprietors was 120, of whom a considerable number belonged to Salem, Mass. The first meeting of the grantees was holden at Danvers, July 17, 1734. The first settlement commenced about the same time by Samuel Walton and Samuel Lampson. Others from the county of Essex soon followed, and in 1741, the settlement contained fourteen families. In 1736, the first bridge was built; in 1739, the first meeting house was erected. The town was incorporated Jan. 18, 1760, when it assumed the name of Amherst in compliment to Lord Jeffrey Amherst, an English nobleman, and a general of the British forces in America in the French war. In 1770, part of Monson, a town N. of Hollis, was annexed to Amherst. In 1771, Amherst was selected for the shire town of the county of Hillsborough. Milford, in 1794, and Mont-Vernon, in 1803, were separated from this town. A congregational church was formed Sept. 22, 1741, and on the next day, Rev. Daniel Wilkins, who graduated at Harvard College in 1736, was ordained. He died Feb. 11, 1784, aged 73. Rev. *Jeremiah Barnard*, who graduated at Harvard College in 1773, was ordained as colleague with Mr. Wilkins, March 3, 1780. Rev. *Nathan Lord*, who graduated at Bowdoin College in 1809, was ordained as colleague with Mr. Barnard, May 22, 1816. For a period of more than 80 years, the church has never been vacant. Among the worthy citizens of Amherst who deserve remembrance, may be mentioned Hon. MOSES NICHOLS, who was a colonel under Gen. Stark in the battle of Bennington; who, after the revolutionary war, was a general of the militia, one of the counsellors under the new constitution, and the register of deeds till his death, May 23, 1790, at the age of 50. He was also eminent as a physician. Hon. SAMUEL DANA, a native of Brighton, Ms., a graduate of Harvard College in the same class with the venerable patriot *John Adams*, and the minister of Groton, Ms. from June 3, 1761, to 1775, resided in this town, the last eighteen years of his life. Here he filled the office of judge of probate several years; was a senator in the general court, and sustained a high reputation as an eminent lawyer. He died in April, 1798, aged 58. Hon. WILLIAM GORDON, who graduated at Harvard College in 1779, at the age of 16, was eminent in the profession of the law. He was elected a senator in the legislature in 1794, a representative to congress in 1796, and succeeded the Hon. Joshua Atherton as attorney general in 1801. He was also register of probate several years. He died May 8, 1802, at the age of 39. Hon. ROBERT MEANS, who died Jan. 24, 1823, at the age of 80, was for a long period of time a resident in Amherst. He was a native of Stewartstown, in the county of Tyrone, in Ulster, Ireland, where he was born Aug. 28, 1742. In 1764, he came to this country, where by his industry and application to business, he acquired a large property. In the years 1783, 1784 and 1789, he was elected a representative to the general court from Amherst, in which place he settled prior to the revolution. Three years he was a member of the senate, and in 1786, he filled the office of counsellor for Hillsborough county. Pop. 1622.

AMONOOSUCK, the name of two rivers, the lesser called *Upper*, an the other *Great* or *Lower*. The Upper Amonoosuck rises in the ungranted lands north of the White Mountains, and passing N. E. into Dummer, approaches to within a few miles of the Ameriscoggin; thence turning abruptly to the S. W. it pursues that direction nearly through Piercy, and falls into Connecticut river near the centre of Northumberland. Its whole length is about 50 miles. The valley of the Upper Amonoosuck is 7 or 8 miles in breadth, and more than 20 in length: it is scooped out with great beauty, the surface gently rising to the summits of the mountains on the N. The Lower Amonoosuck rises on the W. side of the White Mountains, and after running a course of 50 miles, falls into the Connecticut just above Haverhill, by a mouth 100 yards wide. At the distance of two miles from its mouth, it receives the Wild Amonoosuck, a stream 40 yards wide, and when raised by freshes, very swift and furious in its course. The waters of the Amonoosuck are pure, and its bed clean; the current lively, and in some places rapid. The valley of the Lower Amonoosuck is about half a mile in width, and was probably once the bed of a lake, its S. W. limit being the rise of ground at its foot, over which the waters descended in their course to the Connecticut. There is a fine fall in this river about 6 1-2 miles from the Notch of the White Mountains, where the descent is 50 feet, cut through a mass of stratified granite.

AMOSKEAG FALLS, in Merrimack river, are 7 miles below the falls at Hooksett. They consist of three pitches, one below the other; and within the distance of half a mile, the water falls between 40 and 50 feet. The vicinity of these falls was much frequented by the Indians. The sachem Wonolanset resided here. The tribe under him was sometimes molested by the Mohawks, who carried terror to the hearts of all the eastern Indians. In time of war between these hostile tribes, the Indians living in the neighborhood of the falls, concealed their provisions in the large cavities of the rocks on the island in the middle of the upper part of the fall. They entertained an idea that their deity had cut out these cavities for that purpose. *See Manchester.*

ANDOVER, post-town, Hillsborough county, is in lat. 43° 27', and is bounded N. by New-Chester, E. by the Pemigewasset, separating the town from Sanbornton, S. by Salisbury, and W. by Wilmot—containing 29,883 acres, or nearly 46 square miles. The Pemigewasset, on its eastern boundary, and the Blackwater in the S. W. part of the town, are the principal streams; but numerous rills and brooks find their way down the hills into the ponds or the two rivers. There are six ponds in Andover, the largest of which are Chance and Loon ponds, both picturesque, and their waters pure. The surface of this town is extremely uneven, and in some parts rocky and barren. The Ragged Mountains pass along the N., dividing the town from New-Chester; and the Kearsarge extends its base along the W. The soil is in many parts of good quality, and pleasant villages are formed in different parts of the town. The 4th N. H. turnpike passes over the N. W. part of Andover. This town was granted in 1746, by the Masonian proprietors, to Edmund Brown and 59 others; and was called *New-Breton,* in honor of the captors of Cape-Breton in 1745—in which expedition several of the grantees were engaged. It retained this name until June 25, 1779, when it was incorporated by its present name. The first inhabitant of Andover was Joseph Fellows, who moved into the place in 1761 : he died March 14, 1811, aged 84. The progress of the settlement was slow; and though a meeting house had been previously erected, no church was organized until 1782. On the 30th Oct. this year a congregational church was formed, and Rev. Josiah Badcock, of Milton, Ms. ordained; he continued to preach until 1809, when he resigned his charge. There are now two societies of freewill baptists, who are ministered to by Elders *Peter Young* and *Nehemiah Sleeper.* A society of universalists was incorporated in 1818. Among the deceased citizens who are remembered with respect by the inhabitants, we may mention Dr. SILAS BARNARD, the first physician in town, a native of Bolton, Mass. who came to this town in 1792; died June 25, 1795 ;—Dr. JACOB B. MOORE, a native of Georgetown, Me. born Sept. 5, 1772 ; settled in Andover in 1796 ; died Jan. 10, 1813. He possessed respectable poetical talents, was a writer on political subjects in the public papers, and was eminent in his profession. Jonathan Weare, Esq. for many years a civil magistrate and highly respected for his integrity, died Jan. 18, 1816, aged 60. Mr. William Blake and Mr. Joseph Noyes were respectable citizens. The latter, at his decease, made a donation to the town of $10,000, for the support of an academy—a building for which has already been erected by his executor. The deaths in this town for

39 years, are 441—annual average 11 : the greatest mortality, in 1802, when 42 persons died of dysentery; and in 1812 and 1818, when a malignant typhus fever prevailed. This town has about 250 dwelling houses. Pop. 1642.

ANTRIM, a post township in Hillsborough county, in lat. 43° 3′, is bounded N. by Windsor and Hillsborough, E. by Contoocook river which divides it from Deering, S. by Hancock, and W. by Stoddard and the N. E. corner of Nelson. It contains 21,743 acres. It is 20 miles from Amherst, 30 from Concord, and 67 from Boston. The E. part of Antrim lies on Contoocook river; and though somewhat hilly, is a tract of productive land, a considerable proportion of which is arable. On the river there are valuable tracts of alluvial land. The North Branch river, so called, a small stream originating from several ponds in Stoddard, furnishes several valuable mill seats, and in some parts of its course, it is bordered by tracts of interval. The W. part of the town is mountainous, but suitable for grass, and affords an extensive range of good pasturage. There are six natural ponds. Gregg's pond, above a mile S. W. from the centre of the town, covers a surface of perhaps 200 acres, and in some places is 80 feet deep, and is well stored with perch and pike. Its outlet, a tributary to Contoocook river, affords several mill privileges. Willard's pond in the S. W. part, is less than Gregg's. The remaining four are small, having from 5 to 20 acres surface. The soil of this town is mostly a deep gravelly loam, favorable for grass, corn, oats, flax, &c. The apple-tree flourishes remarkably well. The forest trees are sugar-maple, beech, black, white and yellow birch, white and swamp ash, red oak, hemlock and spruce. There is very little white pine timber; no butternut, walnut or chesnut. In some places, elms are numerous. There has lately been discovered in the middle branch of Contoocook river, a rock, about 10 feet long and 8 feet wide, covered with a shallow coat of moss, affording sustenance to 21 different kinds of plants and shrubs, three of which produce edible fruit. Antrim at some periods has exhibited a great degree of health; at other times it has been visited with distressing sickness. In 1800, from the 23d of July, to the 23d September, 62 persons died of the dysentery, and 3 others of other disorders. The spotted fever appeared Feb. 7, 1812, in the family of Mr. Samuel Weeks, and from that time to April 10, there occurred 162 cases, of which 35 terminated fatally. Throughout the month of March, it extended itself rapidly in different directions. In some of the first families attacked with it, almost every person was seized; in others only one or two were materially affected. In some cases, it seemed to spread progressively from one family to another, as if communicated from one person to the other, at the same time that in others, it suddenly made its appearance in distant neighborhoods, seizing two or three persons in a family, nearly at once. All classes of people and all ages seemed alike exposed to its attack. Among its victims, was Daniel Nichols, Esq. father to Rev. John Nichols, a native of this town, who graduated at Dartmouth College in 1813; and was ordained at Boston Sept. 3, 1817, as a missionary to India, where he now resides. Antrim derives its name from Antrim in the county of the same name in Ireland. It was incorporated March 22, 1777. The first settlement was made by Dea. James Aiken about the year 1768. Four years elapsed before a second family moved into the place. During these and several succeeding years, he endured various hardships resulting from the want of neighbors and the wilderness state of the country. For some time, he was obliged to go to Peterborough, New-Boston and other places in order to have his grain ground into meal. Dea. Aiken was a native of Londonderry, where he was born in 1731. He died July 27, 1817. He was a professor of the christian religion more than 60 years, and adorned it by a serious and exemplary life. The people here are chiefly attached to the presbyterian form of doctrine and church government. A church of this kind was gathered in 1788. Rev. Walter Little, afterwards Fullerton, who graduated at Dartmouth College in 1796, was ordained Sept. 3, 1800; dismissed Sept. 1804. Rev. John M. Whiton, who graduated at Yale College in 1805, was ordained Sept. 28, 1808. Pop. 1330.

ASHUELOT or ASHWILLET, a river in Cheshire county, which has its source in a pond in Washington. It runs in a southerly course through Marlow and Gilsum to Keene, where it receives a considerable branch issuing from ponds in Stoddard. From Keene it proceeds to Swanzey, where it receives another considerable branch which originates in Jaffrey and Fitzwilliam. It pursues its course southerly and westerly through Winchester into Hinsdale, where, at the distance of about 3 miles from the S. line of the state, it empties into the Connecticut. Some attempts have been made to render this river navigable for boats. So far as they have extended, they have been successful. The obstructions in the river from Keene to within six miles of its mouth have been removed; two sets of locks constructed, and it is now considered passable through this distance. But whether the great expense which will attend the removal of the obstructions, and canalling the remaining six miles will not prevent further progress, and therefore render useless what has already been effected, is yet questionable.

ATKINSON, a post-town in Rockingham county, lat. 42° 51′, is about 5 miles in length, 4 1-4 in breadth, and bounded N. by Hampstead, E. by Plaistow, S. by Haverhill, Ms. W. by Salem and Londonderry. It contains 6839 acres, lying 36 miles from Boston, 30 from Portsmouth, and 32 from Concord. The surface of Atkinson is uneven; the soil of a superior quality, and well situated. The cultivation of the apple has received much attention here, and the finest fruit is produced. Atkinson comprises a portion of the lands conveyed by the Indians, Nov. 15, 1642, to the inhabitants of Pentuckett, (now Haverhill). The deed was signed by two noted sachems, Passaquo and Saggahew, with the consent of Passaconaway, their chief. When the dividing line between this state and Massachusetts was finally settled, the tract comprising Plaistow fell within the limits of this state, and Atkinson, on account of difficulties respecting the location of the meeting house at the S. extremity of the town, was set off from Plaistow Aug. 31, and incorporated Sept. 3, 1767, by its present name, in honor of Theodore Atkinson, a member of the council and a large landholder. The first settlements were made in 1727 or 1723, by Benjamin Richards, of Rochester, in this state, and Jonathan and Edmund Page and John Dow, from Haverhill, Ms. Several of the first settlers lived to a great age. The Rev. Stephen Peabody was the first and only settled minister in Atkinson. He was a native of Andover, Ms. born Nov. 11, 1742; graduated at Harvard University in 1769; was ordained Nov. 25, 1772, when the congregational church was formed, and remained in the ministry until his death, May 23, 1819. He was related by marriage to the late President Adams, having married for his second wife the sister of Mrs. A. He took an active part in the revolution, and served as chaplain in the regiment under Col. Poor, stationed at Winter-Hill. The academy in this town is one of the oldest and most respectable institutions in the state; it was incorporated Feb. 17, 1791. "In a large meadow in this town, there is an island, containing 7 or 8 acres, which was formerly loaded with valuable pine timber and other forest wood. When the meadow is overflowed, by means of an artificial dam, this island rises in the same degree as the water rises, which is sometimes six feet. Near the middle of this island, is a small pond, which has been gradually lessening ever since it was first known, and is now almost covered with verdure. In the water of this pond, there have been fish in plenty; which, when the meadow hath been flowed, have appeared there, and when the water hath been drawn off, have been left on the meadow; at which time the island settles to its usual place." The correctness of this account of the floating island, given by Dr. Belknap, and which was furnished him by the Rev. Mr. Peabody, has been doubted; but there are persons still living who can substantiate the fact. The artificial dam is now in ruins. Pop. 563.

B.

BACK RIVER. *See Bellamy Bank.*

BAKER'S river, a considerable stream in Grafton county, is formed of two branches. The N. branch has its source near Moosehillock mountain in Coventry. It runs southerly through Warren into Wentworth, where it unites with the S. branch which originates in Orange. After the union of these branches, the river pursues a S. E. and an easterly course through the S. part of Rumney and the N. part of Plymouth, where it forms a junction with Pemigewasset river just above Plymouth village. It was on this river, in the township of Rumney, that General Stark was captured by the Indians, on the 28th of April, 1752. *See Rumney.*

BARKER'S LOCATION, a tract of land in Coos county, containing 3,020 acres, granted Oct. 21, 1773, to Capt. Joshua Barker, of Hingham, Ms. It now composes a part of Lancaster, to which it was annexed June 22, 1819.

BARNSTEAD, post-town, Strafford county, in lat. 43° 21′, is bounded N. E. by Alton, N. W. by Gilmanton, S. W. by Pittsfield, S. by Strafford, and contains 26,000 acres. It is 36 miles from Portsmouth, 26 from Dover, and 20 from Concord. Barnstead is not mountainous, but has large swells of land. The soil is easy and productive; the original growth, pine, oak, beech, maple, &c. There are several ponds in this town—the largest are the two Suncook ponds, which lie near each other, Brindle pond, and Half-moon pond, on Alton line. These waters are stocked with fish, and are discharged into the Suncook. Barnstead was granted May 20, 1727, to the Rev. Joseph Adams and others. Settlements commenced in 1767. A congregational church was organized Aug. 5, 1804; and Rev. *Enos George* settled on the 26th Sept. following. Elder David Knowlton was settled over the freewill baptist society in 1804; died 1809, and was succeeded by Eld. *Nathaniel Wilson*. The social library in this town was incorporated in 1807, and contains 180 volumes. The number of deaths since 1804, has been 204. Pop. 1805.

BARRINGTON, post-town, in Strafford county, lat. 43° 12′, is 20 miles from Portsmouth, 10 from Dover, 30 from Concord, 65 from Boston; bounded N. E. by Farmington and Rochester, S. E. by Madbury, Lee and Dover, S. W. by Nottingham and Northwood, and N. W. by Strafford. The surface of Barrington is somewhat broken and rocky, the soil being principally a gravelly loam. The oak ridges, however, are a sandy loam, or hazel mould, and are very good for tillage. The town is abundantly supplied with ponds, of which there are no less than thirteen of considerable magnitude, from whence issue streams affording excellent mill-seats. At one of these mill-seats, on the Isinglass river, is a perpendicular fall of 30 feet, with a sufficient supply of water for an extensive factory. The rocks in this town are principally granite, are composed of feldspar, quartz and mica, and have a granular structure. In the composition of these rocks, quartz predominates. In some of them, very perfect and beautiful crystals of quartz, and in others, tourmaline and graphite are found. Bog iron ore is also somewhat abundant, and was formerly wrought here. There is, about two miles from the centre of the town, a remarkable cavern or fissure in a rock, commonly called the *Devil's den*. The entrance is on the side of a hill, and is sufficiently large to admit a person in a stooping posture. Having entered 5 feet in a horizontal direction, there is a descent of 4 or 5 feet, on an angle of 45°, large enough only to admit the body of a middling sized man. After squeezing through this passage, you enter a chamber 60 feet in length, from 10 to 15 in height, and from 3 to 8 in width.—Communicating with this, are several other fissures of equal height, and from 10 to 15 in length, which, wanting sufficient width, remain unexplored. In religious sentiment the inhabitants of this town are principally congregationalists and baptists. Over the congregational church, which was formed soon after the settlement of the town, Rev. Joseph Prince was settled in 1755; dismissed in 1768. Rev. David Tenney was settled in 1771; dismissed 1778, and soon after died. Rev. Benjamin Balch was settled in 1784, and died in 1815. The church is now vacant. Barrington was incorporated May 10, 1722, and the settlement commenced in 1732. The town is healthy—of the first settlers, fourteen, who were between 80 and 90 years of age, were alive in 1815. Barrington was originally 13 miles in length, 6 1-2 in breadth and in 1810 contained 3564 inhabitants; but in 1820 the town was divided, and the western section incorporated into a new town of the name of Strafford—thus reducing the territory and population more than one half. Present pop. 1610.

BARRON'S ISLAND. *See Piermont.*

BARTLETT, post-town, Coos county, is in lat. 44° 4', 45 miles from Lancaster, 75 from Concord, and 85 from Portsmouth. It lies at the foot of the White Mountains, with Adams on the N., Chatham on the E., Conway and the public lands on the S. and W. It has an area of about 13,000 acres. Its soil is various, and on the Saco, in some parts, good. This river meanders through the centre of the town, which is also watered by other streams. Bartlett was incorporated June 16, 1790; and received its name in honor of Gov. Bartlett. Pop. 511.

BATH, a post-township in Grafton county, on Connecticut river, in lat. 44° 10', is bounded N. by Lyman, E. by Landaff, S. by Haverhill, and W. by Ryegate, Vt., containing 22,827 acres. It is 42 miles N. E. of Dartmouth College, 82 N. N. W. of Concord and 148 from Boston. Bath is pleasantly situated in the vale of the Connecticut, between the Green mountains on the W., and the White Mountains on the E., by which it is effectually shielded from high winds and long storms. The Amonoosuck river waters the S. E. part, affording many fine mill seats and water privileges. It falls into Connecticut river at the S. W. angle of the town. It receives in its course, about 4 miles from its mouth, the Wild Amonoosuck river, which rushes down the lofty Moosehillock. The head of boat navigation on Connecticut river is in Bath. It is interrupted by a very majestic fall of water, at which a dam is erected and several mills built. The Amonoosuck has a very convenient fall at the village, calculated to accommodate machinery to any extent. At the principal village, there is a considerable bridge over the Amonoosuck, of 350 feet in length—built in 1807. There is a ferry across the river at the falls. Perch pond, having a surface of about 100 acres, is situated in the S. part of the town. At the S. W. corner of Bath, Gardner's mountain rises by a very bold ascent from the confluence of Connecticut and Amonoosuck rivers, and runs a N. course through the whole town, separating the inhabitants, who have no communication but by one pass in the mountain. Its height is generally about 500 feet. On this mountain, are various appearances of iron and silver ore. Strata of rock have been opened near the lower village, the most of which will dissolve on being immersed in warm water. Alum and copperas have been made from this rock. The rocks here are principally granite, slate and flint. The soil on the hills is generally a reddish loam, on a bed of marl or hard pan. In the valleys, it is alluvial. In some parts, are clayey soils; in others, sandy. There are but few swamps. About one sixth part of the whole town is interval land. The native forests, in the valleys and on the flats, are white pine, hemlock, spruce, elm, and some cedar; on the hills, maple, beech, birch, oak and mountain ash. Much improvement has been made in the agriculture of this place. Gypsum has been found highly useful on all the soils, except cold and wet land. The surplus produce is carried to Boston, Salem and Portland. In 1811, the spotted fever visited this

H

place, but did not prove very fatal. The annual average number of deaths is about 20. There is a social library, containing upwards of 200 volumes. The original charter of Bath was granted Sept. 10, 1761, to Rev. Andrew Gardner and 61 others. In March, 1769, it was re-chartered to John Sawyer and others, on the assumption of the forfeiture of the first charter. The first settlement was made in 1765, by John Herriman from Haverhill, Ms. In 1766 and '67, Moses Pike and the family of Mr. Sawyer commenced settlements. A presbyterian church was formed in 1778, which was dissolved in 1791, and a congregational church organized, embracing 19 members. Rev. *David Sutherland*, a native of Edinburg, was installed Oct. 24, 1805. In 1811, a revival of religion occurred, which added to the church 77 members; and in 1820 and '21, a further addition of 101 members was made to the church. There are some baptists and methodists in this town. Pop. 1498.

BEAN HILL. See *Northfield*.

BEARCAMP, a river, which is formed of several branches rising on the south sides of Sandwich and Burton mountains. The two principal branches unite in Ossipee, and fall into the Ossipee lake on its western border.

BEAVER BROOK, the name of several streams in this state. The largest has its source in a small pond in Unity, and running W. falls into the Connecticut in Charlestown. One other rises in Mont-Vernon, and falls into the Souhegan; and another passes from Stewartstown through Colebrook.

BEAVER RIVER, has its principal source in Beaver pond, a beautiful body of water, in London-derry. It passes S. through Pelham, and falls into the Merrimack in Dracut, nearly opposite the mouth of Concord river, in Mass.

BEDFORD, a post-township in Hillsborough county, is situated on Merrimack river, in lat. 42° 53'. It is bounded N. by Goffstown, E. by Merrimack river, which divides it from Manchester and the N. part of Litchfield, S. by the township of Merrimack, and W. by Amherst and New-Boston, containing 20,660 acres. It is 8 miles from Amherst, 21 from Concord and 52 from Boston. Merrimack and Piscataquog are the only rivers in this town. The latter passes through its N. E. corner, where there is a pleasant and flourishing village, which will be noticed under *Piscataquog Village*. In the W. part of this town, the land is uneven and abounds with stones, but the qualities of the soil are warm and moist. The E. part, bordering on the Merrimack, is pine plain, with some very productive intervals. The principal forest trees are white, red, and black oak, walnut, chesnut, maple, birch, pine, hemlock, &c. Of the white oak, great quantities of ship timber have been obtained, and conveyed to Charlestown, Ms. by means of the river and Middlesex canal. Great attention is paid to the cultivation of hops; and there are raised in some years, 100,000 lbs. The agricultural and general condition of this town has of late become flourishing. Linen and woollen are the principal manufactures, of which there have been made cloths of a quality equal to foreign importations. On the W. line of Bedford, are a remarkable gulf and precipice, which are regarded as objects of curiosity. A considerable brook passes over the precipice, and falls about 200 feet within the distance of 100 yards. Here are found several excavations in solid stone, which are sufficiently large to contain many persons. Sibbins' pond is in the E. part of the town. Strictly speaking, there are three ponds, which appear to be united by their waters beneath the surface of an extensive bog, which floats upon the surface and rises and falls with the water. These ponds, taken together, are about 80 rods in diameter, and abound with most kinds of fresh water fish. There is in Bedford, a social library incorporated in 1802. Those who have received a collegiate education from this town, are at *Dartmouth College*, Joseph Goffe, 1791; John Vose, 1795; Benj. Orr, 1798; Joseph Bell, 1807; John Walker, 1808; William Gordon, 1811; William Orr, 1815; Adam Gordon, 1817; John Aiken, 1819; Thornton McGaw, 1820; Adams Moore, 1822: at *Yale College*, Isaac Orr, 1818; Robert Riddle, 1818; Freeman Riddle, 1819; Robert Orr, 1820: at *Middlebury College*, Isaac O. Barnes, 1820. In mineralogy, this town affords a great variety of specimens. Iron ore is found in different places and in several varieties. Sulphuret of iron, imbedded in common granite, and red oxide of iron combined with alumine, are common. Black lead, (graphite) pyritous copper, schorl, hornblende, epidote, talc, mica, black, yellow and green, gneiss, crystallized quartz, &c. are found here. Fifty years since, iron was manufactured in considerable quantities at the mouth of Crosby brook. Within a few years, iron ore in large quantities has been transported to Billerica and other forges out of town. Bedford was one of the Narraganset townships granted by Massachusetts in 1733, to the surviving officers and soldiers, and the heirs of those deceased, who were engaged in King Philip's war in 1676. The number of grantees was 120, all of whom except one belonged to Massachusetts. It was first called *Narraganset No. 5*, or *Souhegan East*. The first settlement commenced in the winter of 1737, by Robert and James Walker, who, the ensuing year, were followed by Col. John Goffe, Matthew Patten, Esq. and Capt. Samuel Patten. Several of the early settlers emigrated from the north of Ireland. The first child born in town was Silas Barron, son of Capt. Moses Barron—he was born Jan. 16, 1741. The town was incorporated by charter from Gov. Wentworth, May 19, 1750. Bedford was the residence of many Indians in former times. In 1745, as James McQuade and Robert Burns, who had been to Penacook to purchase corn for their families, were returning home, they killed McQuade in Pembroke; but Burns escaped by running in a zig-zag direction, by which means, he baffled the fire of the pursuers, and returned in safety to his family. On the bank of Merrimack river, opposite Goffe's falls, is a spot of ground, about ten rods long and four wide, which is supposed to have been an Indian burial place. The surface of the bank is about 40 feet above the river. Human bones at various times have been washed from the bank. In the summer of 1821, Drs. Woodbury and Riddle obtained a part of three skeletons from this place. Some of the bark in which they had been deposited remained. One of them appeared to have been put in the ground in a sitting posture. All of their heads lay towards the south. One was supposed to be a female. The hair was entire, and was done up in a bunch on the back part of the head in a manner similar to that practised at the present day. A presbyterian church was formed in 1757. Rev. John Houston was ordained about the same time, and remained the minister till 1778. From this period the church was vacant, but enjoyed occasional preaching, till Sept. 5, 1804, when *Rev. David McGregore*, who graduated at Dartmouth College in 1799, was ordained. Hon. MATTHEW PATTEN, a gentleman of very respectable character, the second judge of probate in Hillsborough county, and one of the first settlers, died in this town. Hon. JOHN ORR, who died in Jan. 1823, at the age of 75, was a distinguished citizen of this town. He was in the battle of Bennington under Gen. Stark, and received a wound in the early part of the engagement. Pop. 1375.

BELLAMY BANK, a river, one branch of which issues from Chesley's pond in Barrington, and the other from low and marshy lands in the vicinity ; these unite in Madbury, and after meandering through the town, the waters fall into the Pascataqua, on the W. side of Dover Neck, where the stream is called *Back* river.

BELLOWS FALLS, a remarkable fall, in Connecticut river, in the township of Walpole, and formerly known by the name of the Great fall. The breadth of the river, above the fall, is 22 rods ; in some places not more than 16. A large rock divides the stream into two channels, each about 90 feet wide, on the top of the shelving bank. When the water is low, the eastern channel appears crossed by a bar of solid rock, and the whole stream falls into the western channel, where it is contracted to the breadth of 16 feet, and flows with astonishing rapidity. There are several pitches, one above another, in the length of half a mile, the largest of which is that where the rock divides the stream. Notwithstanding the velocity of the current, the salmon pass up this fall, and are taken many miles above ; but the shad proceed no farther. Over this fall, in the year 1785, a bridge of timber was constructed by Col. Enoch Hale, Its length was 365 feet, and was supported in the middle by the great rock. In 1792, this was the only bridge across Connecticut river, and now, in 1823, there are, in this state, sixteen bridges. In crossing the bridge from this town to Rockingham, Vt. the traveller has an interesting and sublime view of these falls.

BETHLEHEM, township, in Grafton county, in lat. 44° 15′, is bounded N. by Whitefield and Dalton, E. by Bretton-Woods and ungranted land, S. by Franconia and Concord, and N. W. by Littleton, containing 28,608 acres. It is watered by Great Amonoosuck river, which takes its rise at the notch of the White Mountains, and runs in a W. and N. W. direction through nearly the centre of this town. A branch of the same river runs through the southerly part into Franconia. The mountains are called Round and Peaked. The soil produces good crops of grass and grain. There is plenty of pine timber and sugar maple. Iron ore, both of the mountain and bog kind, has been occasionally found. Two mineral springs have been discovered. Bethlehem was settled in 1790, by Jonas Warren, Benjamin Brown, James Turner, Thomas and

John Hatch, Nathan and Amos Wheeler, Nathl. Snow and Lot Woodbury. It was incorporated Dec. 27, 1799. A congregational church was formed Oct. 15, 1802; a baptist church in Sept. 1800; and a freewill baptist, June 26, 1813. The number of members in each of the baptist churches is 46; in the congregational, 23. Pop. 467.

BISHOP'S BROOK rises in the S. E. part of Stewartstown, and meanders N. W. through the town into Connecticut river.

BLACKWATER river, so called from its dark appearance, is formed by two small streams, one of which rises in Danbury, and the other issues from Pleasant pond in New-London. These branches unite soon after crossing the W. line of Andover, and form the Blackwater, which passes with considerable rapidity through the S. W. part of that town; from thence through the W. part of the towns of Salisbury and Boscawen into Hopkinton, where it empties into Contoocook river.

BLIND WILL'S NECK, is a point of land formed by the confluence of the Isinglass and Cocheco rivers, in the south part of Rochester. *Blind Will* was a sagamore of the Indians living about the Cocheco. During the war with King Philip, the enemy having made their appearance in the vicinity, he was sent out by Maj. Waldron with seven other Indians, to make discoveries. They were all surprised by a company of Mohawks—two or three escaped, and the others were killed or taken. Will was dragged away by his hair, and being wounded, perished on the neck, which has since borne his name.

BLOODY POINT, on the Newington side of the Pascataqua river, is so called from a quarrel which took place in 1631, between the agents of the two companies of proprietors about a point of land convenient for both; and, there being at that time no government established, the controversy would have ended in blood, had the parties not been persuaded to refer the dispute to their employers.

BLUE HILLS, the name generally appropriated to the first range of mountains in the state, commencing in Nottingham and extending through Strafford, Farmington and Milton; the several summits are distinguished by different names, as Teneriffe, Saddleback, Tuckaway, &c. *See towns just mentioned.*

BOAR'S HEAD. *See Hampton.*

BOSCAWEN, a post-township in Hillsborough county, is situated between Concord and Salisbury, on the W. side of Merrimack river, in lat 43° 19'. It is 7 miles in length and about the same in breadth, and contains an area of 32,230 acres. It is bounded N. by Salisbury, E. by the Merrimack, which divides it from Northfield and Canterbury, S. by Concord and Hopkinton, and W. by Warner. Boscawen is 8 miles from Concord, 52 from Portsmouth, 68 from Boston, and 514 from Washington City. Besides the Merrimack, the west part of this town is watered by Blackwater river, running nearly parallel with the former, through the whole extent of the town and about five miles distant from it. It is not a large stream, but very important, both on account of the fertile fields of champaign on its borders, and the numerous water privileges it affords. It empties itself into Contoocook river in Hopkinton. Over this river and the various other streams, this town supports more than two miles

H2

of plank bridges, including their abutments. There are two ponds of some note. Great pond, near the centre of the town, is 1 mile in length, and 1 mile in width. Long pond, in the west part, is 2 miles long and from 1-2 to 3-4 of a mile wide. There are mill seats at the outlet of each. The soil seems to admit of three divisions, the interval, plain and highland. The intervals on the Merrimack are, in many places, widely extended and were originally very fertile; the plains border on the intervals and have a thinner soil; the highland, which comprises about five sevenths of the whole town, lies in large swells extending from north to south. The natural growth is white oak and other hard wood. It is of a deep, productive soil, affording many excellent farms delightfully situated. The surface of Boscawen, when viewed from its highest parts, appears uncommonly level. There are few spots where stones abound. There are no morasses nor stagnant waters. From the numerous streams of living water, and from the peculiar direction of the swells of the hills, this town probably derives that pure air and uniform temperature which are so conducive to health. The number of deaths for the eleven years ending January 1, 1819, was 269. There are 15 school districts, which have on an average about 35 scholars to each, and 15 school-houses. For the attention paid to education in this place, much credit is due to the Rev. Dr. Wood, who has entered at the different colleges between 80 and 90 young gentlemen, of whom 31 have been engaged in the ministry. The Boscawen social library was founded in 1792; incorporated Dec. 2, 1797, and contains 220 volumes. This town has a musical society, an auxiliary to the American education society, one for the education of heathen youth, two female gleaning societies, a moral, an agricultural, and two female cent societies, which are annually extending their aid to the objects which they respectively embrace. The principal village is in the east section of the town. It has between 30 and 40 dwelling houses, situated on a spacious street nearly two miles in length, very straight and level. Here the eye of the observant traveller is attracted and delighted by the fertile intervals and windings of the river Merrimack. There is another village forming on a pleasant eminence near the west meeting-house. Boscawen was granted by Massachusetts in 1733, to 91 proprietors, who held their first meeting May 2, 1733, at Newbury. The proprietors gave to it the name of *Contoocook*, after the Indian name of the river. It received its present name, when it was incorporated April 22, 1760, from Edward Boscawen, a celebrated English admiral then on the American station. The first settlement commenced early in the season of 1734 by Nathaniel Danforth, Andrew Bohonnon, Moses Burbank, Stephen Gerrish, and Edward Emery. Others soon followed to the number of 27 families. Abigail Danforth was the first child born in the town. These families were secured against the hostile encroachments of the Indians by a log fort, 100 feet square and 10 feet high, built by the proprietors in 1739. In this fort the inhabitants lived in garrison more than twenty-two years. They had previously built a log house for religious worship and their public meetings. In 1746, the Indians made a predatory incursion on the inhabitants; killed Thomas Cook, his son, and a man of color, and took Elisha Jones prisoner. In 1754, they killed Timothy Cook, and took Enos Bishop into captivity to Canada, from whence he escaped about a year afterward and returned home. Mr. Jones died in captivity. An island, at the mouth of Contoocook river, between this town and Concord was the scene of the well known exploit of Mrs. Hannah Duston, which may be described in this place. On the 15th of March, 1698, the Indians made a descent on Haverhill, Mass., where they took Mrs. Duston, who was confined to her bed with an infant only six days old, and attended by her nurse, Mary Niff. The Indians took Mrs. Duston from her bed and carried her away with the nurse and infant. They soon despatched the latter by dashing its head against a tree. When they had proceeded as far as this island, which has been justly called Duston's island, on their way to an Indian town situate a considerable distance above, the Indians informed the women that they must be stripped and run the gauntlet thro' the village on their arrival.—Mrs. Duston and her nurse had been assigned to a family consisting of two stout men, three women, and seven children, or young Indians, besides an English boy who had been taken from Worcester. Mrs. Duston, aware of the cruelties that awaited her, formed the design of exterminating the whole family, and prevailed upon the nurse and the boy to assist her in their destruction. A little before day, finding the whole company in a sound sleep, she awoke her confederates, and with the Indian hatchets despatched ten of the twelve. One of the women whom they thought they had killed made her escape, and a favorite boy they designedly left. Mrs. Duston and her companions arrived safe home with the scalps, though their danger from the enemy and from famine in travelling so far, must have been great. The general court of Massachusetts made her a grant of £50 and she received many valuable presents. The time when the church was formed in this place has not been ascertained. The ministers who have successively presided over it have been as follows: Rev. Phinehas Stevens, ordained October 8, 1740, and died Jan. 19, 1755. Rev. Robie Morrill, ordained Dec. 29, 1761; dismissed Dec. 9, 1766; and died Sept. 23, 1813, aged 79. Rev. Nathaniel Merrill, ordained Oct. 19. 1768, and dismissed April 1, 1774. Rev. *Samuel Wood*, D. D. ordained Oct. 17, 1781. The second congregational church was formed Sept. 10, 1804, and Rev. *Ebenezer Price* was installed on the 26th of the same month. George Jackman, Esq. of this town is entitled to respectful notice. He was the first town clerk and continued in office 36 years. He was appointed a justice of the peace under George II. and continued such under all the successive changes of government to 1818—he was a selectman 22 years, a representative to the general court, and a delegate to the state convention. He is still living at an advanced age.

Bow, a township in Rockingham county, lat. 43° 8', was granted May 20, 1727, to Jonathan Wiggin and others, and was originally laid out nine miles square, comprehending a great portion of the territory now constituting Pembroke and Concord; but at present it contains about 16,000 acres, bounded N. E. by Merrimack river which divides it from Pembroke, S. E. by Hooksett, S. W. by Dunbarton, N. W. by Concord, and a part of Hopkinton. The soil is very uneven and hard, but productive when well managed. There is but one pond of any size, called Turee pond. Turkey river empties into the Merrimack at Turkey falls, near the N. E. part of Bow. About a mile below are Garven's falls, now passable by locks on Bow side. Bow canal is situated on the Merrimack 3 miles below Concord; the perpendicular measurement around which it is carried is 25 feet—its length 1-3 of a mile. It passes through a ledge of granite, and is for the most part imperishable. Its cost was $13,860; and about $2000 of its first income were appropriated towards clearing channels through Turkey falls, &c. The Londonderry turnpike passes through the E. part of this town; and the Londonderry Branch turnpike, through the centre of the town from Hooksett to Hopkinton. The baptist church in Bow was first organized in 1795; and Rev. Benjamin Sargent was ordained in 1797 over the church and society, where he continued till 1801, when he removed to Pittsfield, and has since died. Rev. Thomas Waterman ministered to the people from 1804 to 1807; during which period a new church had been formed of baptists and congregationalists, and subsequently dissolved, the two denominations forming distinct societies. The latter is now very small. From 1807 to 1815, the baptist church was without any pastor. July 3, 1816, the baptist church was re-organized; and on the 13th Feb. 1817, Rev. *Henry Veazey* was settled.—The church now consists of about 60 members. The meeting-house is situated on a commanding elevation, and is a handsome building. Bow is a very healthy town—the average number of deaths for ten years not exceeding 12. Pop. 935. The venerable SAMUEL WELCH, mentioned in page 12, among the instances of longevity in this state, was born at Kingston, N. H. September 1, 1710; and is now (March, 1823) living in this town. His father was from Ipswich, Mass.; his grandfather, one of the original emigrants from England to that place. This old man has outlived all his connexions—he has lived more than half the time since the landing of the pilgrims at Plymouth! The early part of his life was spent at Kingston; he subsequently lived at Pembroke; but for the last 50 years he has resided at Bow, in an obscure corner and steadily cultivated his little farm, till the frosts of a century had whitened his locks, and the chills of a hundred winters had benumbed his frame. His life has been marked by no extraordinary vicissitude—he was never in battle, or in any public service; he has been a man of industry, temperance and health. In person, he is rather above the middle size—of Grecian features, with dark expressive eyes; and his locks are of a clayey white, looking as if they had already mouldered in the grave. His face is fair, though wrinkled with the cares of a century and an eighth. His frame is now feeble, and he is unable to walk. His mental faculties, however, seem but little impaired, and he is an interesting person in conversation.

BOWBACK, a mountain. See *Stratford.*

BRADFORD, a post-township in Hillsborough county, is situated about mid-way between the Merrimack and Connecticut rivers in lat. 43° 14'. It is bounded N. by Fishersfield and Sutton, E. by Warner, S. by Henniker and Hillsborough, W. by Washington, containing nearly 19,000 acres, of which about 500 are of water. It is 31 miles from Amherst, 28 from Concord and 80 from Boston. This town is watered by small streams, which principally issue from ponds, of which the largest is Todd's pond, lying in Bradford and Fishersfield. This pond is supplied with water from the hills and mountains in Fishersfield. In it are a number of floating islands, which are deemed objects of curiosity. Its outlet forms the northern branch of Warner river.—Pleasant, or Bradford pond, is on the E. side of the town. It is about 550 rods long and 150 wide. It communicates with Warner river by an outlet at the N. end of it. In this pond are several islands, which, with the rugged declivities on the E. bank, the waters below, and the cottages and cultivated fields on the west bank, present to view, in the summer season, a wild and variegated landscape. Many parts of Bradford are hilly. A large proportion of the town, however, lies in a valley, about three miles in width. Near the Sunapee mountains, on the N. W., is an extensive plain more than a mile long, and about half a mile wide. The soil differs in quality. It is light, loamy or rough. In the easterly part are valuable stone quarries. The number of deaths from 1809 to 1817, inclusive, was 146; the least annual number was 4; the greatest, 29. There is a number of societies designed to aid in promoting charitable objects. There is also a respectable library.—Bradford was granted to John Peirce and George Jaffrey in ——. Its first settlement was made in 1771, by Deac. William Presbury, and his family. He lived here three years before any other families arrived. It was soon settled by several inhabitants from Bradford in Mass., from which circumstance it derived its name. It was incorporated Sept. 27, 1787, and is mentioned in the act as including New Bradford, Washington Gore, and part of Washington. The congregational church was formed in 1803. Rev. Lemuel Bliss was ordained March 5, 1805; died July 4, 1814, aged 38. Rev. *Robert Paige* was ordained May 22, 1822. There is a freewill baptist society, over which Rev. *Jonathan Rowe* was settled in 1821. There is also a small society of episcopalians. Pop. 1318.

BREAKFAST HILL. See *Rye.*

BRENTWOOD, post town, Rockingham co., in lat. 43°, is bounded E. by Exeter, N. by Epping, W. by Poplin, S. by Kingston; and contains 10,465 acres. The soil is better adapted to grass than grain, although some improvements have been made in its qualities. Exeter river passes nearly through the centre of the town, and there are other streams of less magnitude connecting with it. Pick-pocket falls, on Exeter river, are in this town, and near them are situated an extensive cotton factory, and a number of mills. A card factory has recently been established here, which promises to be of great utility; and also an iron furnace for casting machinery. Quantities of iron ore have been found, and it was formerly worked with success. Vitriol, combined in masses with sulphur, have also been found here. Brentwood was incorporated June 26, 1742. A congregational church was organized in 1752, and Rev. Nathaniel Trask ordained: he died in 1789. Rev. Ebenezer Flint succeeded him, was installed in 1801, and died in 1811. Rev. *Chester Colton*, the present minister, was settled in 1815. There is a society of baptists here, over whom Elder Samuel Shepard was settled in 1775; died 1816. And also a number of friends. Pop. 892.

BRETTON-WOODS, a township in Coos co., lat. 44° 17′, lies at the base of the White Mountains, on the N. W., having Jefferson and Whitefield N., Whitefield and Bethlehem W., and the ungranted lands, and Nash and Sawyer's Location on the S. It has a territory of 24,640 acres; and was granted Feb. 8, 1772, to Sir Thomas Wentworth, Bart. Rev. Samuel Langdon, and 81 others. Its surface is uneven, and its appearance dreary. There are but 19 inhabitants. Pondicherry mountain lies on the N. between this town and Jefferson. John's and Israel's rivers receive several branches from Bretton-Woods; and the head streams of the Amonoosuck from the surrounding mountains unite in passing through the town.

BRIDGEWATER, a township in Grafton county, in lat. 43° 39′, was originally part of New-Chester, and was incorporated Feb. 12, 1788. It is bounded N. by Plymouth and Hebron, on the E. by Pemigewasset river, dividing it from part of Holderness and New-Hampton, on the S. by Bristol, and on the W. by Newfound pond, which separates it from Alexandria. Bridgewater has no rivers or ponds deserving notice. The soil is well adapted to grazing, and few townships in its vicinity exceed it in this respect. The Mayhew turnpike passes through the W. part, near Newfound pond, and the main road from Concord to Plymouth through the E. part near Pemigewasset river. There is a social library, small, but well selected. The first settlement was made in 1766, by Thomas Crawford, Esq. when the tract comprised the whole of New-Chester, Bridgewater and Bristol. He is still living at an advanced age. His brother Jona. Crawford and several others soon became settlers. A congregational church was formed in 1817. Previous to this time the members of it were in connexion with the one at Hebron. There are also baptist and freewill baptist churches. Pop. 727.

BRISTOL, post township in the S. E. part of Grafton county, in lat. 43° 35′, is bounded N. by Bridgewater, E. by Pemigewasset river, which separates it from N. Hampton, S. by Smith's river, which separates it from New-Chester, W. by Alexandria; containing 9000 acres, exclusive of ponds. It is 90 miles from Boston, 16 S. from Plymouth, and 30 N. from Concord. The land is hilly, but has, in general, a good soil. Newfound pond, about 6 miles in length and from 2 to 3 miles in width, lies in this town and in Hebron. Its waters are discharged through Newfound river, a stream about 2 miles long and 100 feet wide, into Pemigewasset river. At the confluence of these rivers is a pleasant village, having 14 dwelling houses, 2 stores, other buildings and a number of valuable mill seats. Bristol is connected by a toll bridge with New-Hampton.—The Mayhew turnpike passes through this town. Here has lately been discovered, about 3 miles from the village, a large body of plumbago, or black lead, (graphite,) of superior excellence. It has been examined by Drs. Mitchell and Dana, Professors at New-York and Hanover, who pronounce it to be of the best kind hitherto discovered in our country. The land in which it is found, has been purchased by Mr. Charles I. Dunbar, of Massachusetts. Bristol was taken from Bridgewater and New-Chester, and incorporated June 24, 1819. The first settlement was made in 1770, by Col. Peter Sleeper, Benj. Emmons and others. There is an incorporated methodist society. The church was formed in June, 1818. Pop. 675; polls in 1821, 133.

BROOKFIELD, township, Strafford county, lat. 43°32', is bounded N. W. by Wolfeborough, E. by Wakefield, S. E. by Middleton, the line passing in a zig-zag direction over Moose mountain, W. by New-Durham; and contains 13,000 ac. It is 45 miles from Concord, and 90 from Boston; was originally a part of Middleton, from which it was separated and incorporated Dec. 30, 1794. The soil is good. Cook's pond, about 1 mile long and 3-4 mile wide, is the source of the W. branch of Salmon-Fall river. There is also another small pond, covering about 15 acres, directly on the top of Moose mountain, which has always about the same quantity of water, and a variety of fish in it. The first settler was Nicholas Austin, and Richard Hanson built the first framed house—dates unknown. There never has been a minister settled in town; but there is a small society of baptists. The inhabitants have a social library. There are no manufactories, taverns or stores. The number of rateable polls is 128. Pop. 740.

BROOKLINE, a township on the S. line of the state, in lat. 42° 44', is bounded N. by Milford, E. by Hollis, S. by Townsend and Pepperell, in Mass., W. by Mason, containing 12,664 acres, 240 of which are water. It is 7 miles from Amherst, 35 from Concord, and 43 from Boston. Nisitissit is the only river in Brookline. It rises in the N. E. part of Mason; passes through the S. part of Milford into Brookline, pursuing a S. E. course to Potanipo pond. From the pond it runs S. E. to Hollis, passing through the S. W. corner of that town into Pepperell, where it empties into Nashua river. Potanipo, or Tanapus pond is situated near the meeting-house. It is about a mile long and one third of a mile wide. This town has but few natural advantages for its improvement in wealth and importance. The population since 1790 has increased more than one third. The number of births for 5 years were as follows, viz. 1808, 25; 1809, 22; 1810, 23; 1811, 12; 1812, 29; total, 111. The number of deaths the same years was, in 1808, 5; 1809, 5; 1810, 8; 1811, 4; 1812, 5; total 27, from which it appears, that the births in 1812 exceeded the whole number of deaths for 5 years. Brookline formerly belonged to Massachusetts, and was included in the Dunstable grant. It was incorporated March 30, 1769, by the name of *Raby*. In Nov. 1798, the name was altered by an act of the legislature to Brookline. A congregational church was formed about the year 1797. Rev. Lemuel Wadsworth, who graduated at Brown University in 1793, was ordained Oct. 11, 1797; died Nov. 25, 1817, aged 48. Pop. 592.

BURNHAM'S RIVER. *See Lyman*.

BURTON, a township in Strafford co., is in lat. 43° 56′, and is bounded E. by Conway, S. E. by Eaton, S. by Tamworth, N. and W. by ungranted lands. It is 12 miles long from E. to W., and about 5 in width, containing about 36,700 acres. Distant from Concord, 75 miles; from Gilford, 45; and 75 from Portsmouth. The principal river is Swift river, which passes from W. to E. through Burton, into the Saco at Conway. There are several small streams in different parts of the town, furnishing convenient mill privileges. These streams were once the residence of numbers of the beaver, otter, &c. There are several lofty hills and mountains in Burton, the highest of which is called Chocorua, and is visible from a great extent of country. It received its name from *Chocorua*, an Indian, who was killed on the summit by a party of hunters in time of peace, before the settlement of the place. The predominant rock of these hills is granite—a soft, decomposing variety, in which the crystals and grains of feldspar are very large, and suffer a rapid decomposition, by which the whole is disintegrated and broken down. The loose stones consist mostly of rolled masses of granite, quartz, feldspar, and some specimens of hornstone. A bed of bog ore of iron is also found here. The soil is fertile, being a sandy loam, mixed occasionally with coarse gravel. There are some fertile interval lands on the borders of the Swift river. The original growth here is maple, birch, ash, pine, &c. The prosperity of this town has been considerably retarded by a peculiar disease which afflicts neat cattle. Young cattle cannot be reared, nor can cows or oxen be kept here for a series of years, without being attacked by a singular and fatal distemper. It commences with a loss of appetite—the animals refuse hay, grain and salt—become emaciated—an obstinate costiveness attends, but the abdomen becomes smaller than in health, and is diminished to one third its original bulk. After these symptoms have continued for an indefinite period, a brisk scouring comes on, and the animals fall away and die. Though superstition may have found a reason in the dying curse of the murdered Chocorua, philosophy has not yet ascertained a satisfactory cause for the disease. It is probably owing to the properties contained in the waters of Burton. This town was granted Nov. 6, 1766, to Clement March, Joseph Senter and others; it constituted a part of Grafton county until Nov. 27, 1800, when it was annexed to the county of Strafford; and is still numbered among those towns in this state which have never settled a clergyman. Pop. 209.

C.

CAMBRIDGE, in Coos county, lat. 44° 37′, is an uninhabited township, of 23,160 acres, granted May 19, 1773, to Nathaniel Rogers and others. It is bounded N. by the township of Errol and Umbagog lake, E. by the state of Maine, S. by Success and Paulsburg, and W. by Dummer. This tract has an uneven surface, but might be advantageously cultivated. Several streams rise here, and fall into the Ameriscoggin, which passes through the N. W. part of the town.

CAMPTON, a post-township in Grafton county, in lat. 43° 49′, is bounded N. by Thornton, E. by Sandwich, S. by Holderness and

Plymouth, W. by Rumney, containing 27,892 acres. It is 50 miles from Concord and 75 from Portsmouth. Its surface is broken and uneven, abounding with rocky ledges, and having several mountainous tracts. Besides Pemigewasset river, running N. and S. through nearly the centre of the town, it is watered by Mad and Beebe's rivers, which fall into the Pemigewasset on the E., and by West Branch river and Bog brook on the W. The land in the valleys is generally good, and there is some good interval. The high land, when not too rocky, is good for grazing. The forest trees are mostly deciduous. There is some hemlock, pine and spruce. No white oak or pitch pine is found N. of the centre of the town. Iron ore of an inferior quality is found in some places. There are many orchards, but apple-trees decay much sooner than in more southern situations. The towns of Campton and Rumney were both granted in Oct. 1761, to Capt. Jabez Spencer of East Haddam, Conn., but he dying before a settlement was effected, his heirs, in conjunction with others, obtained a new charter, Jan. 5, 1767. The first settlement was made in 1765, by two families of the names of Fox and Taylor. The proprietors held their first meeting Nov. 2, 1769, and the inhabitants theirs, Dec. 16, 1771. From the circumstance of the first proprietors building a *camp* when they went to survey Campton and Rumney, this town derives its name. In the revolutionary war, this town, though in its infancy, furnished nine or ten soldiers, five of whom died in the service, and three were living in 1822. The congregational church was formed June 1, 1774. Rev. Selden Church, who graduated at Yale College in 1765, was ordained in Oct. 1774; dismissed in 1792. Rev. John Webber, who graduated at Dartmouth College in 1792, was installed in Feb. 1812; dismissed March 12, 1815. Rev. Amos P. Brown was ordained Jan. 1, 1817; dismissed in 1822. There are some baptists, regular and freewill, and some methodists. Pop. 1047.

CANAAN, post-town in Grafton county, in lat. 43° 40′, bounded N. by Dame's gore, which separates it from Dorchester, E. by Orange, S. by Enfield, and W. by Hanover. It is situated on the height of land between the rivers Connecticut and Merrimack. It is 16 miles E. from Dartmouth College, 30 S. E. of Haverhill, 25 S.W. from Plymouth, and 40 N. W. from Concord. The only stream of consequence is the Mascomy, which rises in the N. W. part of Dorchester, and after a meandering course of 8 or 10 miles, falls into Mascomy pond in Enfield. Indian stream river rises in the S. E. corner of Dorchester, and running about 8 miles, mingles with the waters of Mascomy, near the centre of the town. Heart pond, so called from its figure, is situated in the centre of the town, and upon a swell of land so elevated, that at a distance, it presents the appearance of a sheet of water on a hill. It is about 500 rods in length and 200 in width, and the only natural curiosity of any note, is the mound or bank of earth which nearly surrounds this pond. It is from 4 to 5 feet high, and from its uniform height and regular construction, would seem to be the work of art; but from frequent annual observation, it is found to have been produced by the drifting of the ice when breaking up in the spring. Besides this, there are

Goose, Clark's, Mud and Bear ponds. The Grafton turnpike passes within a few rods of Heart pond, on the west shore of which is the meeting-house and a pleasant village. The land is not so broken as in some of the adjoining towns. There is but little not capable of cultivation. The soil is tolerably fertile, and produces wheat, rye, corn, flax, &c. Canaan was granted by charter, July 9, 1761, to 62 persons, all of whom except ten belonged to Connecticut. It derived its name from Canaan in that state. The first permanent settlement was made in the winter, in 1766 or 7, by John Scofield, who conveyed what effects he possessed the distance of 14 miles over a crust of snow upon a hand-sled. Among others of the first settlers, were George Harris, Thomas Miner, Joshua Harris, Samuel Jones and Samuel Meacham. The first proprietors' meeting was holden July 19, 1768. The first church, which was of the baptist denomination, was formed in 1780. Rev. Thomas Baldwin, D. D. was ordained to the pastoral care of it, in 1783, and removed to Boston in 1790. Rev. Joseph Wheat was settled in 1813. There is a respectable congregational society, incorporated in 1820, over which Rev. *Charles Calkins* presides. There is also a small society of methodists. Pop. 1198. Jonathan Duston, a native of Haverhill, Mass., a grandson to the intrepid Hannah Duston, mentioned under *Boscawen*, died here, July 4, 1812, aged 93.

CANDIA, post-township, Rockingham county, was detached from the N. part of Chester and incorporated Dec. 17, 1763. It was named by Governor Benning Wentworth, who was once a prisoner on the island of Candia, (the ancient Crete) in the Mediterranean sea. Candia is in lat. 43° 8'—is 6 miles long, 4 wide, and contains 15,360 acres, with 1273 inhabitants. Its soil is naturally hard of cultivation; but the industry of the inhabitants has made it fruitful. It was originally covered with a thick growth of oak, ash, maple, birch, &c. The site of this town is elevated, and commands an extensive view of the rich scenery of the adjacent country—the White Hills, the Wachusett, and other mountains, the lights on Plum-island, and the ocean being visible. From its elevation it probably derives its health; and there are now living in the town more than 60 persons between 70 and 100 years of age. Annual average of deaths for six years past, 23. In the W. part of the town is a ridge of land extending from N. to S. which is the highest elevation between Merrimack river and the ocean. On the E. side of this ridge, two branches of Lamprey river take their rise. The first settler was William Turner, who moved into the limits now comprising the town in 1748. In 1755, John Sargent and several others commenced settlements. This town among others contributed largely to the attainment of independence; and the names of 69 soldiers of the revolution are found on its records. There is a respectable congregational society in this town, over whom have been settled, Rev. David Jewett in 1771, removed 1780; Rev. Joseph Prince in 1782, removed 1789; Rev. Jesse Remington in 1790, died in 1815; Rev. Isaac Jones in 1816, dismissed 1818. Rev. *Abraham Wheeler* was installed in 1818. There is also a society of free-will baptists in Candia, and people of other denominations. Here are 12 schools during about half the year; and their regulations promise much usefulness. There are two social libraries; a moral society; a female charitable society, which contributes annually 20 dollars for religious purposes. The inhabitants are mostly industrious farmers, many of whom are wealthy.

CANTERBURY, a post-town, in the county of Rockingham, is in lat. 43° 21'; and bounded N. E. by Gilmanton, S. E. by Loudon, S. by Concord, W. by Merrimack river, which divides it from Boscawen, and N. by a ridge called Bean's Hill, separating the town from Northfield. Canterbury, though an uneven township, is not mountainous. The soil is generally good; the more uneven parts affording excellent pasturage. There are no large streams in this town; but several ponds give rise to smaller streams, furnishing good mill sites, and near which are cut great quantities of hay. Two bridges over the Merrimack connect this town with Boscawen. Canterbury was granted May 20, 1727, to Richard Waldron and others; and formerly comprehended Northfield and Loudon. It now contains an area of 26,345 acres. The town was settled soon after the grant was obtained; and for a long time the inhabitants were exposed to the inroads of the savages. The husbandman cleared and tilled his land under the protection of a guard, uncertain whether the seed he committed to the ground might not be watered by his blood, or that of an enemy. In 1738, two men of the names of Shepherd and Blanchard, going a short distance from the garrison then kept in town, were surprised by a party of seven Indians, who rose from behind a log not more than two rods from them, and all fired upon them, but without effect. Shepherd and his comrade then fired upon their assailants, but to no purpose. Shepherd then made his escape; while Blanchard, less fortunate, fell into the hands of the Indians, who wounded and mangled him in such a manner that he survived but a few days. During the French and Indian war, the latter made, several attempts upon the inhabitants of this town. At one time they entered the house of Thomas Clough; and finding no one within, they pilfered some of its contents. A negro belonging to Clough, and a lad of the name of Jackman, being at work not far distant, the Indians made them captives, and took them to Canada, where they remained till the close of the war, in 1749. Jackman was recently living in Boscawen. In April, 1752, two Indians, named Sabatis and Christi, came into Canterbury, where they were hospitably entertained by the inhabitants for more than a month. At their departure, they forced away two negroes, one of whom made his escape, and returned. The other was taken to Crown Point, and there sold to an officer. The next year, Sabatis, with another Indian, called Plausawa, returned to Canterbury; where, being reproached for misconduct on his former visit, Sabatis and his companion behaved in a very insolent manner. Much excitement was produced against them. Some persons treated them freely with strong drink; one pursued them into the woods, and taking advantage of their situation, killed them, and, assisted by another person, buried them. They were so slightly buried, however, that their bodies were dug up by beasts of prey, and their bones lay upon the ground. The two men concerned in the murder of these Indians belonged to Salisbury; where they were soon after apprehended and carried to Portsmouth for trial. A bill was found against them by the grand jury, and they were confined in irons; but on the night previous to their appointed trial, an armed mob from the country, with axes and bars, forced the prison and carried them off in triumph. Exertions were made to detect the ringleaders of the mob, but without effect. Although the people of Canterbury were occasionally supplied with preaching from the earliest settlement of the place, no church was formed until 1761; when the Rev. Abiel Foster was ordained; he was dismissed in 1779. Rev. Frederick Parker was ordained in 1791, and died in 1802. Rev. *William Patrick* was ordained in Oct. 1803—at which time the church consisted of about 20 male, and 40 female members: it has since considerably increased. Elder *Winthrop Young* was settled over the free-will baptist society in 1793. The Hon. ABIEL FOSTER deserves a particular notice. He possessed in a great degree the esteem and confidence of the people; and soon after he left the pastoral care of the church, he was called to arduous duties as a magistrate and legislator. In 1783, he was elected to Congress; and for three years was a member of that body under the old confederation. He was successively returned a member for nearly all the time until 1804; when he retired to private life and domestic tranquillity. He was an ardent lover of his country; and faithfully served his constituents—by whom his memory will long be cherished. He died in Feb. 1806. Canterbury, from its elevated situation, has ever been a healthy town. The average number of deaths for the last 12 years has been 17; greatest number in any one year, 24; least, 9. Pop. in 1820, 1696.

Shakers' Village.—In the S. E. part of this town, on an elevated and beautiful site, is the village of the "SHAKERS"—a sect of christians first known in this country in 1774, when *Ann Lee*, the founder of the sect, with several others, arrived at New-York from Liverpool. The church at Canterbury was gathered in the year 1792, under the ministration of Elder *Job Bishop*, who is still their minister; although the society first embraced their religious faith about ten years previous to that time. At present it consists of more than two hundred members. They have a meeting-house open at all times of public worship, where any discreet and decent spectator is allowed to attend. They have a Deacons' office, where all their public business is transacted, and where strangers are at first received on their visits to the society. They have also nine dwelling houses, of two and three stories, and several workshops both for men and women. Their mills and various kinds of machinery are moved by water on an artificial stream. They manufacture many articles for sale, which are remarkable for neatness and durability. Their gardens are perhaps the most productive of any in the country; and indeed all their improved lands exhibit the pleasing effects of industry and rural economy. They have for years supplied this section of the state with garden seeds, and take much pains to propagate those of the best kind. They occupy more than 1500 acres of land, lying principally in a body, which they have 'consecrated to the Lord,' and which they enjoy in common. They cheerfully pay their proportion of the public taxes, and share all the burthens of government, except the bearing of arms, which they deem to be contrary to the gospel; and in return they claim from government only that protection and support guaranteed to other citizens. The income of their manufactures, together with their agricultural products, yields their temporal support; and what they become possessed of more than is necessary to their wants, they devote to charitable purposes, agreeably to their church covenant. Fifty-six persons, old and young, have departed this life in the society since it was first organized—a period of forty years. This number is small, in comparison with the mortality of other parts of the state; and furnishes strong proof how much temperate habits tend to prolong life. It should be mentioned as a practice highly creditable to this sect, that the members of their societies never make use of ardent spirits except in cases of sickness, being aware of the evils intemperance brings upon society. Another practice not unworthy of imitation is, they refuse to be trusted even in the smallest sum. They transact their secular concerns with much probity and uprightness; and though they may have suffered reproach from their singularity of life and manners, they have become a proverb for industry, justice and benevolence. The peculiar doctrines of this sect, which have often been misrepresented, are noticed in vol i. *Historical Collections*, to which the reader is referred.

CAPE HORN, mountain. See *Northumberland*.

CARDIGAN, a mountain. See *Orange*.

CARR'S MOUNTAIN. See *Ellsworth*.

CARTER'S MOUNTAIN—between Adams and Chatham.

CATAMOUNT, mountain. See *Pittsfield*. There is also a hill of this name in Allenstown.

CENTRE-HARBOR, post-town, Strafford county, lat. 43° 41', is situated between Winnepisiogee and Squam lakes, bounded N. E. by Moultonborough, S. E. by Meredith, S. W. by New-Hampton, N. W. by Holderness and Squam lake. It has an area of 7,550 acres, and is distant 40 miles from Concord, 70 from Portsmouth, and 110 from Boston. Measley pond and Squam lake are partly in this town; the latter furnishes fine trout, and has several islands valuable for grazing. The soil is very good, mostly a rich loam. The original growth is oak, maple, beech, birch and pine. The town is pleasantly situated, and its local position probably gave rise to its name. The first settlements were made by Ebenezer Chamberlain in 1765, and Col. Joseph Senter, in 1767. A congregational church was formed here in 1815, over which Rev. *David Smith* was ordained 1819. There are portions of the inhabitants of other denominations. Pop. 486.

CHADBOURNE AND HART'S LOCATION, in the county of Coos, is a narrow tract on both sides the river Saco, extending from the notch of the White Mountains to a tract granted to Mr. Royse—it contains 3446 acres. The grant was made April 27, 1772, to Thomas Chadbourne and George Hart of Portsmouth. The tenth N. H.

turnpike passes through this tract from the Notch to the town of Bartlett. Pop. 65.

CHARLESTOWN, a post-township, and one of the shire towns in Cheshire county, is situated on Connecticut river, in lat. 43° 15′, and is bounded N. by Claremont, E. by Unity and Acworth, S. by Langdon and Walpole, and W. by the W. bank of Connecticut river, on which it extends about 13 miles. It contains an area of 21,400 acres. It is 51 miles from Concord, 100 from Boston, 100 from Albany, 110 from Hartford, Conn. and 18 miles from Windsor, Vt. The only rivers in Charlestown, are the Connecticut and Little Sugar rivers. In the former, there are three islands within the limits of this town, the largest of which contains about ten acres and is called Sartwell's island. The others contain about six acres each, and have a rich loamy soil. Sartwell's island is under a high cultivation. There are no falls in this river within the limits of Charlestown, which interrupt the boat navigation, although some little inconvenience is experienced in low water from what are called "Sugar river bars." Little Sugar river waters the north part of Charlestown and empties into Connecticut river about two miles south of the S. line of Claremont. This town has but few factory or mill privileges. The soil is extremely various. West of the great road leading from Walpole to Claremont, are not less than 1500 acres of fine interval land, generally of a deep, rich and loamy soil, and favorable for the culture and growth of most of the various kinds of grass and grain. In the east and northeast parts of the town, the soil of the upland is good—the natural growth of wood, consisting principally of birch, beech, oak, maple and hemlock. There is a ridge of hard, broken, and in some parts stony, land, east of the river road, extending almost the whole length of the town, and which is considered unfit for settlements. The south part of the town appears to have a different soil, and is favorable for yielding the lighter grains. The practical farmers here, for several years past, have used annually not less than 30 tons of plaster of Paris. It is generally applied with much benefit to interval lands. The agricultural products in 1820, were 25,000 lbs. of butter, 36,000 lbs. of cheese, 175,000 lbs. of beef, 180,000 lbs. of pork, 5000 lbs. of flax, and 895 barrels of cider. Charlestown contains two parishes, which are divided by a line running from Cheshire Bridge S. 87° E. to the corner of Acworth and Unity. In the south parish, there is a handsome village, delightfully situated, at the distance of about half a mile from Connecticut river, and parallel with it. It contains an elegant brick meeting-house erected in 1820, 70 feet by 60, and 32 in height, a court house and 56 dwelling houses, built with much taste and arranged with regularity. —In the north parish is a meeting house and a small village. There are 13 school districts, in which has been annually expended for the last ten years $800, for the instruction of about 500 scholars. In each parish is a social library. That in the south parish was incorporated in 1812, and contains above 250 volumes; that in the north parish was incorporated in 1818, and is but small. Cheshire bridge, about two miles N. of the S. meeting-house, connects this town with Springfield, Vt. From this bridge, Cheshire turnpike leads southerly through the principal village to Keene. Charlestown turnpike passes from this village through Acworth, and intersects the 2d N. H. turnpike in Lempster. Charlestown was granted by Massachusetts, Dec. 31, 1735, by the name of *Number* 4, which is sometimes applied to it at the present day. The grantees, 63 in number, belonged to Northampton, Hadley, Hatfield, Deerfield and Sunderland in Massachusetts. Their first meeting was holden at Hatfield, April 5, 1737. The first settlers were several families by the name of Parker, Farnsworth, and Sartwell from Groton, Mass. The next were the families by the name of Hastings from Lunenburg, and Stevens from Rutland. In 1743, a fort was built under the direction of Col. Stoddard of Northampton. In 1744, the first mills were erected. In 1746, they were burnt by the Indians, and were rebuilt in 1751. The Cape Breton war began in 1744. This town being more than thirty miles from any settlement suffered severely. In 1747, the inhabitants were compelled to abandon the town. In April of the same year, Capt. Stevens was ordered by Gov. Shirley to occupy the fort with thirty men to defend the frontiers. The boundary line between this province and Massachusetts was settled in 1741, and Charlestown was located in N. H. On the 2d July, 1753, No. 4 was incorporated by the name of Charlestown. The charter was granted by Gov. Benning Wentworth to Joseph Wells, Phinehas Stevens and others who were purchasers under the old grantees. In 1754, the French war commenced—and the inhabitants were obliged to take up their residence in the fort. In 1768, Mr. Samuel Stevens was the first who was chosen representative to the general court. The first meeting-house was built the same year. In 1771, Charlestown was made one of the shire towns of Cheshire county. In 1781, a number of towns on the west of Connecticut river seceded from New-Hampshire and joined Vermont, and one of the legislative sessions of the new state was holden at Charlestown. The Indian depredations on this town demand a few notices. The first settlers of Charlestown, like the first inhabitants of almost every frontier town in New-England, were, prior to 1760, the victims of savage cruelty. For twenty years after the first settlement, their neighbors on the N. were the French in Canada, on the W. the Dutch, near the Hudson, on the E. the settlements on Merrimack river, and on the S. few were found until arrived at Northfield in Massachusetts, a distance of more than 40 miles. The Indians were at peace but a small portion of that time. From their infancy, the settlers had been familiar with danger and had acquired a hardihood unknown to posterity. When they attended public worship, or cultivated their lands, they sallied from the fort prepared for battle, and worshipped or labored under the protection of a sentinel. In their warfare, the Indians preferred prisoners to scalps, and few were killed but those who attempted to escape, or appeared too formidable to be encountered with success. The Indians, made their first hostile appearance in No. 4, April 19, 1746, when the mills were burnt and John Spafford, Isaac Parker and Stephen Farnsworth were taken prisoners and carried to Canada. May 4th, the same year, Seth Putnam was killed; and on the 24th of the same month, a company under Capt. Paine, from the S. part of Worcester county, arrived for the defence of the place. A part of the soldiers had the curiosity to view the spot where the unfortunate Putnam fell. The Indians rushed between them and the fort, and five were killed. August 3, 1746, a man by the name of Phillips was killed. In Nov., the town was deserted except by six men, who kept the fort until winter, and then left it. In the month of March, Capt. Stevens, with 30 men, took possession of the fort and defended it against the attack of 400 French and Indians.—June 17, 1749, Obadiah Sartwell was killed while ploughing, and Enos Stevens, a boy, son of Capt. Stevens, was taken prisoner. On the 29th of August, 1754, the Indians made their first appearance after the commencement of the French war. At early dawn, they attacked the house of Mr. James Johnson, who, with his wife, her sister and three children, and two men, Peter Labarree and Ebenezer Farnsworth, lodgers in the house, were taken prisoners. On the 2d day, about 15 miles from Charlestown, in the wilderness, Mrs. Johnson was delivered of a daughter, whom she named *Captive*, who afterwards married Col. George Kimball. Of the sufferings, detentions and release of Mrs. Johnson, a minute account has long been before the public, and has lately been re-published in the *Historical Collections*, for 1822. In 1756, Lieut. Moses Willard, the father of Mrs. Johnson, was killed. He was at work within sight of the fort with his son Moses. Him the Indians pursued and wounded with a spear. He made his escape, carrying the spear with him into the fort. He lived respected until Aug. 17, 1822, when he was gathered to his fathers, aged 84 years. In 1757, the mills were again burnt, and Sampson Colefax, David Farnsworth and Thomas Adams were taken prisoners. In 1758, Asahel Stebbins was killed, his wife, Isaac Parker and a soldier were captured. Sept. 8, 1760, Joseph Willard, his wife and children, were taken prisoners. After a march of a few miles, their infant child was destroyed. Mr. Willard was son of Rev. Mr. Willard of Rutland, Ms. who was killed by the Indians. It is believed that this was among the last depredations of the Indians in New-England. The prisoners taken from Charlestown were all carried to Canada by lake Champlain, and sold to the French. Nearly all of them were redeemed by government or their friends. The first child born in Charlestown was Elizabeth, the daughter of Isaac Parker;—she was born 1744; died in 1806, aged 62. Charlestown has been favored with a number of eminent men, a few of whom will be mentioned. Capt. PHINEHAS STEVENS was one of the first settlers. The town, when in its infancy, was protected by his intrepidity. He was a native of Sudbury, Mass. from whence his father removed to Rutland. At the age of 16, while his father was making hay, he, with three little brothers followed him to the meadows. They were ambushed by the Indians, who killed two of his brothers, took him prisoner and were preparing to kill his youngest brother, a child four years old. He, by signs to the Indians, made them understand if they would spare him, he would carry him on his back—

and he carried him to Canada. They were redeemed and both returned. He received several commissions from Gov. Shirley, and rendered important services in protecting the frontiers. In 1747, when Charlestown was abandoned by the inhabitants, he was ordered to occupy the fort with 30 men. On the 4th of April, he was attacked by 400 French and Indians, under Mons. Debeline. The assault lasted three days. Indian stratagem and French skill, with fire applied to every combustible about the fort, had not the desired effect. The heroic band were not appalled. They refused to capitulate. At length an interview between the commanders took place. The Frenchman shewed his forces and described the horrid massacre that must ensue unless the fort was surrendered. "My men are not afraid to die," was the answer made by Capt. Stevens. The attack continued with increased fury until the end of the third day, when the enemy returned to Canada, and left Capt. Stevens in possession of the fort. Capt. Stevens, for his gallantry on this occasion, was presented by Sir Charles Knowles with an elegant sword, and from this circumstance the township, when it was incorporated, took the name of Charlestown. Capt. Stevens died in Nov. 1756, in the service of his country. Samuel Stevens, Esq. the only surviving son of this brave man was the first representative of the town to the general court, and is at the age of 87 years, the present register of probate for Cheshire county. Col. WILLIAM HEYWOOD, who was one of the ten males of the congregational church formed in 1761, filled the office of town clerk 42 years; lived to an advanced age and died in Feb. 1803. Col. SAMUEL HUNT, an active military officer in the French and revolutionary wars, settled here in 1759, and was sheriff of the county till his death in 1779. Hon. SIMEON OLCOTT, who graduated at Yale College in 1761, commenced the practice of law in this town. He was chief justice of the court of common pleas, and of the superior court, and senator in Congress from 1801 to 1805. He died in 1815, aged 79. Hon. BENJAMIN WEST, son of Rev. Thomas West, and brother of Rev. Dr. Samuel West of Boston, resided here more than 40 years. He was born April 8, 1746, graduated at Harvard College in 1768, settled here in the practice of law in 1772, and died in July, 1817, aged 71. At the bar, he ranked among the first of his profession. His application, learning and integrity gave him great and merited influence. The ecclesiastical history is brief. The first minister was Rev. John Dennis, who, on account of the Indian war, was ordained at Northfield, Mass. Dec. 4, 1754. He was dismissed March 31, 1756. Rev. Bulkley Olcott, who graduated at Yale College in 1758, was ordained May 28, 1761, about which time the church was re-organized or a new one formed. He died June 26, 1792. Rev. Dan Foster, though not ordained here, supplied the pulpit from 1796 to his death, in 1809. Rev. *Jaazaniah Crosby* was ordained Oct. 17, 1810. The north parish has no church formed. Pop. 2110.

CHATHAM, township, Coos co. in lat. 44° 8′, is situated on the E. side of the White Mountains, and adjoining the line which divides this state from Maine. It has Conway on the S., Bartlett and Adams on the W., Mount Royse on the N. Chatham was granted to Peter Livius and others, Feb. 7, 1767; it now contains, in addition to its original territory, what was formerly called Warner's location—in all about 26,000 acres. There are several ponds in Chatham, and some considerable streams. The surface is mountainous and rocky, and can never sustain a great population. Between Chatham and Adams, Carter's mountain rises so high as to prevent the opening a road between the two towns; so that in holding an intercourse with the rest of the county, the inhabitants are obliged to pass through part of the state of Maine. Pop. 298.

CHESTER, a post-township of Rockingham county, in lat. 42° 59', is bounded N. and E. by Raymond, Candia and Hooksett, E. by Poplin and Sandown, S. by Londonderry, and W. by Manchester. Its greatest length is about 12 miles; its greatest breadth is about 6 1-2 miles, and its least breadth, but little exceeds two. It is distant 17 miles from Exeter, and 30 from Portsmouth; 17 from Haverhill, and 43 from Boston; 23 from Amherst, and 23 from Concord. A branch of Exeter river, called "The Branch," flows through the N.E. part of Chester, beside which, there is no stream deserving mention. Massabesick pond is the largest body of fresh water in the county, and contains about 1500 acres. It consists of two nearly equal parts, each about 3 miles in length, and from 200 to 400 rods in breadth, united by a strait of about 250 rods in length, which is at one point so narrow, that the Londonderry turnpike passes it by a bridge. The line between this town and Manchester passes more than 2 miles through the westerly half of this pond. A considerable portion of this town possesses a good soil, and many of the large swells yield in fertility to none in the state. There are several large and valuable meadows. In this town are two caves, sometimes visited by strangers. That which was earliest noticed, is situated in Mine hill, near the east side of Massabesick pond, on the old road from Chester to Concord. The entrance is about 5 feet high and 2 1-2 wide. The cavern extends into the hill in a northern direction about 80 feet, of sufficient dimensions to admit a person to pass. Its form is very irregular, and its height and breadth various, from 2 to 12 feet and even more. After dividing into several branches, it is gradually lost in numerous small crevices in the rocks, which appear to be gneiss, and which possess in some parts a slight taste of alum. The other is in the westerly side of Rattlesnake hill, in the S. W. part of the town, in a ledge of coarse granite, nearly 40 feet high. It has two entrances. The north entrance is about 11 feet high and 4 broad. The width of the cave then increases gradually for about 15 feet, where its height is 8, and its breadth from 6 to 12 feet. Its direction there changes to the right, and its width varies from 5 1-2 to 9 feet, and its height from 6 to 7, to the other entrance which is about 7 feet high and 9 wide. Its whole length is about 35 feet. Plumbago or black lead is found in this town of good quality and in considerable abundance. Native sulphur is also found in small quantities, imbedded in tremolite. Granite and gneiss are the prevailing rocks, and handsome specimens of graphic granite are sometimes found. The village in this town has about 35 dwelling houses, and a meeting-house, beside other buildings, stores, &c., standing chiefly on a long street. It is the principal place of business in this part of the county, and is situated on an elevated rise, and commands one of the most extensive prospects in New-England. From this hill, the ocean, though more than 20 miles distant, may, in a clear day, be distinctly seen. There are in this town two meeting-houses, one for congregationalists, erected in 1773, and furnished with a town-clock and a bell, and one for presbyterians, erected about 1735, but since much enlarged. The schools are usually taught here from 5 to 8 months in each year. A social library was incorporated in 1798, and contains about 325 volumes, many of which are well selected and valuable works. The Chester turnpike extends about 15 miles from the village in Chester to Pembroke street. The mail passes and repasses three times in each week, and stages daily, on these roads from Concord to Boston. A weekly mail from Brattleborough, Vt. to Portsmouth, passes through this town. In October, 1719, about 80 persons, chiefly from Hampton and Portsmouth, associated for the purpose of obtaining a grant of a township in the "Chesnut country"—placed three men on the land to keep possession, and petitioned for a grant. After some difficulty, they obtained a grant of a tract of land ten miles square, Aug. 26, 1720. The settlement was immediately commenced by several persons from Rye and Hampton—of whom Samuel Ingalls, Jonathan Goodhue, Jacob Sargent, Ebenezer Dearborn, Robert Smith, B. and E. Colby, John and S. Robie, seem to have been most active and useful; and by several families which had recently emigrated from the north of Ireland. From 1722 to 1726, the settlement was retarded by an Indian war. The Indians, however, did no injury to this town, except that they took Thomas Smith and John Carr, who, after travelling about 30 miles into the woods, made their escape while the Indians were asleep, and arrived in safety at a garrison in Londonderry. Several garrison houses were maintained in this town till after the peace of 1749. On the 8th of May, 1722, the town, which had previously been called *Cheshire*, was incorporated by its present name. The charter included more than 120 square miles of territory. The first meeting under it was holden March 28, 1723. Until 1728, the town meetings were usually holden in one of the old towns in the province, and almost all the town officers, though proprietors, were not inhabitants of the town. Until 1735, the business of the town and of the proprietary was transacted at the town meetings. Separate meetings were afterwards holden. In 1729, the town voted to erect a meeting-house, which was so far completed, that the town meetings were afterwards usually holden in it. In the following year, they settled Rev. Moses Hale, who was removed in 1734. In this year, the first settlers, who were presbyterians, formed a society and settled Rev. John Wilson, after the rules of the Kirk of Scotland. In 1738, they erected a meeting-house. They resisted every attempt to settle a congregational minister, and after the settlement of Rev. Ebenezer Flagg, which occurred in 1736, many of them refused payment of their taxes for his support. Two of them, James Campbell, and John Tolford, were arrested by the collector and committed to jail in Exeter. After a tedious lawsuit, they obtained a decision in their favor, and in 1740, the two congregations were authorised to hold separate meetings with corporate powers. Rev. Mr. Flagg, of the congregational church died Nov. 14, 1796. Rev. Nathan Bradstreet had been settled as colleague in 1793, and resigned in 1818. Rev. Joel R. Arnold succeeded March 8, 1820. Rev. Mr. Wilson, of the presbyterian church, died Feb. 1, 1779 : he was born in the county of Ulster, in the N. of Ireland—to which his ancestors had emigrated from Scotland. He came to America in 1729, and preached 45 years to his church. After his death the church was vacant 24 years. Rev. Zaccheus Colby was installed Oct. 13, 1803, removed in 1809 ; and was succeeded by Rev. Clement Parker Feb. 19, 1817. A baptist church was organized in Chester, Dec. 16, 1819. In 1740 the first schoolhouse was built. In 1748, Capt. Abel Morse was chosen the first representative. In 1750, it was voted, that the S. W. part of the town should be set off with a part of Londonderry and the land next Amoskeag into a separate parish, which was incorporated in 1751 by the name of *Derryfield*. In 1753, the W. part of the town was set off as a distinct parish, and has been since known as the *Long-Meadows*. In 1762, that part of the town called *Charmingfare* was set off as a parish, and in the year following was incorporated by the name of Candia. 1763, the north parish, or *Freetown*, was set off as a parish or town, and in 1765, incorporated by the name of Raymond. In 1822, a part of Chester was disannexed with other tracts to form the town of Hooksett—reducing the population to 1946. The aborigines had a settlement of 10 or 12 wigwams, on an island in Massabesick pond, vestiges of which, it is said, may still be seen.—The throat distemper, which prevailed in 1735, and which proved mortal in 21 cases, is the only dangerous epidemic with which this town has been visited. The first child of English parents born in this place was a daughter of Samuel Ingalls ; she died recently in Candia aged over 90 years. John Sargent was the first boy born here ; he died in Candia between 70 and 80 years of age. The first framed house erected in this town, is still standing and is now occupied as a tavern. Many of the first settlers lived to a very great age.

CHESTERFIELD, a post-township in Cheshire county, in lat. 42° 53', is bounded N. by Westmoreland, E. by Keene and Swanzey, S. by Winchester and Hinsdale, W. by Brattleborough and Dummerston, Vt. containing 29,437 acres. It is 11 miles from Keene, 65 from Concord, and 90 from Boston. This town is generally hilly and uneven. Few towns on Connecticut river have so little interval land. For the whole six miles that it lies upon the river, the hills approach near the river's side. There is much good upland, well adapted for grazing, and the production of Indian corn. The chief articles carried to market are beef, pork, butter and cheese. Connecticut river passes through the western bounds of Chesterfield. Cat's-Bane brook is a stream of great importance, as it furnishes many mill seats. Spafford's lake is a beautiful collection of water, situated about one mile N. of the meeting-house. It is about 8 miles in circumference, containing a surface of 526 acres. It is fed by springs in its bosom. Its waters are remarkably clear and pure, its bed being a white sand. In this lake, there is an island of about six acres, which forms a delightful retreat for students of the academy in the summer. On its E. side issues a stream called Partridge's brook, sufficiently large to carry the machinery of a cotton factory, sawmills, &c. The factory has 800 spindles. Forty looms, operated by water, have been lately built. West river mountain lies in this town and Hinsdale. It is supposed to have been once subject to a volcanic eruption, and there is at present a considerable quantity of lava near its crater. Some of the early inhabitants perceiving an aperture in the mountain, and supposing it led to a silver mine, obtained a lease of that part which contained the supposed mine. The lease requires the lessees to dig, at least three days in each year, that it may not become void. At this time, they have dug principally through a rock between 90 and 100 feet, following the course of the crater downward. It is said by those who live near the mountain, that it frequently trembles, and a rumbling noise is heard in its bowels. Chesterfield has three villages. The principal one, through which the stage road passes, leading from Hartford to Hanover, is situated near the centre of the town and 3 miles E. of Connecticut river. Here are several dwelling houses, the meeting-house and a flourishing academy, which was opened Aug. 14, 1794. It has no funds, but the school has continued every year since it commenced, under the direction of a preceptor and 11 trustees. Until within a few years, this was the only academy in Cheshire county. Chesterfield was granted Feb. 11, 1752, to 12 persons of the name of Willard and 52 others. The first settlement was made Nov. 25, 1761, on the banks of the Connecticut by Moses Smith and William Thomas, with their families. The next spring, Abel Emmons and Simon Davis moved into town. At that period, the river afforded abundance of shad and salmon, and the forests were well stocked with deer, bears and other game, so that the inhabitants did not experience those privations so common in the new settlements on the E. The first child born in town was Mary Thomas—born in 1762, and is now living. The congregational church was formed in 1771. Rev. *Abraham Wood*, who graduated at Harvard College in 1767, was ordained Dec. 31, 1772. He is the oldest minister in New-Hampshire. There is a baptist society, incorporated June 21, 1819; also a universalist society, incorporated June 22, 1818. Mrs. Hannah Bayley, widow of Josiah Bayley, formerly of Lunenburg, Ms. died here in Nov. 1822, aged 104 years and 3 months. Hon. LEVI JACKSON, who was for several years a representative and senator in the legislature, and a member of the executive council in 1816 and 1817, was a native of this town. He was born June 29, 1772, graduated at Dartmouth College in 1799, and died Aug. 30, 1821, aged 49. He was six years preceptor of the academy. Pop. 2110.

CHICHESTER, post-town, Rockingham county, lat 43° 15', is situated 8 miles E. of Concord; bounded N.E. by Pittsfield, S.E. by Epsom, S, W, by Pembroke, N.W. by Loudon and a part of Concord, and comprises 11,978 acres. It was granted May 20, 1727 to Nathaniel Gookin and others; but the settlement was not commenced until 1758, when Paul Morrill settled in the woods. The soil is good, and richly repays the cultivator—there is little waste land, nor are there any considerable elevations. Bear hill in the N. part of the town, which is covered with a cultivated soil, is the principal eminence. The E. of the town is watered by the Suncook river, which affords its mill seats and some productive interval. Several smaller streams flow into this river from the S. side of the town. Linkfield pond is in Chichester, from which flows a small stream S. W. into the Soucook. The turnpike from Concord to Portsmouth passes through this town. In 1791, a congregational church was organized and Rev. *Josiah Carpenter* ordained. There is also a religious society formed of members of different religious sentiments, but agreeing in worship. In various parts of the town are still to be seen traces of Indian settlements; and implements of stone, chisels, axes, &c. have frequently been found. The vicinity was once the residence of a powerful tribe, the Penacooks, and their plantations of corn, &c. were made on the banks of the Suncook. Pop. 1010.

CLAREMONT, a post township in Cheshire county, situated in lat. 43° 23′, on Connecticut river, is bounded N. by Cornish, E. by Newport, S. by Unity and Charlestown, W. by Weathersfield, Vt. containing 25,830 acres. It is 12 miles N. of Charlestown, 47 W. of Concord, 97 from Portsmouth and 100 from Boston. This town is watered by Connecticut and Sugar rivers, besides numerous brooks and rivulets. Sugar river originates from Sunapee lake; passes through part of Wendell, the whole of Newport, and through nearly the centre of this town, where it unites with the Connecticut. Red-water brook waters the N. E. part of the town and empties itself into Sugar river. Claremont is a fine undulating tract of territory, covered with a rich gravelly loam, converted into the best meadows and pastures. The hills are sloping acclivities, crowned with elegant summits. The intervals on the rivers are rich and luxuriant. The agricultural products in 1820, were 30,000 lbs. of butter, 55,000 lbs. of cheese, 135,000 lbs. of beef, 170,000 lbs. of pork, 7,500 lbs. of flax, and 1100 barrels of cider. Three tons of pearlashes were made the same year. The houses and buildings present a very favorable appearance, and indicate the wealth and prosperity of the town. There is but one elevation which comes under the name of mountain. This is near Newport and is called Green mountain. There is one small pond lying in this town and Newport. There is, besides the mills, &c. in the statistical table, a woollen factory, owned by Dr. Leonard Jarvis, which manufactures between 4000 and 5000 yards of broad cloth annually. There is also a valuable paper mill establishment, owned by Col. Stevens.— There is a communication with Weathersfield by means of Ashley's and Sumner's ferries. Just below Ashley's ferry, is Hubbard's island, 240 rods long and 40 wide. There are several bridges over Sugar river. The second N. H. turnpike extends from the lottery bridge in Claremont to the plain in Amherst, a distance of about 50 miles. Claremont was granted Oct. 26, 1764, to Josiah Willard, Samuel Ashley and 68 others. It received its name from the country seat of

Lord Clive, an English general. The first settlement was made in 1762, by Moses Spafford and David Lynde. In 1763, and 1766, several other inhabitants arrived. In 1767, a considerable number of the proprietors, and others from the towns of Farmington, Hebron and Colchester, in Connecticut, made settlements in different parts of the town. The first native of Claremont was Elijah, son of Moses Spafford—he was born in 1763. Among the early inhabitants, to whose enterprise the town was essentially indebted for its prosperity, may be mentioned Samuel Cole, Esq. who graduated at Yale College in 1731, and was for many years very useful as an instructor of youth. He died at an advanced age. Dr. William Sumner, a native of Boston, who came to this place in 1768 from Hebron, Conn., was a resident several years in Claremont, where he died in March, 1778. Col. Benjamin Sumner, who was many years a civil magistrate, died in May, 1815, aged 78. Col. Joseph Waite, who was engaged in the French and Indian war, was captain of one of Rogers' companies of rangers, and commanded a regiment in the revolutionary war, died in Oct. 1776. Capt. Joseph Taylor, who was engaged in the Cape Breton, French, and revolutionary wars, who was, with one Farwell, taken prisoner by the Indians, in the summer of 1755, carried to Canada, and sold to the French, resided in Claremont, and died in March, 1813, at the age of 84. Hon. Samuel Ashley moved to this town in 1782. He was in the wars of 1745 and 1755. He sustained several civil offices, and was judge of the court of common pleas. He died in Feb. 1792. The early inhabitants were about equally divided in their attachment to episcopacy and congregational principles. The churches of these denominations may be considered as coeval. The first minister of the congregational society was Rev. George Wheaton, who was ordained Feb. 19, 1772; died June 24, 1773, aged 22. Rev. Augustine Hibbard was settled in Oct. 1774; was dismissed in 1785. Rev. John Tappan, ordained March 7, 1796; dismissed Sept. 1802. Rev. Stephen Farley, ordained Dec. 24, 1806; dismissed April, 1816. Rev. Jonathan Nye, ordained June 6, 1821. The first minister of the episcopal society was Rev. Ranna Cossit, who sailed for England for holy orders in Dec. 1772. He was ordained by the bishop of London, and returned the next year, and took charge of the church in this town. He was recalled by the bishop to the island of Cape Breton in 1785. Rev. Daniel Barber succeeded him in August, 1775, and was dismissed in Nov. 1818. The church, which is called Union church, one of the largest in the state, is in a flourishing condition, containing 180 communicants, and is under the care of Rev. James B. Howe, who was settled in April, 1819. There are two churches, one built in 1773; the other in 1812, in which public worship is attended alternately. A baptist society was formed in 1785, and the next year, Rev. John Peckens was ordained. He was dismissed in 1788. Rev. John Peake, now of Barnstable, Ms., succeeded Mr. Peckens. There is a methodist society, formed in the year 1809. Rev. Caleb Dustin, who died in 1821, was their pastor several years, and was highly respected. There is a number of universalists, who have occasional preaching. A small society of Roman catholics, in this and the neighboring towns, have lately received Rev. *Daniel Barber*, formerly the episcopalian minister here, who was ordained at the Roman catholic church in Boston, as a missionary for this state, Dec. 3, 1822. The late Hon. CALEB ELLIS was a resident in this town. He was a native of Walpole, Ms., graduated at Harvard College 1793. He read law principally in the office of Hon. Joshua Thomas of Plymouth, Ms.; came to reside in Claremont about 1800. In 1804, he was chosen a member of congress from this state; in 1809 and 1810, a member of the executive council; in 1812, an elector of president and vice-president of the U. S. In 1813, he was appointed judge of the superior court, in which office he remained till his death, May 9, 1816, aged 49. Pop. 2290.

CLEAR STREAM, river, rising in the mountains of Dixville, N. of Millsfield; it passes through the centre of Errol, into the Ameriscoggin, about three miles W. of Umbagog lake.

COCHECO, or QUOCHECHO, river, has its rise from several small streams in New-Durham, which unite in Farmington, whence the river meanders through Rochester, there receiving the Isinglass, a tributary, and thence passes through Dover into the Newichwannock or Salmon-Fall river, the principal branch of the Pascataqua. The Cocheco is a beautiful river, and very important to the inhabitants of Rochester and Dover.

COLEBROOK, post-town, Coos county, lat. 44° 51', is bounded N. by Stewartstown, E. by Dixville, S. by Columbia, W. by the Connecticut river, and contains 25,000 acres. It is watered by the Mohawk river and Beaver brook. The soil here is rich, and very generally capable of culture. Intervals of good quality stretch along the Connecticut, and the uplands, gentle of ascent, are also fertile. Colebrook was originally granted to Sir George Colebrook and others, and was incorporated Dec. 1, 1790. The people are enterprizing and happy. Pop. 469.

COLD RIVER. *See Acworth.*

COLLEGE LANDS, in the county of Coos, consisting of two grants by the state to the trustees of Dartmouth College. The first was made Feb. 5, 1789, and contains 40,960 acres, situated on the Connecticut river N. of Stewartstown. The second grant was made June 18, 1807, consisting of 23,040 acres, located N. of the tract granted to George Wentworth. The lands are of considerable value, but as yet have but 33 inhabitants.

COLUMBIA, post-town, in the county of Coos, in lat. 44° 48', lies on the E. bank of Connecticut river, 30 miles N. of Lancaster. It has Colebrook on the N., Dixville and Ervin's Location on the E. and Stratford on the S. The surface of the town is quite uneven, the mountains of Stratford lying along the S. From these a number of streams descend northwesterly into the Connecticut, yielding an abundance of water for the soil, and furnishing many fine mill seats. There are also several small ponds in town—on the borders of one, called Lime pond, vast quantities of shells are found, from which a species of lime is made that answers for some uses. The forest trees in Columbia are what may be called hard wood, in distinction from evergreens. Some spruce, fir and pine, however, are found in Columbia, but in no abundance. The want of the latter is felt by the inhabitants. This place was granted Dec. 1, 1770, and named *Cockburne* in honor of Sir James Cockburne, of London, a grantee. It was incorporated Dec. 16, 1797; and its name altered to Columbia June 19, 1811. This town originally comprised about 32,000 acres. Wales' Location, containing 5822 acres, has since been annexed. Pop. 249.

CONCORD, post-town, in the county of Rockingham, is the seat of the state government. It is pleasantly situated on both sides the river Merrimack, along which spread some rich intervals. Concord is in lat. 43° 12', N. and is bounded N. W. by Canterbury and Boscawen, N. E. by Loudon and Chichester, S. E. by Pembroke and Bow, and S. W. by Hopkinton. It comprises 40,919 acres, of which about 1800 are water. There are 5 ponds in Concord, two on the E. of the Merrimack, and three on the W. The largest is Turkey pond in the S. W. part of the town, containing about 700 acres, the waters of which form the Turkey river, a stream of some importance, passing S. into Bow. Long pond, in the W. part of the town, contains about 500 acres, the waters of which pass into the Merrimack below Sewall's island. Turtle pond lies E. of Long pond and near the line of Loudon; it contains about 200 acres, and its waters pass into the Merrimack through the valley E. of the river. The others are Snow pond, N. W. of Turtle pond, and Horse-shoe pond near the meeting-house. The river Soucook forms the S. E. boundary of Concord, from Chichester to its junction with the Merrimack below Garven's falls. The Contoocook is a considerable river, entering near the W. corner of the town, and uniting with the Merrimack on the N. W. line, forming at its junction the island celebrated as the spot where Mrs. Duston made a desperate escape from a party of Indians in 1698.* But the Merrimack is the principal river in this region, and is not only the ornament and beautifier of the landscape, but the source of health and profit to the inhabitants. It meanders nearly through the centre of the town, enriching the tracts of interval on its borders. The intervals here are of no great width, and the remark is applicable, we believe, to the whole valley of the Merrimack, which is far inferior in extent and beauty to that of the Connecticut. Soon after entering the town, the river passes over the rapids called Sewall's falls, below which is situated Sewall's island, thus called from an early proprietor. The current of the river from this island is not rapid, and has no natural obstructions, until it reaches Turkey and Garven's falls at the S. E. extremity of the town. Locks are here constructed, and the navigation of the river has been open during the boating seasons for several years. The river here is about 100 yards wide, but occasionally the spring and autumn freshes have covered the interval adjoining the principal village, presenting to the eye a body of water of a mile in width. These freshes, though often destructive to crops, fences, &c. are of no disadvantage to the soil, on which they deposit a rich sediment. During the greatest freshes, the river has risen nearly 20 feet above the ordinary level, but this is un-

*See Boscawen.

common. There are two bridges thrown across the river in this town: the Federal, or Upper bridge, and Concord, or Lower bridge. At these bridges are situated the storehouses of the Boating Company on the river. The intercourse with Boston, opened by way of the canals on the Merrimack, has been of considerable advantage to the country. The navigation to this town was opened in 1815, and the quantity of goods annually brought up has averaged from 1000 to 1500 tons. The freight downward has been more extensive, consisting of the produce of the country, lumber, and other heavy or bulky articles. For the first three years the business on the river exceeded that for the three last; but there is a prospect that it will hereafter be much increased. The principal village, and the seat of most of the business of the town, extends along the western bank of the Merrimack nearly two miles from S.E. to N.W. It is very pleasantly situated, and from its convenient situation has become a place of considerable trade. The state-house,* state-prison, town-house and meeting-house are situated in this village. There are 170 dwelling-houses, 18 stores, 7 taverns, several mechanic shops, 5 printing-offices, 5 bookstores and 2 binderies. On the E. of the river is another considerable village, very pleasantly situated ; and a village is also forming in the W. part of the town. The soil of this town presents all the varieties common to this region, and is in some parts fertile. The highlands extending back from the river are very productive, and were originally covered with oak, chesnut, maple, &c. The plains are alluvial and covered with a growth of pine. Large masses of excellent granite are found in Concord, and the public edifices there are erected of this material. Iron ore exists in small quantities, and was formerly wrought by the inhabitants. The tract comprising the town of Concord, (originally called *Penacook,*) was granted by Massachusetts, Jan. 17, 1725, to Benjamin Stevens, Ebenezer Eastman and others, and included seven miles square. In the following year settlements were commenced, and the tract divided into lots ; a block house was also erected, to serve for a place of worship and as a garrison of defence. In 1727, Capt. Ebenezer Eastman moved his family into this place. In 1728, the S. boundaries of the town were extended, as an equivalent for lands within the limits before granted to Gov. Endicott, and claimed by heirs of Judge Sewall. The first child born at Penacook, was Dorcas, a daughter of Edward Abbot, Feb. 15, 1728. Edward, son of the same, and the first male, was born Dec. 27, 1730. In 1733, the plantation was incorporated by the name of *Rumford.* From about this period till 1762, a controversy existed between the proprietors of Rumford and Bow, the latter claiming under a grant from New-Hampshire a great portion of the town of Rumford. The question was decided on appeal to the King in Council in 1762 ; and Rumford was incorporated by New-Hampshire, June 7, 1765, by the name of *Concord.* No considerable attacks were made by the Indians wandering in this region, until the commencement of the war of 1744. During several years thereafter, the inhabitants were in constant danger and alarm, and lived in garrisons. On the 7th of Aug. 1746,

*See page 41.

the Indians killed Jonathan and Samuel Bradley, Obadiah Peters, John Bean and John Lufkin; and took several others into captivity. The party were travelling toward Hopkinton. The conflict was obstinate, and a greater number of Indians were killed.* The enemy hovered in the neighborhood during the war; killed a Mr. Esterbrooks Nov. 10, 1746, and committed various depredations upon the cattle and other property of the inhabitants. Rev. Timothy Walker, the first minister, was settled Nov. 18, 1730; and died Sept. 2, 1782, aged 77. Rev. Israel Evans was ordained July 1, 1789; dismissed in 1797. Rev. *Asa M'Farland*, D. D. was ordained March 7, 1798; and his church consists of nearly 400 members. An episcopal society was formed here in 1818; and in the same year a baptist church, over which Rev. *William Taylor* was settled in 1819. There is also a society of friends. The first paper established in this town was the "Courier of New-Hampshire," commenced by George Hough Jan. 6, 1790; discontinued Oct. 30, 1805. "The Mirror," by Moses Davis, was commenced in 1792; discontinued in 1799. Elijah Russell established the "Republican Gazette," Feb. 5, 1801, and discontinued it in 1802. The "Concord Gazette," by Hoit & Tuttle, commenced July 6, 1806, and discontinued in 1819. The "*New-Hampshire Patriot*," by Isaac Hill, commenced April 18, 1809. The "Concord Observer," since altered to "*New-Hampshire Repository*," was established by George Hough, Jan. 1, 1819; and transferred to John W. Shepard, the present publisher, April 1, 1822. The "*New-Hamp-*

*See History of Concord, published by Jacob B. Moore.

shire Statesman," by Luther Roby, commenced Jan. 6, 1823. A Literary Journal, conducted by the authors of this Gazetteer, was commenced in 1822, and is still published by J. B. Moore. This town has generally enjoyed an unusual exemption from disease. For the last 31 years, the deaths have been 845, averaging about 27 per annum. Of these about one 12th part have lived to the age of 80 years and upwards—several to nearly 100. Epidemics have scarcely ever prevailed here. The small pox appeared in 1775, but was checked by timely precaution. In 1812, 13, 16 and 17, the spotted fever made its appearance, and a number fell its victims. Among the early inhabitants and distinguished citizens of this town, we may mention the Rev. TIMOTHY WALKER, the first minister. He was a native of Woburn, Ms., graduated at Harvard College in 1725. During 52 years, which he spent in the ministry here, his labors were abundantly successful. Hon. TIMOTHY WALKER, son of the preceding, was born in 1737; graduated at Harvard in 1756; was entrusted with various civil offices by his townsmen, and in 1776 was one of the committee of safety for the state. He commanded a regiment of minute men in New-Hampshire —was afterwards paymaster of the state forces, and served a campaign under Gen. Sullivan. He was a member of the convention which formed our constitution in 1784—was afterwards several years a legislator; and for some time sustained the office of chief-justice of the common pleas. He died May 5, 1822, aged 85. BENJAMIN ROLFE, Esq. an early and distinguished settler, died March 20, 1772. Dr. EZRA CARTER, the first physician, and a person universally esteemed, died Sept. 17, 1767, aged 48. Dr. PHILIP CARRIGAIN, an eminent physician and valuable citizen, died in 1806. Deacon JOHN KIMBALL, esteemed for a life of unobtrusive usefulness and piety, died Dec. 31, 1817, aged 78. Hon. THOMAS W. THOMPSON, a distinguished inhabitant, died Oct. 1, 1821, aged 57. Numerous other individuals, beloved for services to the community, might be mentioned, had we room in this brief sketch. The celebrated BENJAMIN THOMPSON, (known to the world as *Count Rumford*,) was a native of Woburn, Ms. and settled here in early life. In 1775, he went to England, was employed as clerk in the office of an English nobleman, who eventually procured for him a colonel's commission. He served in the British armies until 1784, when his philosophical inquiries having attracted attention in foreign countries, he was promoted to the rank of lieutenant-general of horse, in the service of the Duke of Bavaria. Here he distinguished himself in introducing discipline and economy among the troops; and during his residence in Bavaria made successful efforts in the public service, and particularly in ameliorating the condition of the poor. On leaving the German service, the Duke created him a count, taking his title from the name of the town where he had spent most of his youth. Count Rumford afterwards visited England, where he received the honors of knighthood, and enjoyed the favor of the public. He died in France in 1814, at the age of 60 years. More particular notices of Count Rumford and others may be found in the History of Concord, before referred to. This town has for many years been the seat of the state government. Terms of the superior court, courts of sessions and probate courts are now to be holden at this place. Concord is 62 miles from Boston, 45 from Portsmouth, 40 from Dover, 70 from Haverhill, 55 from Keene, and 505 from Washington City. Pop. 2838.

CONCORD, a post town in Grafton county, in lat. 44° 12', is bounded N. by Littleton and Bethlehem, E. by Franconia, S. by Landaff, and W. by Lyman, containing 29,130 acres. Its S. W. angle terminates at Bath. It is 20 miles from Haverhill, 28 from Lancaster, and 90 from Concord, the seat of government. It is watered by Amonoosuck river, running through the whole extent of the town, and by several smaller streams. Across the Amonoosuck, the town supports three bridges. There are several ponds, the most noted of which is called Mink pond, lying in the S. part of the town, affording mill seats at its outlet. The soil admits of three divisions, the meadows or intervals on Amonoosuck river, which are generally very productive; the plain land of a light, thin soil, requiring considerable manure or plaister to make it productive; and the uplands of a strong deep soil, which afford many good farms. Blueberry mountain is the principal elevation. This town for several years increased greatly in population, having from 1800 to 1810, nearly doubled its numbers. The Franconia iron factory lies near the eastern border of this town. All the ore which supplies the furnace is dug from a quarry in the S. E. part of the town, about 4 miles from the furnace. Two veins of ore have been opened, one of which is 300 feet in length and 120 in depth. The other lies in horizontal strata, 50 feet of which are under an arched roof of stone, affording a convenient shelter for the miners against the inclemency of the weather. Large quantities of limestone are found here—lime-kilns have been erected, in which are burnt 500 hogsheads of lime annually. Maple sugar is manufactured and clover seed is raised in considerable quantities. This town was first granted Aug. 6, 1763, to Joseph Burt and others by the name of Concord. Afterwards it was granted to Leonard Whiting and others, Nov. 20, 1768, by the name of *Gunthwaite*, which name it retained several years. It afterwards assumed the name of Concord. There is a freewill baptist society, over which Elder *Joshua Quimby* was ordained in Sept.1800, and a methodist society under the pastoral care of *Ozias Savage*.

CONNECTICUT, lake, the source of one of the principal branches of Connecticut river, is situated N. of the 1st grant to Dartmouth College, in lat. 45° 2′; and is 5 1-2 miles in length, and 2 1-2 in width. It is supplied by several small streams, rising in the highlands north of the lake.

CONNECTICUT, river, one of the finest streams in New-England, has two principal branches, both having their origin in New-Hampshire and the mountainous tracts on the north. The head of the N. W. branch is near the extreme northern limit of this state. This branch originates from a chain of mountains which proceeds northeasterly to the gulf of St. Lawrence. Between its source and 45° of N. lat., it is the boundary between New-Hampshire and Lower Canada, and in that distance is joined by the N. E. branch. The Connecticut extends about 170 miles on the western border of N. H., and its western shore forms the boundary between this state and Vermont. The different directions of this river and the towns which border it in these states, may be seen by referring to the map. The breadth of the Connecticut, when it first washes Vermont is about 150 feet; and in the course of sixty miles, it increases to about 390 feet. In Massachusetts and Connecticut, the breadth may be estimated from 450 to 1050 feet. The depth of the channel of the river below the head of boat navigation, may be generally stated to vary from 5 to 12 feet. This river is navigable for vessels drawing ten feet water, 36 miles to Middletown; for small sloops 50 miles to Hartford; and by means of canals and other improvements, it has been rendered passable for boats to the Fifteen Mile falls, 250 miles further. There are many rapids in the Connecticut. Those of Bellows Falls in Walpole are the most distinguished, for a description of which see *Bellows Falls*. The falls of Queechy just below the mouth of the river Waterqueechy from the west; the White River falls, a little below the village of Hanover; and the Fifteen Mile Falls, the foot of which is near the head of boat navigation, are the other most considerable rapids in this state. In its course through Massachusetts, are falls at Montague and at South Hadley, and in the state of Connecticut, are Enfield falls. The perpendicular height of the falls which have been overcome by dams and locks between Springfield in Mass., and Hanover in N. H., a distance of 130 miles, is about 200 feet. Bars of gravel and sand extend across this river in various places, over which, boats with difficulty pass in low water. Upon one of those gravel bars between the towns of Deerfield and Montague, it is even fordable during that period. In this state, Connecticut river receives as tributary streams, Upper Amonoosuck, Lower Amonoosuck, Israel's, John's, Mascomy, Sugar, Cold, and Ashuelot rivers. From Vermont, beginning at the north boundary, it receives Nulhegan, Pasumpsick, Wells, Wait's, Ompomponoosuck, White, Waterqueechy, Black, William's, Sexton's, and West rivers. There are from 20 to 30 bridges over the Connecticut between its source and its mouth, of which there are 16 in this state. The intervals are generally spread upon one or both sides of this river, nearly on a level with its banks, and extending from half a mile to five miles in breadth; but its borders are in some places high, rocky, and precipitous. With respect to its length, utility, and beauty, this is beyond all comparison, the finest river in the eastern states, and forms, indeed, a distinguished feature of the country. In the spring, it overflows its banks, and through an extent of 300 miles, forms and fertilizes a vast tract of rich meadow. While it advances the fertility, and serves to transport the produce, it is always adding beauty and grandeur to the prospect, by its majestic movement through an extensive country, variegated with pleasant and happy villages.

CONTOOCOOK river, a stream of considerable length and importance, waters most of the towns in the W. part of the county of Hillsborough. It has its origin from several ponds in Jaffrey and Rindge, and in its course north, receives numerous streams from Dublin, Peterborough, Sharon, Nelson, Stoddard, Washington, Antrim, Deering and Hillsborough. In Hillsborough it takes a N. E. and easterly direction, and proceeds through Henniker to Hopkinton, where it receives Warner and Blackwater rivers. From Hopkinton, it pursues a meandering course through Concord, and discharges itself into the Merrimack between Concord and Boscawen. Near the mouth of this river is Duston's island, celebrated as the spot where Mrs. Duston destroyed several Indians in 1698.

CONWAY, post-town, Strafford county, situated on Saco river, in lat. 43° 57′, bounded N. by Chatham and Bartlett, W. by Hale's location and Burton, S. by Eaton and E. by the State line, which separates it from Brownfield and Fryeburgh, Me.—is six miles square,—contains 28,040 acres, and is 72 miles from Concord, 75 from Portsmouth, 118 from Boston and 52 from Portland. Swift river, a considerable and very rapid stream, Pequawkett river, and a stream taking its rise in Walker's pond, the two last affording mill privileges, discharge themselves into Saco river in this town. Saco river here is from 10 to 12 rods wide and about 2 feet deep; its current rapid and broken by falls. This river has been known to rise 27 and even 30 feet in the course of 24 hours. At such times, it does great injury by destroying fences and cattle, which happen to be exposed to its fury. The largest collections of water in Conway are a part of Walker's pond, and Little Pequawkett pond, which lie in the south part of the town. The latter is about 360 rods in circumference. Pine, Rattlesnake, and Green hills, are considerable elevations on the north-east-orn side of the river. There is a detached block of granite on the southern side of Pine hill,—the largest perhaps in the state. A spring near the centre of the town on the bank of Cold brook, strongly impregnated with sulphur, has been visited frequently by the infirm, and in many instances found beneficial. There are also in this town large quantities of magnesia and fuller's earth. The soil may be divided into interval, plain, and upland. The interval along the river is from 50 to 220 rods wide, and was originally covered with white pine and sugar maple. The plain, when properly cultivated, produces large crops of corn and rye. The upland is rocky and requires much labor to subdue it properly. The natural growth was oak, beech, and maple. The "Conway and Bartlett library" was incorporated in 1802, and contains 175 volumes. The congregational church was formed Oct. 28, 1778, by Timothy Walker, Abiel Lovejoy, Thomas Russell and Richard Eastman. Rev. Nathaniel Porter, D. D. was settled Oct. 28, 1778, and dismissed by the church in 1815. The baptist church was formed Aug. 26, 1796. Richard R. Smith was ordained Oct. 20, 1796; dismissed Sept. 5, 1799. Roswell Means settled Sept. 1799; dismissed June 6, 1807. Samuel Simmons hired Dec. 7, 1807; continued till Jan. 28, 1811. Elder *Ebenezer Bray* moved to Conway and took the pastoral care of this church in April 1813. The present number of members is 55. There is also a society of methodists. James and Benjamin Osgood, John Dolloff, Ebenezer Burbank, and some others, formed settlements in Conway during the years 1764, 5 and 6. Oct. 1, 1765, Daniel Foster obtained a grant of this township on condition that each grantee should pay a rent of one ear of Indian corn annually for the space of ten years, if demanded. The first proprietors' meeting was holden in Chester, Dec. 10, 1765. Thomas Merrill, who was also the first justice of the peace, was chosen town and proprietors' clerk, which office he held 20 years. Ten of the original shares were re-granted in 1772. Three locations on the southern extremity of the town containing 2000 acres each were annexed in 1800. Pop. 1365.

CORNISH, a post-township in the N. part of Cheshire county, lat. 43° 28', is bounded N. by Plainfield, E. by Croydon, S. by Claremont, and W. by Windsor, Vt. containing 23,160 acres. It is 17 miles from Charlestown, 50 from Concord and 108 from Boston. Connecticut river waters the W. part of this town, and by means of a bridge, connects Cornish with Windsor. The soil is generally fertile. The town is hilly with the exception of that part which lies on the river. Blow-me-down and Briant's brooks are the only streams of any magnitude—these afford a few good mill privileges. The agricultural products in 1820, were 28,000 lbs. of butter, 65,000 lbs. of cheese, 122,000 lbs. of beef, 155,000 lbs. of pork, 8,300 lbs. of flax and 1056 barrels of cider. Cornish was granted June 21, 1763, to Rev. Samuel McClintock, of Greenland, and 69 others. The first meeting of the proprietors was holden at Greenland August 15, of the same year. The first meeting of the freeholders and other inhabitants was holden at Cornish, March 10, 1767. The town was settled in 1765, by emigrants chiefly from Sutton, Massachusetts. When they arrived, they found a camp, for many years known by the name of "Mast Camp." It was erected for the accommodation of a company employed in procuring masts for the royal navy. The first settlers found a Mr. Dyke and his family in this camp. Capt. Daniel Putnam, afterwards a respectable inhabitant and many years clerk of the town, had resided here the year previous. Cornish was one of the sixteen towns which seceded from New-Hampshire, and joined Vermont in 1778. It was in this town, that a convention of delegates from several towns on both sides the river, assembled Dec. 9, 1778, and agreed to make the following proposals to N. H., viz. either to agree with them on a dividing line, or to submit the dispute to Congress, or to arbitrators mutually chosen. The proceedings of this town in relation to the controversy with Vermont may be seen by referring to Collections Historical and Miscellaneous, No. 5, for May, 1823. A congregational church was formed, and Rev. James Welman was settled over it in 1769. He was dismissed in 1785. Rev. *Joseph Rowell* was ordained in Sept. 1800. A baptist church was formed June 24, 1791, and Rev. Ariel Kendrick commenced preaching here in 1801. An episcopalian society was formed in Dec. 1793, by Rev. John C. Ogden. It was incorporated Dec. 24, 1795, by the name of "Trinity Church." Rev. *George Leonard* has been the rector several years. Pop. 1701.

CORWAY PEAK, or *Chocorua*, a mountain. See *Burton*.

COVENTRY, a township in Grafton county, in lat. 44° 2′, is bounded N. by Landaff, E. by Peeling, S. by Warren, W. by Haverhill, containing 33,290 acres. It is 70 miles from Concord and 100 miles from Portsmouth. This town is watered by branches of Oliverian brook and Wild Amonoosuck rivers. In the S. E. part of Coventry is one of the most considerable elevations in Grafton county. Moosehillock mountain ranks among the highest mountains in N. H. Owl-head mountain lies in the W. part of this town and on the E. boundary of Haverhill. Coventry presents a rough and mountainous aspect, and the soil in several parts is not capable of cultivation. There are however some very productive farms. This town was granted Jan. 31, 1764, to Theophilus Fitch and others, and was settled after the commencement of the revolutionary war. In 1790, it contained but 80 souls, and from that time to the present, the increase of population has been very slow. Pop. 315.

CROYDON, a township in Cheshire county, situated in lat. 43° 27′, is bounded N. by Grantham and Springfield, E. by Springfield and Wendell, S. by Newport, and W. by Cornish. It contains 26,000 ac.; and is 100 miles from Boston, 44 from Concord. The N. branch of Sugar river waters this town, and there are several streams which issue from small ponds and assist in forming this branch of Sugar river. Croydon mountain is of considerable elevation, and extends in a N. E. direction through the town from its S. W. extremity. There are 2 small ponds on this mountain. The soil of Croydon is moist and rocky, but it produces excellent grass, besides wheat, rye, corn, &c. The agricultural products in 1820, were 22,000 lbs. of butter, 30,000 lbs. of cheese, 51,000 lbs. of beef, 75,000 lbs. of pork, 4,400 lbs. of flax, and 400 barrels of cider. The Croydon turnpike passes through nearly the centre of this town. There is a social library, which contains 170 vols. There has as yet been but one native of the town educated at college. Croydon was granted by charter to Samuel Chase and others May 31, 1763. It was settled in 1766 by inhabitants from Grafton and Sutton, Ms. A congregational church was formed Sept. 9, 1778. Rev. *Jacob Haven* was ordained June 18, 1788. Pop. 1060.

D.

DALTON, post-township, in Coos county, lat. 44° 22′, is situated on the banks of the Connecticut river, directly below Lancaster, by which and Whitefield it is bounded N. E.; S. by Bethlehem, S. W. by Littleton, N.;W. by Lunenburgh, Vt. The great, or Fifteen-Mile Falls, in this river commence in Dalton, and rush tumultuously along the north-west boundary of this town, and of Littleton and Lyman. The town is also watered by John's river and several large brooks. The western and southern parts of this town are hilly. The land in its natural state was covered with a thick growth of maple, beech, birch, ash, some hemlock and spruce; and along the borders of John's river the majestic white pine abounds. The soil on the highlands is deep and well adapted to grazing—is generally good and in some parts easy of cultivation. Blake's pond, the only one in town, lies at the S. E. corner. Moses Blake and Walter Bloss were the first settlers of Dalton, and with their families, for a long time the only inhabitants. Coffin Moore was the third settler. Dalton was incorporated Nov. 4, 1784, and received its name from Hon. Tristram Dalton, a grantee. It comprises an area of 16,455 acres, and has 347 inhabitants.

DANBURY, a township in the S. part of Grafton county, in lat. 43° 33′, is bounded N. by Orange, N. E. by Alexandria, S. E. by New-Chester, S. W. by Wilmot, and N. W. by Cushing's Gore and contains about 19,000 acres. It lies in the form of a diamond. It is 93 miles from Boston and 30 from Concord. This town is generally hilly, although there are some intervals. In the N. E. part is a large hill. The eastern section is watered by Smith's river. The Grafton turnpike passes through the W. extremity. The first settlement was made in Nov. 1771, and the first settler is still living. The settlements were first made in the E. part of the town and have extended over the whole tract of territory excepting the N. E. Danbury was incorporated June 18, 1795. Pop. 467.

DARTMOUTH COLLEGE. See *Gen. View, p.* 31, *and Hanover.*

DEAD river, in Coos county, rises in the lands N. of the tract granted to Gilmanton and Atkinson academies, and after receiving several branches, it falls into the Margallaway river near the S. E. corner of 2d grant to Dart. College.

DEERFIELD, post town, Rockingham county, lat. 43° 8′, was originally a part of the township of Nottingham, from which it was disannexed and incorporated Jan. 8, 1766. It is bounded N.W. by Epsom N. by Northwood, E. by Nottingham, S. by Raymond and Candia, W. by Allenstown—and contains 28,-254 acres. Pleasant pond, a beautiful body of water, lies partly in this town and partly in Northwood; its waters are very clear, and on

L

the margin, especially at the westerly end, are large quantities of fine white floor sand. Shingle pond lies at the S. W. part of this town, and affords fish of various kinds. Moulton's pond is situated at the W. part of the town: this pond, although small, is noted on account of its having no visible inlet, and therefore is supposed to be supplied by a subterraneous passage, as the water is always of nearly an equal depth; the outlets of this pond run in opposite directions, one N. into Suncook river in Epsom, and the other into Lamprey river near the centre of the town. This pond is also remarkable on account of its having been often sounded without discovering any bottom. A branch of Lamprey river passes S. and S. E. through Deerfield. The surface of this town is uneven, the soil durable, and fertile, although hard to cultivate. The growth of wood is rock-maple, white maple, beech, birch, red oak, pine, hemlock, elm, and various other kinds. The Tuckaway, between Deerfield and Nottingham, the Saddleback between Deerfield and Northwood, and Fort mountain on the W., are the principal elevations. In the W. part of this town, on the southerly side of a ridge of rocks which extend 3-4 of a mile, is a natural formation in the rock, for sixty years designated as the "Indian Camp." Its sides are irregular, and t he top is covered by a canopy of granite projecting about 14 feet, affording a shelter from the sun and rain. On the E. side of this camp is a natural flight of steps, or stones resembling steps, by which persons may easily ascend to the top of the rock. This town was once a place of favorite resort for deer and other animals—great numbers of which were taken. While the petition for the town was pending, a Mr. Batchelder killed a deer, and presenting it to Gov. Wentworth, obtained the act under the name of *Deer-field*. The town was settled in 1756 and 1758, by John Robertson, Jacob Smith, Isaac Shepard, Benjamin Batchelder and others. During the Indian wars, the inhabitants lived in garrison, but no serious mischiefs were experienced. The names of 18 persons from this town who died in the revolution, are preserved. The congregational society was formed in Dec. 1772, and Rev. Timothy Upham ordained; he died Feb. 21, 1811, aged 64. Rev. *Nathaniel Wells* was ordained July 1, 1812; and his church consists of 82 persons. Rev. Eliphalet Smith, a follower of Whitefield, preached here before the settlement of Mr. Upham, but afterwards removed. The baptists here have a convenient meeting-house, but no stated preacher. A freewill baptist church was formed May 5, 1799, and consists of about 60 members, but they have no regular preaching. The number of deaths in this town for the last 21 years has been 456, average 22 annually. The greatest mortality was in 1815, when the spotted fever prevailed, and 55 persons died; the least, in 1806, '17 and '22—13 only occurring in each of these years. Wid. Sarah Godfrey died here Feb. 7, 1821, at the age of 100 years 5 months. Hon. RICHARD JENNESS, respected as a magistrate, representative, senator and judge of the common pleas, died July 4, 1819, aged 73. JOSEPH MILLS, an officer in Col. Cilley's regiment during the revolution, afterwards a magistrate and representative, died in June, 1809, aged 60. Pop. 2133.

DEERING, a post-township in Hillsborough county, in lat. 43° 4', is bounded N. by Hillsborough and Henniker, E. by Weare, S. by Francestown and Society Land, and W. by Antrim, containing 20,057 acres. It is 23 miles S. 57° W. from Concord, 23 from Hopkinton, and 66 from Boston. It is diversified with hills and valleys; is well watered, and its soil is favorable for the several purposes of agriculture. There are three ponds, Dudley, Pecker's, and Fulton's. Dudley pond near the N. line, is 140 rods long, and 50 wide, and receives part of its waters from a pond in the south part of Henniker. Pecker's, near the centre, is 180 rods long and 65 wide. These ponds are sources of the N. branch of Piscataquog river. Fulton's pond, about half a mile S. S. W. of the outlet of Pecker's pond, is 50 rods long and 20 wide. The 2d N. H. turnpike, and the road from Boston to Amherst, Montpelier and Montreal, pass through the S. W. part of this town. Besides the enumeration in the county statistical table, there is an iron factory with a trip-hammer, in which hoes are manufactured.— Pot-ashes and bricks are made in a considerable quantity. The agricultural products for the market are principally carried to Boston and Salem. There is a social library containing 140 volumes. There is a cent society, and a number of members belonging to the N. H bible and missionary societies. Deering was incorporated Jan. 17, 1774. The name was given by Gov. John Wentworth, in honor of his wife, whose name before marriage was Frances Dering or Deering. The first permanent settlement was made in 1765, by Alexander Robinson. Soon after, he was followed by William Mc'Kean, William Forsaith, Thomas Aiken, William Aiken, Francis Grimes and others. The first settlers were from Amherst, Chester, Londonderry and Newbury. Some of them are still living. A congregational church was formed by Rev. Solomon Moore and Rev. Jona. Barns, in Dec. 1789. Rev. Messrs. Gillet, C. Page, and D. Long, preached here, but neither were settled. A second congregational church was formed in 1801, over which Rev. William Sleigh was ordained Oct. 22, the same year. He was dismissed in 1807. Rev. *Jabez P. Fisher*, though not settled, preaches in this place.— Pop. 1415.

DEER ISLANDS, in Connecticut river, between Lyman and Barnet, are five in number, and were granted Jan. 16, 1769, to John Hurd of Portsmouth. The largest contains 38 acres.

DIAMOND river, has its principal source in Diamond pond in Stewartstown. From thence it passes through Dixville, and after receiving several tributaries, falls into the Dead river near its junction with the Margallaway.

DIXVILLE, a township, in Coos county, was granted in 1805 and '10 to the late Col. Timothy Dix, jr. of Boscawen; and had in the latter year 12 inhabitants. It comprises 31,023 acres, is an uneven township, and bounded N. by the grants to Dartmouth College and Atkinson and Gilmanton Academies, E. by College lands and Wentworth's location, S. by Millsfield and Ervin's location, W. by Columbia, Colebrook and Stewartstown. Numerous streams meander through this town from the surrounding heights. There were in 1820 but *two* inhabitants.

DORCHESTER, a township in Grafton county, in lat. 43° 46', is situated on the highlands between Connecticut and Merrimack rivers, 12 miles from the former, and 8 from the latter. It is bounded N. by Wentworth, E. by Groton, S. by Dame's Gore, separating it from Canaan, W. by Lime, containing 23,040 acres. It is 23 miles from Haverhill, 50 from Concord, and 90 from Portsmouth. The principal streams are the S. branch of Baker's river, a branch of Mascomy, and Rocky branch. The first rises in Groton, and has a N. course through this town. On the borders of this stream are some narrow tracts of interval. The branch of Mascomy flows from Smart's pond in a S. direction to Canaan, there uniting with the principal stream. There are two considerable ponds, both in the W. part, the largest of which is about 1 mile long, and one fifth of a mile wide. There are two elevations called mountains, one at the N. W. corner; the other at the S. E. extremity. The soil in some parts is very fertile; particularly the intervals on the branch of Baker's river. The highlands are very uneven, and the greater part rocky. The school districts, of which there are eight, average 25 scholars to each. There are three religious societies, methodist, baptist, and congregationalist. The former has a meetinghouse erected in 1800. The baptist church and society was formed in 1819. The two first charters of this town were forfeited by the nonfulfilment of the conditions they required. The third was granted May 1, 1772, to 72 persons, and the settlement began about the same time. The first settlers were Benjamin Rice and Stephen Murch from Hanover, originally from Connecticut. The settlement advanced slowly, and there are now large tracts of vacant land in town. Pop. 584.

DOVER, is one of the principal towns and shire of the county of Strafford, in lat. 43° 12', situated about 10 miles N. W. from Portsmouth, and lies upon the great road leading through the eastern part of the state of New-Hampshire from Boston to Portland. On the E., it is separated from Elliot in Maine by the Pascataqua; has the town of Somersworth on the N. E. and N., Rochester on the N. W., Barrington on the W. and Madbury on the S. W., running to a point in the S. Its two principal streams are the Cocheco, and Bellamy Bank river, more commonly called by the inhabitants *Back* river. They take a S. E. course through the town, and unite with other waters to form the Pascataqua. Passing over this town in any direction, the traveller finds no rugged mountains, nor extensive barren plains, but occasionally ascends gentle swells of land, from the height of which, the eye meets some delightful object; a winding stream, a well cultivated farm, or a distant village. In the S. part of the town is a neck of land about 2 miles long and half a mile broad, having Pascataqua on one side, and Back river on the other. Along this neck, till of late, lay the principal road leading from this town to Portsmouth. From the road on either hand, the land gradually descends to the rivers. It commands a very delightful, variegated, and extensive prospect of bays, adjacent shores, and distant mountains. On this neck, the first settlement of the town was made in 1623, by a company in England, who styled themselves the "company of Laconia." It was their design to plant a colony, and establish a fishery around the Pascataqua; for which purpose they sent over with several others Edward and William Hilton, fishmongers, of London. These men commenced their operations on the neck at a place by the Indians called *Winichahanat*, which they called *Northam*, and afterwards *Dover*. For several years, this spot embraced the principal part of the population of the town; here was erected the first meeting-house, afterwards surrounded with an entrenchment, and flankarts, the remains of which are still visible; here the people of what is now called Somersworth, Durham, Lee, and Madbury, then Dover, assembled to worship, and to transact their public business. In process of time, the business and population of the town began to centre around Cocheco falls, about 4 miles N. W. from the neck. These falls are in the river whose name they bear, and give to the water that passes over them a sudden descent of 32 1-2 feet.— Situate at the head of navigation, about 12 miles from the ocean, having a fertile country on the north, west, and south, they are considered among the most valuable in New-England. Around these falls the present village of Dover is situated. It contains about 100 dwelling-houses, 2 meeting-houses, a court-house, jail, academy, 1 printing office, a library, bank, and manufactories of various kinds. The academy is pleasantly situated on the S. bank of the Cocheco, built of brick, and well adapted for the accommodation of two schools. At present it is struggling with the difficulties attending a want of funds. The newspapers published in Dover have been the "Political Repository & Strafford Recorder," commenced July 15, 1790; discontinued Jan. 19, 1792. "The Phœnix," from Jan. 23, 1792, to Aug. 29, 1795. "The Sun," &c. commenced Sept. 5, 1795, and was succeeded by the "Strafford Register" in ——. The "*New-Hampshire Republican*," by Chas. W. Cutter, commenced Jan. 8, 1823. The library here belongs to an incorporated society, and contains about 350 volumes. The principal manufactories in this place belong to a company of gentlemen incorporated in 1820, and styled the "Dover Cotton Factory Company." Their capital is $500,000. About 3 miles above Cocheco falls, on the same stream, they have a cotton factory, which carries 2,500 spindles, employs 86 looms, 120 persons, and produces per week 10,000 yds. sheeting and shirting. At the falls a brick building was erected in 1820 to be used as a rolling and slitting-mill, a nail factory and a machine shop. About 1000 tons of iron are here rolled and slit, and 700 tons manufactured into nails annually. A new factory has just been erected, designed to contain 4,000 spindles, 120 or 130 looms, and calculated to produce, when in operation, 20,000 yards per week. Near this, are six sites for factories or mills, equally as good as those now occupied. That these factories, and others in contemplation, will exert an important influence on the business and wealth of the town, is confidently expected. The friends were established here at an early period, and formerly comprised about one third of the population. The congregational society is the most ancient of any in Dover. The church with which it is united in the support of public worship was organized in 1638, about 15 years after the first settlement of the town. According to the usage of many churches at that time, it elected as officers a pastor, ruling elders and deacons. No account is found of ruling elders in the church here later than 1662. At that time there were three —Nutter, Wentworth and Starbuck. Wentworth preached occasionally, and was ancestor to the several governors of the name. There being no well defined and efficient government, civil or ecclesiastical, adopted by those who first settled N. Hampshire, the people of Dover were subject to a variety of troubles,—not the least considerable of which originated immediately from the character of their ministers. The first who appeared among them and probably the first who preached the gospel in New-Hampshire, was Mr. Leverich, a worthy puritan. He was sent from England by the Lords Say and Brooke, with a promise of support; but the encouragement given proving too small, he removed to the south.— Between the period of his removal and 1642, we find as preachers here George Burdet, Hanserd Knollys and Thos. Larkham; all of whom appear to have been destitute of a moral character. Being relieved of these men, the people were for some time destitute of preaching. In 1642, Daniel Maud, a pious minister, was settled, who died in 1655. He was succeeded by Rev. John Reyner, who came from England, and was minister of the church at Plymouth from 1636 till 1654. He continued at Dover until his death, April 3, 1669. His successor was Rev. John Reyner, jun., who graduated at Harvard College in 1663; was ordained in 1671. Rev. John Pike was his successor, and died in March, 1710. Rev. Nicholas Sever succeeded, but was soon dismissed on account of an impediment in his speech. Rev. Jonathan Cushing was ordained Sept. 1717; died March, 1769. Rev. JEREMY BELKNAP, the historian of New-Hampshire, was ordained colleague with Mr. Cushing Feb. 1767; and in 1786, was dismissed, and removed to Boston. Rev. Robert Gray was ordained Feb. 1787; removed May, 1805. Rev. Caleb H. Sherman, ordained May, 1807, was dismissed May, 1812; at which time Rev. Joseph W. Clary was ordained. The methodist society in this town was incorporated in 1819. This town in its early years was greatly frequented by the Indians; and experienced many sufferings in their repeated attacks upon the inhabitants. In 1675, Maj. Waldron by a stratagem secured about 200 Indians at Dover, who had at times exhibited signs of hostility. Seven or eight of them, who had been guilty of some atrocities, were immediately hanged, and the rest sold into slavery. The Indians abroad regarded this act of Waldron as a breach of faith, and swore against him implacable revenge. In 1689, after a lapse of 13 years, they determined to execute their project. Previous to the fatal night (27th of June) some hints had been thrown out by the squaws, but they were either misunderstood or disregarded; and the people suffered them to sleep in their garrisons as usual. In the stillness of night the doors of the garrisons were opened, and the Indians, at a concerted signal, rose from their lurking places, and rushed upon the defenceless inhabitants. Waldron, though 80 years of age, made a gallant defence, but was overwhelmed by the superior numbers of his adversaries, who literally cut him to pieces. In this affair, 23 persons were killed, and 29 made prisoners. Jan. 25, 1691, a young man in the woods near Dover was fired upon by a party of

Indians. A body of citizens immediately went in pursuit, and killed or wounded nearly the whole party. This excited a temporary terror among the Indians; but July 26th, 1696, they attacked the people returning from worship, 3 were killed, several wounded and taken prisoners. In Aug. 1704, Mark Giles was killed, and the people waylaid on their return from meeting. In 1706, William Pearl and Nathaniel Tibbets were killed; and in 1710, Jacob Garland met a similar fate. In the spring of 1711, this town was again attacked by the Indians; and in April, 1712, a Mr. Tuttle was killed. Aug. 29, 1723, the Indians again made their appearance at Dover, surprised the house of Joseph Ham, whom they killed, taking 3 of his children into captivity. As the particulars of the Indian attacks upon the inhabitants of this town are faithfully related by Dr. Belknap, whose history should be in the hands of every reader, we deem it unnecessary, even had we room, to go into detail. Garrison houses, having narrow windows, port holes, a projecting upper story and walls of solid timbers, are yet standing in Dover quite entire. Pop. about 3000.

DREWSVILLE, a pleasant village on Connecticut river, in the town of Walpole, containing 30 dwelling houses, 250 inhabitants; a large cotton factory in successful operation, 3 stores, a school-house, a spacious hotel, and a post-office. Fifteen years since, the place where this neat and pleasant village is situated, contained but a single dwelling, surrounded by pines and oaks, and presenting to the eye of the traveller the secluded retreat of a hermit.

DUBLIN, a post-township in Cheshire county, in lat. 45° 54′, is bounded N. by Nelson and Hancock, E. by Peterborough, S. by Jaffrey, W. by Marlborough and Roxbury, containing 26,560 acres. It is 10 miles from Keene, 50 from Concord and 70 from Boston.— Dublin is situated on the height of land between Connecticut and Merrimack rivers. Its streams are small; those on the W. side run into the Ashuelot, those on the E. into Contoocook river. There is a pond near the middle of the town called Centre pond, one mile in length and about the same in breadth. In the N. part is North pond. A large portion of the Grand Monadnock lies in the N. W. part of Dublin, and near the centre of the town is Breed's mountain.— Monadnock was formerly covered with a growth of small timber and shrubbery, but fires having run over it at different times, it presents little more than ragged rocks. Between the rocks, however, there are low whortleberry bushes, which produce great quantities of fruit of a very rich flavor. The season for ripening is the latter part of August, and to those who ascend the summit at this season, they are peculiarly grateful. The soil is rocky and hard of cultivation. The land in general is much better for grazing than tillage. There is a handsome congregational meeting-house built in 1818, standing on such an elevation, that the rain which falls from the W. roof runs into the Connecticut, and that from the E. roof into the Merrimack. The baptist meeting-house is in the N. W. part of the town. There are 10 school districts, which average about 50 scholars to each district. The late Rev. Edward Sprague bequeathed nearly 8000 dollars for the support of public schools, the annual interest of which is to be applied to this object. He also left the town $5000, the interest of which paid quarterly, is to be applied to the support of an ordained congregational minister who shall statedly preach in Dublin. Besides this liberal provision for the support of the gospel, the town has $3000 arising from the sale of ministerial lands, and the interest of this sum is to be applied to the same purpose. There is a social library, incorporated in 1797, and containing 110 volumes. There is a ladies' library instituted in 1802, containing 140 volumes. The Dublin musical society was incorporated in June, 1821. Dublin, originally called *Monadnock No. 3*, was granted Nov. 3, 1749 to Matthew Thornton, Sampson Stoddard and others. It was incorporated by charter, March 29, 1771. The first settlements were in 1762 by John Alexander, Henry Strongman, and William Scott, who were natives of Ireland, from the capital of which country, the town was called Dublin. Other settlers, principally from Massachusetts, soon arrived, of whom were Thomas, John and Eli Morse, Benjamin Mason, Samuel Twitchell, Moses Adams, Silas Stone, and William McNee. The congregational church was formed June 10, 1772, and Rev. Joseph Farrar was ordained at the same time. He was dismissed Jan. 7, 1776. Rev. Edward Sprague was ordained November 12, 1777, and died Dec. 16, 1817, aged 68. Rev. *Levi W. Leonard* was ordained Sept. 6, 1820. The baptist church was organized Nov. 5, 1785. Rev. *Elijah Willard* was ordained June 5, 1793. This church is composed of members belonging to Dublin and several of the adjacent towns. The following persons have received a public education, all at Dartmouth.

Asa Bullard, 1793; Amos Twitchell, 1802; Amos Allen, 1808; Ebenezer Morse, 1810; Samuel Morse, 1811; Thomas Hardy, 1812; Daniel Elliot, 1813. The number of deaths for 6 years preceding 1822, was 94. Pop. 1620.

DUMMER, township, Coos co. is in lat. 44° 37′, bounded N. by Millsfield and Errol, E. by Cambridge, S. by Paulsburgh, W. by Kilkenny, and comprises 23,040 acres. It was granted March 8, 1773, to Mark H. Wentworth, Nathaniel A. Haven and others; is watered by the Amonoosuck and Ameriscoggin; and contains but 27 inhabitants.

DUNBARTON, a post-township in Hillsborough county, in lat. 43° 5′, is bounded N. by Hopkinton and Bow, E. by Bow and Hooksett, S. by Goffstown and W. by Weare, containing about 21,000 acres. It is 7 miles from Hopkinton, 9 from Concord, and 65 from Boston. The situation of this town is somewhat elevated, though there are but few hills, nor any mountains. The air is clear, the water is good, and the health of its inhabitants is seldom interrupted by sickness. The forest trees are principally chesnut, pine and oak. The soil is good, peculiarly suited for corn, wheat and orcharding. Almost every lot in town is capable of making a good farm. The farmers here have good buildings and are excellent husbandmen. There are few towns in the county, in passing through which, we see so many good houses as in Dunbarton. The advantages in point of water privileges are not great. There is a social library incorporated in 1793, containing about 180 volumes. There are several charitable and religious associations. The inhabitants are principally descendants of Scotch Irish, so called, from the N. of Ireland. Most of the first settlers came from Londonderry in this state, but several were originally from Scotland and Ireland. Their posterity still retain many traits of character peculiar to that people. Dunbarton was granted in 1751, to Archibald Stark, Caleb Page and others, by the Masonian Proprietors. It was first called *Starks-Town*, in honor of the principal proprietor. Its present name is derived from *Dumbarton* in Scotland, from whence Stark emigrated. The first settlement was made about 1749, by Joseph Putney, James Rogers, William Putney and Obadiah Foster. These families settled in the E. part of the town. Capt. Caleb Page, from that part of Haverhill, now Atkinson, was one of the first settlers—was proprietors' clerk many years, and held several of the first offices in town after it was incorporated. Archibald Stark resided in Manchester. He was a man of considerable influence and possessed a large landed property. Two of his sons, William and Archibald, were early settlers. William held several civil offices and was colonel of the militia. William Stinson was born in Ireland, came to Londonderry with his father. He was much respected and was a useful man. James Rogers was from Ireland, and father to Major Robert Rogers. He was shot in the woods, being mistaken for a bear. [See *Hist. Collections* Vol. 1, p 240.] The congregational church was formed June 18, 1789, by Rev. Messrs. Waters and Cram. Rev. *Walter Harris* was ordained August 26, 1789. There have been two periods of attention to religion in this place, viz. in 1792—3, when 80 were added to the church, and in 1816, when there was an increase to its number of 40. Pop. 1450.

DUNSTABLE, a post-township in Hillsborough county, in lat. 42° 44′, is bounded N. by the town of Merrimack, E. by Merrimack river, which separates it from Nottingham-West, S. by Tyngsborough and Dunstable, Ms. and W. by Hollis, containing 18,878 acres. It is 13 miles from Amherst, 34 from Concord, and 34 from Boston. The soil has considerable variety. It is easy of cultivation, and is generally productive. The east part of the town lying on the river presents a very level surface. The W. parts are more divided into hills and valleys, but the whole township may be considered far from being hilly or mountainous. It is watered by the Nashua river, a fertilizing stream, which rises in the state of Massachusetts, and Salmon-Brook, a small stream which originates from several ponds in Groton. Both of these empty into Merrimack river, the former at Nashua village, the latter about one and a half miles below. On Salmon brook are 2 grist mills, 1 saw mill, 1 fulling mill, and 4 triphammer shops, at which are annually manufactured 1500 dozen of hoes, besides scythes, axes, &c. The road form Boston to Amherst passes through this town nearly parallel with the Merrimack. There is a handsome meeting house, erected in 1812, and a number of dwelling houses, which constitute a pleasant village. In the N. E. part of the town on Nashua river is the largest village in town, and the place of greatest business. (See *Nashua Village.*) There is a library containing about 300 volumes. Dunstable is the oldest town in Hillsborough county. It was granted about the year 1672 to five individuals, and included Litchfield, a corner of Londonderry, Nottingham-West, Tyngsborough and Dunstable in Mass., Pepperell, as far as the original line of Groton, Townsend, Hollis, Brookline, and all that part of Milford, Amherst and Merrimack, S. E. of Souhegan river. It was settled about the time it was granted. Its name was given in compliment to Mrs. Tyng, who, it is said, came from Dunstable, in Bedfordshire, Eng. Her husband, the Hon. Edward Tyng, emigrated to New-England about 1630 ; settled in Dunstable soon after its incorporation, and died in Dec. 1681, aged 90. The names of Weld, Blanchard, Waldo, Cumings, French, Lovewell, Farwell, Lund and Colburn were among the early inhabitants of the town, which, in 1680, contained 30 families. Dunstable was for a long time a frontier town, and the first settlers were many times annoyed by the Indians in the successive wars in which this country was engaged with them. In the war with the famous Narraganset sachem, this town was much exposed, and some of the inhabitants fled to older settlements. In the spring of 1702, the town was attacked, and several persons, with the Rev. Thomas Weld, the first minister, were killed. In 1724, two men being missing, a scout of eleven went in quest of them, who were fired upon by thirty of the enemy, and nine of them were killed. The other two made their escape, though one of them was badly wounded. In Lovewell's war, the company from this town under the brave Capt. John Lovewell, acquired an imperishable name. Their successes at first and misfortunes afterwards have been often repeated and are generally known. They were for many years kept in fresh remembrance by a popular song, which, after the lapse of a century, has not yet sunk into oblivion. From this homely effusion of gratitude to the memory of such heroic spirits, the praises of the "worthy Capt. Lovewell" and his coadjutors, often resounded from the humble cottage of the poor and the stately mansion of the opulent. Dunstable belonged to Massachusetts till the divisional line between the two provinces of Mass. and N. H. were settled in 1741. It was incorporated by N. H. April 1, 1746. The congregational church was gathered in 1685. Its original members were Rev. Thomas Weld, Jonathan Tyng, John Cumings, John Blanchard, Cornelius Waldo, Samuel Warner, Obadiah Perry and Samuel French. Rev. Thomas Weld, from Roxbury, who graduated at Harvard College in 1671, was ordained Dec. 16, 1685, and was killed by the Indians in April or May, 1702. Rev. Nathaniel Prentice, who graduated at Harvard College in 1715, was the successor of Mr. Weld. He died Feb. 25, 1737. Rev. Josiah Swan, who graduated at Harvard college in 1733, was ordained Dec. 27, 1738, and was dismissed in 1746. Rev. Simon Bird, from Dorchester, was ordained Aug. 31, 1747 ; dismissed 1751. The settlement of Mr. Bird caused a division in the church and town. A new church was formed, and another meeting house erected. After his dismission the two churches were united. Rev. Joseph Kidder, from Billerica, a graduate from Yale College in 1764, was the next minister. He was ordained March 18, 1767 ; his civil contract was dissolved June 15, 1796 ; he died Sept. 6, 1818, aged 77. Rev. Ebenezer P. Sperry was ordained as colleague with Mr. Kidder, Sept. 3,

1813, and dismissed in April, 1819. Hon. JONATHAN BLANCHARD, who was a delegate from N. Hampshire to the continental congress, during the confederation of the states, was a native and resident in this town. In conjunction with the Rev. Dr. Langdon, he published a map of New-Hampshire, which was inscribed to the Hon. Charles Townsend, Esq., his Majesty's secretary at war, and one of the privy council. He was the judge of probate in Hillsborough county, and was much in public business till his death in 1788. Pop. 1142.

DURAND, an incorporated township in the county of Coos, lat. 44° 22' is situated directly under the north end of the White Mountains its S. E. corner bounding on the base of Mount Madison, the E. peak of the range. It has Maynesborough on the N., Shelburne E., and Kilkenny W. It contains about 26,680 acres. Branches of Israel's and Moose rivers pass through Durand. The soil is in some parts good, but the town increases slowly in its settlements. It was granted Aug. 20, 1772, to John Durand and others, of London. Joseph Wilder and Stephen Jillson were the first settlers. Pop. 78.

DURHAM, a post-town in Strafford co., adjoining Rockingham, in lat. 43° 7', is bounded N.E. by Madbury, E. and S. E. by Little and Great Bays, S. by New-Market, and W. by Lee, comprising 14,970 acres. The situation of this town upon the Pascataqua and its branches, is very favorable both as to water power and transportation. Oyster river, one of the branches of the Pascataqua, issues from Wheelwright's pond in Lee, and after running nearly its whole course in Durham, furnishing in its progress several convenient mill seats, falls into the main river near Pascataqua bridge. The tide flows in this branch up to the falls near the meeting-house in the village, where business to a large amount is annually transacted. This village contains 68 dwelling-houses, and about 550 inhabitants; and is a very central depot for the lumber and produce of the adjacent country; the water carriage hence to Portsmouth being as convenient as from the head of the tide of any other branch of the Pascataqua. Lamprey river, another branch of the Pascataqua, runs through the westerly part of this town over several falls remarkably well adapted for mill seats into the town of New-Market, where it falls into the Great Bay. The soil of this town is generally hard and stony, lying for the most part throughout the town upon a chain of granite ledges, which appear to be of primitive formation—but where it meets with proper cultivation, it is very productive in the usual crops adapted to this climate. Upon both sides of Oyster river, a deep argillaceous loam prevails, which is peculiarly favorable to the production of the grasses, of which very heavy crops are cut, and hay is an article of considerable export. The extensive ledges before alluded to have been the source of much profitable employment to the inhabitants of this town. From the excellent quality of the stone, the skill with which it is prepared, and the convenience of water carriage, there has been a constant demand from many of the neighboring towns for underpinning, steps, mill-stones, &c. A large block of detached granite in the southeast part of this town was formerly placed in a very singular situation. Its weight was 60 or 70 tons, and it was poised so exactly upon two other stones as to be visibly moved by the wind. It was some years since dislodged from this extraordinary position by the barbarous curiosity of some visitors, who after much labor succeeded in prying it from its balance by levers. About one half of that part of Pascataqua bridge N. of Goat Island is within the limits of this town. The town is very well accommodated with other bridges and roads. Durham was originally a part of Dover, and included in Hilton's patent; but soon after its settlement was formed into a distinct parish by the name of *Oyster river*, from the stream which passes through it. From the abundance of excellent oysters found in its waters, this river probably derived its name, and it was a famous rendezvous of the Indians, especially at the point about a mile from the junction of Oyster river with the Pascataqua. In September, 1675, the Indians made an attack at Oyster river, burned two houses, killed several men and carried away two captives. Two days after this attack they made another, destroyed several houses and killed two persons. In 1694, when a large part of the inhabitants had marched to the westward, the Indians who were dispersed in the woods about Oyster river, having diligently observed the number of men in one of the garrisons, rushed upon eighteen of them, as they were going to their morning devotions, and having cut off their retreat to the house put them all to death except one, who fortunately escaped. They then attacked the house, in which there were only two boys beside the women and children. The boys kept them off for some time and wounded several of them. At length the Indians set fire to the house and even then the boys would not surrender till the Indians had promised to spare their lives. The latter however perfidiously murdered three or four children, one of whom they fixed upon a sharp stake in the view of its mother. The women and children were carried captive, but one of the boys made his escape the next day. The next spring the Indians narrowly watched the frontiers to determine the safest and most vulnerable points of attack. The settlement at Oyster river was selected for destruction. Here were twelve garrisoned houses, amply sufficient for the reception of the inhabitants, but not apprehending any danger, many of the families remained in their unfortified houses, and those who were in the garrisons were but indifferently prepared for a siege, as they were destitute of powder. The enemy approached the place undiscovered and halted near the falls. One John Dean, whose house stood near the falls, happening to rise very early for a journey before the dawn of day, was shot as he came out of his door. The attack now commenced on all points, where the enemy was ready. Of the twelve garrisoned houses five were destroyed, Adams,' Drew's, Edgerly's, Meader's, and Beard's. The enemy entered Adams' without resistance, where they murdered fourteen persons, whose graves can still be traced. Drew surrendered his garrison on promise of security, but he was put to death. One of his children, only nine years old, was compelled to run through a line of Indians as a mark for their hatchets. Edgerly's garrison was evacuated, the people having fled to their boats, one of whom was mortally wounded in attempting to escape. Beard's and Meader's were also evacuated and their inhabitants escaped. The unfortified houses were all set on fire, the people being either put to death or captured in them. Some escaped, concealing themselves in the bushes and elsewhere. Thomas Edgerly having hid himself in his cellar preserved his house, though it was twice set on fire. The house of John Buss the minister was destroyed, together with his valuable library. He was absent at the time, and his wife and family fled to the woods. Many other cruelties were perpetrated, when the Indians fearing that the inhabitants from the neighboring settlements would collect against them, retreated, having killed or captured between 90 and 100 persons and destroyed 20 houses, 5 of which were garrisoned. In 1703, the Indians made another incursion and killed one man. In 1704, several persons were murdered by them; and in 1705, a small party attacked the house of John Drew, where they put eight people to death and wounded several others. May 22, 1707, two men were captured from Durham, and two others were murdered as they were on a journey from that town to Dover. In September following, a party of Mohawks attacked a company of people, who were at work in the woods under the direction of Capt. Chesley. At the first fire they killed 7 and wounded another. Chesley, with his few surviving companions, continued a brisk fire on the enemy, and for some time kept them off, but at length fell, overpowered by numbers. He was deeply lamented as a brave officer. In 1724, the Indians made another incursion into this town, formed an ambush near the road and murdered several persons. Minute accounts of these disasters are given in Belknap's Hist. N. H., to which the reader is referred. The first preacher who statedly officiated in Durham was John Buss; but he never was ordained. He died 1736, at the age of 108. Rev. Hugh Adams settled March 26, 1718; dismissed 1739. Rev. Nicholas Gilman settled in 1741; died 1748. Rev. John Adams settled 1748; dismissed 1778. Rev. Curtis Coe settled Nov. 1, 1780; dismissed 1806. Rev. Federal Burt was ordained June 18, 1817. There are also methodist and baptist societies in this town. Durham social library was incorporated June 20, 1815, and contains upwards of 400 volumes. The average number of deaths for ten years is 16. Maj. Gen. JOHN SULLIVAN, of the revolutionary army, was a resident of this town, and died here Jan. 23, 1795. He was a native of Berwick, Me.; was a distinguished commander during the war; was president of the state three years, and afterwards district judge of N. H. On all occasions, he proved himself the firm supporter of the rights of the country. Hon. EBENEZER THOMPSON was a native of this town. He sustained several offices during the revolution, and was an efficient legislator and a respectable lawyer. Col. WINBORN ADAMS, of the revolutionary army, was a citizen of Durham. Hon. GEORGE FFROST, of this town was a delegate in Congress for 1776, 7 and 9; a judge of the common pleas in Strafford, and subsequently chief justice of that court. He died at Durham, June 21, 1796, aged 77. Durham was incorporated May 13, 1738. Pop. in 1820—1538.

M

E.

EAST-KINGSTON, a township, in Rockingham county, in lat. 42° 57′, is bounded N. by Exeter, E. by Kensington, S. by South-Hampton, W. and N. W. by Kingston, of which it formerly constituted a part—containing about 3 square miles. Its soil is of an excellent quality, and well adapted to the cultivation of grain and grass. Powow river crosses the S. W. part of this town, having its sources in the ponds of Kingston. The town was incorporated Nov. 17, 1738. Among the first settlers were William and Abraham Smith, who settled near the centre of the town. Rev. Peter Coffin was settled here in 1739; and was dismissed in 1772—since which time they have had no stated preaching. They have a meeting-house, and several school-houses; also mills and machinery sufficient for the use of the inhabitants. Pop. 443.

EATON, post-township, Strafford county, in lat. 43° 53′, ; 71 miles from Concord, 41 from Gilford, 71 from Portsmouth; is bounded N. by Conway, W. by Burton and Tamworth, S. by Ossipee and Effingham, E. by the state of Maine, and comprises 33,637 acres. The soil of the uplands, which are quite uneven, is moderately good, and the plains furnish excellent pine timber. There are no rivers in this town; the mill streams are fed principally by springs and small brooks. Six mile pond is in this town, and is about 3 miles long and from one half to one mile in width—its waters discharge into Ossipee lake. There are several other smaller ponds in this town. Eaton was granted Nov. 7, 1766, to Clement March and 65 others. A baptist church was formed here in 1800, which has now become extinct. There are two free-will baptist societies, the first organized in 1803, the latter in 1821. There is a woollen factory for making sattinetts, &c. and several mills. Pop. 1071. This town is the only instance in the state where the population has doubled within the last ten years. Iron ore in considerable quantity, exists among the ledges in this town, and is judged to be of good quality.

EFFINGHAM, post-town, Strafford county, in lat. 43° 44′, is bounded N.,W. & S.W. by Ossipee, S. by Wakefield, E. by Parsonsfield, Me., and contains about 34,900 acres. There are several mountains of considerable elevation in this town. The Ossipee river passes through this town, over which is a toll-bridge. There is a pond about 400 rods long and 270 wide, situated near this river. Province pond lies between Effingham and Wakefield. Effingham was settled a few years prior to the revolution. It was then known by the name of *Leavitt's Town*. In 1775, it contained no more than 83 inhabitants. It was incorporated Aug. 18, 1778. Rev. Gideon Burt was settled over the congregational church in 1803; dismissed in 1805; and the church is now vacant. A baptist church was formed here in 1808, and consists of 72 members. The Effingham academy was incorporated in 1819, and is a respectable institution. Pop. 1563.

ELLIS' river, rises on the E. side of the White Mountains, in several small streams, near the sources of Peabody river; and separating into two streams which unite in Adams, it falls into the Saco at Bartlett.

ELLSWORTH, township, in Grafton county, in lat. 43° 54′, is bounded N. by Peeling, E. by Thornton, S. by Rumney, and W. by Warren, containing 16,606 acres. It is 52 miles from Concord and 84 from Portsmouth. It is a mountainous tract of territory—the most prominent elevation is Carr's mountain, situated in the N. and extending to the central part of the town. A small stream issues from West Branch pond in the S. E. part of Ellsworth, and runs into the Pemigewasset at Campton. The soil, though in some parts sterile, produces wheat, rye, corn, oats, &c. The forest trees are various kinds, having a considerable proportion of hard wood. Maple sugar is made here, and clover seed is raised in considerable quantities. This town, formerly called *Trecothick*, was granted May 1, 1769, to Barlow Trecothick. There is a small baptist society, over which Israel Blake has presided. Pop. 213.

ENFIELD, a post town in the S. W. part of Grafton county, in lat. 43° 36′, is bounded N.E. by Canaan, S. E. by Grafton, S. W. by Grantham, and W. by Lebanon, comprising 24,060 acres, of which about 2500 acres are water. It is 12 miles S. E. from Dartmouth College, 42 miles from Concord, and 105 from Boston. Its surface is diversified with hills and valleys, and watered by a variety of ponds and streams, stored with fish of every species common to the country. Mascomy pond, which has acquired from travellers the appellation of Pleasant pond, is a beautiful collection of water, 4 miles in length and of various breadth, interspersed with islands and checkered with inlets. Its eastern banks are covered with trees, which, as the hill ascends, gradually rise one above another for some distance. Along the western bank, between the pond and Mont Calm, within a few rods of the water, extends the 4th N. H. turnpike, the whole distance through a beautiful village, shaded to the north on either side by a second growth of trees. Mascomy river, which takes its rise in Dorchester, and runs through Canaan, empties into this pond in the N. W. part. It is supposed to have been once much higher than it now is, and the plain and villages to the south, are supposed to have been the bed of it. This fact is sufficiently evident from the ancient shore still remaining round the pond, about 30 feet above high water, and from logs having been frequently found 12 feet below the surface of the plain once flowed. Its fall appears to have been sudden, by an alteration of the outlet. On the W. bank near the southern extremity, is the Shaker's settlement, too much remarked to need particular description. It is raised on a fertile plain: the structure of the buildings, though not lofty, are neat and convenient: the inhabitants are peculiar in their manners and dress, in their economy and religion. They occupy about 1000 acres of land, and their number consists of about 200.— Fifty-eight persons have died since the formation of the society.— They are agriculturalists and mechanics. Garden seeds, wooden ware, whips, corn brooms, leather, and various other articles are manufactured by them. They first made their appearance here in 1782. They were gathered into the order of a church in 1792, under the ministration of Elder Job Bishop. The religious sentiments of the different branches of this community are similar, and the reader will find a more particular notice, (see page 92,) under the head of Canterbury. In the east part of the town is East pond, 1 1-2 miles long and 3-4 of a mile wide. Mud pond is mostly in Canaan. Besides these, there are Spectacles pond, so called from its figure; George pond, and Mountain pond, on the summit of Mont Calm, 200 rods long, and 100 rods wide. At the outlets of these ponds are mills.— At the base of Mont Calm, a mountain in the southerly part of the town, iron ore has been found, which has been pronounced by Professor Dana to be of an excellent quality. The town was formerly called *Relham*, and was incorporated by charter, granted to Jedediah Dana and others, July 4th, 1761.— The first settlers were Nathaniel Bicknell, Jonathan Paddleford and Elisha Bingham. Elias, the son of the last named, was the first male child born in town. The congregational church had Rev. Edward Evans for the first minister. He was settled in Dec. 1799; dismissed in 1805. A free will baptist church was formed July 31, 1816, over which Elder John Sweat presided about 5 years. Elder *Ebenezer Chase* took charge of this church, Jan. 1, 1822, and of the Religious Union Society, formed at that time under the late act of the legislature. "The Religious Informer," and the "Masonic Casket," both conducted by Elder Ebenezer Chase, are published in this town. Jesse Johnson, Esq. was among the first settlers, was a member of the legislature and a justice of the peace till his death in 1800. The late Hon. JESSE JOHNSON, his son, was the first justice of the peace appointed in Enfield, the first representative to the legislature, and one of the first settlers. He was an intelligent and useful citizen. He came to this town when 17 years of age.— When 21, he was elected town clerk, selectman, representative, and was appointed justice of the peace. He was afterwards a member of the state convention, which formed the constitution of N. H.; judge of probate, and judge of the court of common pleas. He died Sept. 23, 1816, aged 53. Pop. 1370.

EPPING, a post-town, in the county of Rockingham, lat. 43° 3′, lies 30 miles S. E. of Concord, 20 miles W. of Portsmouth, and 8 miles N. W. of Exeter. It is bounded on the N. by Nottingham and Lee, E. by New Market, Exeter and Brentwood, S. by Brentwood and Poplin, and W. by Raymond and Nottingham. It was formerly a part of Exeter, and was incorporated Feb. 12, 1741; and in 1742 the inhabitants held their first meeting. The town contains 12,760 acres, being nearly 20 square miles. The soil, in general, is very good, and well suited to raise the various productions that grow in the state. Lamprey river, at the west, receives the Patuckaway, and runs through the whole length of the town. Another river runs through the N. part of the town, and from that circumstance is called North river. The principal roads are in good repair; and the town is gradually making them better. By observations taken at 6 in the forenoon, at 1 and 9 o'clock in the afternoon, from Fahrenheit's thermometer placed in the open air, 13 feet from the ground, and where the sun does not shine on the thermometer, the annual average of heat for 10 years ending 1818 was 44 1-12°. During that period the annual average that fell of [*feet, inches,* 10 20 40 80] rain, was 2 10 6 1 0 0 & of snow, 6   7 2 0 0 1

In September 1783, the town contained 201 dwelling-houses, and 210 barns and framed buildings. The congregationalists, quakers, baptists and methodists have now each a meeting-house. The first house of this kind was raised in the year 1750. The number of inhabitants are fewer than they were 40 years since. This is not owing to sickness or mortality, but to emigration. Most of the people are industrious, frugal agriculturalists; the price of land, for many years, has been higher than in the adjacent towns; and when a farm is sold, which is but seldom, it is usually divided amongst the adjoining neighbors: of course the number of inhabitants as well as farms has diminished. Pop. in 1820, 1158. The present population is 58 to the square mile. Within the last ten years the number of deaths in town has been 161, averaging 16 in a year. Though one fourth of the number died under ten years, the ages of the whole averaged 36 years and 4 months to each person. The town is divided into 8 school districts; and there is a school house in each district suited to the accommodation of the scholars. The money for the support of schools is raised by a town tax, and expended in the several districts in proportion to the tax they pay, and not in proportion to the scholars in the district. In one of the districts a school is kept 9 or 10 months in the year, but in some other districts not more than 3 or 4 months annually. WILLIAM PLUMER, late governor of this state and one of its most distinguished and estimable cizizens, resides in this town. A considerable portion of his life has been employed in the service of the people, in the several stations of representative and senator in the legislature, president of the Senate, speaker of the House of Representatives, representative and senator in Congress, and for four years as chief-magistrate of the state. HENRY DEARBORN, though not born in this town, lived here in early life with his parents for a number of years. He served as an officer in the army of the United States during the whole of the revolutionary war; was afterwards marshal of the district of Maine; representative in Congress; secretary of war of the United States; collector of the customs of the port of Boston and Charlestown; major-general of the army of the United States in the war of 1812, and is now minister of the U. S. at Portugal. JOHN CHANDLER was born in this town, and lived in it many years. He has been representative and senator in the Massachusetts legislature; representative in Congress; brigadier-general in the army of the United States in the war of 1812; president of the senate in Maine; and is now senator in Congress. There are several religious societies of different sects. They are here enumerated, not according to their numbers, but the order of time in which they were established. 1. The congregationalists were the first settlers of the town, and for a number of years all the inhabitants were of that sect. Rev. Robert Cutler was their first minister; he was ordained in 1747, and in 1755 was dismissed. March 8, 1758, Rev. Josiah Stearns was ordained as his successor; he died July 23, 1788 of a cancer, aged 57. In February 1793, Rev. Peter Holt was ordained; and in 1821, at his own request, was dismissed. The members of this society are calvinists. 2. Quakers.—Though few in number they have existed in the town for more than half a century. As early as the year 1769, Jonathan Norris, one of their members, was imprisoned for not paying taxes to support the congregational minister; but the town the next year released the constable from the tax; and after that no distress was made upon the quakers for ministerial rates. Joshua Folsom, a native of the town, for many years was their preacher; he died December 21, 1793, aged 72. His son, Benjamin Folsom, is now their principal speaker. 3. Baptists.— They formed a society and built a meeting-house about 50 years since. About that time the Rev. Dr. Samuel Shepard was ordained as a preacher over the society in Epping, Stratham and Brentwood; in each of those towns he preached every third Sunday. He lived a number of years in Stratham, afterwards removed to Brentwood, where he lived many years, and died there November 1815, aged 77. For more than 50 years he was a useful practical physician. Since his death the society in Epping have had regular preaching a portion of the time. The members of this society are calvinists. 4. Methodists.—A society of this sect has existed in this town for about 20 years, and have had different preachers for a portion of the time. 5. Free-will Baptists.—This sect has been in the town about 6 or 7 years—they are more numerous than the calvinistic baptists, but have no minister settled over them.

EPSOM, post-town, Rockingham county, lat. 43° 12', lies 12 miles E. of Concord, bounded N. by Pittsfield, E. by Deerfield and Northwood, S. by Allenstown, W. by Pembroke & Chichester, & contains an area of 19,200 acres. The surface of the town is generally uneven. The principal eminences are called M'Coy's, Fort, Nat's, and Nottingham mountains. The soil is in general good, and well adapted for grazing or grain. Great and Little Suncook are the only streams deserving the name of rivers; the former passing through the town from the N., the latter a branch from the E. uniting near the centre of the town. Here are three ponds, Chesnut, Round and Odiorne's. The mineralogy and geology of Epsom have been partially explored. Brown oxide, and sulphuret of iron are found, the latter most frequently in its decomposed state. Varieties of quartz, feldspar and schorl are found. An alluvial deposite has been discovered, which Prof. Dana has ascertained to be Terra de Senna—it constitutes a very handsome and durable paint for cabinet work. It is found in the N. part of the town. Epsom was granted May 18, 1727, to Theodore Atkinson and others, inhabitants of New-Castle, Rye and Greenland. Several families had previously moved into town. It received its name from Epsom in England. Rev. John Tucke was ordained here in 1761, and dismissed in 1774. He died while on his way to join the American army as chaplain. Rev. Ebenezer Hazeltine, who was ordained Jan. 21, 1784, died Nov. 10, 1813, aged 59. Mr. H. was born at Methuen, Ms. Oct. 28, 1755, and graduated at Dartmouth College. Rev. *Jonathan Curtis*, who was born at Braintree, (now Randolph) Ms. Oct. 22, 1786, and graduated at Dartmouth in 1811, was ordained Feb. 22, 1815; and his church consists of 115 members. Like all the other frontier towns, Epsom was exposed in its early settlement to the Indians. No serious injuries, however, were sustained. The Indians who subsequently committed some mischiefs at Canterbury, after laying in wait for some time, on the 21st Aug. 1747, took Mrs. McCoy from Epsom, a prisoner, and sold her in Canada, from whence she returned at the close of the war. Depredations were afterwards committed on the cattle in the neighborhood, the greater part of the inhabitants having fled to the garrisons in Nottingham. There is a social library in Epsom, containing 100 volumes. The number of deaths from 1784 to 1813, was 286—annual average 9 1-2. Maj. ANDREW M'CLARY, a native of this town, a gallant and meritorious officer, fell at the battle of Breed's Hill, June 17, 1775. Like the illustrious Roman, he left his plough on the news of the massacre at Lexington, and in the action when he lost his life displayed great coolness and bravery. He was son of Andrew M'Clary, of Ireland, an early settler of Epsom. Hon. JOHN M'CLARY, an estimable citizen, was killed by the fall of a frame while raising, Dec. 13, 1821, at the age of 36 years. He was son of Gen. Michael M'Clary, and had been for several years a representative and senator in the state legislature. Pop. 1336.

ERROL, township, Coos county, in lat. 44° 43', is situated on the W. of Umbagog lake, bounded N. by Wentworth's location, E. by the state of Maine, the line extending through the lake, S. by Cambridge and Dummer, W. by Millsfield. It contains about 35,000 acres, of which 2,500 are water. Several considerable streams here unite with the Ameriscoggin, passing from the N. E. through this town. Errol was granted Feb. 28, 1774, to Timothy Ruggles and others. Pop. 26.

ERVIN'S LOCATION, in Coos county, is a tract of 3468 acres, granted June 2, 1775, to Capt. William Ervin, of Boston. It is bounded N. by Dixville, E. by Millsfield, S. by public lands, W. by public lands and Columbia. It is at present uninhabited.

EXETER, post-township, Rockingham county, in lat. 42° 59', is bounded N. by New-Market, E. by Stratham, S.E. by Hampton and Hampton-falls, S. by Kensington and East-Kingston, and W. by Brentwood and a corner of Epping. The compact part of the town lies about the falls, which separate the fresh from the tide-water of a branch of the Pascataqua, called by the natives Squamscot, and now known by the name of Exeter river. Above the falls, this stream assumes the name of Great river, to distinguish it from one of its smaller branches, called Little river. Great river has its source in Chester, whence it runs through several towns before it meets the tide-water in the centre of Exeter. On this river are many valuable mill privileges; and there are already erected upon it in Exeter, 1 cotton manufactory, 1 woollen, 3 corn mills, 3 saw mills, 2 oil mills, a paper manufactory and a bark mill: and on the same stream, just without the limits of the town, are a saw mill, a corn mill, and a cotton manufactory of 800 spindles, owned in Exeter. On Little river, there is 1 carding machine. In addition to these, there is an establishment for morocco dressing, where 20,000 skins are annually prepared, and 6 tanneries, some of them extensive. The town is pleasantly situated on the banks of the river, and contains two congregational churches, one baptist, a court-house, two printing offices, a bank with a capital of $100,000 and an academy. Its soil is in general good, though comprehending every variety, from that of the best quality to the least productive. Like most towns in the state, it is essentially agricultural, and the improvement in the style of husbandry within the last fifteen years has been very great; and within the same period, the number of industrious and enterprising mechanics, to whom Exeter is now indebted for her prosperity, has been very rapidly increasing. The sum raised for the support of schools for many years, has been $1000 annually; and the average annual expenditure for the improvement of highways during the last ten years, $1300. The poor are supported on a farm purchased for that purpose in 1817; since which time, this new system has been in successful operation, and has not only rendered their condition much more comfortable, but reduced the expense of their support rather more than one third. The same establishment answers the purposes of a house of correction. Phillips' Exeter academy was founded by the liberal donations of John Phillips, LL. D. in 1781, who at his death, in 1795, bequeathed to the institution a large portion of his estate. It is under the control of a board of seven trustees, three of whom only can reside in Exeter. Its instructors are a principal, a professor of mathematics and natural philosophy, and an assistant. Lectures are delivered to the students by a theological instructor, who superintends this part of their education; and sacred music and writing, taught by separate instructors. The number of students is usually between 80 and 90. No one under the age of 10 is admitted to the Latin department, and twelve is the age commonly required for admission to the English. The former embraces a full course of studies preparatory for college, with provision for those who choose to advance farther; and the latter is arranged with a view to a complete education in English literature and science. The present principal, BENJAMIN ABBOT, LL. D. has discharged the duties of that office with distinguished ability for more than thirty years. The building stands on a plain, near the centre of the town, and is well provided with accommodations for the different branches of instruction, and a large hall for declamation and the annual exhibitions. There are three terms in a year, with a vacation of three weeks each. A considerable part of the funds is devoted to the purpose of aiding the poorer class of students. The settlement of Exeter commenced in 1638, by John Wheelwright and others, who formed themselves into a body politic, chose their magistrates, and bound the people to obedience. Their laws were made in popular assemblies; and the combination thus entered into subsisted about three years. Wheelwright in 1629 had purchased of the Indians the country between the Merrimack and Pascataqua, extending back about 50 miles. In consequence of his antinomian opinions, he had been banished the colony of Mass., and sought refuge here. In 1642, Exeter was annexed to the county of Essex; and Wheelright, who was still under sentence

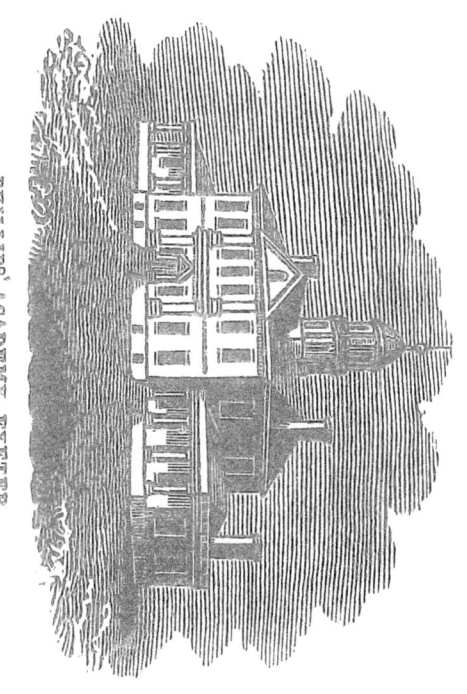

PHILLIPS' ACADEMY, EXETER.

of banishment, with a few adherents, removed to Maine. In 1643, upon a new arrangement of the counties, Exeter came under the jurisdiction of the county of Norfolk. Various changes occurred until the final adjustment of the lines in 1741, suspended all excitement on the subject of territorial limits between Mass. and N. H. Exeter, like most of the early settlements, suffered from the attacks of the Indians. In 1675, one person was killed between Exeter and Hampton, and another made prisoner; and other mischiefs were perpetrated. In 1695, two men were killed. In 1697, the town was providentially saved from destruction. A body of Indians had lain in ambush, intending to make an assault on the following morning. By an accidental alarm, caused by a gun fired to frighten a few women and children, who went into the fields after strawberries contrary to the advice of their friends, the people were brought together in arms. Seeing this, the Indians supposed they were discovered, and precipitately retreated, killing one person, wounding another and taking away a child. No further injuries were committed until 1707, when another person was killed at Exeter. In the spring of 1709, William Moody, Samuel Stevens, and two sons of Jeremy Gilman were taken at Pickpocket mill in Exeter. In 1710, they ambushed and killed Col. Winthrop Hilton, a meritorious citizen, with two others, taking two prisoners. Soon after this, they took four children and John Wedgewood from Exeter, and killed John Magoon. In April, 1712, a Mr. Cunningham was killed; and depredations were made upon the property of the inhabitants. It does not appear that Exeter suffered much from the Indians after this period. The first church in Exeter was probably the first formed in this state; it was founded in 1638, by Rev. John Wheelwright, a brother-in-law of the celebrated Anne Hutchinson, and cotemporary with Oliver Cromwell at the university. Wheelwright removed to Wells, Me. in 1643, was afterwards minister at Hampton; and died at Salisbury in 1680. The church at Exeter was broken up; and a new church was afterwards organized, at what period it is uncertain. Over this church were successively ordained Rev. Samuel Dudley in 1650, who died in 1683, aged 77;—Rev. John Clarke, graduated at Harvard college in 1690; ordained 1698; died in 1705, aged 35;—Rev. John Odlin, in 1706; died 1754, aged 72; —Rev. Woodbridge Odlin, in 1743; died 1776, aged 57;—Rev. Isaac Mansfield, in 1776, who was removed in 1787; and Rev. *William F. Rowland* in 1790. The second congregational church was formed in 1748, and Rev. Daniel Rogers, a descendant of the martyr John Rogers, ordained, who died in 1785, aged 79. His successors were Rev. Joseph Brown, ordained 1792 and removed 1796; and Rev. *Isaac Hurd*, ordained in 1817. Rev. *Ferdinand Ellis* is the ordained minister of the baptist church in this place. Hon. SAMUEL TENNEY, M. D. graduated at Harvard College in 1772; was an original member of the N. H. medical society, and its vice president several years; a member of the Amer. Acad. of Arts and Sciences; an honorary member of the Mass. Med. Soc.; was elected corresponding member of Mass. Hist. Soc. Oct. 8, 1792; was elected a member of Congress in 1800, 1802, and 1804. He died in 1815, aged —. He was a man of science and learning. Gen. NATHANIEL PEABODY was an original member of the N. H. Med. Society; was a member of the old Congress; a senator in 1792; and speaker of the House in 1793. Hon. NICHOLAS GILMAN was a member of the old Congress, a senator in 1804, and President of the Senate; a senator in Congress from 1805, to his death in 1814. He died in Philadelphia; and is the only member of Congress, from this state, who died in office. Gen. NATHANIEL FOLSOM was a member of the old Congress; and a valuable revolutionary officer. Hon. JEREMIAH SMITH, a native of Peterborough, was one of the first representatives to Congress under the federal government, was appointed Judge of S. C. of N. H. in 1802, was chief justice, and continued such till 1809, when he was elected governor. He was appointed chief justice of S. J. C. in 1813. In 1804, he received the honorary degree of LL. D. from Dart. Coll.; in 1807, the same from Harvard. Hon. JOHN TAYLOR GILMAN, a descendent of one of the principal settlers at Exeter, was an active supporter of the revolution; a member of the old Congress; filled at times the offices of representative and state treasurer; and for fourteen years, between 1794 and 1816, was governor of the state. In 1794, he received the honorary degree of LL. D. from Dartmouth College. Exeter has at all periods of its history possessed eminent and useful men; and some of the first lawyers and jurists, antiquarians and scholars, have received their early education at its literary institution. Pop. in 1820, 2114.

F.

FARMINGTON, post-town; Strafford co., lat. 43° 20', was formerly a part of Rochester, but was incorporated as a distinct town Dec. 1, 1798. It has Milton on the N. E. Rochester S. E., Strafford S. W., New-Durham N. W.—its area about 21,000 acres. It is distant from Concord in a line E. N. E. about 25 miles, but by the road usually travelled nearly 40; from Portsmouth, in a direct line, N. W. by N. 26 miles. This is rather a broken township, much of the soil being rugged, but found to be productive when properly subdued by human industry. The interval is inconsiderable, though very fertile on the banks of the Cocheco, which meanders through the N. E. part of the town. The Blue Hills or Frost Mountains, extend nearly through the town under different names from N. to S. From the summit of the ridge in the S. E. part, here called Mount Washington, ships may be seen by the naked eye off Portsmouth harbor; while to the north and west the White Hills and the Monadnock, with hundreds of smaller mountains meet the eye of the beholder.—There is not far from the village in Farmington, a rock supposed to weigh from 60 to 80 tons, so exactly poised on other rocks, that it may be caused to vibrate several inches by the hand. There is a decent meeting-house in Farmington; and a congregational church has recently been formed under the care of Rev. *James Walker*. There are many other professing christians of different denominations, but no church has been organized except that of the congregationalists. At the bank of the Cocheco, a little more than a mile S. E. from the principal village, is a place called the *Dock*—so named from the circumstance that the first settlers usually deposited their lumber here to be floated down the river. This name is sometimes ignorantly applied to the village. Hon. AARON WINGATE, for many years a member of the legislature, a counsellor from 1797 to 1803, and for some time chief-justice of the common pleas in Strafford, died here in 1822, aged 78 years. Pop. 1716.

FISHERSFIELD, a post-town in Hillsborough county, in lat. 43° 18', is bounded N. by New-London, E. by Sutton, S. by Bradford, W. by Goshen and Wendell, containing 19,332 acres. It is 23 miles from Hopkinton, 40 from Amherst, 35 from Concord, and 95 from Boston. Though this town has a large proportion of water, yet there is no considerable stream within its limits. The S. part of Sunapee lake lies in the N. W. part. Todd pond, situated at the S. E. angle, 500 rods in length, and 60 in width, affords a small branch to Warner river. Chalk pond is in the N. part, from which issues a small stream communicating with Sunapee lake. In the W. part of the town, there is a considerable elevation of hills, and the land in that section is broken, but is suitable for grazing. The growth of wood in Fishersfield is rock maple, beech, birch, spruce and hemlock. The land is generally mountainous, and the soil hard and rocky. This town, according to Dr. Belknap, was originally known by the name of *Dantzick*, and contained in 1775 only 130 inhabitants, Sutton being joined in the enumeration. It did not at first belong to Hillsborough county, but was annexed to it at the time of its incorporation, Nov. 27, 1778. It received its name from John Fisher, who afterwards went to England. The first settlement was made in the year 1762 by Zephaniah Clark, Esq.—There is a society of freewill baptists. Pop. 874.

FITZWILLIAM, a post-township, in Cheshire county, in lat. 42° 45', is bounded N. by Troy, E. by Rindge, S. by Royalston and Winchendon, in Massachusetts, and W. by Richmond. It originally contained 26,900 acres, but by an act of the legislature, passed June 23, 1815, 4200 acres of land were disannexed from Fitzwilliam, and now constitute part of Troy. Fitzwilliam is 13 miles from Keene, 60 from Concord, and 65 from Boston. Camp and Priest brooks, running in a S. direction, are the principal streams. South pond, 230 rods long and of various width; Sip's pond, 200 rods long and 100 wide; Rockwood's pond and Collin's pond, are the only natural collections of water. The surface of this town is hilly. The soil is rocky. The natural growth on the upland is maple, beech, birch, oak, pine and hemlock; on the low lands, pine, hemlock, and spruce. There is a considerable quantity of very productive and highly valuable meadow land. The soil is suitable for grazing and tillage. Beef, pork, butter and cheese are the staples. The farmers have of late turned their attention to the raising of sheep, and the making of woollen cloths, and this branch of industry is becoming an object of profitable attention. Near the centre of the town is a large hill, remarkable for the beautifully romantic prospect it affords. Gap mountain, which, at a distance, appears to be part of the Monadnock, and on which are found various kinds of stones suitable for whetstones, lies partly in Troy and partly in the N. E. part of Fitzwilliam. Five turnpike roads, meet at the village, viz. one from Keene and Winchester each, one to Templeton, leading to Worcester, and one to Rindge and Winchenden each, both leading to Boston. These roads have all been built within a few years, and for the projection and completion of most of them, the public is indebted to the public spirit and enterprize of the late James Robeson, Esq. The village contains one meeting-house, 2 stores, an extensive tannery, several other mechanic shops, and 20 dwelling-houses. Fitzwilliam was originally called *Monadnock No.* 4, and was granted Jan. 15, 1752, to Roland Cotton and 41 others, but the grantees incurred the forfeiture of the grant, and it was re-granted to Samson Stoddard and 22 others. The first settlement was made early in 1760, by James Reed, John Fassett, Benjamin Bigelow and others. It was incorporated May 19, 1773, when it was named from the Earl of Fitzwilliam. A congregational church was formed March 27, 1771, on which day, Rev. Benjamin Brigham, who graduated at Harvard college in 1764, was ordained. He died June 11, 1799, aged 57. Rev. Stephen Williams succeeded Mr. Brigham, Nov. 4, 1800; dismissed Nov. 1802; died at Woodstock, Conn. 1822, aged 60. Rev. *John Sabin*, who graduated at Brown University in 1797, was ordained March 6, 1805. The number in his church is 150. In 1816, an elegant meeting-house was erected at the expense of $7000; dedicated Nov. 6. On the night of the 17th Jan. 1817, it was struck by lightning, and entirely consumed. In the same year, another, 65 by 57 feet, was erected on the same spot and dedicated Nov. 1817. The number of deaths from 1802 to Nov. 21, 1822, inclusive, was 334. Brig. Gen. JAMES REED, a revolutionary patriot, whose merits as an officer and a man will be long remembered, was a citizen of this town. Pop. 1167.

FOX POINT, in Newington, the place where a party of Indians under Hoophood, a sagamore, in May, 1690, destroyed several houses, killed 14 persons, and took 6 prisoners.

FRANCESTOWN, a post-township in Hillsborough county, in latitude 42° 59′, is bounded N. by Deering, E. by New Boston and Weare, S. by Lyndeborough and Greenfield, and W. by Greenfield and Society-Land, containing 18,760 acres. It is 12 miles from Amherst, 55 from Hanover, 27 from Concord, and 60 from Boston. The two S. branches of Piscataquog river rise in this town; the largest branch from Pleasant pond; the other from Haunted pond. The former branch passes near the village in Francestown. Pleasant and Haunted ponds are considerable collections of water, the former being about 350 rods square; the latter 300 rods in length and 225 in width. The land is uneven, and in many parts stony, but the qualities of the soil are warm and moist. There are some small intervals which are very productive. The original growth here was beech, birch, red oak, maple, hemlock and pine. The streams of water are not large, and almost every mill is situated on rivers that take their rise from hills and ponds within the limits of the town. But three of the mill privileges may be considered as valuable. The highest land is Crotched mountain, the summit of which is more than 600 feet above the level of the common in the centre of the town. One of the summits of this mountain is covered with wood; the other is almost a solid ledge of rocks, affording a very extensive prospect to the S.W. There is, in the easterly part of this town, on the farm of Mr. Daniel Fuller, a very extensive and valuable quarry of free-stone (steatite.) It was accidentally discovered by Mr. Fuller while ploughing in the field, and was first worked in 1804. It is of a dark greyish color, and when polished, strongly resembles the variegated marble of Vermont. It is soft, adhesive, and easily manufactured. Its specific gravity, from recent experiments, is found to exceed considerably that of common granite. When separated from the quarry, it is worth $2,50 per cubic foot. It is transported to Boston in large quantities, where, as well as at the quarry, it is manufactured into stoves, hearths, &c. In the N. part of this town, black-lead, (plumbago, or graphite) has been recently found of a good quality—and in the S. part, near Lewis' mills, some beautiful specimens of rock crystal. The common garnet is met with in various places. On the N. side of Haunted pond, there is a bar of 20 rods in length, 6 feet high, and 3 or 4 feet through, but for what purpose or by what means this barrier was raised, is a matter of conjecture only. The 2d N. H. turnpike passes through near the centre of Francestown. The local situation of this town is very eligible for business, being near the centre of the county, and on the great thoroughfare from Windsor to Boston, and on a leading road from the S. W. of the state to Concord. There is a handsome village, consisting of an elegant meeting house, with a cupola and bell, an academy, two stories high, built of brick, and 25 dwelling houses. The number of deaths from the first settlement to 1790 was about 100. From that time to Jan. 1, 1819, the number was 463. A large proportion of these was infants. The dysentery prevailed in 1799, and 33 persons died of that disorder, which, with 12 other deaths, made the total that year 45,—the greatest number which ever occurred in one year. A congregational church was gathered by Rev. Samuel Cotton, of Litchfield, Jan. 27, 1773. It consisted at first of 18 members, and in 1790, of 148, and in 1821, of 328. Rev. *Moses Bradford*, from Rowley, Ms. who graduated at Dartmouth College in 1785, was ordained Sept. 8, 1790. No other religious society has ever existed here, excepting a small one of Scotch presbyterians, which, in 1792, united with the congregationalists.——Francestown derived its name from *Frances*, the wife of the last Gov. Wentworth. It was not granted to proprietors as most of the early townships were. It includes what was once called New-Boston-Addition and part of Society land, and was incorporated on petition of the inhabitants of those places, as a distinct township, June 8, 1772. The titles were derived from the Masonian proprietors, the land being within the curve line. A part of Lyndeborough was afterwards added to this town. The first settlement was made about 1760, by John Carson, a Scotchman. This town passed several spirited resolves, Oct. 21, 1774, which were published Nov. 18th in the N. H. Gazette, signed by most of the inhabitants then belonging to the place. Richard Batten, who died Aug. 25, 1822, at the age of 85 years, resided in this town more than 40 years. He was captured by the Indians during the last French war, in the year 1757. Although guarded by two warriors, he was able, by superior strength and agility, to effect his escape, but not without the loss of all his clothes. He wandered entirely naked between the lakes George and Champlain for six days, eating nothing but berries and bark. To elude his pursuers, he was obliged to swim across Hudson river three times. Mr. JAMES WOODBURY, who died March 3, 1823, at the age of 85, closed his life in this town. He was an active soldier in the old French war, and engaged by the side of Gen. Wolfe when he was killed at the memorable siege of Quebec. He was one of the truly invincible *rangers* under the immortal Stark, and discharged every duty in a prompt and courageous manner. Pop. 1479.

FRANCONIA, a post-township in the N. part of Grafton county, in lat. 44° 10', containing 32,948 acres, is bounded N. by Bethlehem, E. by ungranted land, S. by Lincoln and Landaff, and W. by Concord. It is 28 miles from Haverhill, 74 N. from Concord, the seat of government, and 140 miles from Boston. A large proportion of this town is mountainous. Its streams are branches of the Lower Amonoosuck river, and rise in the mountainous tracts on the E. There are two ponds in the notch of the mountain and but little lower than the ground on which the public road now passes, both situated in the S. part of the town. The lower one, commonly called Ferrin's pond, is 1-2 a mile long and 1-4 of a mile wide. It is the source of one of the principal branches of Pemigewasset river, called the Middle Branch. The North pond, about a mile long and from 1-2 to 3-4ths of a mile wide, is the source of one of the branches of the Amonoosuck. Numerous elevations of land present themselves in this town. Those adjacent the Notch, are the most prominent. Here nature seems to have left only room for the road, which will probably become the great outlet of the Coos country. What has received the name of the Profile in Franconia is regarded as a singular curiosity. The peak on which it is situated is estimated by some to be 1000 feet in height, rising at an angle of about 80°, presenting a bold and majestic front of solid rock, a side view of which exhibits the profile of the human face, of which every feature is conspicuous. At the foot of the mountain is Ferrin's pond. There are two Iron establishments in this town. The lower works are situated on the S. branch of Amonoosuck river and are owned by the New-Hampshire Iron-Factory Company, incorporated Dec. 18, 1805, which is composed principally of gentlemen in Salem and Boston. Their establishment is very extensive, consisting of a blast furnace erected in 1808, an air furnace, a forge and trip-hammer shop. There are also near or connected with the establishment, grain and saw mills, a large store, several shops, and other buildings, with 12 dwelling houses, which make a small village. The ore is obtained from a mountain in the east part of Concord, three miles from the furnace, and is considered the richest in the United States, yielding from 56 to 63 per cent; and the mine is said to be inexhaustible. About 12 or 15 tons of iron are made in a week, and 60 men on an average are employed annually. There is a highly impregnated mineral spring, about two miles from the furnace. About one mile from the Lower works, are the Upper works, owned by the Haverhill and Franconia company, but their operation is not very extensive. Franconia, originally called *Morristown*, was granted Feb. 14, 1764, to Isaac Searle and others. The first permanent settlement was made in 1774, by Capt. Artemas Knight, Lemuel Barnett, Zebedee Applebee, and others. Pop. 373.

G.

GEESE islands, in Connecticut river, in the town of Haverhill, five in number, the largest of which contains about 49 acres. The others contain in all about 15 acres. They were granted to Benjamin Whiting of Charlestown, Jan. 3, 1769.

GILFORD, township, Strafford county, in lat. 43° 32′, is situated on the S. of Winnepisiogee lake, which forms its N. boundary. On the E. lies Alton, S. Gilmanton, and W. Long bay and Winnepisiogee river, which separate the town from Meredith. It contains an area of about 23,000 acres, and has 1816 inhabitants. The soil is generally productive. There are two ponds in this town, Little and Chattleborough. Gunstock and Mile's rivers, rising in Suncook mountains and flowing N. into the lake, are the principal streams. The N. source of the Suncook river is on the S. of these mountains, which extend in a lofty pile over the E. part of the town, from Gilmanton line nearly to the lake. There are two islands in the lake belonging to Gilford, one of which has been connected to the main land by a bridge 30 rods in length. This town, which was formerly a part of Gilmanton, was incorporated June 16, 1812. It was settled in 1778, by James Ames and S. S. Gilman. Elder *Richard Martin* was settled here in 1798, over the first free-will baptist society. Elder Uriah Morrison was ordained over a baptist society in 1808, and died in 1817, aged 36 years. Elder *William Blaisdell* was ordained in 1809, and is the pastor of the christian baptist church. There are also societies of congregationalists and universalists. Here are two meeting-houses, open to all denominations; a new and promising academy, incorporated in 1820; 11 schools during almost 5 months in the year; a valuable paper manufactory, established by Aaron Martin, besides other useful mills and machinery. Four bridges across the Winnepisiogee connect the town with Meredith. The village at this place is thriving and pleasant, consisting of 30 dwelling houses, the court-house, paper-mill, &c. A term of the superior court is now held at this place annually. Pop. 1816.

GILLIS & FOSS' GRANT, a tract of territory containing 33,272 acres, in Grafton county, in lat. 43° 54′, is bounded N. by ungranted land, E. by Burton, S. by Sandwich, and W. by Thornton. It was granted June 29, 1819, to Josiah Gillis, Moses Foss, jun. and others. It is watered by Mad river, which rises among the mountainous tracts on the N.; runs S. W. about 20 miles, and falls into Pemigewasset river in Campton. Swift river has its source in this grant, pursues an E. course through Burton into Conway, where it unites with Saco river. There are two ponds, and several considerable elevations. Moses Foss, jun. commenced the settlement a few years since. It has but about 20 inhabitants.

GILMANTON, post-town, Strafford county, is situated in lat. 43° 25', 17 miles from Concord, 44 from Portsmouth, 78 from Boston, and 522 from Washington City. It is bounded N. by Gilford, E. by Alton, S. E. by Barnstead, S.W. by Loudon, Canterbury and Northfield, N. W. by Winnepisiogee bay and river, which separate it from Sandbornton, and contains 63,500 acres. Beside the Winnepisiogee, this town is watered by the Suncook and Soucook rivers, which have their sources in this town. The Suncook rises in a pond near the top of one of the Suncook mountains, elevated 900 feet above its base. The water of this pond falls into another at the foot of the mountain, of 1 mile in length and 1-2 mile wide. Passing from this, it falls into another, covering about 500 acres, from which, it meanders through the town, receiving several streams in its course. The Soucook rises from Loon, Rocky and Shellcamp ponds, in the S. part of the town. This town is very hilly and rocky. The N. part bounds upon Suncook mountains, from which a chain of hills extends S., dividing the head springs of the Suncook and Soucook. The soil is hard, but fruitful, when properly cultivated. The geology of this town presents many varieties. Quartz, crystallized, yellow and red ferruginous, irised and granular, is frequently found. Hornstone, schorl, in their varieties, occur in several places. Mica slate, gneiss and sienite abound. Sulphur occurs on the W. bank of the middle branch of the Soucook; red and yellow ochre are found in various parts. Iron ore exists here, and works were erected in 1768, at the *Iron Works' Village*, but after a few years, were abandoned. There are several springs in this town, termed mineral—one of which has proved efficacious in cutaneous and bilious affections. This town was granted May 20, 1727, to 24 persons of the name of Gilman, and 152 others. Its settlement was protracted in consequence of the frequent depredations committed by the Indians during the continued wars of this period. After the reduction of Canada, the fear of the Indians in a great measure subsided; and in Dec. 1761, Benjamin and John Mudgett with their families settled here. Orlando Weed joined in 1762, and they were soon followed by several other families. Dorothy Weed, the first child, was born here Oct. 13, 1762. The baptist church was organized Nov. 16, 1773; Elder Walter Powers was ordained June 14, 1786, and dismissed in 1806. In 1811, the church was divided, one portion of which now constitutes the Gilford church. June 10, 1818, a new baptist church was formed, and is under the pastoral care of Rev. *Phineas Richardson.* The congregational church was formed Nov. 30, 1774, and Rev. Isaac Smith ordained. He died March 25, 1817, at the age of 72, and in the 43d year of his ministry. Rev. *Luke A. Spofford* was ordained June 9, 1819. There are respectable societies of friends and methodists in Gilmanton, and 4 free-will baptist churches—three of which have stated ministrations. The one formed in 1810, is under the care of Elder *Peter Clark;* the others, two of which were organized in 1816, are under the care of Elders *Abel Glidden* and *John*

Knowles. The academy in this town, founded in 1794, and endowed with $5,500 and one fourth of a township of land, is a flourishing institution. "The social library of Gilmanton" was incorporated in June 1801, and contains 150 volumes; the "Gilmanton Academy social library," incorporated June 1815, contains 160 volumes. The average number of deaths for 10 years past, is 40. Gen. JOSEPH BADGER, one of the first settlers, was the first magistrate in town; for many years representative, and for some time previous to his death judge of probate for the county of Strafford. He was an estimable and useful citizen. Pop. in 1810, 4,338. Gilford was disannexed in 1812; and the population in 1820 was 3527.

GILSUM, a small township in Cheshire county, situated about 10 miles from Connecticut river, in lat. 43° 1', is bounded N. by Alstead and Marlow, E. by Stoddard and Sullivan, S. by Keene, and W. by Surry. It contains 9,456 acres. The land is generally uneven and stony; but there is some good arable land free from stone. The soil is, in many parts, fertile, and produces good crops of grass, grain, &c. The agricultural products in 1820, were 8,500 lbs. of butter, 11,000 lbs. of cheese, 19,000 lbs. of beef, 30,500 lbs. of pork, 2000 lbs. of flax, and 300 barrels of cider. Ashuelot river runs through this town and affords a good supply of water for mills. Gilsum was first granted Dec. 8, 1752, to Joseph Osgood, Jacob Farmer and others, and was called *Boyle*. It was regranted by the name of Gilsum, July 13, 1763, to Messrs. Gilbert and Sumner and others. From the combination of the first syllables of the names of these men, it derives the name of Gil-sum. The first settlement was made in 1764 by Josiah Kilburn, from Hebron in Conn. The other early settlers were Pelatiah Pease, Obadiah Wilcox, Ebenezer Dewey, Jonathan Adams, &c. most of whom were from Conn. The congregational church was gathered in 1772. Rev. Elisha Fish was installed May 29, 1794; died March 28, 1807. Divisions in religious sentiment succeeded the death of Mr. Fish. In 1816, the congregational church and society were incorporated, the members of which have assumed no sectarian name, but call themselves christians. There are some methodists and some universalists, which, with the other denominations, live in peace and harmony. Pop. 601.

GLYNVILLE, or Littleton village, is pleasantly situated on both sides of Amonoosuck river, in the S. part of the town of Littleton. It is 40 miles from Plymouth, 15 from Bath, 17 from Lancaster, and 5 from the Franconia Iron works. Here is a good situation for mills, &c., the bed of the river being for a considerable distance of solid rock, with a sufficient fall and a plenty of water. In this village, there are a store, tavern, post office, and such professional men and mechanics as are necessary. There is a social library, called Glynville library, incorporated in 1813.

GOFFSTOWN, a post-township, in Hillsborough county, in lat. 43° 2', is bounded N. by Dunbarton, E. by Manchester and Hooksett, S. by Bedford, W. by New-Boston, containing 29,170 acres. It is 12 miles from Amherst, 16 from Concord, and 55 from Boston. Merrimack forms part of the E. boundary. Piscataquog river, the tributary branches of which unite near the W. line of the town, runs through its centre in an E. direction, and falls into Merrimack river at Piscataquog village in Bedford. Large quantities of lumber are annually floated down this river to the Merrimack, and most of the mill privileges are derived from this valuable stream. There are two considerable elevations in the S. W. part of the town, which obtained from the Indians the name of *Un-can-nu-nuc*. Douglass, vol. i. page 458, spells it *Oncanouil*, but the orthography commonly adopted, and which conveys the present pronunciation, is Unconoonock. Excepting these elvations, Goffstown is less broken by hills than most of the circumjacent towns. On the rivers abovementioned are considerable tracts of valuable interval. Back from the rivers, commence extensive plains, less rich in soil than the intervals, but easy of cultivation, and producing abundant crops of Indian corn and rye. From these plains, the land rises on each side of Piscataquog river into large swells, in some parts rocky, but affording excellent grazing land and good tillage. The principal forest trees are oak, pine of several sorts, hemlock, beech and maple. A great number of masts for the Eng. navy has been furnished from this place. They are still an article of export, but their stock is nearly exhausted. In this town, there is an extensive cotton factory. There is a public school which has been in operation two years. Three persons have received a collegiate education, viz. Kilburn Johnson, Charles F. Gove, L. B. and James Shirley. The two last were graduated at Dartmouth college in 1817 and 1818. The late Mr. James Aiken, of this town, bequeathed $4000, which, on a certain contingency, is to form a permanent fund for supporting an academy here. In 1816, a society, called the Religious Union Society, was incorporated for the support of religious instruction. To this society, Hon. Thomas W. Thompson, deceased, devised about 170 acres of land, towards a fund for supporting the gospel ministry in this town. A congregational church was formed in 1771. Rev. Joseph Currier, who graduated at Harvard college in 1765, was the first pastor. He was dismissed in 1774. Rev. Cornelius Waters, a graduate of Dartmouth in 1774, was ordained in 1781; dismissed in 1795. In 1802, a presbyterian congregational church was organized, and Rev. David L. Morril, a native of Epping, was ordained March 3. He was dismissed July 10, 1811, and has since been distinguished as a legislator, both in our state government and the government of the U. S. Rev. *Benjamin H. Pitman*, from Newport, R. I. was ordained in Oct. 1820. A baptist church was formed in 1820, of which Rev. *John B. Gibson* was constituted pastor. There are two meetinghouses, one built in 1765; the other in 1815. The last is a handsome edifice, and is furnished with a bell. Goffstown was in former times a favorite resort of the Indians, who found ample means of support in the abundance of fish in its limits. It was granted by the Masonian proprietors in 1748, to Rev. Thomas Parker, of Dracut, and others. The year of its first settlement we have not ascertained. It was incorporated June 16, 1761, by the name of Goffstown, in honor, it is said, of Col. John Goffe, for many years a resident of Bedford, and the first judge of probate in Hillsborough county. Dr. JONATHAN GOVE, a man distinguished for his urbanity, his talents and professional skill, resided in this town. He was graduated at Harvard college in 1768, and at the time of his death, was one of the oldest practitioners of medicine in the county. He was many years an active member of the legislature. Pop. 2173.

GOSHEN, a post-township, in Cheshire county, in lat. 43° 17', is bounded N. by Newport and Wendell, E. by Fishersfield, S. by Washington, and W. by Lempster and Unity, containing 12,023 acres. It is 42 miles from Concord. Croyden turnpike passes through Goshen. From Sunapee mountain, lying in the E. part of this town, spring many small streams, which unite in forming Sugar river. Rand's pond is in the N. E. part of the town. The soil is particularly calculated for the production of grass. The natural growth consists of maple, birch, beech, hemlock and spruce, and some oak. From the maple, sugar is manufactured in considerable quantities. The agricultural products in 1800, were 11,000 lbs. of butter, 15,000 lbs. of cheese, 22,000 lbs. of beef, 48,000 lbs. of pork, 8,100 lbs. of flax, and 200 barrels of cider. This town has a library of about 90 volumes. Goshen was formed of territory belonging to Newport, Wendell, Fishersfield, Washington, Lempster and Unity. It was incorporated Dec. 27, 1791. The first settlement was made in that part taken from Wendell, about the year 1769, by Capt. Benjamin Rand, William Lang, and Daniel Grindle, whose sufferings and hardships were very great.—The crops of the first settlers were greatly injured, and sometimes entirely destroyed by early frosts. In such cases, they procured grain from Walpole and other places. At a certain time of scarcity, Capt. Rand went to that place after grain, and being detained by a violent snow storm, his family was obliged to live without provision, for six days, during which time Mrs. Rand sustained one of his children 5 years old, by the milk from her breast, having a short time before buried her infant child.—In the spring of 1813 the spotted fever swept off many of the inhabitants. A congregational church was formed in February 1802, consisting of 7 members, and a baptist society was formed October 12, 1803, consisting of 12 members, which has increased to 53. Pop. 687.

GOSPORT, one of the isles of Shoals, formerly called *Appledore* and afterwards *Star-island*, contains about 150 acres. Gosport was early invested with town privileges; in 1728 paid £16 as its proportion of the province tax of £1000; had a meeting-house, and subsequently a fort on its W. point. Its business has now greatly lessened. Rev. John Tucke was settled on this island in 1732; died Aug. 12, 1773. A further notice of this island, is contained in that of the Isles of Shoals.

GRAFTON, a township in Grafton county, in lat. 43° 34', is bounded N. E. by Orange, S. E. by Cushing's Gore, separating it from Danbury, S. W. by Springfield, and N. W. by Enfield, containing 21,993 acres, of which 500 are water. It is 36 miles from Concord, and 13 S. E. from Dartmouth College. It is watered by branches of Smith's and Mascomy rivers. Heard's river, a small tributary to Smith's river, waters the S. E. part. There are 5 ponds. The largest, containing from 200 to

300 acres, is called Grafton pond. Two are named Mud ponds. The surface of Grafton is very hilly, in some parts very mountainous; and the soil is so rocky as,in many places, to be unfit for cultivation.— There are, however, some good tracts of land. The Grafton turnpike, leading from Andover to Orford Bridge, passes through the E. part; and the 4th N. H. turnpike, from Concord to Hanover, through the W. part. On the former is a small village, containing 14 dwelling houses, a store, school house, tavern, attorney's office and several mechanic establishments. Grafton contains 175 dwelling houses and about 185 families. Since 1807, 136 families have emigrated to the states of New-York, Ohio, and other places. From Sept. 1815, to 1822, there died 72 persons. At the last period there were living 51 persons above 60, 19 above 70, and 4 above 80. In this town, there is a remarkable ledge, called the Pinnacle, on the S. side of which, the ground rises by a gradual ascent to the summit; but on the N. side, it falls nearly 150 feet, within the distance of 6 or 8 feet. Clay is found in several places. Isinglass, as it is commonly called, is found in a state of great purity in Glass Hill mountain. It adheres in the form of lamina to rocks of white and yellow quartz. The usual size of these lamina is about 6 inches square, but some have been found much larger. It requires much labor to obtain this glass, which, when prepared, is transported to Boston, and from thence exported to England. It is found on the E. side of the mountain, which is 200 feet high. Grafton was granted Aug. 14, 1761, to Ephraim Sherman and others. The first permanent settlement was made in May 1772, by Capt. Joseph Hoyt, from Poplin. Capt. Alexander Pixley and wife were the second family who settled here. Capt. Jacob Barney, now 48, was the first native of the town. The baptist church in the N. part of the town, was formed in 1785.— Rev. Oliver Williams was ordained Sept. 27, 1786; died Aug. 15, 1790, aged 39. Rev. Joseph Wheat was installed in Aug. 1801; dismissed in 1815. Rev. Ephraim Crocket, ordained in May, 1816; removed Jan. 20, 1817. Rev. *Stephen K. Wescott*, ordained Oct. 6, 1819. The south church had David Fisher and Uriah Smith for preachers. A freewill baptist church was formed about the year 1817—it has about 40 members. Pop. 1094.

GRANTHAM, a township in Cheshire county, in lat. 43° 13', is bounded N. by Enfield, E. by Springfield, S. by Croydon, W. by Plainfield, which separates it from Connecticut river. It contains an area of 24,900 acres. It is 12 miles S. E. from Dartmouth college, and 45 N. W. from Concord. There are 7 or 8 ponds, the largest of which lies in the S. E. part of the town and is called Eastman's pond, and contains nearly 300 acres. Another, lying near the centre of the town, contains nearly 200 acres. Croydon mountain extends through the westerly part of Grantham in a direction from S. W. to N. E. The soil is productive when well cultivated, especially on the W. of the mountain. It seems to be more favorable for wheat than any other species of grain. The mountain affords good pasturage, and the lower land yields grass in abundance. The agricultural products in 1820 were, 21,000 lbs. of butter, 30,500 lbs. of cheese, 61,000 lbs. of beef, 72,000 lbs. of pork, 8,600 lbs. of flax, and 450 barrels of cider. The town is well watered by numerous brooks and rivulets which principally issue from Croydon mountain. On the E. side of the mountain is a spring supposed to possess medicinal qualities, visited by hundreds of valetudinarians in the summer season. In the N. W. corner of the town is a bed of paint, which after being clarified, makes a paint similar to spruce yellow, or, by being burnt, is similar to Spanish brown. On the summit of Croydon mountain, is a natural pond, containing about 50 acres. This town was first granted July 11, 1761, but the proprietors not fulfilling the conditions of the charter, it was forfeited. In 1767, it was re-granted to Col. William Symmes and 63 others, by the name of *Grantham*. It was afterwards called New-Grantham, and has, within a few years, been changed, by act of the legislature, to its former name. The inhabitants on the W. side of the mountain are connected for religious purposes with Meriden parish, in Plainfield, over which Rev. *Dana Clayes* was ordained July 4, 1821. On the E. side of the town is a society of methodists. Pop. 1032.

GRANT'S ISLAND, in Connecticut river, opposite Lime, contains 24 acres, and was granted to Benjamin Grant of Lime, April 5, 1767.

GREAT-BAY, a name appropriated to two bodies of water in this state. The largest is that lying E. of New-Market, formed by the united waters of Squamscot, Winnicot and Lamprey rivers. It is 4 miles wide; and at some seasons is picturesque as connected with the surrounding scenery. This bay has Newington on the E., Greenland and Stratham on the S., New-Market and Durham W.; its waters pass N. E., through Little Bay, where Oyster river unites with the current which passes into the Pascataqua. Great-Bay, between Sanbornton and Meredith, is an extensive body of water, connected with Winnepisiogee lake, and discharging its waters into Winnepisiogee river. Round and Long Bays are situated between the lake and Great-Bay, and there are two small bays on the river below.

GREAT-ISLAND. *See N. Castle.*

GREENFIELD, post-township, in Hillsborough county, in lat. 42° 57', is bounded N. by Francestown and Society-Land, E. by Francestown and Lyndeborough, S. by Lyndeborough and Temple, W. by Peterborough and Hancock, containing 16,904 acres. It is 14 miles from Amherst, 38 from Concord, and 62 from Boston. Contoocook river forms part of the W. boundary, and separates this town from Hancock. The soil has considerable variety, but is generally fertile. It contains a great variety of forest trees—nearly all the kinds found in the county. The hills afford excellent pasturage; the valleys and plains are favorable for grain. Hops are raised in great abundance. A part of Crotched mountain rises from the N. part, and part of Lyndeborough mountain from the S. and E. sections of this town. There are some valuable meadows. In one of them, owned by Maj. Whittemore, have been found many Indian relics, from which, it is conjectured that it was a favorite spot of the sons of the forest. There are five ponds; the largest about one mile in length, and one third of its length in width. There are several small fertilizing streams. Greenfield has a pleasant village of about 30 houses—it has a social library, containing 200 volumes. The first settlement commenced in 1771, by Capt. Alexander Parker, Major A. Whittemore, Simeon Fletcher and others. It was incorporated June 15, 1791. The name of Greenfield was given to it by Major Whittemore. A congregational church was formed August 13, 1791. Rev. Timothy Clarke, who graduated at Dartmouth college in 1791, was settled Jan. 1, 1800; dismissed in 1811. Rev. John Walker, who graduated at Dartmouth college in 1808, was ordained Feb. 5, 1812; dismissed in 1822. Pop. 974.

GREENLAND, post-town, Rockingham county, 43° 2′, is situated 5 miles W. S. W. from Portsmouth, 45 from Concord, 51 from Boston. It is bounded N. by the Great-Bay and Newington, E. by Portsmouth and Rye, S. by North-Hampton, W. by Stratham, and contains 6,335 acres. The soil is remarkably good, and at present in a high state of cultivation. The orchards and gardens of this town are valuable, and yield annual profits to the farmers. Greenland, originally a part of Portsmouth, was incorporated as a distinct town in 1703. Settlements commenced early, and in 1705, there were 320 inhabitants. Rev. William Allen, the first minister of Greenland, was ordained July 15, 1707; died Sept. 8, 1760, aged 84. Rev. Samuel M'Clintock, D. D. was ordained colleague with Mr. Allen, Nov. 3, 1756; died April 27, 1804, aged 72. Rev. James Armstrong Neal, ordained May 22, 1805, died July 18, 1808, aged 34. Rev. *Ephraim Abbot* was ordained Oct. 27, 1813; and the church consists of about 40 members. The methodist church in Greenland was formed in 1809, and is under the pastoral care of Rev. *Alfred Metcalf*. George Brackett, Esq. of this town has given a fund in trust of $5000—200 dollars of its annual income to be applied to the support of the congregational minister for the time being, and the remainder for missionary purposes. The number of deaths for 30 years is 204 —an average of less than 7 per year. From 1712 to 1753, the baptisms in Greenland were 1092, averaging more than 26 each year, while the deaths during that period were less than 10 per annum. The births for the last 10 years have trebled the number of deaths. Of 204 deceased during 10 years past, 64 lived to the age of 70 and upwards. Rev. SAMUEL M'CLINTOCK, D. D. who died in the 48th year of his ministry, was born at Medford, Mass. May 1, 1732; graduated at the New-Jersey college in 1751; ordained in 1756; and died April 27, 1804, aged 72.— His father was a native of Ireland. Dr. M'Clintock was a sound divine, eminent as a preacher, and distinguished for his attachment to the cause of his country. He served as chaplain in the army of the revolution. Pop. 634.

GROTON, a township in Grafton county, in lat. 43°44′, is bounded N. by Rumney, E. by Hebron, S. by Orange and W. by Dorchester, containing 16,531 acres. It is 10 miles from Plymouth, 45 miles from Concord and 15 miles from Hanover. The N. part is watered by a branch of Baker's river, and the southerly part has several small streams which fall into Newfound lake. There is but one pond of any consequence lying wholly in this town, and that is situated about a mile N. E. of the meeting house. Groton was granted July 8, 1761, to George Abbot and others by the name of *Cockermouth.* It was re-granted, about five years afterwards, to Col. John Hale and others. The first settlement was commenced in 1770, by James Gould, Capt. Ebenezer Melvin, Jonas Hobart, Phinehas Bennet and Samuel Farley. They endured many hardships during the succeeding winter, having failed in raising their provisions. About the year 1779, a congregational church was formed, and Rev. Samuel Perley, who graduated at Harvard College in 1763, was settled. He was dismissed in 1785. Rev. Thomas Page was ordained in 1790, over a large church collected from this and other towns, and remained the pastor until his death, May, 3, 1813. Rev. *William Rolfe* was settled in 1804. This town was incorporated by the name of Groton, Dec. 7, 1796. Pop. 686.

H.

HALL'S stream, rises in the highlands which separate this state from the British dominions, and forms the N. W. boundary between New-Hampshire and Lower Canada from its source to its junction with the Connecticut at Stewartstown.

HALE'S location, Coos county, is situated W. of Conway, bounded S. by Burton, W. and N. by ungranted lands. It consists of 1215 acres, granted Dec. 27, 1771, to Maj. Samuel Hale, of Portsmouth, and contains 20 inhabitants,

HAMPSTEAD, post-town, Rockingham county in lat. 42° 53′, lies partly on the height of land between Merrimack and Pascataqua rivers—bounded N. by Hawke and Sandown, E. by Kingston, S.E. by Plaistow, S. by Atkinson, W. by Londonderry, and contains 8,350 acres, 400 of which are water. Most of the waters descend S. W. into the Merrimack through Spiggot river, which flows from Wash pond near the centre of the town. Angly pond is in the N. E. of the town, the waters of which pass into the Powow river. Island pond in the S. W. part of the town, contains a valuable farm of 300 acres, the property of Hon. N. Gilman of Exeter. Hampstead is an ill-shaped town, having about 30 angles. The soil is a hard, strong land, favorable to the growth of oak, walnut and elm, with some chesnut, maple, &c. The tract composing this town was, previous to the establishment of the state boundaries in 1741, considered as a part of Haverhill and Amesbury, and was called *Timber-Lane.* A part was also called *Haverhill District.* About 1728, a Mr. Emerson from Haverhill made a settlement in the S. part near a brook, and at that time, it is reported, only one Mr. Ford and two Indians lived in the place. About the same time, a Mr. Heath and a few others moved into the place. The town was granted by Gov. Benning Wentworth, Jan. 19, 1749, and named by him after a pleasant village five miles N. of London, Eng. He reserved the island before mentioned for his own farm. In the early settlement of the town, a dispute arose between Kingston and Hampstead, respecting certain grants made by Amesbury before the state line was run, which was finally settled by Hampstead paying £1000 old tenor, and the grant of Unity to Kingston made by the governor July 13, 1764. About 1750, the meeting-house was erected, and Rev. Henry True ordained June 3, 1752 : he died May 22, 1782, after having lived a pious and useful life. Rev. *John Kelly,* was installed Dec. 5, 1792. Daniel Little, Esq. was the first magistrate of Hampstead, and a useful man. Richard Hazzen, Esq. who run the state line, was a man of piety and liberal education. Col. Jacob Bailey, afterwards one of the first settlers of Newbury, Vt. was an eminent citizen. Hon. John Calfe was a native of this place, for 29 years a justice of the peace, 25 years on the bench of the court of common pleas, and for 25 years clerk of the House of Representatives. He was a useful and a good man. He died Oct. 30, 1808, aged 68. Pop. 751.

HAMPTON, post-town, Rockingham county, lies on the sea-coast, in lat. 42° 57′, bounded N. E. by North-Hampton, S. E. by the Atlantic, S. W. by Hampton-Falls, N. W. by Hampton-Falls and part of Exeter. Distant 13 miles from Portsmouth, 7 from Exeter, and 50 from Concord. It comprises a surface of 8,130 acres; 1800 of which are salt-marsh, 650 sand banks between the marsh and high water mark of the sea—leaving only 5,680 acres of upland. The land is rather level, gently declining to the sea and marsh, but of good quality. It is well adapted to tillage and mowing; but there is not sufficient pasturing for the stock generally kept, and the young cattle, &c. are pastured in the neighboring towns. Hampton is pleasantly situated; many eminences in the town affording romantic views of the ocean, Isles of Shoals, and sea-coast from Cape-Ann to Portsmouth. Its beaches have long been the resort of invalids and parties of pleasure—and are little inferior to the famous Nahant beach near Boston. *Boar's Head* is an abrupt eminence extending into the sea, and dividing the beaches about half-way between the river's mouth and the N. E. corner of the town. On the N. beach, are 26 fish-houses, from which the winter and summer fisheries have been carried on with much success. At one fare the boats frequently land from 20 to 30 tons of cod ; and although the fishermen venture to sea in whale boats and wherries to the distance of 4 or 5 leagues, in very cold and boisterous weather, it is said no person was ever lost. Great quantities of the winter fish are carried frozen into the interior, and to Vermont and Canada. Previous to the revolution, and for many years after until timber in the vicinity became scarce, one or more brigs or ships, from 150 to 350 tons burthen, were annually built in the ship-yard of the Hon. Christopher Toppan, under his superintendance, and several vessels were owned here engaged in the W. I. trade. Several vessels of from 60 to 100 tons have been lately built. Several vessels of this description are now employed from Hampton river as coasters and in the mackerel fishing. Two convenient wharves are situated about 1 1-4 miles from the centre of the town. Hampton now affords a good market, and its trade is evidently increasing. The Indian name of this town was *Winnicumet ;* it was first settled in 1638, by emigrants from the county of Norfolk, Eng. The first house was erected in 1636, by Nicholas Easton, and was called the boundhouse. The town was incorporated in 1638, and then included within its limits what now constitutes the towns of North-Hampton, Hampton-Falls, Kensington and Seabrook. In 1638, the first congregational church in New-Hampshire was established at Exeter.

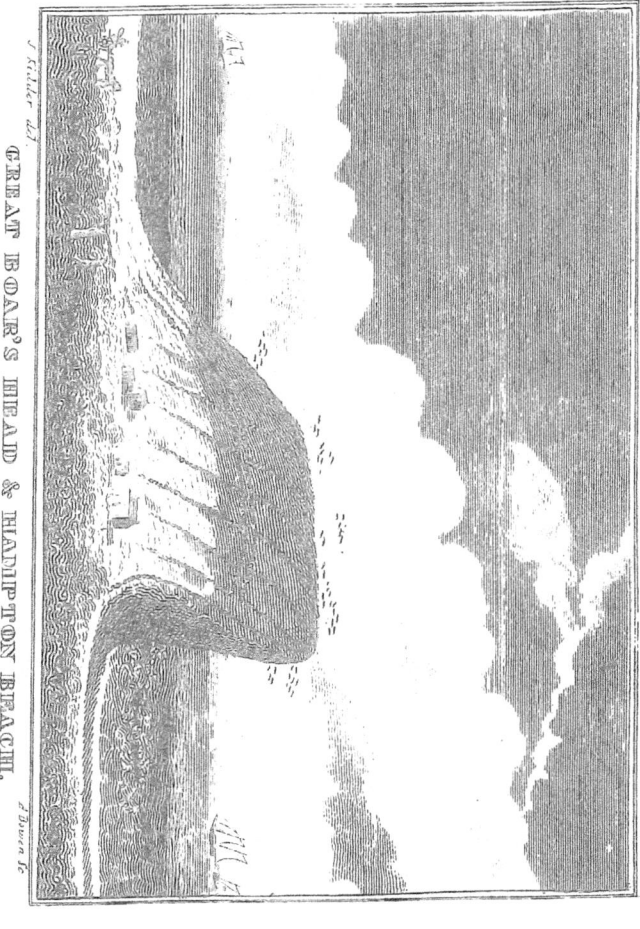

GREAT BOAR'S HEAD & HAMPTON BEACH.

The second church was gathered this year in Hampton, over which have officiated the following clergymen: Rev. Stephen Bachelor, ordained 1639; removed 1641. Rev. Timothy Dalton, ordained 1639; died 1661. Rev. John Wheelwright, ordained 1647; afterwards removed. Rev. Seaborn Cotton, born at sea in Aug. 1633, and graduated at Harvard college in 1653, was ordained 1660, and died 1686, aged 53. Rev. John Cotton, ordained 1696, died in 1710, at the age of 57. Rev. Nathaniel Gookin, ordained 1710, died in 1734, aged 48. Rev. Ward Cotton, ordained 1734, was removed in 1765. Rev. Ebenezer Thayer, ordained 1766, died in 1792, aged 58. Rev. Jesse Appleton, D. D. was ordained in 1797; was elected president of Bowdoin college in 1807, and died Nov. 12, 1819. Rev. *Josiah Webster* was ordained in 1808. Rev. Timothy Dalton, the second minister of the town, gave by deed to the church and town of Hampton, for the support of the gospel ministry, several pieces of land lying in the township. Of this land the towns set off have had their proportion by an amicable adjustment of their claims. Several years since, through the influence of the Hon. Christopher Toppan, deceased, this town sold several pieces of unproductive land included in the above gift, and vested the proceeds in public securities then worth 3s9 to 5s. on the pound lawful. This fund has been kept by the town; and its income with parsonage rents, exclusive of the parsonage occupied by the settled minister, amounts to $450 per annum. The estate appropriated to this purpose is about $12,000. There is a baptist society in Hampton, incorporated in 1817, under the care of Eld. *John Harriman*. This town was formerly the scene of Indian depredations. On the 17th Aug. 1703, a party of Indians killed 5 persons in Hampton, among whom was a widow Mussey, celebrated as a preacher among the friends. Hampton Proprietary School was incorporated in 1810; it has a large and convenient building, and promises extensive usefulness. In 1735 and 6 the throat distemper prevailed in this town, and 55 persons fell its victims. It was also fatal in other towns, and nearly 1000 were swept away with the disease within fourteen months. This fatal sickness returned again in 1754, during which, and the succeeding year, more than 50 persons died in Hampton. The town has, however, been remarkable for its general health, and the longevity of its inhabitants—a very unusual number having lived to from 80 to 100 years. But one adult has died here within the last twenty years of fever; and more than three to a hundred now living are more than 75 years of age; several more than 90. The Hon. CHRISTOPHER TOPPAN died here in Feb. 1819, aged 84: he was a very useful and distinguished citizen. He was grandson of Rev. Christ. Toppan of Newbury. His father, Dr. Edmund Toppan, married a daughter of Col. Wingate, and settled in Hampton as a physician. Mrs. Sarah Toppan, his relict, died in 1801, having lived respected and honored nearly a century. Col. Wingate left a numerous family, and among his descendants are numbered some of our most distinguished characters. Gen. JONATHAN MOULTON was an inhabitant of this town, and died in 1788: he was a large proprietor in lands; and several flourishing towns in the interior of the state owe their early settlement to his exertions and influence. Pop. 1098.

HAMPTON-FALLS, post-township, Rockingham county, lat. 42° 57′, is situated 45 miles from Concord, 41 from Boston, and 16 from Portsmouth. It is bounded N. E. by Hampton, S. E. by the marshes, S. by Seabrook, W. by Kensington, N. W. by Exeter, and contains 7,400 acres. The soil is generally similar to that of the contiguous towns, moderately good, and pleasantly situated. Hampton-Falls was originally a part of Hampton, from which it was separated and incorporated in 1712; and the same year, the first minister, Rev. Theophilus Cotton, was settled; he died in 1726, aged 45. Rev. Joseph Whipple, ordained in 1727, died in 1757, at the age of 57. Rev. Josiah Bayley succeeded him in that year; died in 1762, aged 29. Rev. Paine Wingate was settled in 1763, and removed in 1771. Rev. Samuel Langdon, D.D. was settled in 1781, and died Nov. 29, 1797, aged 75. He was several years Pres. of Har. Coll. Rev. *Jacob Abbot* ordained Aug. 15, 1798. There is also a small society of baptists. The malignant throat distemper prevailed here in 1735—36, and destroyed a great number of persons, principally youth. Pop. 572.

HANCOCK, a post-township in Hillsborough county, in lat. 42° 59′ is bounded N. by Antrim, E. by Society-Land, and Contoocook river which divides it from Greenfield, S. by Peterborough and Dublin, and W. by Nelson, containing 19,372 acres. It is 35 miles from Concord, 22 from Amherst and 19 from Keene. The soil is various, but generally productive. The W. part of the town is mountainous, but affords excellent pasturing and many good farms. The other parts of the town are agreeably diversified with plains, hills and valleys. On the Contoocook, and some of its tributary streams, there are several tracts of excellent interval. It may with propriety be said to be a good farming town. There are two considerable ponds, one of which is in the centre, a few rods N. of the meeting-house, called Norway pond; the other in the S. W. corner of the town, and, from its shape, is called Half-moon pond. Besides these, there is a small pond called Mud or Hosley's pond, lying between Half-moon and Long, or Hunt's pond, the last of which is very large and situated in this town and Nelson. These ponds contain fish of various kinds. There is an elegant meeting-house erected in 1820, on the same spot where the former one was accidentally burnt down, Oct. 28, 1819. The pews in this edifice, exclusive of several reserved for public use, were sold at auction in one day for 7000 dollars. The meeting-house is pleasantly situated near the centre of the town, on a handsome plain, in a thriving village, in which are two taverns, three stores, and is well supplied with mechanics of different kinds; two physicians and one attorney at law. In this town, there are one cotton factory, one potash manufactory, and one for the manufacture of elegant fowling pieces and rifles, many of which are annually made here, and from their excellence are in great demand. There are nine schoolhouses. That in the village, is built of brick two stories high, the upper story of which was designed, and is well adapted for a public school or academy, to which use it is generally applied. There is a social library containing upwards of 200 volumes. Hancock is justly considered a healthy place. There has been no prevailing sickness since the summer of 1800, when the dysentery, in the short period of nine weeks, swept off 56 persons, most of whom were children and youth. The whole number of deaths that year was 64. The annual average number for the last 20 years has been about 14. For several years past, nearly one half of the deaths has been caused by consumption. Hancock was incorporated Nov. 5, 1779. It was named after Gov. Hancock of Boston, who was one of the original proprietors. The first settlement was begun by John Grimes in May, 1764. In the succeeding autumn, he removed with his family to Peterborough; remained there through the winter, and returned in the spring of 1765, which may be considered the first permanent settlement. Within four or five years from that time, John Aspey, George M'Cloud, Moses Morrison and William Lakin, with their families, settled in this place. From this period, the settlements greatly increased by emigrants from Groton, Hollis, Londonderry, New-Ipswich, Peterborough and other places. The first settlers suffered many of the hardships and privations incident to new settlers, but less, perhaps than some others, inasmuch as most of the towns adjoining had been previously partially settled. The congregational church here was organized Aug. 28, 1788, and then consisted of ten males and seven females. It now contains about 100 members. Rev. REED PAIGE, from Hardwick, Mass. was ordained Sept. 21, 1791; died July 22, 1816, aged 52 years. He was justly esteemed a learned, pious, able and faithful minister; a good citizen, an honest and upright man; a firm patriot, and zealous and able advocate of his country's rights, which very much endeared him to the people of his charge, who frequently elected him to represent the town in the state legislature, of which he was a member at the time of his death. Rev. *Archibald Burgess*, was ordained as the successor of Mr. Paige, Dec. 25, 1822. Pop. 1178.

HANOVER, a post-township in Grafton county, in lat. 43° 42', is bounded N. by Lime, E. by Canaan, S. by Lebanon and W. by Norwich, Vt. containing 27,745 acres. It is 53 miles N. W. from Concord, 102 from Portsmouth, 114 from Boston and 495 from Washington city. In this town, there is no river nor any considerable stream besides the Connecticut. Mink brook, running in a S. W. direction, Slate brook in a W. course, and Goose-Pond brook in the N. E. part of the town, are among the principal streams. Neither of these are large enough for permanent mill privileges. There are several small islands in Connecticut river within the limits of Hanover, the largest of which is Parker's island containing about 20 acres. There are no natural ponds. The original growth of wood is maple, beech, birch, ash, bass, hemlock, spruce and pine. When the town was settled, the greatest proportion of forest trees was what is denominated *hard wood*. The surface of Hanover is agreeably diversified with hills and valleys, and the greatest part is suitable for farms. There is but a small proportion of waste land, less, perhaps, than in any other town in Grafton county. It is estimated that nearly one half is under improvement. Moose mountain is a considerable elevation, extending across the town from N. to S. at the distance of about five miles from Connecticut river. Grafton turnpike passes through the N. E. part of Hanover to Orford. A handsome bridge connects the S. W. part of the town with Norwich. The principal village is in the S. W corner of the town, on a beautiful and extensive plain, half a mile from Connecticut river, and 180 feet above the level of its waters. Vegetable substances are found in different parts of this plain at a depth of from 50 to 80 feet. The number of houses is upwards of 70, the best of which are erected round a square level area of 12 acres. The remainder stand on different streets, leading from the green in all directions. On the N. side of the green is a spacious meeting-house; on the S. a brick tontine, four stories high, and 150 feet long. The number of deaths in this village, of which the population is 633, in 1821, was three. The annual average for the last 16 years has been about seven. It is perhaps as healthy as any place of its size in New-England. A spring of excellent water was brought in 1821, a distance of 1 3-4 mile in leaden pipes, at an expense of $3,500. There are 6 law offices, two taverns, two bookstores, one apothecary's shop and five English and W. I. goods' stores. In this pleasant village is located Dartmouth college, of which an account is given in the *General View*, page 31. The College buildings are a handsome edifice of wood, 150 feet by 50, three stories high, (*See plate*) containing 34 rooms for undergraduates, and 6 rooms for other purposes; an edifice of brick, styled Medical House, 75 feet long and 32 wide, three stories high, (*See annexed View*) containing a laboratory, an anatomical museum, a minerological cabinet, two lecture rooms, and six rooms for students; and a convenient chapel. A greenhouse has lately been erected, which will soon be furnished with an ample collection of botanical specimens. Though a more central situation for the only collegiate institution in the state would be on some accounts highly desirable, yet it has often been remarked, that the location of Dartmouth college is peculiarly favorable to study and the preservation of morals. Circumstances conducive to these objects in addition to establishments wisely arranged for the pursuits of literature, are to be found in the salubrity of the situation, the uniform temperature of the climate and the pleasantness of the village, which is neither too populous nor too solitary. Among the worthy men who have finished their earthly career in this place, may be mentioned Rev. ELEAZAR WHEELOCK, D. D. who died April 24, 1779, aged 68; Hon. JOHN WHEELOCK, LL. D. President of the college 35 years, who died April 4, 1817, aged 63; Hon. BEZALEEL WOODWARD, who died Aug. 1804; Rev. JOHN SMITH, D. D. who died April, 1809; Hon. JOHN HUBBARD, who died in Sept. 1810; and Rev. FRANCIS BROWN, D. D. who died July 27, 1820, aged 36. These gentlemen were all connected with the college. The first newspaper printed in Hanover was published by Alden Spooner. "The Eagle or Dartmouth Centinel," was commenced July 22, 1793, by Josiah Dunham, A. M. and continued by different publishers till 1799. "The Dartmouth Gazette," by Moses Davis, commenced Aug. 27, 1799, discontinued in 1820. The "Dartmouth Herald," by Bannister & Thurston, commenced June 21, 1820; discontinued July 25, 1821. Hanover was grant-

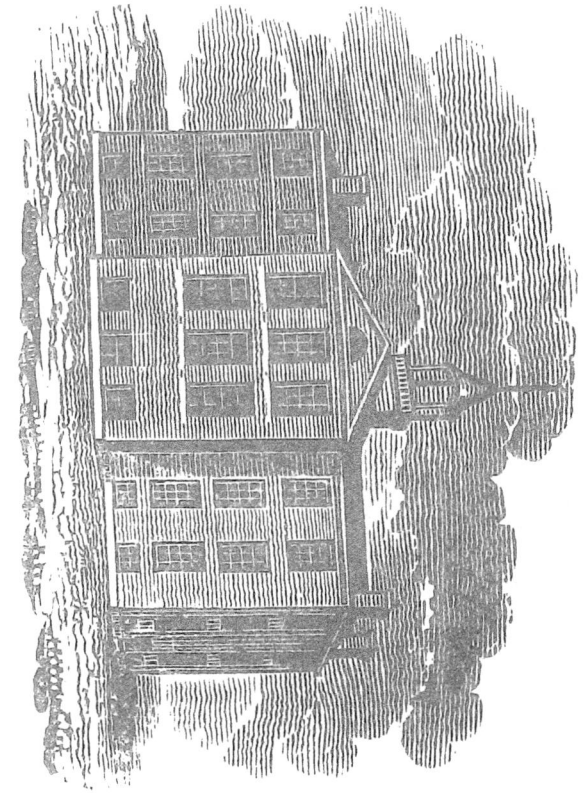
MEDICAL COLLEGE, HANOVER.

ed by charter, July 4, 1761, to eleven persons of the name of Freeman and 52 others, principally belonging to Connecticut. The first settlement was made in May, 1765, by Col. Edmund Freeman, from Mansfield, Conn. In 1766, Benjamin Davis and Benjamin Rice from the same place, and Gideon Smith and Asa Parker, became settlers. All of the first settlers were from Connecticut and most of them were from the towns of Mansfield and Coventry. In 1770, Dartmouth college was established here by Dr. Wheelock. At that time there were 20 families in town. A church was gathered in the college by Dr. Wheelock in Jan. 1771. Those who have successively officiated in this church, which still exists, are Rev. Messrs. Wheelock, Ripley, Smith and *Shurtleff*. The first settled minister of the church and town was Rev. Eden Burroughs, who was installed in Sept. 1772. He continued in the ministry until a division arose, which occasioned the foundation of a new church and society, over which Rev. Samuel Collins was installed in Nov. 1788. He was dismissed in 1795. Rev. Dr. Burroughs was dismissed in 1809. Soon after, these churches were united, and now form one congregational church, over which Rev. *Josiah Towne* was ordained in June, 1814. There is a baptist church, over which Rev. Abel Bridgman was settled in 1791; died 1800. Rev. Isaac Bridgman, settled in 1800; died 1815. Pop. 2222.

HART'S ISLAND, in Connecticut river in the township of Plainfield, contains 19 acres.

HAVERHILL, a post-town, and the half shire town in Grafton county, in lat. 44° 3′, is bounded N. E. by Bath, E. by Coventry, S. W. by Piermont, and W. by Newbury, Vt. containing 34,340 acres. It is 31 miles from Plymouth, 70 from Concord, 27 from Dartmouth college, and 132 from Boston. It is watered by Oliverian brook, passing through the S. part and falling into Connecticut river above Bedel's bridge, and by Hazen brook passing the centre of the town, and falling into the Connecticut near the Great Ox Bow, in Newbury. Haverhill is a pleasant town, though but thinly inhabited for several miles in the centre along the main road. The soil is loam mixed with gravel and suited to every species of cultivation. There is a quarry of granite suitable for mill stones, for buildings, &c. and a bed of iron ore, on the W. side of Coventry bordering this town. Haverhill is divided into two parishes, the south and north, in each of which is a congregational church and a meeting-house. The principal village is at the S. W. angle of the town, and known by the name of *Haverhill Corner*. There is a beautiful common in this village, laid out in an oblong square, around which the buildings regularly stand. The site is a handsome elevation, overlooking the adjacent country many miles N. and S., and not less than 6 or 7 miles E. and W. From the street, the ground slopes with unusual elegance to the west; and is succeeded by large intervals. The prospect here is delightful. This village contains 46 dwelling-houses, 34 of which are two stories high, and one, three stories high, built of brick, and two of the others are built of brick; a court-house which is a brick edifice, 53 feet by 43, with a projection 20 feet by 10; an academy, Grafton bank, printing office, post office, 8 stores, 2 taverns, jail, &c. Five stage coaches now arrive at this village, twice in a week each, four of which are mail coaches. There is a pleasant village forming at the N. W. angle of the town, on a street nearly a mile in length, straight and very level. The Haverhill academy was opened in Sept. 1793, and incorporated Feb. 11, 1794. The lower story of the court-house is appropriated to its use. There is a social library, incorporated June 17, 1817. The newspapers published here have been "The Coos Courier," which commenced April 21, 1808, and the "New-Hampshire Intelligencer," which commenced in 1820, by Sylvester T. Goss, who also publishes the "Evangelist," a religious paper. Nathaniel Coverly published a paper for about 6 months prior to 1800; and 3 or 4 numbers of a magazine were published by Mosely Dunham. Haverhill was granted by charter, May 18, 1764, to John Hazen and 74 others. Its first settlement was made in 1764, by Capt. John Hazen, who settled on the Little Ox Bow, near where there had formerly been an Indian fort and burying ground, and where many Indian skulls and relics have been found. Several of the early settlers were from Newbury and Haverhill, Ms. and from the last place, this town derived its name. Its former name was *Lower Cohos.* The first court was holden here, Oct. 21, 1773. The first minister was Rev. Peter Powers, the first male child born in Hollis, who was settled over Haverhill and Newbury, Vt. in 1765, and was dismissed in 1784. He died at Deer Isle, Me. in 1799. The first congregational church, in the S. parish, was formed Oct. 30, 1790. Rev. Ethan Smith was ordained Jan. 25, 1792; dismissed June 23, 1799. Rev. John Smith was ordained Dec. 23, 1802; dismissed Jan. 14, 1807. Rev. Grant Powers, from Hollis, ordained Jan. 4, 1815. The church contains 93 members. There is a 2d church in the N. parish. There is a society of methodists, consisting of three classes. Hon. MOSES DOW was one of the most distinguished citizens of this place. He was born in Atkinson; obtained a collegiate education by his own exertions, was graduated at Harvard college in 1769. After studying the profession of law, he practised as an attorney five years at Haverhill, Ms.; five years at Plymouth, N. H., from whence he removed to this town, where he practised until within a few years of his death. He was, more than 30 years, register of probate, was a colonel, a brigadier general, speaker of the house of representatives, senior senator in 1791, and one of the judges of the court in Grafton county, which office he sustained till his death, March 31, 1811, at the age of 64. Hon. CHARLES JOHNSTON, who died March 5, 1813, aged 76, resided here. He was a valuable officer in the revolution, and was many years, judge of probate in Grafton county. Hon. James Woodward and Hon. Ezekiel Ladd were among the early settlers, and were judges of the old county court. Pop. 1600.

HAWKE, township, formerly a part of Kingston, Rockingham co., is in lat. 42° 57′, and bounded N. by Poplin, E. by Kingston, S. by Kingston and Hampstead, W. by Sandown, and contains 7000 acres. It was incorporated Feb. 22, 1760, and derived its name from a British admiral. In 1775, there were 500 inhabitants more than there has been at any time since. The soil is uneven, but in some parts good. Squamscot river passes over the N. W. corner of Hawke. Long pond lies in the E. part, and Cub pond on the W. side, adjoining Sandown. The first settlements were made by Jonathan Sanborn, Jacob Hook and others between 1735 and 1739. Rev. John Page was ordained over a congregational church here Dec. 21, 1763, and died of the small pox Jan. 29, 1782, aged 43. Since that time no minister has been settled. The average annual number of deaths for the last ten years, has been 5. Hawke has a convenient meetinghouse, and three schools. Pop. 421.

HEBRON, a township in Grafton co., lat. 43° 42' is bounded N. by Rumney and Plymouth, E. by Plymouth, S. by Bridgewater, Alexandria and Orange, W. by Groton. It contains 13,350 acres, of which one eighth part is water. It is 9 miles from Plymouth and 40 from Concord. A considerable part of Newfound lake lies in the S. E. part of this town. The Mayhew turnpike passes through the E. part, and for some distance near the lake and parallel with it. It has no river, nor any important streams. Nearly one half of this town was included in the grant of Cockermouth, now Groton. The remaining part was taken from Plymouth. It was incorporated June 15, 1792. In 1801, the inhabitants erected a handsome meeting-house, but have had no settled minister. Pop. 572.

HENNIKER, a post-township in Hillsborough county, in lat. 43° 10', is bounded N. by Warner and Bradford, E. by Hopkinton, S. by Deering and Weare, and W. by Hillsborough, containing 26,500 acres. It is 27 miles from Amherst, 15 W. from Concord, and 75 from Boston. Contoocook river passes easterly through its centre and divides the town into nearly equal portions of territory and population. Its course is rather circuitous, and in many places presents scenes of considerable interest and beauty. Few places afford better prospects for the successful operation of any sort of water machinery than this. There are several ponds of considerable size. Long pond is the largest being between 1 and 2 miles in length, and from 40 to 80 rods wide—situated 1 mile N. of the centre village. Craney hill is the principal elevation, and embraces a large portion of territory on the S. side of the town. It is mostly in a state of cultivation. Henniker, in its soil and productions, can justly claim a character for as much variety and fertility as any town in the county. The soil of the hills is favorable for wheat—the valleys produce good crops of corn. The roads here have been much improved within a few years, and the bridges are kept in good repair. In 1818, a bridge across the Contoocook was constructed at an expense of $2000, having its abutments and principal pier of split granite, and fastened together with iron bolts. There is a social library, incorporated Nov. 30, 1803, containing 170 volumes. Those who have received a collegiate education are, at Dartmouth college, Tilly Howe, 1783; Elisha Morrill, 1799; David C. Proctor, 1818; James C. Goss, 1820: at Union college, Solomon Ward: at Harvard college, Timothy Darling, 1822. The number of deaths for 20 years preceding Aug. 1822, was 370, making an annual average of 18 1-2. The greatest instance of longevity was Mary Wallace, aged 95. In 1815, 31 persons died of the spotted fever. Henniker was granted July 16, 1752, by the Masonian proprietors, under the name of *Number* 6, to James Wallace, Robert Wallace and others of Londonderry. Its settlement commenced in 1761 by James Peters. A large proportion of its earliest inhabitants were from Marlborough, Mass. It was incorporated Nov. 10, 1768, when it received its present name from governor Wentworth, in honor of his friend Henniker, probably John Henniker, Esq., a merchant in London and a member of the British parliament at that time. The congregational church was formed June 7, 1769, and consisted of 9 members. Rev. Jacob Rice, a graduate of Harvard college, was ordained at the same time; dismissed Feb. 21, 1782. He is now the minister of Brownfield, Me.; and at the age of 83, is active in the discharge of his parochial duties. Rev. *Moses Sawyer*, graduated at Dartmouth college in 1799, was ordained May 26, 1802. Hon. ROBERT WALLACE, who was one of the early settlers, was long known in the various capacities of representative, senator, counsellor, and associate judge of the court of common pleas. An unusual proportion of his life, which was continued to the age of 66 years, was employed in public service. The man is rarely found who had fewer enemies at home or abroad, and who maintained through life a more unsullied reputation than Judge Wallace. He died in Jan. 1815. Pop. 1900.

HILLSBOROUGH, a post-township in Hillsborough county, in lat. 43° 9′, is bounded N. by Bradford, E. by Henniker, S. by Deering and Antrim, W. by Windsor and part of Washington, containing 27,320 acres. It is 23 miles from Amherst, 15 from Hopkinton, 24 from Concord and 70 from Boston. This town is well watered. Contoocook river passes through the S. E. corner, and affords several excellent water privileges. Hillsborough river has its source from ponds in Washington; runs in a S. E. course through the whole extent of Hillsborough, receiving the outlets of several ponds on the E. and forms a junction with the Contoocook, on the S. line of this town. The largest pond, called Lyon pond, is nearly a mile in length, and two thirds of a mile wide. This, with other considerable ponds, make a surface of about 500 acres of water. The land here is uneven, but it affords many good farms. There is a small pleasant village on the 2d N. H. turnpike which passes N. W. through this town, containing a number of dwelling-houses, stores, mills, a post office, and tavern. The meeting-house is 2 miles N. of this village. A post office was established here in 1803. There is a cotton and woollen factory, which has been incorporated. Hillsborough was formerly known by the name of *Number* 7 of frontier towns. The time it was originally granted is not ascertained. The first settlement was made in 1741, by James M'Calley, Samuel Gibson, Robert M'Clure, James Lyon and others, said to have been from Boston and its vicinity. James M'Calley was married, and his wife was the only woman in town the first year. The first children born in Hillsboro' were John M'Calley & —— Gibson, who intermarried, and received as a gift, a tract of land, from the principal proprietor. The Cape Breton war in 1744 was the means of breaking up the settlement; which was not resumed until a few years prior to 1759. In the interval, the town was granted by the Masonian proprietors to Col. John Hill, of Boston, from whom it derives its name. It was incorporated by charter, Nov. 14, 1772. A congregational church was formed Oct. 12, 1769. Rev. Jonathan Barns, who graduated at Harvard college in 1770, was ordained Nov. 25, 1772; dismissed Oct. 20, 1803; and died Aug. 3, 1805. Rev. Stephen Chapin, (now D.D.) who graduated at Harvard college in 1804, was ordained June 19, 1805; dismissed May 12, 1808. Rev. Seth Chapin, who graduated at Brown University, R. I., was ordained Jan. 1, 1812; dismissed June 26, 1816. Rev. *John Lawton*, from Windham, Vt. was installed Nov. 7, 1821. A baptist society was formed May 21, 1813, and the church gathered August 31, 1820. Pop. 1982.

HILTON'S POINT, on the Pascataqua, forms the S. E. extremity of Dover; and is so called from the circumstance of the original settlers, Edward and William Hilton, establishing themselves at this place. *See Dover*.

HINSDALE, a post-town in the S. W. corner of Cheshire co., in lat. 42° 48', is bounded N. by Chesterfield, E. by Winchester, S. by Northfield in Massachusetts, and W. by Vernon and Brattleborough in Vermont, containing 14,000 acres. It is 75 miles from Concord, 96 from Boston, 86 from Hartford, Conn., and 86 from Albany. It is well watered with springs and rivulets of the purest water. The Connecticut washes its western border; and the Ashuelot runs through the centre, forming a junction with the Connecticut, a little below the great bend, called Cooper's point. Kilburn brook rises in Pisgah mountain, runs S. and falls into Ashuelot river. Ash-swamp brook rises in West river mountain, runs a S. W. course, and falls into the Connecticut, near the site of Hinsdale's fort. There are several islands in the Connecticut in this town. On the N. line of Hinsdale, is West river mountain which extends from the banks of the Connecticut E. across the whole width of the town. Its greatest elevation is at the W. end. President Dwight states the height above low water mark to be from 800 to 900 feet. In this mountain is found iron ore, and some other minerals and fossils; but to what extent or value they exist, it has not been ascertained. Some years since, there was a slight volcanic eruption, but nothing of that kind has appeared of late. N. of Ashuelot, on the E. line of the town, is Pisgah mountain. S. of Ashuelot, is Stebbin's hill, a tract of excellent land, and principally in a high state of cultivation. The intervals here are extensive, and of an excellent quality. Between the intervals and the hills in the N. part of the town, is a large tract of plain, which is well suited for corn, rye and clover. The forest trees are yellow, pitch and white pine, interspersed with white and yellow oak, chesnut and walnut. The principal roads through this town, are the sixth N. H. turnpike which crosses in a W. and N. W. direction from Winchester to Brattleborough, and the stage road from Northfield to Chesterfield. In 1802, a bridge was built over Connecticut river opposite Brattleborough village. It was rebuilt in 1820, and is a firm, commodious and elegant structure. In 1818, a new bridge was built over Ashuelot river, in the centre of the town. On the point of a hill, not far from Connecticut river, there is to be seen the remains of an Indian fortification, constructed prior to the settlement of the town. There is a deep trench drawn across the hill to separate it from the plain back, and is continued to the river. All that is known respecting this ancient fortification is from vague and uncertain tradition. Hinsdale was incorporated Sept. 3, 1753. It received its name from Col. Ebenezer Hinsdale, one of the principal inhabitants, who was highly esteemed for his virtue and talents. It was originally a part of Northfield, and was granted by the government of Massachusetts, and was settled as early as 1683. It included in its limits, Vernon till Vermont became a separate state. The former name of this place was *Fort Dummer* and *Bridgman's Fort*. This town encountered all the difficulties of the Indian wars, and struggled with other hardships incident to frontier settlements, begun in the wilderness and remote from cultivated lands. The early settlers were protected by fort Dummer, Hinsdale's fort, Shattuck's fort and Bridgman's fort; but these were insufficient to shield them from the hostile incursions of the Indians. On the 24 June, 1746, a party of 20 Indians came to Bridgman's fort, 2 miles below fort Dummer, and attacked a number of men who were at work in a meadow. William Robbins and James Parker were killed; Daniel How and John Beeman taken prisoners; M. Gilson and Patrick Ray wounded, but recovered. How killed one of the Indians before he was taken. In 1747, they burned Bridgman's fort, killed several persons and took others from that place. In Oct., Jonathan Sawtell was taken prisoner. July 3, 1747, they waylaid a mill in Hinsdale. Col. Willard having come to the mill with a guard of 20 men, for the purpose of grinding corn, and having placed his guards, they were soon fired upon. The colonel gave such loud, and repeated orders to attack the enemy, that they fled with the greatest precipitation, leaving behind them their packs and provisions. On June 16, 1748, in crossing from Col. Hinsdale's to fort Dummer, Nathan French, Joseph Richardson, and John Frost were killed; seven others were captured, one of whom, William Bickford, died of his wounds. In 1755, they attacked a party, who were at work in the woods; killed John Hardiclay and John Alexander, and took Jonathan Colby; the others escaped to the fort. On the 27th of July, they ambushed Caleb Howe, Hilkiah Grout, and Benjamin Gaffield as they were returning from their labor in the field. (See Belknap vol. ii. p. 295, and ditto vol. iii. p. 277.) The congregational church was formed in 1763. Rev. Bunker Gay, who graduated at Harvard college in 1760, was ordained in 1763; died Oct. 19, 1815. A baptist church was formed in 1808, which has been under the pastoral care of Rev. Jeremy Parker. Pop. 890.

HOLDERNESS, post-township in Grafton county, in lat. 43° 44', is bounded N. by Campton, E. by Sandwich, Moultonborough and Centre-Harbor, S. by Centre-Harbor and New-Hampton, and W. by Pemigewasset river, separating it from Bridgewater and Plymouth. It contains 24,921 acres. It is 65 miles from Portsmouth and 40 from Concord. The soil is hard and not easily cultivated, but, when subdued, is tolerably productive. The prevailing wood is oak, mixed with pine, beech and maple. From the sap of the sugar maple, (*acer acchari-num*) a considerable quantity of sugar is annually made. The Pemigewasset imparts a portion of its benefits to this place, and there are various other streams which serve to fertilize the soil, and to furnish mill seats. Squam river, the outlet of Squam ponds, runs in a S. W. direction and empties into the Pemigewasset near the S. W. angle of the town. This stream affords excellent mill privileges, having on it, 1 saw and grain mill, 2 paper mills, 2 carding machines, 1 triphammer and 1 bark mill. There are three ponds or lakes. Squam lake, lying on the borders of this town, Moultonborough, Sandwich and Centre Harbor, is about 6 miles long, and from 4 to 5 wide. Squam pond, lying wholly in Holderness, is about 2 miles long, and 1-2 a mile wide. White Oak pond is about 1 mile long. The road from Plymouth through this place to Winnepisiogee lake, and along the borders of that lake to Wolfeborough is highly interesting; displaying scenery which is scarcely equalled in this part of our country. Holderness was first granted by charter, Oct. 10, 1751, to John Shepard and others, but this charter was forfeited because its conditions were not fulfilled by the grantees. It was again granted Oct. 24, 1761, to John Wentworth and sixty-seven others, all of them, it is said, professing the doctrines of the church of England. The first settlement was made about the year 1763, by William Piper from Durham, or its vicinity. Others of the early settlers were from Barrington. In this place, there is an episcopal church, over which, Rev. *Robert Fowle* has officiated for more than thirty years. He was graduated at Harvard college in 1786; and was ordained at Portsmouth by bishop Seabury, in 1791. There are some congregationalists, baptists, and methodists. Hon. SAMUEL LIVERMORE commenced a settlement in this town in 1765; was one of the grantees, and by purchase, became proprietor of about half of the township. He was a native of Waltham, Mass., where he was born May 14, 1732, O. S. He graduated at Princeton college in 1754; studied law with the Hon. judge Trowbridge, and was admitted to practice in the S. J. C. of N. H. in Jan. 1757. He settled in N. H. in 1758, and in 1769 was appointed King's attorney general. After the assumption of government by the people, he was in the office of attorney general. He was, several years, a delegate to the old congress. In 1782, he was appointed chief justice of the superior court. From 1792 to 1802, he was a senator of the U. S., which office he resigned on account of declining health. He died in May, 1803, aged 71. Pop. 1160.

HOLLIS, a post town, in Hillsborough county, in lat. 42° 44', is bounded N. by Milford and Amherst, E. by Dunstable, S. by the state line of Mass., W. by Brookline, containing 19,620 acres. It is 8 miles from Amherst, 36 from Concord and 42 from Boston. Nashua river waters the S. E. part, and Nisitissit crosses the S. W. extremity. There are four ponds, known by the name of Flint's, Penichook, Long, and Rocky ponds. This town contains a variety of soils. On the Nashua is some excellent interval. In the N. and S. E. parts are considerable tracts of pine land. There is a pleasant village near the centre of the town, on a somewhat elevated, having a some congregational meeting-house, a number of dwelling houses, stores, a post office, an attorney's office, and other buildings. There is a society, formed in 1801, and incorporated in 1814, for raising a fund which shall be adequate to support the gospel in this place. Its amount of funds is over $2000. There is a social library containing 120 volumes. This town has produced a large number of persons who have received a collegiate education. The following is a list of them, viz. At *Harvard College*, Rev. Peter Powers, 1754; Rev. Josiah Goodhue, 1755; Rev. Henry Cumings, D.D. 1760; Joseph Emerson, 1774; Dr. Samuel Emerson, 1785; Josiah Burge, 1787; Rev. Daniel Emerson, 1794; Rev. Joseph Emerson, 1798; Benjamin M. Farley, 1804; Benjamin Burge, M.D. 1805; John Proctor, 1813; Rev. William P. Kendrick, 1816; George F. Farley, 1816; Taylor G. Worcester, now in senior year.—At *Dartmouth college*. Rev. Samuel Worcester, D.D. 1795; Rev. Abel Farley, 1798; Rev. Mighill Blood, 1800; Rev. David Jewett, 1801; Rev. Caleb J. Tenney, 1801; Jonathan Eastman, 1803; N. Hardy, 1803; Rev. Stephen Farley, 1804; Rev. Eli Smith, 1809; Rev. Grant Powers, 1810; Rev. Leonard Jewett, 1810; Dr. Noah Hardy, 1812; Luke Eastman, 1812.—At *Yale college*. Joseph E. Worcester, 1811; Rev. Ralph Emerson, 1811.—At *Brown university*. Rev. Daniel Kendrick, 1809; Luther Smith. At *Middlebury college*. William Tenney, 1808; Rev. Fifield Holt & Solomon Hardy.— At *Tennessee college*. Eli Sawtell. Besides these, all of whom were natives of Hollis, are several who have received honorary degrees from the New-England colleges. Rev. Noah Worcester received the degree of D. D. from Harvard college in 1818, and Rev. Thomas Worcester that of A.M. from Dartmouth college, in 1806. The oldest person living in the preceding list is the venerable Dr. Cumings of Billerica, who has been the minister of that place more than 60 years. The number of deaths for 25 years ending in 1818, was 567. One in nine lived to the age of 80 years or upwards. Mrs. Ulrick, a native of Ireland, died here in 1789, at the age of 104—was active till after she was an hundred. The original name of Hollis was *Nisitissit*, its Indian name. It was afterwards the West Parish of Dunstable. The first settlement was made by Capt. Peter Powers in 1731. Peter Powers, his son, was the first child born in town. It was incorporated April 3, 1746. The name is either derived from Thomas Hollis, a distinguished benefactor of Harvard college, or from the Duke of New-Castle, whose name was Hollis. The congregational church was formed in 1743. Rev. Daniel Emerson, from Reading, who graduated at Harvard college in 1739, was ordained April 20, 1743; died Sept. 30, 1801, aged 85. Rev. *Eli Smith*, who graduated at Brown University in 1792, was ordained as colleague with Mr. Emerson, Nov. 27, 1793. The number of communicants is about 270. The late NOAH WORCESTER, Esq, was a resident in this town. For a notice of him, see *Historical Collections* for 1822, p. 260. Pop. 1543.

HOOKSETT, post town, in Hillsborough county, in lat. 43° 5,′ is bounded N. by Bow and Allenstown, E. by Deerfield and Candia, S. by Chester and Manchester, and W. by Goffstown. It is nine miles from Concord, 12 from Hopkinton, and 54 from Boston. The river Merrimack, whose course here is nearly N. and S. passes through this town, a little W. of the centre. Here are those beautiful falls, known by the name of Isle of Hooksett Falls. The descent of water is about 16 feet perpendicular in 30 rods. A high rock divides the stream, and a smaller rock lies between that and the western shore. From an eminence, called the Pinnacle, on the W. side, there is a delightful landscape; the water above and below the falls, the verdant banks, the cultivated fields, and the distant hills in the back ground, form a picturesque scene, which relieves the eye of the traveller from the dull uniformity of a road not rendered remarkably pleasant. The soil in a considerable portion of this town is not of the most fertile character, but there are some excellent farms under a good state of cultivation, and the interests of agriculture receive more attention than formerly. There is a small village on the W. side of the river, containing two taverns, two stores and a number of dwelling-houses and mechanics' shops. The Londonderry turnpike passes through this village. There is a strong and well built bridge over Merrimack river. Hooksett canal is in this town. It is 1-4 of a mile long—the fall is 16 feet perpendicular. It cost $6,210. Hooksett was detached from Chester, Goffstown and Dunbarton, and incorporated as a separate town in June, 1822. No enumeration has been made of the number of inhabitants. The number of voters is 150. A large and extensive cotton factory is soon to be built on the E. side of the river, which will add to the business and wealth of the place.

HOPKINTON, a post town, and one of the seats of justice in Hillsborough county, is situated in lat. 43° 11′, and is bounded N. by Warner and Boscawen, E. by Concord, S. by Bow, Dunbarton and Weare, and W. by Henniker. It contains 26,967 acres. It is 28 miles N. of Amherst, 7 W. of Concord, 46 N. E. of Keene, 30 S. E. of Newport, 50 W. of Portsmouth and 65 N. N. W. of Boston. Contoocook river flows from Henniker into the southwesterly part of this town, and meanders in a N. E. direction. In its course it receives Warner and Blackwater rivers and several large brooks, and empties into Merrimack river at Concord. On these streams are some valuable tracts of interval and meadow lands, which were laid out in small parcels, and are principally owned by persons who have upland farms. Widely extended hills comprise a considerable part of the surface S. of Contoocook river. They were formerly covered with a heavy growth of deciduous trees, interspersed with evergreens; but these swells now exhibit many well cultivated farms. The declivities and vales are now found the most easy lands for cultivation, producing fine crops of grass, corn, rye, &c. The hills on the N. of the river were formerly covered with white, black, and yellow oak. The intervening grounds and some bordering on the S. side of the river, were well clad with the various kinds of pine and other trees. The inhabitants are accommodated with numerous well made common roads, which are kept in very good repair; but those of the greatest public travel through the town have been located anew in many places and are not well made. The Londonderry Branch turnpike extends about two miles through the S. E. part of the town. There is a pleasant village, 7 miles from the state-

P

house in Concord, containing a congregational meeting house, a spacious town and court house, a jail, 42 dwelling houses, 4 stores and 4 attorneys'. offices. There are in the town a second congregational meeting house, a baptist meeting house, 5 grist mills, 5 saw mills, 2 clothing mills, 1 trip hammer, and 2 mills for circular sawing clapboards. There is a social library, containing 130 volumes. Hopkinton was granted by Massachusetts, Jan. 16, 1735, to John Jones and others, of Hopkinton in that state, and was called *Number* 5, and afterwards *New-Hopkinton*. The first settlement was made about 1740, by emigrants from Hopkinton, Ms. In consequence of the French and Indian war, which commenced in 1744, the inhabitants were compelled to leave the place, and the settlement was not resumed till after the conclusion of that war. This town suffered from Indian depredations. On the 22d of April, 1746, six Indians, armed with muskets, tomahawks, knives, &c., broke into a garrison, and took prisoners eight persons, while in their beds, viz. Mr. Woodwell, his wife, two sons and a daughter, Samuel Burbank, and his two sons, Caleb and Jonathan. *See Hist. Coll. for* 1822, *p.* 284. Abraham Kimball was the first male child born in town—he was born April 18, 1741. He is now (1823) living in Peacham, Vt. at the advanced age of 82 years. On the 13th of April, 1753, while going from Kimball's garrison to Putney's garrison, he was taken by the Indians, who, also, at the same time, took Samuel Putney, a man 60 years of age. On the 3d day after they were taken, the Indians being on the hills, W. of Boscawen plains were so suddenly attacked by some of the inhabitants of Boscawen, that they fled, leaving Putney in the rear, and Kimball escaped through the help of a dog, who seized an Indian while in the act of drawing his tomahawk to kill Kimball. Nov. 30, 1750, Henry Mellen and others received a grant from the Masonian proprietors which occasioned a long and perplexing dispute with the proprietors of Bow. It was finally settled by the incorporating charter, which was granted Jan. 11, 1765. The congregational church was gathered Nov. 23, 1757, and Rev. James Scales was ordained the same day. " The ordination was solemnized in Putney's fort, so called, and the numerous spectators attended the solemnity abroad in the open air, the weather being very warm, calm and pleasant for the season." Mr. Scales was dismissed July 4, 1770, and Rev. Elijah Fletcher, from Westford, who graduated at Harvard College in 1769, was ordained Jan. 27, 1723. He died April 8, 1786, aged 39. Rev. Jacob Cram was ordained Feb. 25, 1789; dismissed Jan. 6, 1792. Rev. Ethan Smith was installed March 12, 1800; dismissed Dec. 16, 1817. Rev. *Roger C. Hatch*, who graduated at Yale College in 1815, was ordained Oct. 21, 1818. The baptist society was formed the 8th of May, 1771. The episcopal society, by the name of Christ's Church, was established in 1803, and admitted to the union with the other churches in the state, and to a seat in convention, on the 17th of Aug., in the same year. Pop. 2437, of whom 520 are electors.

I.

INDIAN STREAM, Coos co., the principal and the most northerly source of Connecticut river, rises in the highlands near the N. limit of the state, and pursues almost a direct S. W. course to its junction with the E. branch flowing from lake Connecticut.

ISINGLASS river takes its rise from Long pond in Barrington and Bow pond in Strafford, and after receiving the waters of several other ponds, unites with the Cocheco near the S. part of Rochester.

ISRAEL'S river, is formed by the waters which descend in cataracts from the summits of Mounts Adams and Jefferson, and running N. W. it passes through Durand and Jefferson, discharging itself into the Connecticut near the centre of Lancaster. It is a beautiful stream, and received its name from Israel Glines, a hunter, who with his brother frequented these regions long before the settlement of the county.

ISLES OF SHOALS, a name appropriated to a cluster of islands, 8 in number, situated 9 miles S. E. of the Portsmouth light-house, 21 N. E. of Newburyport lights, and in lat. 42° 59'. The line which divides this state from Maine, passes through these islands, leaving Haley's, Hog, Duck, Cedar, and Malaga isles on the N. E. in Maine, and Gosport, or Star-island, White and Londonner's isles on the S. W. in New-Hampshire. The largest is Hog island, containing 350 acres. Star island contains 150; Haley's, 100; and the largest of the others about 8—the smallest 1 acre. These islands were discovered by the celebrated John Smith, in 1614, and were named by him *Smith's Isles.* They are a bed of rocks, raising their disjointed heads above the water, and for the most part covered with a thin soil—their appearance is inhospitable; and but for their advantageous situation for carrying on the fisheries, would probably never have been inhabited. Upon all the islands are chasms in the rocks, having the appearance of being caused by earthquakes. The most remarkable is on Star island (Gosport,) in which one Betty Moody secreted herself when the Indians visited the island and took away many female captives; and thence called to this day "*Betty Moody's hole.*" For more than a century previous to the revolution, these islands were populous, containing from 300 to 600 souls. They had a court-house on Haley's island; a meeting-house, first on Hog island, and afterwards on Star island. From 3 to 4 thousand quintals fish were annually caught and cured here, and 7 or 8 schooners, besides numerous boats, were employed in the business. The business of these islands has since very greatly decreased; there are now 66 inhabitants in Gosport. William Pepperell and a Mr. Gibbons, from Topsham, Eng. were among the first settlers at the Shoals—the former an ancestor of the celebrated Sir William Pepperell. Previous to 1641, a meeting-house was erected on Hog island, and regular preaching was thereafter had until 1775—though Rev. John Tucke was the only clergyman ordained. He continued to preach from his ordination in 1732, till his death Aug. 12, 1773. A woman, of the name of Pusley died in Gosport, in 1795, aged 90. In her life time she kept two cows. The hay on which they fed in winter, she used to cut in summer, among the rocks, with a *knife* with her own hands. Her cows, it was said, were always in good order. They were taken from her, but paid for, by the British, in 1775, and killed, to

J.

JAFFREY, a post-township, in Cheshire county, in lat. 42° 50', is bounded N. by Dublin, E. by Peterborough and Sharon, S. by Rindge and Fitzwilliam, W. by Troy and Marlborough, containing 25,600 acres. It it 62 miles N. W. from Boston and 46 S. 46° W. from Concord. The Grand Monadnock is situated in the N. W. part of this town and in Dublin. (See *Monadnock mountain*.) Innumerable streams of water issue from the mountain. Those which issue from the western side, discharge themselves into the Connecticut river; those from the eastern form the head waters of Contoocook river. The largest stream rises about 100 rods from the summit, and descends in a S. E. direction. With this brook, the thirsty and fatigued visitors of the mountain associate the most pleasing recollections. Thirty years since, Monadnock was nearly covered with evergreen wood of considerable growth. By the repeated ravages of fire, it now presents to the distant beholder, nothing but a barren and bald rock. But on ascending, we find plats of earth sufficient to give growth to the blueberry, cranberry, mountain ash, and a variety of shrubs. Some caves are discovered, which excite curiosity. They appear to have been formed by large fissures, and by extensive strata being thrown from their primitive state, and forming different angles with each other and with perpendicular precipices. The uneven soil of Jaffrey, affording numerous meadows and early and rich pasture, is peculiarly adapted to raising cattle. There are several ponds in this town. Out of the no small grief of the good old woman.

three, issue streams sufficient to carry mills erected near their outlets. In the largest, which is 400 rods long and 140 wide, is an island comprising about 10 acres. The 3d N. H. turnpike passes through this town in a S. E. direction—on this turnpike a mail stage runs six days in a week. About 1 1-2 miles S. E. of the mountain is the "Monadnock mineral spring." Some conveniences have been made for the use of the waters. The spring is slightly impregnated with carbonate of iron and sulphate of soda. It preserves so uniform a temperature, as never to have been known to freeze. Where the spring issues from the earth, yellow ochre is thrown out. Upwards of 30 tons have been transported to Boston and its vicinity, and a considerable quantity yet remains. In this town are a meeting-house, built in 1775, near the centre and principal village, a cotton and woollen factory, an oil mill, three grain and saw mills, and several stores. The purchasers of Mason's title to this town granted it to 40 persons, in 1749, who held their first meeting at Dunstable, Jan. 16, 1750. The first permanent settlement was made in 1758 by one Grout and John Davison. It had been attempted in 1753 by Richard Peabody, Moses Stickney and a few others, who remained but two or three years. The first child was born in town in 1753—a son of Moses Stickney. Jaffrey was incorporated in 1773, receiving its name from George Jaffrey, Esq. of Portsmouth, one of the Masonian proprietors. Its former name was *Middle Monadnock*, or *No. 2*. The deaths for the last 10 years have averaged 13 a year, about one to 100. In 1780, a congregational church was formed, and in 1782, the Rev. *Laban Ainsworth*, a graduate of Dartmouth college in 1778, was ordained as pastor. There are here a social library, a ladies' library and a reading society, having in all about 300 volumes; also charitable associations. Pop. 1339.

JEFFERSON, post-town, in the county of Coos, comprising 26,076 acres of land and water, is bounded N. by Lancaster, E. by Kilkenny, S. by Bretton Woods, W. by Whitefield. The turnpike road from Lancaster to Portland passes through this town; and another road passing through Durand and N. of the White Mountains, branches from the turnpike here. Pondicherry pond, in this town, is about 200 rods in diameter, and is the principal source of John's river. Pondicherry bay is about 200 rods wide and one hundred long. The name is derived from that of the mountain between Jefferson and Bretton-Woods. Mount Pliny lies in the easterly part of this town, and around its base there is excellent grazing and tillage land. On the S. W. side of this mountain are several fine farms, which command a most delightful view of the White Mountains. The W. part of the town is low, and too wet for cultivation. Israel's river passes through Jefferson from S. E. to N. W., and here receives a considerable branch. Jefferson was granted, under the name of *Dartmouth*, Oct. 3, 1765, to John Goffe; and re-granted June 26, 1772, to March H. Wentworth and others. The town was first settled by Col. Joseph Whipple, Samuel Hart and others about the year 1773. It was incorporated Dec. 8, 1796, by the legislature of this state, and received its present name, in honor of the illustrious Jefferson. During the war of the revolution, Col. Whipple was here captured in his own house by a party of Indians, headed by a white man. He requested and obtained leave to go into another room to change his apparel, and to take some necessary articles for his march to Canada. Seizing the opportunity, he escaped from a back window, fled to the woods, where he eluded the search of his pursuers, and safely arrived among other inhabitants. A Mr. Gotham, who then lived with the colonel, made his escape at the same time, and taking directly for the river, was fired upon while crossing it on a log; the ball, however, did not reach him. The party plundered the house, and supplying themselves plentifully with provisions, departed without further outrage. There are two school districts in this town. There is no settled minister, though a regular baptist church was sometime since formed and now exists. Pop. 252.

JOHN'S RIVER, has its principal source in Pondicherry, a pond of considerable magnitude in Jefferson. Its most southerly branches rise in Bretton-Woods, Whitefield and Dalton, and its northerly in Lancaster. These branches unite with the main stream in Dalton, which falls into the Connecticut about 60 rods above the head of the Fifteen-Mile falls—where its mouth is about 30 yards wide. This river, and Israel's, in Lancaster, derived their names from John and Israel Glines, two brothers, who hunted beaver and other animals on these rivers previous to the settlement of any part of the county.

K.

KEARSARGE mountain, in the county of Hillsborough, is in lat. 43° 22', and situated between the towns of Sutton and Salisbury, extending into both towns. The line between Wilmot and Warner passes over the summit. Kearsarge is elevated 2461 feet above the level of the sea, and is the highest mountain in Hillsborough county. Its summits are now a bare mass of granite, presenting an irregular and broken surface; the sides are covered with a thick growth of wood. The prospect from this mountain is in a clear sky very wide and beautiful.

KEENE, a post-town, and the half shire in Cheshire county, in lat. 42° 57′, is bounded N. by Surry and Gilsum, E. by Sullivan and Roxbury, S. by Swanzey, S. E. by Marlborough, W. by Chesterfield and Westmoreland, containing by charter six miles square. But its limits have been reduced by contributions to Sullivan and Roxbury, both receiving large tracts from this town. It is 80 miles from Boston, 60 from Dartmouth College, 43 from Windsor, 40 from Amherst, and 55 from Concord. The soil consists of three kinds, viz. meadow or interval, light sandy plains, and upland. The latter lies on the outskirts of the town, bounding on the E., W. and N. a flat or valley, consisting of the first and second kinds, and 3 miles in width and the same in extent from N. to S. This valley is divided in the centre by the Ashuelot river, and from the unusual extent of level which it presents, variegated by cultivation, affords a fine prospect to the traveller approaching it from the high land, by which it is surrounded. Ashuelot river has its source in a pond in Washington, and discharges itself into the Connecticut at Hinsdale, 20 miles distant from Keene. (See *Ashuelot river*.) Keene has been called one of the "prettiest villages" in New-England; and President Dwight in his travels, pronounces it one of the pleasantest inland towns he had seen. The principal village is situated on a flat, E. of the Ashuelot, nearly equidistant from that and the upland. It contains the meeting house, court house, bank, post-office, and 120 dwelling houses, besides a number of large stores and mechanic shops. It is particularly entitled to notice for the extent, width, and uniform level of its streets. The main street, extending one mile in a straight line, is almost a perfect level, and is well ornamented with trees. The buildings are good and well arranged. There is another village in the W. part of the town, containing a baptist meeting house and 15 or 20 dwelling houses.—Keene is a place of considerable business. It has an extensive bookstore and bindery, connected with a printing establishment; two glass factories established in 1814; and several stores unusually large for the country. The first newspaper published here was the "New-Hampshire Recorder," by James D. Griffith. It commenced in 1787; discontinued March 3, 1791. "The Cheshire Advertiser" succeeded Jan. 1, 1792; was published one year, by Mr. Griffith. "The Columbian Informer," by Henry Blake, commenced April 3, 1793; was followed August, 1799, by "The Rising Sun," published by C. Sturtevant, jr. & Co. till August, 1798. The "New-Hampshire Sentinel," by John Prentiss, commenced in March, 1799, and next to the Gazette and Journal at Portsmouth, is the oldest paper in the State.— Keene was originally granted by Massachusetts. Its first settlement commenced about the year 1734, by Jeremiah Hall, Elisha Root, Nathaniel Rockwood, Seth Heaton, Josiah Fisher, Nathan Blake and others. Its original name was *Upper Ashuelot*. It was incorporated with its present name, April 11, 1753, which is derived from an English nobleman, perhaps Sir Benjamin Keene, British minister at Spain and contemporary with Gov. B. Wentworth, who granted the charter. In 1736, the settlement had so increased that a meeting house was erected, and in two years after, a minister was settled. But the usual scourge, which attended the frontier settlements, visited this town. In 1745, the Indians killed Josiah Fisher, a deacon of the church; in 1746, they attacked the fort, the only protection of the inhabitants. They were however discovered by Capt. Ephraim Dorman in season to prevent their taking it. He was attacked by two Indians, but defended himself successfully against them, and reached the fort. An action ensued, in which John Bullard was killed; Mrs. M'Kenney, who being out of the fort, was stabbed and died; and Nathan Blake taken prisoner, carried to Canada, where he remained two years. Mr. Blake afterwards returned to Keene, where he lived till his death, in 1811, at the age of 99 years and 5 months. When he was 94, he married a widow of 60. The Indians burnt all the buildings in the settlement, including the meeting house. The inhabitants continued in the fort until April 1747, when the town was abandoned. In 1753, they returned, and recommenced their settlements.—In 1755, the Indians again attacked the fort. Their number was great, and the onset violent, but the vigilance and courage of Capt. Syms successfully defended it. After burning several buildings, killing cattle, &c. they withdrew. This was in June. In July, they again invaded the town, but with little success. The congregational church was formed Oct. 18, 1738. Rev. Jacob Bacon, a native of Wrentham, Ms. who graduated at Harvard college in 1731, was ordained when the church was gathered. He remained the minister until April, 1747, when the settlement being broken up, he went to Plymouth. He died at Rowley in 1787, aged 81. Rev. Ezra Carpenter, a graduate of Harvard college in 1720, was settled over Keene and Swanzey, Oct. 4, 1753; continued his relation to Keene till 1760. Rev. Clement Sumner, who graduated at Yale college in 1758, was ordained June 11, 1761; dismissed April 30, 1772. Rev. Aaron Hall, who graduated at Yale college in 1772, was ordained Feb. 19, 1778; died Aug. 12, 1814. Rev. David Oliphant, ordained May 25, 1815; dismissed Dec. 1, 1817. Rev. *Zedekiah S. Barstow*, a graduate of Yale college in 1813, was ordained July 1, 1818. The church consists of nearly 200 members. There have been 1185 baptisms. A baptist church was formed in 1816. Rev. Ferris Moore was ordained over it, Dec. 30, 1819; dismissed March, 1821. Col. ISAAC WYMAN, an active and influential man, marched the first detachment of men from this town in the war of the revolution, and was present at the battle of Breed's Hill. Pop. 1895.

KENSINGTON, township, Rockingham co., lat. 42° 47′, is bounded N. by Exeter, E. by Hampton-Falls, S. by South-Hampton, W. by East-Kingston—and is 45 miles from Boston, 40 from Concord. It is nearly of a square form, and comprises 7,045 acres. This town has no streams of any note; its surface is pretty even. There is but one pond, and that is small, but deep and muddy. Kensington was settled at an early period, and was originally a part of Hampton, from which it was detached and incorporated April 1, 1737. It contained more inhabitants at the commencement of the revolution than it does at present. The congregational church was established about the year 1737. The pastors who have been successively settled over it, are Rev. Jeremiah Fogg, ordained Nov. 1737, and died Dec. 1, 1789; Rev. Napthali Shaw, ordained Jan. 30, 1793, dismissed in 1812; Rev. Nathaniel Kennedy, ordained Jan. 13, 1813, dismissed June, 1816. Beside the congregationalists, there is a baptist society and some friends. There is a social library, incorporated in 1798. The Rev. Timothy Hilliard, late pastor of the first church in Cambridge, was a native of this town, born in 1746. He graduated at Harvard college, first settled at Barnstable, and afterwards at Cambridge, where he died May 9, 1790. Pop. 709.

KILKENNY, Coos county, lat. 44° 27′, is an irregular township, bounded W. by Jefferson and Lancaster, N. by Piercy, E. by Paul's-burgh, Maynesborough and Durand, S. by ungranted land. It contains 15,906 acres. This place was granted to Jonathan Warner, Esq. and others June 4, 1774, and contains but 24 inhabitants—they are poor, and for aught that appears to the contrary, must always remain so, as they may be deemed actual trespassers on that part of creation, destined by its author for the residence of bears, wolves, moose, and other animals of the forest! An exception, however, may possibly be made in favor of a narrow strip of land along the S. boundary of the town. Pilot and Willard's mountains, so called from a dog and his master, cover a considerable part of this town. Willard, a hunter, had been lost two or three days on these mountains, on the E. side of which his camp was situated. Each day, he observed, his dog Pilot left him, as he supposed, in pursuit of game; but towards night he would constantly return. Willard being on the second or third day nearly exhausted with fatigue and hunger, put himself under the guidance of his dog, who in a short time conducted him in safety to his camp.

KINGSTON, post-township, Rockingham county, is situated in lat. 42° 55′ 15″, and bounded N. by Brentwood, E. by East-Kingston, S. by Newtown and Plaistow, W. by Hampstead and Hawke. It is distant from Concord 37 miles, from Exeter 6, from Portsmouth 20; and contains 12,188 acres, of which 800 are supposed to be water. There are several ponds in this town. The largest is Great pond, which lies on the W. of the village, and contains upwards of 300 acres, with an island of 10 or 12 acres, covered with wood. Country pond, in the S. E. and partly in Newtown, contains about 200 acres, and has also an island of 6 or 8 acres covered with wood. The other ponds are called Little, Moon, Long and Barberry ponds. Near the centre of the town is an extensive plain, on which is situated the principal village, the meeting-house, and the academy. There are no high hills in Kingston; those called the Great hill and Rockrimmon are the highest The former is on the post-road to Exeter; the latter on the W. of the plain near Hawke line, and is a body of granite extending over 20 or 30 acres, mostly covered with soil and a growth of wood. On its

W. side is an abrupt descent of nearly 100 feet to the plain. The soil of Kingston is generally loamy bottomed on sand and gravel, though in some places clay predominates. The plain is a rich loam and very fertile. The rocks are mostly granite, although green porphyry, and fragments of many other kinds may be seen. No metallic ores have been discovered excepting iron, and that principally bog ore, found in Great pond and the swamps. This was formerly wrought in considerable quantities, but with no great success. In some places red and yellow ochre have been found of a quality suitable for paint. The natural growth of wood was principally of the various kinds of oak and other hard timber, with cedar in the swamps. The charter of Kingston was granted by Lt. governor Usher, Aug. 6, 1694, to James Prescott, Ebenezer Webster and others, from Hampton. The grant also comprehended what now forms the towns of East-Kingston, Hawke, and Sandown. Soon after the grant was made, the proprietors erected garrison houses on the plain, and commenced the cultivation of their lands. They were discouraged, however, from the dangers and difficulties of the succeeding hostilities, and many of them returned home within two years. After the war closed, they renewed their enterprize, but it was not until 1725, that they were able to procure the settlement of a minister. Before the settlement of Hampton, the Indians resorted there for the variety of fish found in the ponds. During the wars, they were extremely troublesome to the inhabitants, and several were killed. In 1707, Stephen and Jacob Gilman, brothers, were ambushed between Kingston and Exeter, but fortunately escaped to the garrison. In 1712, Stephen Gilman and Ebenezer Stevens were wounded at Kingston, the former taken and put to death. Sept. 7, 1724, Jabez Colman and his son were killed while at work in their field. Four children were also taken, one escaped, and the others were afterwards redeemed. Many Indian implements, with some ancient French coin, have been ploughed up in the vicinity of the ponds, such as jasper and quartz arrow-heads, axes, gouges, and hammers of different kinds of stones. This town is generally healthy, though it has afforded no remarkable instances of longevity. Rev. Ward Clark was the first settled minister of Kingston, though religious services had been regularly performed for several years previous to his settlement by Rev. Mr. Choate from Ipswich. Mr. Clark was ordained in 1725, and died in 1737, aged 34. He was succeeded by Rev. Joseph Secombe, a learned divine, who died in 1760. In the year following, Rev. Amos Tappan was ordained; he died in 1771. In 1776, Rev. Elihu Thayer, D. D. was installed, who preached until 1812, and died aged 65. Rev. *John Turner*, was installed over a new congregational society in 1818. Major EBENEZER STEVENS, one of the early settlers, was a very distinguished and useful citizen; and such was his integrity and benevolence, that differences among the people were submitted to his decision with perfect confidence. He sustained many important public functions, and discharged every duty with ability and faithfulness. His descendants now live in Kingston. This town was also the residence of the Hon. JOSIAH BARTLETT, one of the first worthies of the state, and an eminent physician. He commenced his practice in Kingston in 1761, and soon acquired a reputation for great skill, particularly in the treatment of the *cynanche maligna*, or throat distemper, then so prevalent and mortal. His public career commenced in 1765, and from that time to his death he was an unwearied advocate and supporter of the liberties of America. He was for some time chief justice of the colony, afterwards president of the state, and the first governor under its free constitution. He died May 19, 1795, at the age of 65 years. Pop. 847.

L.

LAMPREY river rises on the W. of Saddleback mountain in Northwood. Taking a S. course it passes into Deerfield and thence into Raymond, where it receives a W. branch from Candia. Taking a S. direction it receives the waters of Jones' pond in Raymond; and thence, as it flows through Epping, the Patuckaway river unites with it. In its course through Lee and Durham, it receives the waters of North, Little and Piscassick rivers, and meets the tide about 2 miles above the Great Bay.

LANCASTER, a post-town, in the county of Coos, is situated in lat. 44° 29', on the southeastern bank of Connecticut river, which forms and washes its N. W. boundary, a distance of ten miles. It is bounded S. W. by Dalton, S. by Whitefield and Jefferson, E. and N. E. by Kilkenny and Northumberland; and lies distant 110 miles W. from Portland, 130 N. from Portsmouth, 95 almost due N. from Concord, and 75 above Dartmouth College—containing about 23,480 acres. Besides the Connecticut, which is deep and about 22 rods in width while it passes through Lancaster, the town is watered by Israel's river and several considerable brooks. Across this river a bridge and three dams are thrown; the waters from the last of which turn four grist and two saw-mills, three carding machines, and two fulling mills. There are several ponds in Lancaster, the largest of which is called Martin-meadow pond, from Martin, a hunter. This communicates with Little pond. The one covers perhaps 150, and the other 40 acres; and both are situated in the southern part of the town. Lancaster is situated near lofty mountains, but is not itself mountainous. There are three hills in the S. part of the town, called Martin meadow Hills; and the land in the S. E. part lies too high up the mountains for cultivation. The soil along the Connecticut is alluvial, the meadows extending back nearly three-fourths of a mile; and at the mouth of Israel's river much farther. To these succeed a border of white pine or spruce land, which is generally level and productive when properly cultivated. The next region was covered in its natural state with a thick growth of sugar maple, beech, bass, ash, and other deciduous forest trees. In many places, however, the spruce and fir abound, particularly in the low lands, with here and there a cedar swamp. The larch and mountain ash are not unknown to the inhabitants of Lancaster, as the one occupies considerable tracts between the meadows and the high lands, and the other is scattered among the other timber and underbrush. The village, or most compact part of the town, lies on a street extending from the bridge across Israel's river northwardly. There is a considerable number of buildings on the southerly side of the river, and on that side stands the meeting-house. At the northerly end of the street stand the court-house and jail. Previous to their incorporation, Lancaster, Northumberland and Stratford in this state, and Lunenburg, Guildhall and Maidstone, Vt. were designated by the Indian name of *Coos*, which signifies crooked, and was originally applied to that part of the Connecticut on which these towns are situated. Lancaster was granted to Capt. David Page and others, July 5, 1763. In the fall of that year, he, with his family, and Edward Bucknam and Emmons Stockwell, moved into the town. They were its first settlers, and suffered the hardships which always attend emigrants to new countries. David Page, son of the gentleman first mentioned, had marked a path through the woods from Haverhill to Lancaster, a distance of 48 miles, in June of that year; and this path was followed by the family in the month of September following to Lancaster. At that time, there was not a single inhabitant on the whole route. The war of the revolution tended to retard the settlement of the town. Every person above Captain Stockwell's, before mentioned as one of the first settlers, left the country, and fled for safety to the older settlements. He patriotically resolved to stay and abide the consequences; and by his example induced several others to do likewise. After the war closed, the town settled with considerable rapidity, and has since gradually increased in wealth and population. The number of deaths in Lancaster, from July 1794, to June 1814, was 121. In July 1794, about thirty years after the settlement of the place, a congregational church was gathered, and on the 18th Sept. following, Rev. *Joseph Willard* was installed as pastor. The town at that time contained thirty-six families. Besides his church and congregation, there is a regular baptist, and a methodist church in town: but no minister is settled over either. There are also christians of other denominations in town, but none who have regularly organized churches, or places of public worship. Pop. 644.

LANDAFF, a township in Grafton county, in lat. 44° 7', is bounded N. E. by Concord and Franconia, E. by Lincoln, S. W. by Coventry, and W. by Bath, containing 29,200 acres. Its distance from Haverhill Corner is about 12 miles, and from Concord 90 miles. Wild Amonoosuck river runs from S. E. to N. W. through the S. part of the town and nearly parallel the whole distance with the S. W. boundary line.—Through the north-westerly extremity passes the Great Amonoosuck river. Landaff mountain in the E. part, Cobble Hill in the centre, and Bald hill in the W. are the principal elevations. The meeting house is near the N. W. part of the town. The soil in some parts is very fertile, and there is a number of good farms. Landaff was granted Jan. 3, 1764, to James Avery and others, but the grantees not fulfilling the conditions of the charter, it was, agreeably to the usage then practised, declared by the governor and council to be forfeited. It was then granted to Dartmouth College; but after the revolution, the first grantees renewed their claim, alleging that the adjudication of the forfeiture was irregular. One or two cases were tried by the proper judicature, and the lands awarded to the first proprietors. Its settlement had commenced under the patronage of the government of D. College, which was at considerable expense in building mills, opening roads and clearing lands, when, by the decision of the proper tribunal, this institution was compelled to abandon all their improvements.— Subsequent grants to the college, however, in some measure made up their loss. A baptist church was formed here in 1788. There are freewill and methodist societies, which have occasional preaching. Pop. 769.

LANGDON, post-township, Cheshire co., in lat. 43° 10', is bounded N. by Charlestown, E. by Acworth, S. by Alstead and Walpole, W. by Walpole and Charlestown, containing 9,891 acres. It is 17 miles from Keene, 50 from Concord. The principal village is 3 miles E. from Connecticut river, and 6 from Bellows Falls. The soil here is adapted to grain of various kinds, and flax.— The agricultural products in 1820. were 12,000 lbs. butter, 16,000 lbs. cheese, 46,000 lbs. beef, 65,000 lbs. pork, 6,200 lbs. flax, with 337 bbls. cider. Cheshire turnpike, leading from Charlestown to Keene, passes through Langdon. A considerable branch of Cold river passes S. W. through the whole extent of this town, and unites with the main branch near the S. line. Langdon, named in honor of the late Gov. Langdon, was incorporated Jan. 11, 1787. Its settlement commenced by Seth Walker, in 1773; Nathaniel Rice and Jonathan Willard, in 1774. A congregational church was formed Nov. 8, 1792; and a universal church April 5, 1805, over which Rev. Abner Kneeland was ordained Oct. 30, 1805; dismissed in 1810. In 1817, Rev. *Robert Bartlett* commenced preaching in this place. A new congregational church and society were formed in 1820. Pop. 654.

LEBANON, post town, in Grafton county, on Connecticut river, in lat. 43° 38', is bounded N. by Hanover, E. by Enfield, S. by Plainfield, W. by Hartford, Vt. containing 23,000 acres. It is 4 miles S. of Dartm. College, 49 from Concord, 90 from Portsmouth, and 110 from Boston. Besides the Connecticut on its W. border, this town is watered by Mascomy river, running from E. to W. through its centre, and affording many valuable mill seats and a constant supply of water. Over this river, the 4th N. H. turnpike corporation supports 5 bridges, and the town 4. The soil here is alluvial. The intervals on the Connecticut extend back from the river about half a mile. There are meadows or intervals on Mascomy river. To these succeed a border of white pine and oak. The next division is sugar maple, birch, beech, bass, ash, hemlock, &c. The mountain ash is found in almost all the hilly parts of the town. The principal village is situated on a plain near the central part, at the head of the falls of Mascomy river. It contains between 40 and 50 families, has a meeting-house, 2 school-houses, 3 stores, 2 taverns, and a number of mechanics. There is a social library containing upwards of 300 vols. The Croydon turnpike intersects the 4th N. H. turnpike in this village. The former runs S. E.; the latter from E. to W. There are falls in the Connecticut in this town, which have been locked and canalled by a company called the White River Company. Lyman's bridge connects this town with Hartford, Vt. A medicinal spring has lately been discovered. A lead mine has been opened, and there has been lately found on Enfield line, near the outlet of the Great pond, a vein of iron ore, composed of the magnetic oxide, mixed with the pyrites. Lebanon was granted July 4, 1761, to 62 proprietors, belonging to Norwich, Mansfield and Lebanon, Conn. The first settlers were William Downer, William Dana, Levi Hyde, Charles Hill, Silas Waterman, Nathaniel Porter, from the towns just mentioned. It was the first town settled on Connecticut river to the N. of Charlestown. The first settlers were a hardy, brave people, tenacious of their principles; many of them were men of strong minds, good habits, correct principles, and good common education. A congregational church was formed in 1771. Rev. Isaiah Potter was installed in 1772, and died in 1817. A baptist church was formed in 1782 by Rev. Jedidiah Hibbard. A universalist society was formed in 1813. Thomas Waterman, Esq., now a resident in town, was the first male child born in Lebanon. Pop. 1700.

LEE, post-town, in the S. part of Strafford county, is in lat. 43° 7,' and bounded N. by Madbury, E. by Durham, S. by New-Market and Epping, W. by Nottingham and Barrington, and comprises an area of 11,625 acres, 300 of which are water. In the N. part of the town lies Wheelwright's pond, containing about 165 acres, and forming the principal source of Oyster river. This pond is remarkable for the sea or white perch formerly taken here by angling in large quantities, weighing 2 and 3 lbs. From the N. E. extremity of Epping, Lamprey river enters Lee, and after a serpentine course of about 7 miles, it passes into Durham. Other parts of he town are watered by Little, North, and Oyster rivers. There are in Lee 3 bridges over Lamprey river, 3 over Little, 2 over North, and 6 over Oyster rivers. The N. H. turnpike from Portsmouth to Concord, passes over the N. part of the town; and there are 40 miles, 300 rods of public highway, mostly in good repair, supported by the inhabitants. Here is a woollen factory, besides other mills and machinery; also a social library incorporated in 1814, containing about 100 volumes. The freewill baptists and friends have each a meeting-house. The first settled minister was Rev. Samuel Hutchins. Elders Elias Smith and Richard Martin, preached here subsequently; and Eld. *John Osborne*, is the present pastor. Lee was originally a part of Durham, and was incorporated Jan. 16, 1766. Pop. 1224.

LEMPSTER, post-township in Cheshire county, in lat. 43°, 14', is bounded N. by Unity, E. by Goshen and Washington, S. by Marlow and W. by Acworth, containing 21,410 acres. It is 40 miles from Concord and 90 from Boston. The surface is, in general, uneven, and the eastern part is mountainous, it being the W. border of the height of land between Merrimack and Connecticut rivers. The soil is moist—and better suited for grass than for grain. The agricultural products in 1820 were 16,000 lbs. of butter, 25,000 lbs. of cheese, 55,000 lbs. of beef, 61,000 lbs. of pork, 2100 lbs. of flax, and 220 barrels of cider. The town is well watered, although its streams are small. One branch of Sugar river, and the S. and W. branches of Cold river afford conveniences for water machinery. Near the W. boundary line is a pond 320 rods long and 80 wide. Sand pond lies in this town and Marlow. It is 420 rods long, and 70 wide. Dodge's pond, near the centre of Lempster, contains about 50 acres. There is a factory for dressing cloth, one of the best in the county, which dresses about 8000 yards of cloth annually. Here is a social library, containing about 300 volumes. Lempster was granted by charter, October 5, 1761, to Richard Sparrow and 61 others. It was settled about 1770, by emigrants from Connecticut. A congregational church was gathered in Nov. 1761, in which there have been 173 admissions and 614 baptisms. Rev. *Elias Fisher* was ordained Sept. 26, 1787. There is a methodist society of about 30 members. Pop. 950.

LIME, a post township, Grafton co., in lat. 43° 48', is bounded N. by Orford, E. by Dorchester, S. by Hanover, W. by Thetford, Vt. containing 28,500 acres. It is 6 miles S. from Orford, and 54 miles from Concord. The soil here is similar to that of other towns on Connecticut river, with this difference, that there is a less proportion of interval, and a less difference between that directly adjoining the river and the other parts of the town. There are three small streams passing through Lime and emptying into Connecticut river. There are two small ponds, the largest of which is called Ports pond, lying W. of the turnpike and about one mile N. of the meeting-house.— There is a mountain, called Smart's mountain, lying in the N. E. part of the town. Near the centre of Lime is the town-house, a large building, in which public business is transacted. There are 2 meeting houses, the congregational, built in 1811, at an expense of $6000, exclusive of the bell, weighing 13 cwt. —the baptist, which is situated on the turnpike leading through this town, and is 2 miles above the centre village. There is a handsome parsonage belonging to the congregational society. There is a social library of 300 volumes, incorporated in Dec. 1797. The annual number of deaths for 20 years past has varied from 12 to 32—average 20 per annum. Lime was granted by charter, July 8, 1761, to Theodore Atkinson and others. It was settled May 20, 1764, by Walter Fairfield, John and William Sloan and others from Connecticut. It received its name from *Lyme* in that state. The difference of orthography is owing to the mis-spelling of the name in the charter. The congregational church was formed in 1772. Rev. William Conant was ordained in Dec. 1773; died March 8, 1810, aged 67. Rev. Nathl. Lambert was installed Jan. 1811; dismissed Septem. 6, 1820. Rev. *Baxter Perry* was ordained Jan. 1821. There are 163 communicants, of whom 78 were added to the church in one year. There is a baptist church which was formed in 1810. Capt. John Sloan and his wife, about 90 years of age each, were living in 1822. Hon. JONATHAN FRANKLIN, who has been a member of the council and representative in the legislature, has resided in this town 46 years. Pop. 1824.

LINCOLN, a mountainous township in Grafton county, lat. 44° 4', is bounded N. by Franconia, S. by Peeling, E. by Thornton and ungranted lands, W. by Landaff, containing 32,456 acres, and is 70 miles N. from Concord. The middle branch of the Pemigewasset passes through nearly the centre of the town. It has its source in Ferrin's pond, in the S. part of Franconia. There are several ponds, viz. Bog, Fish and Loon ponds. There are many elevations, of which Kinsman's mountain is the most considerable. In the N. part of the town are two large gulfs, made by an extraordinary discharge of water from the clouds in 1774. The numerous "slips," as they are called, from the mountain are worthy of notice. They commence near the summit of the mountain, and proceed to its base, forcing a passage through all obstructions. The soil here in many parts is unfit for cultivation. The vegetable productions are often injured or destroyed by frosts. Wild animals, such as bears, racoons, foxes, sables, otters, deer, &c. are very numerous. Lincoln was granted Jan. 31, 1764, to James Avery and others; but its settlement did not commence till several years after the revolution. Instead of increasing, it rather decreases in population, and has but 20 or 30 inhabitants.

LITCHFIELD, in Hillsborough county, a small fertile township on the E. bank of Merrimack river, in lat. 42° 50', is bounded E. by Londonderry and Nottingham-West, S. by Nottingham-West, W. by Merrimack river, containing 8426 acres. It is 8 miles from Amherst, and 30 from Concord. This town has an excellent soil, and produces in great abundance wheat, rye, corn, oats, &c. Its original growth of forest trees was oak, elm, birch, butternut, walnut, bass, thornbush, and some pine. Large quantities of lumber have been transported down the Merrimack to Newburyport, or through the Middlesex canal to Boston. There are two ferries, Thornton's, near the meeting-house, on the post road from Amherst to Portsmouth; and Read's, 3 miles above. Here are 3 school districts; and a social library, containing 150 volumes. Litchfield was taken from Dunstable and incorporated by the government of Mass. in 1734. It was chartered by N. H., June 5th, 1749. It was originally known by the Indian name of *Natticott*, and by the English one of *Brenton's Farm*, being granted by the general court of Massachusetts as early as 1656. The settlement commenced about 1720, by a few families from Billerica. Some of the early settlers were from Chelmsford. The congregational church was gathered, and Rev. Joshua Tufts ordained in 1741; he was dismissed in 1744. Rev. Samuel Cotton, from Newton, was ordained in Feb. 1765; dismissed in 1784; died at Claremont in 1819. A church was formed in the presbyterian order in 1809, and Rev. Nathaniel Kennedy was settled April 12. He was dismissed in April, 1812. Rev. Enoch Pilsbury was ordained Oct. 25, 1815; died Feb. 15, 1818, aged 30. The Hon. WYSEMAN CLAGETT closed his life in this town. He was a native of England, came to this country before the revolution commenced, and sustained several important offices. He was attorney general under the provincial and state governments, and filled the office with dignity and honor. Pop. 465.

LITTLE-HARBOR. See *Portsmouth*.

LITTLETON, post township, in Grafton county, on Connecticut river, lat. 44° 15', is bounded N. W. by Concord and Waterford, Vt., N. E. by Dalton, S. E. by Bethlehem, S. W. by Lyman, containing 26,000 acres. Its extent on Connecticut river is about 14 miles. It is 18 miles from Lancaster, 39 from Plymouth, 30 from Haverhill Corner, and 100 from Concord. Connecticut river, in passing down the rapids called Fifteen-Mile falls, extending the whole length of Littleton, runs in foaming waves for miles together, which render it impossible to ascend or descend with boats in safety. There are 3 bridges over the Connecticut in Littleton. Amonoosuck river waters the S. part, having on its banks small tracts of excellent interval. There is a pleasant village on this river in the S. part of the town. (*See Glynville.*) There is but one pond, situated on the S. W. line and partly in Lyman, called Partridge pond. Raspberry, Black, Palmer's and Iron mountains are the most prominent elevations. They are covered principally with sugar maple, beech, birch, bass, white ash, and in some places intermixed with red oak. Hemlock abounds in the S. W. part. Near Amonoosuck river, there is a mineral spring, the water of which is said to be similar to the Congress spring at Saratoga. The land comprehending Littleton was first granted Nov. 17, 1764, by the name of *Chiswick.* It was re-granted Jan. 18, 1770, by the name of *Apthorp,* and contained by admeasurement 40,850 acres, including the territory now composing Dalton. Nov. 4, 1784, Apthorp was divided, and the towns of Littleton and Dalton incorporated. The first settlement was made about 50 years since by Capt. Nathan Caswell, who was in 1822 living in Canada. The first child born in town was his son, who was named Apthorp. The congregational church was formed in 1803. Pop. 1096.

LONDONDERRY, post-township in Rockingham county, adjoining the E. line of the county of Hillsborough, is in lat. 42° 53′, and bounded on the N. by Chester and Manchester, W. by Manchester, Litchfield, and Nottingham-West, S. by Nottingham-West, Windham, and Salem, and E. by Atkinson, Hampstead, and Sandown. It originally contained 64,000 acres, of which 20,000 are now included in the towns of Windham, Salem, Nottingham-West, and Manchester. A small but flourishing village is situated near the centre of the town on the Londonderry turnpike, at the intersection of the northern and southern, eastern and western mail routes. This village is 15 miles N. W. from Haverhill, Mass. 35 from Portsmouth, 38 N. W. from Boston, and 25 S. E. from Concord. The most considerable stream in this town is Beaver brook or river, issuing from Beaver pond, a beautiful body of water nearly circular in form and about 300 rods in diameter, about one mile N. E. from the village. Three miles N. W. from this pond, are three other small ponds, Scoby's, Upper, and Lower Shields'; small streams issuing from these unite and fall into the Beaver brook, on which are extensive and valuable meadows. Cobbet's pond in the S. part of this town, is one of the sources of the Spiggot river. The E. line of the town passes through Island pond, so called from its containing an island constituting an extensive and valuable farm. Londonderry contains very little waste land and it is believed, a more extensive body of fertile soil than any town in the E. section of the state. It contains no high hills or extensive plains, no morasses or stagnant waters of any considerable extent; its surface consists of swells of moderate elevation, with intervening valleys of no considerable breadth. Its healthfulness is indicated by the longevity of an unusual proportion of its inhabitants. The Londonderry turnpike from Concord to Boston, passes about 8 miles within the limits of this town. The Pinkerton academy, in an elevated and pleasant situation on the Londonderry turnpike, near the village, has productive funds to the amount of $14,000; the donation of Major John Pinkerton. The institution has now a fair prospect of becoming extensively useful. Londonderry was settled in 1719, by a colony of presbyterians, from the vicinity of the city of Londonderry, in the N. of Ireland, to which place their ancestors had emigrated about a century before from Scotland. They were a part of 120 families chiefly from three parishes, who with their religious instructors came to New-England in the summer of 1718. In October, 1718, they applied to the government of Massachusetts for the grant of a township, and received assurances, that a grant should be made them, when they should select a place for its location. After some time spent in viewing the country, they selected the tract afterwards composing the town of Londonderry, at first known by the name of *Nutfield*. At this time it was supposed by them to be within the bounds of Massachusetts, the line between that state and the state of New-Hampshire being then unsettled and in dispute. April 11, 1719, sixteen families, accompanied by Rev. James McGregore, one of the clergymen who had emigrated from Ireland with them, took possession of the tract, and on the day of their arrival attended religious services and a sermon under an oak on the E. shore of Beaver pond. In the month of May following, and as early as the necessary arrangements could be made, Mr. McGregore was regularly ordained their minister. The first summer all the settlers united in cultivating a field in common, the produce of which they amicably divided in autumn. Influenced by the opinion, that the best title to the soil in a moral point of view must be that derived by purchase from the aboriginal inhabitants, they in 1720 purchased the title to the tract, which they had located from Col. John Wheelwright, whose ancestor had purchased a tract, of which this was a part, from the tribes of Indians, who were its rightful proprietors. The inhabitants of Londonderry, although it was long a frontier town, were never molested by the Indians. The proprietors of Londonderry, upon application to Gov. Shute and his council for New-Hampshire, received, on the first day of June, 1722, a grant of the tract of land they had located, and a charter of incorporation by the same instrument. This grant was made to 105 persons, and so rapid had been the settlement, that evidence exists to justify the belief, that there were at this time more than sixty families in the town. The early settlers of this town were in general farmers, possessing considerable information for their situation in life, their ancestors having preserved the laudable custom of their Scottish progenitors in procuring for their children instruction in all the branches of learning then taught in common schools. None of them were rich, but many of them brought to Londonderry property sufficient to enable them to make a rapid progress in the improvement of their farms, and to acquire very early all the necessaries and even the conveniences and comforts of civilized life. Few or none of their number were indigent. They introduced with them the culture of the potatoe, a vegetable till then unknown in New-England; and the manufacture of linen cloth, which, though long since declined, was for many years a considerable source of their early prosperity. Mills were erected immediately upon their first settlement, and within the first year a convenient dwelling-house, two stories high was built for their minister. This house, the timber of which is entirely sound and the house in good repair, is now occupied by John Morrison, Esq., a descendant of one of the early settlers. Within two years from the first settlement, a meeting-house was erected, and within six years it appears, that four schools were kept in the town during half the year. Conclusive evidence of the rapid progress of the town exists in the fact, that within nine years from its first settlement, it paid more than one fifteenth part of the state tax although the old and then extensive towns of Portsmouth, Dover, Exeter, and Hampton had been settled more than a century, and several other towns had been long settled. Within five years from the settlement of the town, Mr. McGregore's church consisted of 230 members. Mr. McGregore died March 5, 1729, at the age of 52 years; he was distinguished for talents, a sound judgment, and great prudence, and was eminently useful to the town in regard to its civil concerns, as well as by the discharge of his professional duties. He was succeeded by Rev. Matthew Clark a native of Ireland, who had in early life been an officer in the army and distinguished himself in the defence of the city of Londonderry, when besieged by the army of King James II. A. D. 1688–9. He afterwards relinquished a military life for the clerical profession. He possessed a strong mind, marked by a considerable degree of eccentricity. He died Jan. 25, 1735, and was borne to the grave at his particular request by his former companions in arms, of whom there were a considerable number among the early settlers of this town; several of whom had been made free from taxes, throughout the British dominions by King William, for their bravery in that memorable siege. In 1733, Rev. Thomas Thompson, a native of Ireland, was ordained as the colleague of Mr. Clark, and died Sept. 22, 1798, aged 38. The Rev. William Davidson, a native of Ireland, succeeded him in 1739; and continued in the ministerial office till his death, Feb. 15, 1791, at the age of 79 years. In 1795, he was succeeded by Rev. Jonathan Brown, who was in 1804, dismissed at his own request. September 12, 1810, Rev. *Edward L. Parker*, the present minister of the original, or east parish, was settled. In 1735, the town voted, that the inhabitants of the W. part of the town should become a separate parish; and in 1737, this parish settled Rev. David McGregore, a son of the first minister of the town. In 1739, the parish was incorporated. Mr. McGregore died May 30, 1777, at the age of 67 years: he was a man eminent for piety, talents, eloquence, and devotion to the cause of civil liberty. He was succeeded in 1783 by William Morrison, D. D. a native of Scotland, distinguished for his piety, talents, and liberality of mind. Dr. Morrison died March 9, 1818, at the age of 70, and was succeeded Jan. 16, 1822, by *Daniel Dana*, D. D. The two parishes possess funds to nearly the amount of $20,000, principally of the donation of Maj. John Pinkerton, the same benevolent individual, who endowed the academy designated by his name. This worthy man, whose name and character deserve to be held in veneration, came from

Ireland to Londonderry with his parents in infancy. He was through life distinguished for a laudable economy and persevering industry, and not less so for his charity to the poor and unfortunate. He died in 1818, at the age of 81. There have been in this town many remarkable instances of longevity. Of its early settlers and their children, born within 20 years after the first settlement of the town, more than 100 persons are known to have reached the age of 80 years and upwards. Of this number 25 are known to have been more than 90 years of age; six of the natives of this town, above the age of 90 are now living. One individual, William Scoby, died at the age of 110, and when 100 years old, travelled on foot to Portsmouth, more than 35 miles in one day. A company of 70 men from this town, under the command of Capt. George Reid, were in the battle of Breed's hill, and about the same number were in that at Bennington, in which Capt. David M'Clary one of their citizens, a distinguished and brave officer, was killed. Thirty-one of the natives of this town have received a collegiate education, of whom twenty-two are now alive. Of this number 12 have entered the profession of divinity, and 10 that of the law. Of the natives of this town, who have sustained public offices, military and civil, are Maj. Gen. John Stark and Col. George Reid, officers of the army of the revolution. Joseph M'Keen, D. D. first president of Bowdoin college; Arthur Livermore, Jonathan Steele, and SAMUEL BELL, judges of the superior court; the latter of whom, from 1819 to 1823, was governor of this state and discharged the duties of that station to the universal satisfaction of the people. He is now senator in Congress. Robert Wallace and Hugh Ramsay, judges of the court of common pleas; George Reid, sheriff of the county of Rockingham. Amongst the descendants of the early settlers, are Jeremiah Smith, late chief justice of the superior court; Gen. James Miller, and Col. John M'Neil, distinguished officers in the late war with Great Britain. Amongst those, who, though not natives, were inhabitants from early life, are Matthew Thornton, a delegate from New-Hampshire, to Congress, and one of the signers of the Declaration of Independence, and one of the first judges of the superior court after the commencement of the revolution; and John Prentice, for several years attorney general of the state. Pop. 3127.

LONG BAY, at the head of Winnepisiogee river, lies between Gilford and Meredith. The waters of the lake Winnepisiogee pass through this bay into the river of that name.

LOUDON, post-town, Rockingham county, lat. 43° 19′, is bounded N. W. by Canterbury, N. E. by Gilmanton, S. E. by Pittsfield and Chichester, S. W. by Concord, and contains 28,257 acres. Soucook river passes from Gilmanton S. through Loudon, furnishing valuable mill privileges. There is some good interval on its borders. The soil is various—the natural growth in the E. part of the town sugar maple and beech; in the S. and W. pine, oak and chesnut. Soucook village, the seat of the principal business in town, is in the S. part of the town on a pleasant site E. of the river; it contains 40 buildings, and is 4 miles from the centre meeting-house. Loudon was originally a part of Canterbury; was incorporated Jan. 23, 1773, and the first town meeting was holden March 23, same year. Settlements had been made in 1760, by Abraham and Jethro Bachelder and Moses Ordway. A congregational church was formed in 1784; and in 1789, Rev. Jedidiah Tucker was ordained. He was dismissed in 1810, and died in 1818, aged 57. Rev. *Enoch Corser* was ordained in 1816. There is also a freewill baptist society in Loudon. Pop. 1694.

LOVEWELL'S POND. See *Wakefield*.

LYMAN, a township on Connecticut river, in Grafton county, in lat. 44° 15', is bounded N. W. by Barnet, Vt. N. E. by Littleton, S. E. by Concord, in Grafton county, and W. by Bath. It is 13 miles above Haverhill, 90 miles from Concord, and 155 from Boston. The soil and productions are similar to those on Connecticut river in the N. part of the state. Pine and hemlock are among the prevailing forest trees. There is one considerable elevation, called on the Map of N. H., Gardner's mountain, but generally known by the name of Lyman's mountain. It is in fact a continuation of Gardner's mountain, which extends from Bath through this town in nearly a N. and S. direction. The N. W. branch of Burnham's river has its source from this mountain. The N. E. branch comes from Partridge pond in Littleton and this town. There are several ponds in the E. part of Lyman, through the largest of which, Burnham's river has its course. The lower bar of the Fifteen-Mile falls is in this town. Carleton's falls are several miles below, and below these is Stevens' ferry, which communicates with Barnet. It is said that copper and emery, intermixed with iron ore, have been found here. Lyman was granted Nov. 10, 1761, to a number of proprietors, of whom was Daniel Lyman, from whom it probably received its name. Of the three first families who settled here, there were 20 sons, of whom 19 were living a few years since. Seventeen of them lived in Lyman. The spotted fever in 1812, attacked 70 persons, of whom only one died. Pop. 1270.

LYME. See *Lime*.

LYNDEBOROUGH, post-township in Hillsborough county, in lat. 42° 53', is bounded N. by Francestown, E. by N. Boston and Mont-Vernon, S. by Milford and Wilton, and W. by Temple and Greenfield, containing 20,767 acres. It is 10 miles from Amherst, and 35 from Concord.—It is an elevated township, having a considerable mountain which divides it from E. to W.— There is, in the N. E. part of the town, below the mountain, a plain, over which the 2d N. H. turnpike passes, where there is a small village, pleasantly situated near Piscataquog river. The soil of this town, though stony, is deep and strong. For grazing it is, perhaps, not exceeded by any town in the county. The streams are small, originating principally from sources in the town, and running N. and S. from the mountain. There is one small natural pond, not far from the meeting-house, which stands on an eligible spot S. of the mountain. There is a small foundry for casting articles of hollow ware. There is a social library containing from 200 to 300 volumes. One native, Caleb Huston, has received a collegiate education—graduated at Williams' college in 1812. Lyndeborough was originally granted by Massachusetts to Capt. Samuel King and 59 others, who went on the Canada expedition in 1690. From this circumstance and from some of the proprietors belonging to Salem, it was called *Salem-Canada*. In 1753, Benjamin Lynde, Esq. of Salem, purchased a considerable part of the township, and adjoining lands. From him, the place, when it was incorporated, April 23, 1764, took the name of Lyndeborough. It was settled as early as 1750. The earliest names were Putnam, Chamberlain and Cram, who emigrated from Massachusetts. The congregational church was founded in 1757. Rev. John Rand, who graduated at Harvard college in 1748, was ordained Dec. 3, 1757; dismissed April 8, 1762. Rev. Sewall Goodrich, who graduated at Harvard College in 1764, was ordained Sept. 7, 1768; died in March 1809. Rev. *Nathaniel Merrill*, a graduate of Dartmouth college in 1809, was ordained Oct. 30, 1811. On the 15th Nov. 1809, three children were burnt in a barn, while their parents were attending an installation at Mont-Vernon. In the winter of 1812, the spotted fever prevailed here, of which 13 persons died within about as many days. The number of deaths for the last 10 years has been 160. Pop. 1200.

M.

MAD river rises among the mountains in the ungranted lands of Grafton county, about 10 miles N. of Sandwich. Taking a S. W. course, it crosses the S. E. extremity of Thornton, and falls into the Pemigewasset river near the centre of Campton.

MADBURY, Strafford county, lat. 43° 10′, is a small township of about 12 square miles, bounded N. E. by Dover, S. W. by Durham and Lee, N. W. by Barrington. Its greatest length is about 7 miles, the extreme easterly point extending to the tide water of a branch of the Pascataqua, about 5 miles above Portsmouth. The soil of this town is generally productive. The valleys consist of a proportion of clay, and the higher lands are a mixture of sand and loam, with very few stones. In some parts of the town, bog iron ore has been dug up in considerable quantities, and in some instances red and yellow ochre. Bellamy bank river is the only stream of any magnitude, and Barbadoes pond the only considerable body of water. This pond lies between Dover and Madbury, and is 120 rods long, 50 wide. Madbury formerly constituted a part of the ancient town of Dover; but was set off and incorporated May 31, 1755, by the present name. No church can with propriety be said to have been established. In 1758, Rev. Samuel Hyde commenced preaching, and continued until 1770, but no regular church was organized. Rev. Eliphaz Chapman officiated from 1771 until 1773; when Eld. William Hooper, a baptist, formerly of Berwick, commenced preaching and continued several years. There is one meeting-house in Madbury, but no settled minister. There are a considerable number of friends in this town belonging to the society at Dover. The inhabitants are mostly industrious agriculturalists; and as there are neither stores nor taverns in town, intemperance is not frequent among them. Pop. 559.

MANCHESTER, a township, in Hillsborough county, lies on the E. side of Merrimack river, by which it is bounded on the W. for 8 miles, in lat. 42° 51′. On the N. and E.

it is bounded by Chester, S. by Londonderry and Litchfield. It contains an area of 15,671 acres. There are several streams which have their origin in this town, and which discharge themselves into the Merrimack.—Cohass brook, issuing from Massabesick pond, is the largest. It receives two other small streams from the S. and empties itself at the S. W. angle of the town. Massabesick is a large pond at the E. side of the town, and partly within its limits. Alewives pass from the Merrimack into this pond, by the Cohass brook, the main outlet to the pond. There are several smaller ponds abounding with pickerel and other fish. The soil of a considerable part of the town is light and sandy, originally covered with a thick growth of pine wood. In other parts it is fertile, and is wooded with oak, walnut and maple. The intervals on the river are easy of cultivation and productive. The canal by Amoskeag Falls is in this town, and was projected and constructed by the ingenuity and perseverance of the late Samuel Blodget, Esq. It is a work of great public utility. The fall is about 45 feet perpendicular measurement; and the whole extent, including the channels and dams which form the upper entrance, down to the four locks at the lower end, is nearly one mile. It was completed in 1816, in the most substantial manner, at an expense of $60,000, though a much greater sum had been originally laid out. It has the business that goes by rafting to Newburyport as well as Boston. The falls may not be considered among the least natural curiosities. The river is widened to three times its general width and is divided into several different streams by several small islands.

The water rushes through the various channels over a ragged bottom with great velocity, and the sound it produces is heard for several miles. At the upper part, near the greatest fall, circular holes of various sizes have been worn perpendicularly into the solid rock several feet, some of which holes are more than eight feet diameter. Here, it is said, the Indians in time of war concealed their provisions. At these falls in the months of May, June and July are caught salmon, shad and other fish, but, on account of the obstructions in the river, not in such abundance as formerly. The facility of procuring fish, it is highly probable, drew the attention of the natives to this place, as appearances indicate its having been thickly peopled by them. Various kinds of tools constructed of stone, such as axes, chisels, arrow-heads, &c. are frequently found in the earth near these falls; human bones have also been discovered——all which render it highly probable that this was an important spot to the aboriginals. This town was formed of a part of Londonderry, a part of Chester, and a tract of land called Harrytown, and incorporated Sept. 3, 1751, by the name of *Derryfield*. This name it retained until 1810, when it was changed to Manchester by an act of the legislature. The venerable Gen. JOHN STARK had his residence in this town, where he died May 8, 1822, at the great age of 93 years 8 months and 24 days. He was born at Londonderry, August 28, 1728; was taken prisoner by the Indians, while hunting near Baker's river, in Rumney, April 28, 1752. In 1775, he was appointed a colonel of one of the three regiments raised in N. H.—was engaged on the heights of Charlestown, June 17,—

was at the battle of Trenton in 1776—captured Col. Baum and 1000 of the British at Bennington, Aug. 16, 1777. This event, in the language of President Jefferson, was "the first link in the chain of successes which issued in the surrender of Saratoga." He was soon after appointed a brigadier general of the U. S. army, and, at the time of his death, was the only surviving American general officer of the revolution. The Marquis De la Fayette, was appointed a major general by Gen. Washington, and he is still living in France, at the age of 65. For a memoir of Gen. Stark, see *Hist. Coll. for 1822, p.* 92—116. Pop. 761.

MARGALLAWAY river has its source among the highlands, which separate Maine from Lower Canada, in the N. E. extremity of New-Hampshire, about 30 miles N. from Errol. After a S. course of nearly 20 miles on the western border of Maine, it enters New-Hampshire at the S. E. part of the 2d grant to Dartmouth college, where it forms a junction with the united streams of Dead and Diamond rivers.— Thence after a S. course of about 6 miles to Errol it receives the waters of Umbagog lake. After this junction the main stream is the Ameriscoggin river.

MARLBOROUGH, a post-township in Cheshire county, in lat. 42° 52', is bounded N. by Roxbury, E. by Dublin and Jaffrey, S. by Troy, W. by Swanzey and part of Keene. Before the incorporation of Troy principally taken from this town, it contained 20,740 acres. It is 6 miles from Keene, 55 from Concord, and 76 from Boston. There are several ponds which are the sources of some of the branches of Ashuelot river. The soil is rocky, suitable for grain and flax, and particularly for grass. The 3d N. H. turnpike and the Fitzwilliam Branch turnpike pass through this town. The annual number of deaths for the last 25 years has averaged about 13. Marlborough was granted by charter, April 29, 1751, to Timothy Dwight, Esq. and 61 others. The conditions of the grant not being seasonably complied with on account of the Indian and French war, the claims of forfeiture incurred by the grantees was suspended by another charter, Sept. 21, 1764. The first settlement commenced about 1760, by a Mc.Alister, William Barker, Abel Woodward, Benj. Tucker and Daniel Goodenough. The town was incorporated Dec. 13, 1776. A congregational church was founded in 1778, and Rev. Joseph Cummings was ordained in Nov. the same year. He was dismissed in Dec. 1780. He graduated at Harvard College in 1768. Rev. *Holloway Fish* was ordained Sept. 25, 1793. Lt. Col. Andrew Colburn, an officer killed in the revolutionary war, belonged to this town. Pop. 766.

MARLOW, post-township, in Cheshire county, in lat. 43° 7', is bounded N. by Acworth and Lempster, E. by Washington and Stoddard, S. by Gilsum, W. by Alstead, containing 15,937 acres. It is 15 miles from Keene, and 45 from Concord. Ashuelot river passes through almost the whole length of the town. There are no ponds of note, nor any mountains. The soil is rather wet, but considerably productive. There are large tracts of meadow land on Ashuelot river and other streams, of an excellent quality. The land is generally uneven, but not very rocky. It produces the various kinds of grain— is also very favorable for flax and potatoes. The agricultural products in 1820, were 14,400 lbs. of butter, 21,000 lbs of cheese, 40,000 lbs. of beef, 44,000 lbs. of pork, 3,400 lbs. of flax, with 150 barrels of cider; also 5 tons of pearl-ashes. Marlow was chartered Oct. 7, 1761, to William Noyes and 69 others, residing principally in Lime, Conn. The first settlers were Joseph Tubbs, Samuel and John Gustin, N. Royce, N. Miller, Nathan Huntley, Solomon Mack, Solomon Gee, Eber Lewis and others. The first town meeting was in March, 1766. In 1772, there were 29 families.— The first inhabitants were baptists. They soon formed a baptist church and in Jan. 1778, settled Rev. Caleb Blood, who was dismissed March 9, 1779. Rev. Eleazar Beckwith succeeded, and preached till his death in 1809. There is a methodist society, over which Rev. Paul Dustin was settled by a vote of the town, May 12, 1807. He died Feb. 15, 1811. There is also a society of universalists. Pop. 597.

MASCOMY, a river in Grafton county, rises S. of Smart's mountain, lying in Lime and the N. W. part of Dorchester. It has a S. course through Dame's Gore to Canaan, where it receives the waters of Goose pond and Heart pond, and also its E. branch. It proceeds to Enfield, receiving the waters of several ponds, and there empties itself into Mascomy pond. The outlet of this pond is at its W. extremity in Lebanon, where it becomes a considerable stream, which after a course of 7 miles, falls into the Connecticut river a few miles below Lyman's bridge. See *Enfield.*

MASCOMY pond lies principally in Enfield and partly in Lebanon. It contains a surface of between 2000 and 3000 acres. See *Enfield.*

MASSABESICK, a pond. See *Chester.*

MASON, a township in Hillsborough county, in lat. 42° 45', is bounded N. by Temple and Wilton, E. by Milford and Brookline, S. by Townsend and Ashby in Ms., and W. by New-Ipswich, containing 18,860 acres. It is 15 miles from Amherst, 43 from Concord and 50 from Boston. The surface is uneven; the hills are chiefly large swells, with narrow valleys between them. The streams are rapid. There are no natural ponds. The principal meadows were formerly beaver ponds. Souhegan is the principal stream affording many fine mill seats. The small streams run into Nashua river and into Tanapus or Potanipo pond in Brookline. The soil in the E. part is rather light—the forest trees, white, red and yellow oak, walnut, pine and chesnut. The W. part is mostly a strong deep soil, red or dark loam, but stony. It is good for grass and grain. The natural growth, red oak, hemlock, beech, maple, birch, &c. The soil of the high lands was greatly injured by fires in the forests previous to its settlement. The 3d N. H. turnpike passes through the S. W. part of this town about 3 miles. In Souhegan village, there is a cotton factory in 2 large buildings, one containing 500 spindles, with the necessary apparatus for carding and spinning, including a double speeder; in the other building are 16 power looms. There is also a large woollen factory, containing 5 sets of cards, a spinning machine known by the name of a Brewster, 4 power looms for sattinett, and 6 broad looms, which can turn out 20 yards of broad cloth per day. There is also in this town a starch manufactory, which manufactures

4000 or 5000 bushels of potatoes into starch, per annum. In 1820, 30,000 lbs. and in 1821, 26,000 lbs. of this useful article were manufactured. Eight pounds of starch can be made from one bushel of potatoes. Mason was granted by charter, Aug. 26, 1768. It was formerly known by the name of *No.* 1. The first effort to settle this place was in 1751, and the next year a permanent settlement was made by Enoch Lawrence, from Pepperell, Ms. Deac. Nathan Hall, who died May 7, 1807, aged 92, was an early settler. Jonathan Foster, another early inhabitant, lived to exceed 100 years. The congregational church was formed in 1772, and consisted of 12 males and 9 females. Rev. Jonathan Searle was ordained Oct. 14, 1772; dismissed about 1782. Rev. *Ebenezer Hill*, who graduated at Harvard college in 1786, was ordained in 1790. A baptist church was constituted in 1786, and Rev. *William Eliot* was ordained their pastor. Pop. 1300.

MAYNESBOROUGH, an uninhabited township in Coos county, lat. 44° 27', is bounded N. by Paulsburgh, E. by Success, S. by Shelburne and Durand, W. by Kilkenny. It is 125 miles from Concord; contains 31,154 acres; and was granted Dec. 31, 1771, to Sir William Mayne, bart., Robert, Thomas and Edward Mayne and others, of Barbadoes. The Ameriscoggin passes through the E. part of this town, and the Upper Amonoosuck through the W.

MEREDITH, a post-town, in Strafford county, in lat. 43° 36', is bounded N. by Centre-Harbor and Winnepisiogee lake, N. E. and E. by said lake and river, S. E. by Great bay, S. and S. W. by Sanbornton, W. and N. W. by New-Hampton and Centre-Harbor. This town was incorporated Dec. 30, 1768, and was first called *New-Salem*. It lies distant from Concord about 29 miles; from Portsmouth, 63 miles; and from Washington city, 531 miles. Meredith contains 2 post-offices, 4 houses for public worship, 13 school houses, 2 distilleries, and a convenient number of mills and machines. There is in this town a pond adjoining Centre-Harbor, about 2 miles long and 1 wide, emptying into Great bay, near the village; besides this there are several smaller ponds. There is probably no town in the country more pleasantly and advantageously situated, or of a better soil, than Meredith. The waters of the Winnepisiogee washing the boundaries of a great part of the town, convey many heavy mercantile articles to, and from almost the doors of several of the inhabitants in the summer; and in the winter, the ice serves as a level and easy road. Near the upper or N. W. part of the town, the traveller passing along the road, is presented with a very beautiful landscape. On the E. and S. E. the placid Winnepisiogee, the largest lake in New-Hampshire, with its numerous islands, arrests the eye, and bounds the circle of vision in a S. E. direction. On the N. E. Ossipee mountain rises boldly to view. On the N., the prospect is intercepted by Red hill, a pleasant and noted eminence in Moultonborough, only a few miles distant. At Meredith Bridge is a handsome and flourishing village, and the seat of much business. It is connected with the principal village of Gilford by a bridge over the Winnepisiogee. There are societies of congregationalists and baptists in this town, the former under the care of Rev. *David Smith*;

the latter in charge of Elder Parker Fogg. Hon. EBENEZER SMITH, moved into this town at an early period of its settlement, and was as a father to the new settlers for many years. He was for many years a justice of the peace, and judge of probate; and for two years president of the senate. He died at Meredith, Aug. 22, 1807, aged 73; and will long be remembered with veneration and respect. Pop. 2416.

MERRIMACK, one of the principal rivers of New-England, is formed of two branches. The N. branch called Pemigewasset, rises near the Notch of the White-Mountains, and passes southwardly through a corner of Franconia, Lincoln, Peeling, Thornton and Campton, forming the boundary between Plymouth and Holderness, and also the boundary line between the counties of Strafford and Grafton from the S. corner of Holderness to its junction with the Winnepisiogee. It receives several considerable branches in its course—Mad river in Campton, Baker's in Plymouth; and streams flowing from Squam and Newfound lakes, with numerous small tributaries. The E. branch is the Winnepisiogee, through which pass the waters of the lake of that name. The descent of this branch from the lake to its junction with Pemigewasset, is 232 feet. The confluent stream bears the name of Merrimack, and pursues a S. course, 78 miles, to Chelmsford, Mass.; thence an E. course, 35 miles to the sea at Newburyport. On the N. line of Concord, the Contoocook discharges its waters into the Merrimack. The Soucook becomes a tributary in Pembroke, and the Suncook between Pembroke and Allenstown. The Piscataquog unites in Bedford; the Souhegan in Merrimack, and a beautiful river called Nashua in Dunstable. The principal tributaries are on the W. side of the river, mostly rising in the highlands between the Connecticut and Merrimack. There are numerous falls in this river, the most noted of which are Garven's, in Concord, the falls in Hooksett, and Amoskeag in Manchester. *See Amoskeag, &c.* These falls are all rendered passable by locks, and boat navigation has for several years been extended as far as Concord. There are several bridges over the Merrimack and its principal branches, besides a number of ferries. The Merrimack, whose fountains are nearly on a level with the Connecticut, being much shorter in its course has a far more rapid descent to the sea than the latter river. Hence the intervals on its borders are less extensive, and the scenery less beautiful than on the Connecticut. It is, however, a majestic river; its waters are generally pure and healthy; and on its borders are situated some of the most flourishing towns in the state. The name of this river was originally written *Merramacke* and *Monnomake*, which in the Indian language signified a *sturgeon*. Its width varies from 50 to 120 rods; and at its mouth it presents a beautiful sheet of half a mile in width. For notices of the canals and bridges on this river, *see pp.* 14, 17.

MERRIMACK, a post-town in Hillsborough county, in lat. 42° 51′, is bounded N. by Bedford, E. by Litchfield, S. by Dunstable and W. by Amherst, containing 19,361 acres. It is 6 miles from Amherst, 27 from Concord and 45 from Boston. Merrimack river waters its E. border through its whole extent, opening a communication by water from this place to Boston. Souhegan enters this town from Amherst; pursues a winding course to the Merrimack, where it discharges itself one mile above Thornton's ferry. There are fine water privileges on this stream. At the mouth of it is a valuable factory, which was erected in room of one, owned by Isaac Riddle, Esq. & Sons, which was consumed by fire, June 10, 1818, with a loss of $6000. This factory has lately enlarged its plan of operation, and bids fair to become one of the best establishments of the kind in the county. A small village is situated in its vicinity, which is a place of considerable business. Babboosuck brook, issuing from Babboosuck pond in Amherst, empties into Souhegan river, and Penichook brook from a pond in Hollis, forms the southern boundary. This town presents no remarkable peculiarity of surface. It may be considered a level tract, having but few hills, and those not worthy of particular notice. The soil in various places is very fertile, but a considerable portion of the land is plain. There are some fine intervals on the Merrimack. The wealth and population have not increased as might have been expected from its local advantages. Some of the best and most extensive water privileges the county affords, about 1 1-2 mile from the Merrimack, on Souhegan river, lie unimproved. This town claims the first discovery in this region of making what are called Leghorn bonnets. They were first made several years since by the Misses Burnaps, who are deserving much credit for their enterprize in this species of manufacture. Some of their bonnets have been sold at auction in Boston for $50. This town was formerly called *Souhegan East*. All that part S. of Souhegan river was included in the Dunstable grant. The remainder belonged to Number 5, of the Narraganset townships. (*See Bedford*.) It was incorporated by charter, April 2, 1746, having been settled about 13 years. A Mr. Hassell was among the first settlers, and his daughter was the first person born in town. The first house in this town was built many years before any permanent settlement was made. It was erected on the margin of the river for a house of traffic with the Indians. It was called Cromwell's house, and was occupied by John Cromwell, originally from England, but last from Boston. For some time he carried on a lucrative trade with the Indians, weighing their furs with his foot, till, enraged at his supposed or real deception, they formed the resolution to murder him. This intention was communicated to Cromwell, who buried his wealth and made his escape. Within a few hours after his flight, a party of the Penacook tribe arrived, and not finding the object of their resentment, they burnt his habitation. The time when this occurred is not positively known, but it is inferred that it was after 1679, when it appears his house was standing. The name of Merrimack is derived from the river on which it is situated. A congregational church was formed Sept. 5, 1772. Rev. Jacob Burnap, D. D. from Reading, Ms. who graduated at Harvard college in 1770, was ordained Oct. 14, 1772; died Dec. 26, 1821, aged 75, having admitted to the church 194 members. He was eminently distinguished for his superior knowledge of the original languages, in which the scriptures were written. He was much esteemed for his piety, integrity patience and all the social virtues. Hon. MATTHEW THORNTON, one of the signers of the Declaration of American Independence, resided many years in this town. He died while on a visit at Newburyport, June 24, 1803, at the age of 89. He was a member of the first congress, and many years a judge of the superior court of N. H. a representative, senator and counsellor, and sustained other important offices. For a memoir of him, see *Historical Collections* for 1822, page 87—91. Pop. 1162.

MERRYMEETING bay, an arm of the Winnepisiogee lake, extends about 1800 rods into the town of Alton, and is 27 miles from the navigable waters of the Pascataqua. See *Alton*.

MERRYMEETING pond. See *New-Durham*.

MIDDLETON, post-town, in Strafford co. lat. 43° 29', is bounded N. by Brookfield, E. by Wakefield, S. by Milton, and W. by New-Durham, comprising 9,840 acres. It is a very level township, having no high ground except a part of Moose mountain, which separates it from Brookfield. There are no rivers nor ponds; the soil is rocky; the growth of wood chiefly hemlock and spruce, with some maple and beech. There are 3 schools, and a meeting house. Rev. Nehemiah Ordway, graduated at Harvard college in 1764, was settled here in 1778, remained a few years, and was dismissed. Elder *William Buzzell*, a free-will baptist, is the only preacher. Middleton was incorporated March 4, 1778. The first settlers were from Lee and Rochester. Pop. 482.

MILFORD, a post-town in Hillsborough county, in lat. 42° 59', is bounded N. by Mont-Vernon and Lyndeborough, E. by Amherst, S. by Hollis and Brookline, W. by Mason and Wilton, containing 15,402 acres. It is 2 1-2 miles from Amherst, 31 from Concord, and 47 from Boston. Milford lies on both sides of Souhegan river, which runs through the town from W. to E. forming a rich meadow or interval, from 1-4 to 1-2 a mile wide. The banks of this river are annually overflowed, by which means, the soil, which is black and deep, is much enriched. The forest trees are, on the river, elm, walnut, butternut, &c.; on the highlands, white, red and black oak, chesnut, white and yellow pine, maple, hemlock, &c. This town has excellent water privileges. There is a valuable factory in the village, containing 844 spindles. There are fine orchards, and fruit of an excellent quality and flavor is produced.— Sixty two bushels of apples have been gathered from one tree the same season. The village, pleasantly situated on both sides of the river, contains two meeting-houses, one on each side, one school-house 2 factory buildings, 51 dwelling houses, 3 stores, post-office, &c.— Milford was formerly known as the S. W. parish of Amherst. It was incorporated Jan. 11, 1794, and includes what was anciently called, the Mile Slip and Duxbury school farm. Eighty families were detached from Amherst and several from Hollis, when it was incorporated.— The first settlers were John Burns, William Peabody, Benjamin Hopkins, Caleb Jones, Nathan Hutchinson, Andrew Bradford and others, whose descendants are numerous and respectable. Capt. Josiah Crosby and William Wallace were among the early settlers. The former, a revolutionary officer, died Oct. 15, 1793, aged 63; the latter in 1791, aged 73. There are two religious societies. The congregational church was embodied in 1788, consisting of 19 members. Rev. *Humphrey Moore* was ordained Oct. 13, 1802. The baptist church, consisting of 28 members, was constituted Sept. 5, 1809. It now contains about 100 members. The baptist society have a very neat and handsome meeting house, erected in 1816. Pop. 1243.

MILTON, post-town, Strafford co. in lat. 43° 26′, is bounded N. W. by Middleton and Wakefield, E. by Salmon Fall river, separating it from Maine, S. W. by Farmington, and contains about 25,000 acres.—The Salmon Fall river washes its whole E. boundary, a distance of 13 miles; and a branch of the same river crosses from the S. part of Wakefield, and unites near the centre of the E. boundary. Teneriffe, a bold and rocky mountain, extends along the E. part of Milton, near which lies Milton pond, of considerable size, connecting with the Salmon Fall river. This town was formerly a part of Rochester, from which it was detached, and incorporated June 11, 1802. There is a meeting-house here, but no settled minister. Pop. 1232.

MILLSFIELD, Coos county, is an uninhabited township, in lat. 44° 43′, 7 miles W. of Umbagog lake, and about 35 N. from the White mountains. It is bounded N. by Dixville, E. by Errol, S. by Dummer, W. by Ervin's location and ungranted lands. Clear stream waters its N. extremity, and Phillip's river, with several small streams the other parts. Here are several ponds, the largest is about 300 rods long, 140 wide. Millsfield was granted March 1, 1774, to George Boyd and 81 others; and was named after Sir Thomas Mills, a grantee. It contains an area of 23,200 acres.

MOHAWK river, in Coos county, has its source among the mountains of Dixville, and in its W. course through Colebrook, receives some considerable branches from Stewartstown, among which is Beaver brook. It passes into the Connecticut below the centre of Colebrook.

MONADNOCK mountain, usually called the *Grand Monadnock*, is situated in the towns of Jaffrey and Dublin, in Cheshire county, about 22 miles E. from Connecticut river, and 10 N. of the southern boundary of this state. The direction of the ridge is N. E. and S. W. The mountain is about 5 miles long from N. to S. and 3 miles from E. to W. Its base, according to Judge Winthrop's observations made in 1780, is 1395 feet, and its summit 3254 feet above the level of the sea. According to Professor Dana, who visited the mountain in 1816, its base is 1452.5, and its summit is 3450 above the level of the sea. The mountain is composed of talc, mica, slate, distinctly stratified. Garnet, schorl, feldspar and quartz occur in various parts. On the E. side, plumbago is found in large quantities. Crucibles and pencils have been manufactured from it, but for the latter, it proves not very good. The summit, when seen at a distance of 4 or 5 miles, appears rounded and destitute of those high cliffs and mural precipices belonging to granitic mountains. The prospect from the pinnacle is very extensive; thirty ponds of fresh water, some of which are so large as to contain islands of 8 or 10 acres, may be seen from it, in the immediate vicinity. Near the base of the mountain, is the "Monadnock Mineral Spring." See *Jaffrey.*

MONT-VERNON, a pleasant elevated township in Hillsborough county, in lat. 42° 53', is bounded N. by New-Boston, E. by Amherst, S. by Amherst and Milford and W. by Lyndeborough, containing 7,975 acres. It is three miles, N. W. from Amherst, 28 from Concord and 50 from Boston. There is but one stream of any note, and this is but small: it rises near the north part of Mont-Vernon, and runs through Amherst near the E. extremity of the plain and empties into Souhegan river in the S. part of Amherst. That part of this stream near the mouth was called by the Indians *Quohquinapassakessanannagnog*.— The soil here does not materially differ from that of the circumjacent towns. The forest trees are maple, beech, birch, white and red oak. The situation is elevated, and towards the E. and S. E. there is a considerable prospect. There is a pleasant village situated near the highest point of elevation, having a congregational meeting house, 22 dwelling houses, three stores, &c. The 2d N. H. turnpike passes through this village. There is a social library. This town was originally a part of Amherst, from which it was detached and incorporated Dec. 15, 1803. Its settlement commenced soon after that of Amherst. Isaac Smith, aged 91, and Jonathan Lampson, aged 90, two of the early inhabitants, died here in 1807 and 1815. A congregational church was formed in 1780. Rev. John Bruce, who graduated at Dartmouth College in 1781, was ordained Nov. 23, 1785; died March 12, 1809, aged 52. Rev. Stephen Chapin, who graduated at Harvard college in 1804, was installed Nov. 15, 1809. Having espoused baptist sentiments, he was dismissed in Nov. 1818. Rev. Ebenezer Cheever, who graduated at Bowdoin college in 1817, ordained Dec. 8, 1819; was dismissed April 8, 1823. Dr. DANIEL ADAMS, who commenced and conducted the Medical and Agricultural Register, and is author of a popular system of Arithmetic, school geography, and a number of useful school books, has his residence in this place. Pop. 729.

MOOSEHILLOCK or MOOSEHILOCK, is a noble and lofty eminence in the S. E. part of Coventry, and ranks among the highest mountains in New-England. The altitude of the N. peak above tide water, as estimated by Capt. Partridge from barometrical observations, is 4636 feet—that of the S. peak is 4536 feet. Baker's river has its source on its eastern side.

MOOSE, the name of a mountain situated between Middleton and Brookfield, and also of the mountain in Hanover. See *Brookfield* and *Hanover*.

MOOSE river has its rise on the N. side of the White Mountains near Durand, through which it passes, and unites with the Ameriscoggin in Shelburne. Its source is very near that of Israel's river, which passes W. into Connecticut.

MORIAH, an elevated peak of the White Mountains, situated in the S. part of Shelburne.

MOULTONBOROUGH, post-township, Strafford county, in lat. 43° 44', is situated on the N. W. shore of Winnepisiogee lake, bounded N. by Sandwich and Tamworth, N. E. by Ossipee, S. E. by Tuftonborough, and W. by Centre-Harbor and Squam lake. This town is broken by mountains and ponds. Red Hill, lying wholly within this town, commands notice from the E., S. and W.; and extends about 3 miles from E. to W., between Red

Hill river on the N., Great Squam on the W., Great Squam and Long pond on the S., terminating S. E. by a neck of fine land extending into the Winnepisiogee. Its summit is covered with the *uvæ ursi* and low blueberry bush, which in autumn give the hill a reddish hue, from which circumstance its name was probably derived. A number of oval bluffs rise on its summit, from each of which the prospect on either hand is extensive and delightful. The N. bluff is supposed to consist of a body of iron ore. Slight attempts have been made upon the mass, and the results indicate that an effectual attempt would develope a very rich and valuable bed of ore. Bog ore is found in a brook descending from this bluff. Ossipee mountain extends its base into this town, and is a commanding elevation. On the S. part of this mountain, in Moultonborough, is a mineral chalybeate spring, the waters strongly impregnated with iron and sulphur, and efficacious in cutaneous eruptions. About a mile N. is a spring of pure cold water, 16 feet in diameter, through the centre of which the water, containing a small portion of fine white sand, is constantly thrown up to the height of two feet—the spring furnishing water sufficient for mills. On the stream nearly a mile below is a beautiful waterfall of 70 feet perpendicular. Descending on the left of this fall, a cave is found, containing charcoal and other evidences of its having been a hiding place for the Indians. Red Hill river originates in Sandwich, and passes through this town into the Winnepisiogee. Long pond is a beautiful sheet of water, and connects with the lake by a channel 60 rods in length. Squam and Winnepisiogee lakes lie partly in Moultonborough. The soil of this town is fruitful, though in some parts rocky. The E. winds falling over Ossipee mountain are frequently destructive and always violent. The N. W. winds falling over Red Hill are also violent, and frequently do much damage. Moultonborough was granted by the Masonian proprietors, Nov. 17, 1763, to Col. Jonathan Moulton and 61 others, principally from Hampton. Settlements commenced in 1764, by Ezekiel Moulton and a few others, and in the following year others joined them. The first house for public worship was erected in 1773, and was blown down by an E. wind in Dec. 1819. March 12, 1777, a congregational church was embodied, and in Oct. 1778, Rev. Samuel Perley was ordained, but continued only a few months. Rev. *Jeremiah Shaw*, from Hampton, who graduated at Harvard college in 1767, at the age of 20, was ordained Nov. 17, 1779. In 1816, his civil contract with the town was annulled; yet he still preaches to his church, and people. He is one of the oldest clergymen in N. H., and during his ministry has solemnized more than 400 marriages. Many Indian implements and relics have been found indicating this to have been once their favorite residence. In 1820, on a small island in the Winnepisiogee, was found a curious gun-barrel much worn by age and rust, divested of its stock, enclosed in the body of a pitch pine tree 16 inches in diameter. Its butt rested on a flat rock, its muzzle elevated about 30°. In 1819, a small dirk 1 1-2 feet in length from the point to the end of the hilt, round blade, was found in a new field one foot under ground, bearing strong marks of antiquity. On the line of Tuftonborough, on the shore of the lake, at the mouth of Melvin river, a gigantic skeleton was found about 15 years since buried in a sandy soil, apparently that of a man more than seven feet high—the jaw bones easily passing over the face of a large man. A tumulus has been discovered on a piece of newly cleared land, of the length and appearance of a human grave, and handsomely rounded with small stones, not found in this part of the country; which stones are too closely placed to be separated by striking an ordinary blow with a crow-bar, and bear marks of being a composition. The Ossipee tribe of Indians once resided in this vicinity, and some years since a tree was standing in Moultonborough, on which was carved in hieroglyphics the history of their expeditions. Pop. 1279.

N.

NARMARCUNGAWACK, a branch of the Ameriscoggin, rises in the township of Success, and unites with the main stream in Paulsburgh.

NASH AND SAWYER'S LOCATION, in the county of Coos, lat. 44° 13′, is a tract of 2184 acres, granted May 20, 1773, to Timothy Nash and Benjamin Sawyer, for their labor and expense in exploring a route through the White Mountains. The pass through the notch, the only route by which the inhabitants beyond the mountains, can reach the eastern settlements, without a great circuit, was known to the Indians; but to the people of New-Hampshire it was either unknown, or they had forgotten it. Nash made the discovery, and afterwards admitted Sawyer to a share of the benefits. They were both hunters, and the property was of little service to them. This tract is bounded N. by Bretton Woods, E. by the White Mountains, S. by Chadbourne and Hart's Location, W. by lands ungranted. Pop. 22.

NASH's stream, a branch of the Upper Amonoosuck, has its sources in Stratford and the lands E., and unites with the river in the N. W. part of Piercy.

NASHUA river, a beautiful stream in the S. part of Hillsborough county, has its source in Worcester county, Mass. It is formed of two branches called the N. and S. branches. The N. branch is formed of two streams, one from Ashburnham, the other from Wachuset pond.— The S. branch is composed of Still river, issuing from the E. side of Wachuset mountain, and a small stream from Quinepoxet pond in Holden. These branches are united in Lancaster, from which the main river proceeds in a N. E. course to Harvard, Shirley, Groton, and Pepperell in Mass.; and from thence into N. H. through Hollis, and nearly the centre of Dunstable, where it falls into Merrimack river.

NASHUA village, on the preceding river, in Dunstable, is 11 miles from Amherst, 36 from Boston, and 32 from Concord. It is a place of considerable business, being situated near the Merrimack river, and on the great road from Amherst to Boston, and on the road mostly travelled by teams from Concord to Boston. Its location is pleasant, and it has a number of handsome buildings.

NELSON, post-township, in Cheshire county, in lat. 42° 59′, is bounded N. by Stoddard, E. by Antrim and Hancock, S. by Dublin, W. by Roxbury and Sullivan, containing 22,875 acres, being 40 miles from Concord. This town is situated on the height of land between Connecticut and Merrimack rivers.

The surface is hilly, but good for grazing. The streams are small. In the S. part, a branch of Ashuelot river rises, and from Long pond in this town and Hancock, issues a branch of Contoocook river. The best mill privileges are furnished by streams, issuing from ponds in this town, of which there are four, containing a surface of 1800 acres. There is a cotton factory, in which property to the amount of $10,000 is invested. The principal articles of produce are beef, pork, butter and cheese. The inhabitants are principally farmers of industrious habits. This town was originally called *Monadnock No. 6.* It was granted by the Masonian proprietors; and chartered Feb. 22, 1774, by the name of *Packersfield,* from Thomas Packer, who owned about one half of the township. In June, 1814, the name was altered to Nelson. The first settlements commenced in 1767, by Breed Batchelder, and in 1768, by Dr. Nathaniel Breed. The congregational church was formed Jan. 31, 1781, at which time Rev. Jacob Foster was installed. He was dismissed in 1791. Rev. *Gad Newell,* who graduated at Yale college in 1786, was ordained June 11, 1774. The number of church members in 1822, was 152. Pop. 907.

NEW-BOSTON, post-township, in Hillsborough county, in lat. 42° 58′, is bounded N. by Weare, E. by Goffstown and Bedford, S. by Amherst and Lyndeborough, and W. by Lyndeborough and Francestown, containing an area of 26,536 acres. It is 9 miles from Amherst, 22 from Concord, and 57 from Boston. It is watered by several streams, the largest of which is the S. branch of Piscataquog river, having its source in Pleasant pond in Francestown. This town consists of fertile hills, productive vales, and some valuable meadows. The soil is favorable for all the various productions common to this section of the state, and there are many excellent farms under good cultivation. In the S. part of New-Boston, there is a considerable elevation, called Jo English hill, on one side of which it is nearly perpendicular. Its height, taken from the road through the notch of the hill, is 572 feet. Beard's pond, in the N. E. part, and Jo English pond, in the S. part of this town and the N. part of Amherst, are the only ponds of note. The 2d N. H. turnpike passes through the S. W. corner of this town, near which are the Cristy mills. There is a social library, of 200 volumes, incorporated June 16, 1801. The following natives of this town have received a collegiate education. William Wilson, now a judge of the supreme court of the state of Ohio, William Ferson, Nathaniel Peabody, Rev. Thomas Cochran, Peter Cochran, Robert Cochran, and Rev. Samuel Clark. There is a ministerial fund, of which the annual interest is $344 55. New-Boston was granted by Massachusets, Jan. 14, 1736, to inhabitants of Boston, from which circumstance it received its name. It was incorporated by N. H. Feb. 18, 1763. The first settlement commenced about the year 1733. The names of some of the earliest settlers were Cochran, Wilson, Caldwell, M'Neil, Ferson and Smith. In Sept. 1756, the settlement contained 1 saw and 1 grain mill, 31 dwelling-houses, inhabited by 27 men, 10 women, and 9 males and 10 females under the age of 14 years. The presbyterian church was formed about 1768. The first minister was Rev. Solomon Moor, a native of Newtown,

Limavady, in Ireland, who received his education at Glasgow, in Scotland, and studied theology with professor Leechman of that university. He was licensed to preach, July 26, 1762, and a few years after came to this country. In Feb. 1767, he arrived at New-Boston, and was ordained Sept. 6, 1768; died May 28, 1803, aged 67. Rev. *Ephraim P. Bradford*, who graduated at Harvard college in 1803, was ordained his successor, Feb. 26,1806. There are two baptist churches, over one of which, Rev. *Isaiah Stone* was ordained Jan. 8, 1806. Pop. 1686.

NEW-CASTLE, township, Rockingham county, lat. 43° 5', is a rough and rocky island, situated in Portsmouth Harbor, and formerly called *Great Island*. A handsome bridge, built in 1821, connects this town with Portsmouth. Here is an ancient church, but no preacher.—Rev. Samuel Moody preached here previous to the commencement of the 16th century. He was succeeded by Rev. John Emerson, ordained in 1704; Rev. William Shurtleff, in 1712; Rev. John Blunt, in 1732; Rev. David Robinson, in 174–; Rev. Stephen Chase, in 1750; and Rev. Oliver Noble, in 1784. The church is at present vacant. New-Castle was incorporated in 1693, and contains 458 acres. This island was the seat of business, when ancient *Strawberry Bank* was the mere germe of the town of Portsmouth. Fishing is here pursued with success; and the soil among the rocks, being of good quality, is made to produce abundantly. Fort Constitution and the light-house stand on this island. The position of each is very advantageous. Hon. THEODORE ATKINSON, for a number of years chief-justice of the province, secretary and president of the council, was born at New-Castle Dec. 20, 1697; graduated at Harvard in 1718; died Sept. 22,1789, aged 82. NATHAN PRIEST, Esq. for many years a member of the legislature, died here in 1822. Pop. 932.

NEW-CHESTER, post-township in Grafton county, in lat. 43° 31', is bounded N. by Bristol, Danbury, and Alexandria, E. by New-Hampton and Sanbornton, S. by Andover, W. by Wilmot, being 10 miles in length, and containing 20,000 acres. It is 24 miles from Concord, 44 from Haverhill, 25 from Hanover and 86 from Boston. It is watered by Pemigewasset and Blackwater rivers, and several small streams. Eagle pond is the only one of note. Ragged mountain is a considerable elevation and but little inferior to Kearsarge. Viewed from the summit of the neighboring hills, this town appears very uneven, yet there are many fine tracts converted into productive farms. The soil in some parts is rich and fertile—it is generally good. The forest trees are white pine, birch, beech, hemlock, maple, &c. There is at the S. E. section of the town, a flourishing village, containing an elegant meeting-house, built in 1821, and 20 dwelling-houses, situated on a spacious street 1 mile in length. There are several charitable societies; also a musical society, a social library of 100 volumes, incorporated Dec. 10, 1800. The number of deaths for 3 years ending Jan. 1, 1822, was 47. A Mr. Emerson lived to the age of 96. This town was granted Sept. 14, 1753, to 87 proprietors, who held their first meeting at Chester, and as the greater part of the first inhabitants belonged to that place, it was called New-Chester. The first settlement was in 1768.

by Capt. Cutting Favor, who died March 8, 1822, aged 85, and by Carr Huse, Esq. who was a civil magistrate 35 years, town clerk 33 years, and representative several years, and is now the oldest man in town. New-Chester was incorporated Nov. 20, 1778. In Dec. 1820, six children of Mr. William Follansbee were consumed in the flames of his house, while he and his wife were absent. There is a congregational society, incorporated Dec. 11, 1816. Pop. 970.

NEW-DURHAM, post-town, Strafford county, lat. 43° 26', is bounded N. W. by Wolfeborough and Alton, E. by Brookfield and Middleton, S. E. by Farmington, S. W. and W. by Alton; and contains 23,625 acres. The surface of this town is very uneven, a portion so rocky as to be unfit for cultivation. The soil is generally moist, and well adapted to grazing. There are 5 ponds in New-Durham, the largest of which is Merrymeeting pond, about 10 miles in circumference, from which a copious and perpetual stream runs S. and then N. W. into Merrymeeting bay in Alton. Ela's river flows from Coldrain pond into Farmington, on which is a fine waterfall. The Cocheco also has its source here. Mount Betty, Cropple-crown and Straw's mountains are the principal eminences. On the N. E. side of the latter is a remarkable cave, the entrance of which is about 3 feet wide and 10 feet high. The outer room is 20 feet square; the inner apartments grow smaller, until at the distance of 50 feet they become too small to be investigated. The sides both of the galleries and the rooms are solid granite. They bear marks of having been once united, and were probably separated by some great convulsion of nature. There is a fountain, over which a part of Ela's river passes, which is regarded as a curiosity. By sinking a small mouthed vessel into this fountain, water may be procured extremely cold and pure. Its depth has not been ascertained. Near the centre of the town is Rattlesnake hill, the S. side of which is nearly 100 feet high, and nearly perpendicular. Several other hills in this town contain precipices and cavities, some of considerable extent. New-Durham was granted in 1749, to Ebenezer Smith and others. It was incorporated Dec. 7, 1762, by its present name. Col. THOMAS TASH, who was active in forwarding the settlement, resided here during the last 20 years of his life.—He was born in Durham in 1722; was a brave officer in the French and revolutionary wars; and at the close of the latter, removed to New-Durham, where he died at the age of 87. Rev. Nathaniel Porter was ordained over a congregational church here Sept. 8, 1773, and removed in 1777. Elder Benjamin Randall, the founder of the sect of freewill baptists, commenced his labors here in 1780, and organized a church. He died in 1808, aged 60. Elders *Joseph Boody* and *Jonathan Kenney* are the present preachers. The N. H. Charitable Society was formed here in 1813. Pop. 1168.

NEW-FOUND, the name of a large pond, and a river, in the county of Grafton. *See Bristol.*

NEW-HAMPTON, post-township, is situated in the N. W. corner of Strafford county, lat. 43° 37'; bounded W. by Pemigewasset river, N. by Holderness, E. by Centre-Harbor, S. by Meredith and Sanbornton, and comprises an area of 19,422 acres. Pemigewasset river, which washes the W. boundary is the only stream of magnitude;

and over it is thrown the bridge which unites the town with Bristol. There is a remarkable spring on the W. side of Kelley's hill in this town, from which issues a stream sufficient to supply several mills, &c. This stream is never affected by rains or droughts, and falls into the river after running about a mile. Pemigewasset pond lies on the border of Meredith, and is about 200 rods in diameter. There is another, called Measley pond, and three other smaller ponds. The soil of New-Hampton, though the surface is broken and uneven, is remarkably fertile, producing in abundance most kinds of grain and grass. The industry of the inhabitants has enabled them in years of scarcity to supply the wants of other towns. In the S. part of the town there is a high hill of a conical form which may be seen in almost any direction from 10 to 50 miles—the prospect from the summit of which is very pleasant. The first religious society was a baptist church formed in 1782, of members from Holderness, Bridgewater and New-Hampton, over which was ordained the same year Eld. Jeremiah Ward—he died in 1816. There are two societies of freewill baptists, and several preachers of that denomination. In June, 1800, Rev. Salmon Hibbard was ordained over a small congregational church, and dismissed in 1816. There is also a small society of methodists. There are 3 meeting-houses for different denominations; a flourishing academy lately incorporated, and a social library. In 1763, Gen. Jonathan Moulton of Hampton, having an Ox weighing 1400 pounds fattened for the purpose, hoisted a flag upon his horns and drove him to Portsmouth as a present to Gov. Wentworth. He refused to receive any compensation, but merely as a token of the Governor's friendship and esteem, he would like to have a charter of a small gore of land he had discovered adjoining the town of Moultonborough, of which he was one of the principal proprietors. It was granted, and he called it *New-Hampton*, in honor of his native town. It was incorporated Nov. 27, 1777. Centre-Harbor was set off as a separate town in 1791. The first settler was Samuel Kelley, who moved here in 1775—when the cry of war was heard on the sea-board, and the yell of the savage resounded on the north. The oldest person is Widow Sarah Kelley: she is now 103 years of age. Pop. 1500.

NEWICHAWANNOCK. *See Pascataqua.*

NEWINGTON, a township, Rockingham county, in lat. 43° 5′, is bounded N. E by the Pascataqua, E. by Portsmouth, S. by Greenland and Great Bay, W. and N. W. by Great and Little Bays; and contains 5,273 acres. The soil is generally sandy and unproductive; excepting near the waters, where it yields good crops of grain and grass. At Fox point, in the N. W. part of the town, Pascataqua bridge is thrown over the river to Goat island, and thence to Durham shore. The bridge was erected in 1793, is 2600 feet long, and 40 wide—cost $65,401. Newington was originally a part of Portsmouth and Dover, and was early settled. It was disannexed and incorporated in July, 1764. Rev. Joseph Adams, the first minister of Newington, was graduated at Harvard college in 1710; ordained here in 1715; was settled over the town Dec. 15, 1774, and died May 26, 1783, at the age of 95. He was succeeded by Rev.

Joseph Langdon, ordained Jan. 9, 1788, and dismissed in March, 1810; since which time the church has been vacant. There is a respectable society of methodists, who have occasional preaching. Newington was among the settlements early exposed to the ravages of the Indians. In May, 1690, a party of Indians, under a sagamore of the name of Hoophood, attacked Fox point, destroyed several houses, killed 14 persons, and took 6 prisoners. They were immediately pursued by the inhabitants, who recovered some of the captives and a part of the plunder, after a severe action, in which Hoophood was wounded. RICHARD DOWNING, Esq. who graduated at Harvard College in 1739, was a citizen of this town, and for nearly 40 years its representative. He died at the age of 78. March 5, 1765, Mrs. Elizabeth Hight died in this town, aged 100. Mrs. Sarah Dame was lately living here, at the age of 100, in tolerable health, and able to walk about. Pop. 541.

NEW-IPSWICH, a post-town, in Hillsborough county, in lat. 42° 45', is bounded S. by Massachusetts and W. by Rindge, N. by Sharon and Temple, E. by Mason. It is 6 miles in length and 5 in breadth, and contains 20,860 acres. It is 50 miles from Concord, 70 from Portsmouth, 50 from Boston, 452 from Washington City. The town is watered by many rivulets, but principally by the Souhegan river, which is formed by the junction of two streams; the W. issuing from a small pond on the Pasture mountain, so called; the S. from two ponds in Ashburnham, Ms. near the base of Watatick hill. The Souhegan takes a N. E. course through the town, and after passing several towns empties into the Merrimack. Over it is a stone bridge built in 1817, by the proprietors of the 3d N. H. turnpike. This turnpike, commencing at Bellows falls on Connecticut river, passes through Walpole, Keene, Marlborough, Jaffrey and New-Ipswich to Townsend, Ms. The bridge is 156 feet long, 22 feet wide and 42 feet high, resting in a single arch of split stone—cost $3500. There are 2 woollen factories and 3 of cotton; 1 carding machine distinct from the woollen factories; 1 mill for grinding tanner's bark; 1 oil mill. The first cotton factory built in the state was in 1803, and is among the above mentioned; the former building has been taken down and now rebuilt with brick, 84 feet in length, 40 in width, and 3 stories high; contains 500 spindles, a double speeder, warper, dresser, &c. and 16 looms for weaving sheeting, and will shortly contain apparatus sufficient to employ 50 looms. The 2d factory contains 500 spindles without looms. The 3d, 250 spindles without looms. There are two small ponds, one called Pratt's pond, the other Hoar's pond, containing about 50 acres each. The soil is termed the soil of the *Monadnocks*, yielding excellent pasturage. Under cultivation, Indian corn, rye, oats, barley, potatoes, beans, turnips, &c. are produced in abundance. The number of deaths for 41 years ending Jan. 1, 1822, was 426. The New-Ipswich academy was incorporated June 18, 1789. Its funds amount to $3000. The annual average of scholars is 50. The library consists of 100 volumes, a donation of Samuel Appleton, Esq. a native of the town, who also presented the academy with a pair of globes. There is also an appendage to the library of 100 volumes belonging to the Demosthenean society. The principal village is the centre of the town, in a pleasant and fertile valley running N. and S., and contains between 30 and 40 dwelling houses. Here are the congregational and baptist meeting houses, town house and academy. The public houses are finished in handsome style. Many of the dwelling houses are of brick, and are elegant in appearance. There are 3 houses for public entertainment; four retailing stores, where an assortment of foreign and domestic merchandize is constantly supplied. New-Ipswich was first granted by Massachusetts. It was settled prior to 1749, by Reuben Kidder, Archibald White, Joseph & Ebenezer Bullard, Joseph Stevens and eight others. It was re-granted in April 1750, by the Masonian proprietors, and was incorporated by charter, Sept. 9, 1762. The first settlers had preaching before 1750—a church was gathered and occasionally communed. The first minister was the Rev. Stephen Farrar, a native of Lincoln, Ms. where he was born Oct. 22, 1738. He graduated at Harvard College in 1735; was ordained Oct. 22, 1760; died June 23, 1809, aged 71. Rev. *Richard Hall* succeeded and was ordained March 12, 1812. The baptist church, which separated from the church in Temple, was formed in 1811. Rev. John Parkhurst, who graduated at Harvard college, in 1811, was ordained in 1814; dismissed in 1820. Rev. *Ferris Moore* succeeded Mr. Parkhurst. Many worthy and good men have resided in this town. We have room to notice only a few of them. Reuben Kidder, Esq. one of the first settlers, and the first civil magistrate, died in Sept. 1793, aged 70. Dr. John Preston was the first physician— was eminent in his profession. He was a patriot of the revolution, several times a member of the General Court, and a useful magistrate under the new constitution of the state. He died in Feb. 1803, aged 64. Ephraim Adams and Benjamin Adams, brothers and first settlers, and deacons of the church, were useful men and did much good in society. The former was at the taking of Louisburgh in 1745, was representative many years, and died March 1797, aged 72. Benjamin died May, 1815, aged 86. Hon. CHARLES BARRETT, one of the principal donors to the academy, was a counsellor and senator several years. He died Sept. 21, 1808, aged 63. Hon. EBENEZER CHAMPNEY was the first lawyer in town. He graduated at Harvard college in 1760; came here in 1768; was 16 years judge of probate. Pop. 1278.

NEW-LONDON, a post town in Hillsborough county, in lat. 43° 27′, is bounded N. and E. by Wilmot, S. by Sutton and Fishersfield, W. by Sunapee lake, and N. W. by Springfield, containing about 17,000 acres. It is 33 miles from Concord, 75 from Portsmouth, and 90 from Boston. Lake Sunapee separates this town from Wendell, and is the principal source of Sugar river. There are three considerable ponds. Little Sunapee pond, 1 1-2 miles in length and 3-4 of a mile in width, lies in the W. part and empties its waters into Lake Sunapee. Harvey's and Messer's ponds, near the centre of the town, are the principal sources of Warner river. They are about a mile in length, and 3-4 of a mile in breadth, and are separated by a bog, many parts of which rise and fall with the water. Pleasant pond, in the N. part of New-London, is nearly 2 miles long and 1 wide. The settlements of

New-London are formed principally on three large swells of land, extending through the town in a N. W. direction. The soil is deep and generally good. The growth is maple, birch, beech, white ash, hemlock, &c. In the N. part, are several elevations. In some parts the land is rocky, but there is little not capable of cultivation. There is a musical society, a female cent society, and a social library, incorporated June 9, 1801, of 100 volumes. The number of deaths from April 20, 1809, to July 3, 1822, was 130. The two first settlers were Nathaniel Merrill and James Lamb. They was followed by Eliphalet Lyon and Ebenezer Hunting. John Lamb was the first child born in town—about 1776. New-London was incorporated June 25, 1779. Its first name was *Dantzick*: Dr. Belknap says, *Heidlcburg*. A baptist church was formed Oct. 23, 1788. Rev. *Job Seamans*, who was born at Swanzey, Ms. May 24, 1748, was ordained Jan. 21, 1789. The number of church members is about 200. There is a small society of universalists and some freewill baptists. Two natives of New-London have received a collegiate education, both at Dartmouth College—John H. Slack in 1811, and Benjamin Woodbury in 1817. The damage sustained by the inhabitants in the W. part of this town, by the violent whirlwind of Sept. 9, 1821, was estimated at $9000. Pop. 924.

NEW-MARKET, post-town, Rockingham county, in lat. 43° 3′, is bounded N. by Lee and Durham, E. by Squamscot river and Great Bay, S. by Exeter, and W. by Epping; comprising an area of 11,082 acres. Piscassick river passes through this town into Durham. The Lamprey river washes its N.

E. boundary, as does the Squamscot the S. E. The soil is good, and agricultural pursuits are here crowned with much success. There are several pleasant and thriving villages. New-Market was originally a part of Exeter, and was detached and incorporated Dec. 15, 1727. Rev. John Moody was ordained here in 1730, and died in 1778, aged 73. Rev. Nathaniel Ewer afterwards preached here. Rev. S. Tombs was ordained in 1794; afterwards removed. Rev. James Thurston was ordained Oct. 15, 1800, and soon after removed. The congregational church has since been vacant. Rev. *John Brodhead* is pastor of the methodist church; and Rev. *Thomas Cheswell* pastor of the baptist church. From 1731 to 1770, there were in New-Market 948 baptisms and 554 deaths, averaging about 28 of the former and 14 of the latter annually. New-Market Wesleyan Academy, a flourishing institution, was incorporated June 23, 1818. Mrs. Fanny Shute, who died in this town Sept. 1819, was regarded with respect not only for her excellent qualities, but the adventures of her youth. When 13 months old, she was taken by a party of Indians, carried to Canada, and disposed of to the French—educated in a nunnery, and after remaining 13 years in captivity, was redeemed and restored to her friends. An interesting narrative of her captivity may be found in vol. I, Hist. Coll. p. 116. Pop. in 1820—1083.

NEWPORT, post-town, Cheshire co., lat. 43° 21′, has Croydon on the N., Wendell on the E., Goshen and Unity S., and Claremont W., comprising an area of 25,267 acres, 40 miles from Concord and 96 from Boston. Its central situation, as it regards the towns in the northern half of the county, together with the enterprising spirit of its inhabitants, has rendered it a place of considerable business. Near the centre of the town, and the confluence of the E. and S. branches of Sugar river, on the Croydon turnpike, is a handsome village, of about 30 houses, two meeting houses, four stores, two taverns, a cotton factory and several mechanic shops. A mail stage passes through this town from Boston to Windsor, Vt. 3 times a week. Its soil may be said to be of three kinds, *alluvial* on the borders of the different branches of Sugar river, particularly on the S. and N. branches, forming rich and fertile meadows, extending one fourth of a mile generally from each side of the river; *dry* and *gravelly*, on the low grounds in other parts of the town; and *moist* and cold on the hills and elevated parts. In general, the soil is rich and productive. Sugar river flows through this town, and its three branches unite near the village, whence it passes through Claremont into the Connecticut. On the eastern branch are situated principally near the village, 1 cotton factory, 4 saw mills 2 grain mills, 1 oil mill, 2 clothing mills, 2 tanneries with each a bark mill, and a carding machine. There are besides these in the town 5 saw mills, one grain mill, 1 clothing mill, 1 carding machine and a trip hammer. One grain mill near the village has four runs of stones and two bolts. There are two ponds of small extent—Nettleton's pond in the easterly, and Chapin's pond in the N. W. part of the town. In these, especially in Chapin's pond, trout and other fish are caught. There are a few eminences designated by Bald mountain, Coit mountain, East mountain, and Blueberry hill. Croydon turnpike passes through this town from Lebanon to Amherst, and N. of the village receives Cornish turnpike from Windsor, Vt. The highways are generally in good repair, and the four principal roads leading from the village to the four adjoining towns are generally smooth and level. An academy was incorporated in June 1818; is without funds—and the average number of students attending it is about 35. This town is divided into 14 school districts; in most of which are handsome and convenient school houses. The average number of scholars belonging to these districts is about 40 to each. There are a social library, incorporated in June, 1803, containing about 200 volumes, an instrumental music society, incorporated with a fund of about $300, since expended in the purchase of musical instruments, two female cent societies, two charitable societies, one tract society, a society for educating heathen youth, and a missionary society. Corinthian Lodge of freemasons is located in this town, and was chartered in 1816. Those from this town, who have received a collegiate education, are at *Dartmouth college*, 1794, Abijah Wines; 1804, Uriah Wilcox; 1804, Hubbard Newton; 1808, Benjamin Sawyer; 1809, Horatio Buel; 1811, Hosea Wheeler; 1816, John Wilcox; 1816, William Chapin; Carlton Hurd, 1818; at *Yale college*, 1808, James H. Parmele. Newport was granted by charter, Oct. 6, 1761. The first effort towards a settlement was made in the fall of 1763, by Jesse Wilcox, Ebenezer Merrit, Jesse Kelsey and Samuel Hurd. The first settlers were principally from North Killingworth, Conn. The first birth was a child of Jesse Wilcox and wife, which died in a few days. There are here three churches, one congregational, and two baptist. The congregational church was gathered in 1779. Rev. John Remelee was ordained Jan. 1783; dismissed Feb. 1791. Rev. Abijah Wines was ordained Jan. 1795; dismissed Nov. 1816. Rev. James R. Wheelock, ordained Dec. 2, 1818; dismissed 1823. The congregational society have recently erected an elegant meeting house, which was dedicated March 13, 1823. The first baptist church was formed in 1779. Rev. Biel Ledoyt was settled in 1791; dismissed in 1805. Rev. Thomas Brown, settled 1806; dismissed in 1813. Rev. Elisha Hutchinson succeeded Mr. Brown. Rev. *Solomon Howe* was then called to the care of one church; and, in 1823, Rev. *Ira Persons* was called to the care of the other. Pop. 1679.

NEWTOWN, township, Rockingham county, 40 miles from Concord and 27 from Portsmouth, is in lat. 42° 51′, and bounded N. by Kingston, E. by South-Hampton, S. by Massachusetts, W. by Plaistow, and comprises 5,250 acres. Nearly one third of Country pond lies in Newtown, and two other small ponds connect by outlets with its waters. The soil produces good crops of grain or grass. Joseph Bartlett first settled in this town in 1720, and was soon joined by several others. Twelve years previous to his settlement here, Bartlett was taken prisoner by the Indians at Haverhill, and remained a captive in Canada about four years. Rev. Jona. Eames was settled here in 1759; removed in 1791; died at Wentworth in 1800. The baptist church at Newtown is the oldest of that denomination in this state. Rev. Walter Powers was settled here in 1755, when that church was gathered. Rev. John Peak succeeded him in 1795, who was removed in 1802. Rev. *David Tewksbury* was ordained in 1813. There are methodist and free will baptist societies here. Pop. 477.

NORTHFIELD, post-town, lat. 43° 25′, in the N. W. corner of Rockingham county, is bounded N. by Winnepisiogee river, which divides it from Sanbornton; E. by Gilmanton, S. by Canterbury, W. by the Merrimack, which separates it from Salisbury and Boscawen; and contains about 20,000 acres of land and water. The soil here is in some parts good—that of the best quality lies on the two ridges extending through the town. Chesnut pond lies in the E. part of the town, and its waters flow into the Winnepisiogee three miles from its junction with the Pemigewasset. Sondogardy pond is in the S. part of the town, and flows into the Merrimack. At the N. W. part of the town, near Webster's falls, the Winnepisiogee falls into the Pemigewasset, and the united streams form the Merrimack river. The principal elevation, called Bean Hill, separates the town from Canterbury. The first settlement was made here in 1760 by Benjamin Blanchard and others. Here is a meeting house, open to all denominations. A methodist church was formed here in 1806; and there are some congregationalists and baptists. There is a valuable paper-mill established by Messrs. Crane & Peabody; also a woollen factory, and several mills. An extensive cotton factory has been recently erected, and promises much usefulness. Northfield was incorporated June 19, 1780, and has 1304 inhabitants.

NORTH OF LAT. 45°, is a tract belonging to the state of N. H. extending to the British possessions in L. Canada. It was surveyed in 1805, and contains 160,363 acres. Lake Connecticut and several considerable ponds are situated within this tract; and numerous streams from the mountains unite with the main branches of the Connecticut.

NORTH-HAMPTON, a township, in Rockingham co., lat. 42° 59′, formerly constituting the parish called *North-Hill*, in Hampton, is bounded N. by Greenland, E. by Rye and the sea, S. by Hampton, and W. by Stratham. It is 50 miles from Concord, and contains 8,465 acres.—Here are two small rivers—Little river rises in the low grounds in the N. part of the town, and after running S. E. one or two miles, takes an E. course, falling into the sea between Little Boar's Head in this town and Great Boar's Head in Hampton. The mouth of this river was anciently the boundary between Hampton and Portsmouth. Wisnicut river, rises near the centre of the town, and passes N. W. through Stratham and Greenland into Great Bay. The first settlements commenced early. The first meeting-house was built in 1738, and Nov. 17th, of this year, the inhabitants were made a distinct parish, by the general court. Nov. 26, 1742, the town was incorporated. Rev. Nathaniel Gookin, son of Mr. Gookin of Hampton, and father of Judge Daniel Gookin, was ordained here Oct. 31, 1739; died Oct. 22, 1766, æt. 53. The present meeting-house was erected in 1761. Rev. Joseph S. Hastings was ordained Feb. 11, 1767; removed July 3, 1774. Rev. David M'Clure, D. D. ordained November 13, 1776, resigned Aug. 30, 1785. Rev. Benjamin Thurston, ordained Nov. 2, 1785, was dismissed Oct. 27, 1800. Rev. *Jonathan French* was settled Nov. 18, 1801.

There is an incorporated baptist society; also a female charitable society, and an incorporated social library. Maj. Gen. Henry Dearborn, now American minister at Portugal, was born here Feb. 12, 1750. Rev. Henry Alline, an eccentric clergyman, from Nova-Scotia, died here Feb. 2, 1784, aged 35. In the early periods of the settlement, the people were annoyed by the Indians. Garrisons were erected, to which during periods of danger the inhabitants resorted. About 1677, several persons were killed within the limits of this town. The number of deaths from 1801 to 1821, was 224; baptisms 200. Pop. 764.

NORTH river has its sources in Northwood and Nottingham, and passes S. E. through Nottingham, a part of Lee, and unites with Lamprey river near the N. E. corner of Epping.

NORTHUMBERLAND, township, Coos co., in lat. 44° 33′, is bounded S. W. by Lancaster, S. by Piercy, N. E. by Stratford, W. by Guildhall and Maidstone, Vt. This town is 130 miles from Concord. The soil along the Connecticut is very productive, perfectly free from stone and gravel, and originally covered with a growth of butternut. A portion of the upland is also good, and covered with pine, spruce, fir, ash, maple, &c. Cape Horn, an abrupt mountain of 1000 feet in height, lies near the centre of the town. Its N. base is separated from the Connecticut by a narrow plain, and the Upper Amonoosuck passes near its E. base, as it falls into the Connecticut. Here the meadows are extensive, and are annually covered by the spring floods, presenting the appearance of an inland sea. At the falls in the Connecticut, below the mouth of the Amonoosuck, a handsome bridge connects

Northumberland with Guildhall. A dam is also thrown across the river at this place, at both ends of which grain and saw mills are erected. On the Northumberland side, are a clothing mill and carding machine. The court-house for Essex county, Vt. stands on the N. side of the falls, and on both sides are small villages. The first settlers were Thos. Burnside and Daniel Spaulding, with their families—who moved into town in June, 1767. The meeting-house stands on a plain N. of Cape Horn mountain. There is no settled minister. Near the river, on this plain, a small fort was erected during the revolutionary war, and placed in the command of Capt. Jeremiah Eames, afterwards well known for his usefulness, and the wit and pleasantry of his conversation. Northumberland was incorporated Nov. 16, 1779. Pop. 300.

NORTHWOOD, post township, in Rockingham county, lat. 43° 12', is bounded N. E. by Strafford, S. E. by Nottingham, S. and S. W. by Deerfield, N. W. by Epsom and Pittsfield. It is 18 miles from Concord, 20 from Exeter, 24 from Portsmouth, and contains 17,075 acres of land and water. There are 6 ponds in this town—Suncook pond, 750 rods long, 100 wide; Jenness' pond, 300 rods long, 150 wide; Long pond, about 300 rods long, 50 wide; Harvey's pond, of an elliptical form, 200 rods long, from 40 to 80 wide; a part of Great Bow pond is also in this town, and a part of North river pond; Pleasant pond, and Little Bow pond, the latter having two outlets: the waters passing N. E. into Great Bow pond, the head of Isinglass river; and N. W. into Long pond, the waters thence passing through Suncook pond and river into the Merrimack. The north branch of Lamprey river has its rise in this town near Saddleback mountain, a high ridge between this town and Deerfield. On the E. side of this ridge are found crystals and crystalline spars of various colors and sizes. Graphite exists in small quantities, but of good quality. This town has an elevated site, and commands a distant and varied prospect. The waters flowing from the farm of Jonathan Clarke, Esq. fall into three different rivers, the Suncook, Lamprey and Isinglass rivers. The soil of this town is generally moist, and well suited to grazing.— The N. H. turnpike passes in a direct course from E. to W. 8 miles through this town. Northwood was originally a part of Nottingham and was settled March, 25, 1763, by Moses Godfrey, John Bachelder, Increase Bachelder, from North-Hampton. Solomon Bickford and family from Durham, followed in December. His son, Solomon, was the first child born in Northwood.— Feb. 6, 1773, the town was incorporated. Rev. Edmund Pillsbury, the first minister, was ordained over the baptist church, Nov. 17, 1779, and continued to preach about 18 years. The congregational meeting-house was erected in 1781; and on the 29th May, 1799, Rev. *Josiah Prentice* was ordained. The baptist church was without a pastor from Mr. Pillsbury's secession until Dec. 30, 1805, when Rev. *Eliphalet Merrill* was ordained. Only one native of Northwood (Rev. John L. Blake, who graduated at Brown University in 1812) has received a collegiate education. The late Jonathan Clarke, Esq. was one of the first settlers, and a member of the legislature. Pop. 1260.

NOTCH. See *White Mountains*.

NOTTINGHAM, post-town, Rockingham county, in lat. 43° 07' is 25 miles from Concord, 20 from

Portsmouth, 55 from Boston, and is bounded N. E. by Barrington, S. E. by Lee and part of Epping, S. by Epping and Raymond, and W. by Deerfield and Northwood, comprising 25,800 acres, of which 300 are water. There are several ponds in this town, mostly of small size.—Little river and several other streams rise here; and North river passes through the town. The soil of this town is in many parts good, though the surface is rough and broken. Several mountains extend along the W. part of the town, forming parts of the range called Blue Hills. *Nottingham Square* is a pleasant village on an elevated site, having a meeting-house, post-office, public houses, stores, &c. The N. H. turnpike road passes through the N. part of this town.—Bog iron ore is found here in great quantities; and it is said inexhaustible masses of mountain ore exist in the mountains. Crystals and crystalline spars are found here; and also ochres in small quantities. Nottingham was incorporated May 10, 1722, and settled in 1727, by Capt. Joseph Cilley and others.—A congregational church was formed, and Rev. Stephen Emery settled in 1742, who continued but a few years. Rev. Benjamin Butler succeeded in 1758, and was dismissed Aug. 1, 1770, at his own request. The church has since been vacant. Rev. Mr. Butler was afterwards a civil magistrate until his death, 26th December, 1804. Elder Samuel B. Dyer was some time pastor of the freewill baptist society. During the last Indian war, in 1752, a Mr. Beard, Mrs. Folsom and Mrs. Simpson, wife of Andrew Simpson, were killed by the Indians. They had left the garrison to attend to some business at their houses, situated at a short distance, where they were surprised and put to death. Gen. JOSEPH CILLEY, son of one of the early settlers, entered the army of the revolution at its commencement and commanded the 1st N. H. regiment. He was distinguished for bravery and patriotism during the whole contest. After the liberties of the country were secured, he was several times elected representative, senator and counsellor; and died in Aug. 1799, aged 65. Hon. THOS. BARTLETT was an active revolutionary patriot; one of the committee of safety; lt. col. under Stark at the capture of Burgoyne; commanded a regiment at West-Point in 1780, when the treachery of Arnold betrayed that post. After the close of the war, he was speaker of the house, and a justice of the common pleas; and died June 30, 1807, aged 59. Gen. HENRY BUTLER, was an officer in the army of the revolution, major-general of militia, justice of the peace and senator in the legislature: he died July 20, 1813, aged 62. Descendants of these revolutionary worthies now live in town. Nottingham has been a very healthy town, and many individuals have lived to a great age. The mountainous parts of the town were formerly the haunts of beasts of prey—the fox and wild cat only remain. Rattlesnakes still infest the mountains. Pop. 1126.

NOTTINGHAM-WEST, a post-township, in Hillsborough county, in lat. 42° 44′, is bounded N. by Litchfield and Londonderry, E. by Windham and Pelham, S. by Tyngsborough in Mass., and W. by Merrimack river, which separates it from Dunstable, containing 17,379 acres. It is 17 miles from Amherst, 39 from Boston, and 38 from Concord. The land here is of easy cultivation. On the river are fine intervals, of a deep rich soil, producing in great exuberance and plenty. Distant from the river, the land is hilly and somewhat broken. The forest trees are oak and pine, with some walnut, birch, maple and hemlock. There are two ponds, known by the name of Little Massabesick and Otternick ponds. The former is situated in the N. E. part, and contains about 200 acres. Otternick, in the W. part of the town, between the N. meeting-house and the river, contains about 80 acres. A small stream issues from the last which runs into the Merrimack. There are two libraries in this town. Nottingham-West was included in the grant of Dunstable, and was settled as early as 1710. Some of the early names were Blodget, Winn, Lovewell, Colburn, Hill, Greeley, Cross, Cumings, Pollard, Marsh and Merrill. The first settlements were made on the banks of the river, where the Indians had cleared fields for cultivating corn. The first inhabitants lived in garrisons. While the men were abroad in the fields and forests, the women and children were lodged in these places of security. Few Indians were found here when the settlement was effected, but they frequently made their visits to this place in time of peace; and once in a time of war, they took a man by the name of Cross, who was employed in collecting turpentine, and carried him to Canada, where he remained a prisoner till he was ransomed by his friends. Near the Indian cornfields, have been found cinders of a blacksmith's forge, which have led to the conjecture that they employed a smith to manufacture their implements of war and agriculture. Nottingham-West was incorporated July 5, 1746. An addition to its territory from Londonderry, was made by act of the general court, March 6, 1778. A congregational church was formed Nov. 30, 1737, and on the same day, Rev. Nathaniel Merrill was ordained, whose relation to the church continued till his death in 1796, though his civil contract was dissolved in 1774. Rev. Jabez Pond Fisher succeeded Mr. Merrill; was ordained Feb. 24, 1796, and dismissed May, 1801. A presbyterian church was organized in 1771. Rev. John Strickland was ordained July 13, 1774, and after a few years was dismissed. A baptist church was formed in 1805, over which Rev. Daniel Merrill officiated from 1814 to 1819. In 1816, the congregational church changed their form of government and united with the presbyterians. Pop. 1227.

O.

OLIVERIAN river, in Grafton county, is formed of two branches, both having their sources in Coventry—the E. branch from the W. side of Moosehillock mountain, and the N. branch from Owl head mountain. These branches unite near the E. line of Haverhill, and main stream pursues nearly a W. course through the S. part of the town, and falls into Connecticut river above Bedel's bridge.

ORANGE, a township in Grafton county, in lat. 43° 39', is bounded N. E. by Groton, E. by Alexandria, S. W. by Grafton and W. by Canaan and Dame's Gore, containing by the survey of 1805, about 22,000 acres. In 1820, nearly one third of its territory was annexed to Alexandria. It is 16 miles E. from Dartmouth college and 40 from Concord. In this town are found many mineral substances, such as lead ore, iron ore, &c. There is in the S. E. part a small pond, in which is found a species of paint resembling spruce yellow. Chalk, intermixed with magnesia, is said to be procured from the same pond. In 1810, a valuable species of ochre was discovered. It is found in great abundance, deposited in veins, and of a quality superior to the imported. Large quantities of it are annually prepared for market. One man will dig and refine about 50 lbs. in a day. Clay of an excellent quality is also abundant. The surface of Orange is uneven. The soil in many parts productive. Cardigan mountain lies in the E. part of the town. On the W. side of this mountain was formerly a pest house where hundreds were inoculated for the small pox. Grafton turnpike passes through the S. W. part to Orford. Orange was granted by the name of *Cardigan*, Feb. 6, 1769, to Isaac Fellows and others. Its settlement commenced in 1773–4. Silas Harris, Benjamin Shaw, David Eames, Col. Elisha Bayne and Capt. Joseph Kenney were the first inhabitants. Pop. 300.

ORFORD, a post-township in Grafton county, in lat. 43° 53′, is bounded N. by Piermont, E. by Wentworth, S. by Lime, and W. by Fairlee, Vt. containing 27,000 acres. It lies on Connecticut river, over which is a bridge, connecting this town with Fairlee. Orford is 10 miles below Haverhill, 17 N. of Hanover, 60 from Concord and 120 from Boston. The soil is generally of a fertile character. The large interval farms, watered by the Connecticut, are particularly distinguished for their beauty and fertility. There are two considerable elevations, called Mount Cuba and Mount Sunday, lying near the centre of the town. There are 4 or 5 ponds of considerable size, one of which, called Baker's upper pond, lies within 3 or 4 miles of Connecticut river, and about the same distance W. of the height of land, E. of the river. This pond discharges its waters into another pond, lying partly in Wentworth, and the waters of both empty into Baker's river, near the meeting house in Wentworth. Indian pond lies about 1 mile W. of Baker's upper pond, the waters of which pass to the Connecticut, only 2 or 3 miles distant, offering much the cheapest and most feasible opening for connecting the waters of the Connecticut and Merrimack. Limestone, or the carbonate of lime, is found in great abundance. It is of the primitive kind, coarse grained, and forms a strong and hard cement, multiplying more in slaking and requiring a larger proportion of sand than any other heretofore used. It is found at the foot of a mountain about 400 or 500 feet above Connecticut river. The soap rock, or, as it is' more generally called, cotton stone, is found here in great abundance. A light grey granite rock, much used for mill stones and for building, is found in various places. Galena, or lead ore, of a very fine texture, containing needles of crystallized quartz, or lead, has been recently found, in considerable quantities in sinking a well. Orford contains a pleasant village, situated on the main road. "It is built on a beautiful plain bordered by interval on the W. The hills on both sides of the river, near the centre of the expansion, approach each other so as to form a kind of neck; and with a similar approximation at the two ends, give the whole the appearance of a double amphitheatre, or of the numerical figure 8. The greatest breadth of each division is about 1 1-2 miles; and the length of each between 2 and 3 miles." The houses stand principally on a single street, of 2 or 3 miles in extent. There are 2 congregational meeting houses, one in the village, the other near the centre of the town. The Orford social library was incorporated June 16, 1797, and contains 200 volumes. Orford was granted Sept. 25, 1761, to Jonathan Moulton and others. In June, 1765, a Mr. Cross, with his family from Lebanon, first settled in this town. In Oct. the same year, Gen. Israel Morey, John Mann, Esq and a Mr. Caswell, with their families, from Connecticut, began settlements. A congregational church was gathered Aug. 27, 1770, then consisting of 22 members. Rev. Oliver Noble, who graduated at Princeton college, was ordained Nov. 5, 1771; dismissed Dec. 31, 1777. Rev. John Sawyer, who graduated at Dartmouth college in 1785, was ordained Oct. 22, 1787; dismissed Dec. 1795. Rev. Sylvester Dana, who graduated at Yale college in 1797, was ordained May 20, 1801; dismissed April 30, 1822. Rev. *James D. Farnsworth* was ordained Jan. 1, 1823. A new congregational church, called the W. church, was formed April 30, 1822, and Rev. *Sylvester Dana* was installed Feb. 19, 1823. There is also a methodist church, which has existed about 12 years. Pop. 1568.

OSSIPEE, post-township, Strafford county, in lat. 43° 42′, is bounded N. by Tamworth, E. and N. E. by Effingham, S. E. by Wakefield, S. W. and W. by Wolfeborough, Tuftonborough, and Moultonborough, N. W. by a corner of Sandwich. Ossipee mountain, a rough and broken range, lies in the N. W. part of Ossipee, extending into the adjoining towns. It is 6 or 8 miles in length, and is so elevated, that in E. storms the winds break over the summits, frequently causing much injury to the farms, &c. at its base. Ossipee lake is partly in this town and Effingham: it is a fine body of water of an oval form, covering about 7000 acres, having no island, and its waters clear and beautiful. Ossipee river flows from this lake, forming the bays E. of the lake, from whence it passes through Effingham into the Saco in Maine. Pine river passes through the E. part of Ossipee, and Bearcamp river falls into the lake on the N. W. There are several ponds in Ossipee, the largest of which lies partly in Tuftonborough, and is about 400 rods long. Bear pond in the S. E. part, has no visible outlet. On the farm of Mr. Smith, near the W. shore of Ossipee lake, is a mound of earth 45 or 50 feet in diameter, of a circular form, and about 10 feet high, from which have been taken several entire skeletons, and also tomahawks, &c. exhibiting the strongest evidence that the tribe once so powerful in this vicinity had their principal residence here. (See description of this mound,&c. Hist. Coll. for 1823, p. 45.) Ossipee was incorporated Feb. 22, 1785; has 2 meeting-houses, several stores, mechanics, &c. There is a society of methodists here, but no settled minister. Pop. 1793.

OSSIPEE GORE, a township,was annexed to Effingham, Dec. 23, 1820.

OSSIPEE mountain. *See Ossipee.*

OYSTER river. *See Durham.*

P.

PARKER'S island, in Connecticut river, at Hanover, contains 20 acres.

PASCATAQUA, the only large river whose entire course is in

New-Hampshire, is formed by the junction of several small streams in a wide and deep bed; hollowed out partly by them, and partly by the tide. The names of these streams, beginning at the N. E., are Salmon-Fall, Cocheco, Bellamybank, Oyster, Lamprey, Squamscot, and Winnicut rivers. The five last unite their waters in a large and irregular bay between Durham and Greenland, more resembling a lake than a river. The waters of this bay meet those of Salmon-Fall and Cocheco rivers, coming from the N. W. at Hilton's point, a few miles below Dover. After this junction, they proceed in a direct line to the S. E.; and join the ocean 2 or 3 miles below Portsmouth; embosoming several islands, and forming one of the best harbors on the continent. Few rivers make a more magnificent appearance than this; yet the streams by which it is supplied are small. Salmon-Fall furnishes more than all the rest. This stream is called *Newichawannock* from the falls in Berwick till it receives the waters of the Cocheco; but the name of Pascataqua ought to be applied to the whole of Salmon-Fall river.

PASCATAQUA harbor. *See Portsmouth.*

PAULSBURGH, a township in Coos county, in lat. 44° 30′, is 139 miles from Concord, and about 22 from Lancaster; bounded N. by Dummer and Cambridge, E. by Success, S. by Maynesborough, W. by Kilkenny and Winslow's location. This tract was granted Dec. 31, 1771, to the grantees of Maynesborough, Sir William Mayne and others, and contains 31,154 acres. The Upper Amonoosuck and Ameriscoggin rivers pass through this town. There are several ponds, and some considerable mountains. The town, however, is not very mountainous, and has some low lands. There are at present but 15 families.

PEABODY river has its source in the E. pass of the White Mountains, near the head springs of Ellis' river, a branch of the Saco; and passes N. into the Ameriscoggin.

PEAKS, names of mountains. *See Stratford.*

PEELING, township, in Grafton county, in lat. 44°, is bounded N. by Lincoln, E. by Thornton, S. by Thornton and Ellsworth, and W. by Warren, Coventry and Landaff, containing 33,359 acres. It is 20 miles from Plymouth, and 60 from Concord. Pemigewasset passes through its E. section. The 3 branches of this river unite in the N. part of Peeling. There are several brooks and rivulets which supply this place with a number of mill privileges. The ponds are Elbow pond, near the centre, Russell's pond, in the E., and M'Lellan's pond in the S. E. part of this town. Hills and mountains, interspersed with valleys, give some variety to the surface. Cushman's mountain in the S. W., Black mountain in the N. W. and Blue mountain in the W. are the highest elevations. Among these mountains, branches of the Wild Amonoosuck and Baker's rivers and Moosehillock brook, have their sources. On the last stream, there is a beautiful cascade. There are here two springs, which have been termed medicinal. Peeling was granted to Eli Demeritt, Sept. 23, 1763. Its name was afterwards altered to Fairfield, and from that to Peeling again. It was settled about 1773, by John Riant and others. Lindsey, Osgood, Barron,

Russell, and Bickford, were among the early settlers. There is a baptist society, to which Mr. Thomas Whipple has occasionally ministered. Pop. 224.

PELHAM, post-township, at the S. W. corner of Rockingham county, in lat. 42° 43′, is bounded N. by Windham and Salem, E., S. E. and S. by the state of Massachusetts, W. by Nottingham-West; is distant 37 miles from Concord, 45 from Portsmouth and 32 from Boston, and contains 16,338 acres. Here are 3 ponds, called Gumpas, Island and North ponds. Island pond is the largest, containing 178 acres. 30 acres of Long pond are in Pelham, the remainder in the N. W. corner of Dracut. Beaver river passes through the town, a little E. of the meeting-house. On this river and the tributary streams, there is much valuable meadow; adjoining which are pine lands of an excellent quality for grain, and especially rye. To the E. and W. is hilly land, good for grazing, orcharding and the growth of timber, particularly oak. This land is of a strong soil, and richly repays cultivation. Beside other mills, here is a woollen factory; and 8 or 10 tons of nails are annually cut here. But the inhabitants depend principally on agriculture for the means of support. Much timber and cord-wood are carried annually to the banks of the Merrimack, and thence conveyed to Newburyport, or to Boston through Middlesex canal. Pelham was included in Wheelwright's purchase and in Mason's patent. Although within about 30 miles of the capital of New-England, no settlements were here made during the first century after the landing at Plymouth. The first settlements were made in 1722, by John Butler, William Richardson and others. William Richardson was grandfather of the Hon. judge Richardson; was a native of Chelmsford, where he was born Sept. 19, 1701. The town was incorporated July 5, 1746, about 5 years after the state line was established, by which a part was separated from Dracut. The first house for public worship was built in 1747. Rev. James Hobbs was ordained Nov. 13, 1751, and at the same time a church was formed. Mr. Hobbs died June 20, 1765, aged 40 : he was a native of Hampton, and graduated at Harvard College, 1748. Rev. Amos Moody was ordained Nov. 20, 1765, and dismissed by mutual agreement in 1792; he was born in Newbury, Ms. Nov. 20, 1739, graduated at Harvard, 1759—died March 22, 1819. Some years previous to Mr. Moody's dismission, the town became divided into two societies; another house for public worship was erected, and several candidates employed to preach. But after his dismission the town again united in one society. Rev. *John H. Church* was ordained Oct. 31, 1798. There is a social library in Pelham, incorporated in 1797, with about 200 vols. Pop. 1040.

PEMBROKE, a post-town, Rockingham county, in lat. 43° 10′, lies 60 miles N. W. from Boston, 6 S. E. from Concord. It is bounded W. by Merrimack river, N. W. by Soucook river, which separates it from Concord, N. E. and E. by Chichester and Epsom, S. E. by Suncook river, dividing the town from Allenstown; and contains 10,240 acres. This town is generally well watered. The Suncook on the S. E. boundary, furnishes many valuable water privileges; and on the Soucook, are situated 4 paper mills, the cotton factory of

T

Maj. Stark, and several mills, together with a flourishing village. The public roads are mostly laid out in right angles, dividing the territory into squares. The main street extends nearly on a parallel with Merrimack river in a straight course about 3 miles, and is very pleasant. On this are situated the academy, one of the meeting-houses, and the principal village. Pembroke has a variety of soils, mostly very productive. On the rivers are small but valuable tracts of interval, and from these the land rises in extensive and beautiful swells, yielding in abundance when properly cultivated. The public buildings are a town house, two meeting-houses, and the academy, founded by the liberal donation of the late Dr. Abel Blanchard. It is situated on the main street, and is one of the most flourishing institutions of the kind in New-Hampshire. Pembroke is the ancient *Suncook* of the Indians. It was granted by this name in May, 1727, by the government of Massachusetts, to Capt. John Lovewell, and his brave associates, in consideration of their services against the Indians. The whole number of grantees was 60; 46 of whom accompanied Lovewell in his last march to Pequawkett—the remaining 13 were among the 62 who attended him in his first enterprizes against the Indians. The first survey was made in 1728; and in the following year settlements were commenced by several of the grantees. The settlements increased slowly, in consequence of the frequent alarms from the Indians, who committed many depredations upon their property. James Carr, killed May 1, 1748, (See *Allenstown*,) was the only inhabitant who lost his life by the Indians. The first child born in Pembroke was Ephraim Moore. This town was interested in the long dispute maintained by the proprietors of Bow against the grantees of lands in this vicinity. Nov. 1, 1759, the town was incorporated by its present name. As the original settlers were composed of persons of Scotch and English descent, foundations were early laid for presbyterian and congregational churches. The congregational church was organized March 1, 1737; and Rev. Aaron Whittemore, of Concord, Ms. who graduated at Harvard college in 1734, was settled. He died Nov. 16, 1767, aged 55. No record exists of the organization of the presbyterian church; but Rev. Daniel Mitchell, a native of Ireland, educated at Edinburgh, was ordained Dec. 3, 1760, and died Dec. 15, 1776, aged 69. Rev. Jacob Emery, a native of Andover, Ms. who graduated at Harvard college in 1761, succeeded Mr. Whittemore in the congregational church, Aug. 3, 1768; and was dismissed March 23, 1775. Both churches were vacant from the death of Mr. Mitchell until the ordination of Rev. Zaccheus Colby, March 22, 1780—soon after which the two churches were united. Mr. Colby was a native of Newtown; graduated at Dartmouth college, 1777; and was dismissed May 11, 1803. From this time to 1808, the church was vacant. March 2, 1808, Rev. *Abraham Burnham*, a native of Dunbarton, graduated at Dartmouth college in 1804, was ordained over a newly organized church, of 54 members, which has since increased to more than 170. There are several religious, charitable and literary societies, which are annually extending their beneficial influence. Pop. 1256.

PEMIGEWASSET river. This stream and the Winnepisiogee constitute the Merrimack. It is formed of three principal branches having their sources in Peeling, Franconia, and the ungranted lands S. W. of the White Mountains. These branches unite in Peeling, from whence the main stream passes in a S. direction through Thornton, Campton, between Plymouth and Holderness; Bridgewater, Bristol and New-Hampton; New-Chester, Andover, and Sanbornton, and the S. W. part of Sanbornton and the N. part of Salisbury, where it unites with Winnepisiogee river, and the main stream becomes the Merrimack. From Campton to the S., the towns that lie on the E. of Pemigewasset river, are Holderness New-Hampton and Sanbornton; on the W., Plymouth, Bridgewater, Bristol, New-Chester, Andover and Salisbury.

PEQUAWKETT, written by Belknap, *Pigwacket*, and by Sullivan *Pickwocket*, but the true orthography is found to be Pe-quaw-kett; an Indian name applied to a considerable tract of country, now including Conway, Fryeburg and some of the adjacent towns. It is also the name of a river flowing into the Saco, from two ponds in Eaton; and of a mountain between Bartlett and Chatham, formerly called Kearsarge.

PETERBOROUGH, a post-town, in Hillsborough county, in lat. 42° 52′, is bounded N. by Hancock and Greenfield, E. by Greenfield and Temple, S. by Sharon, and W. by Jaffrey and Dublin, containing 23,780 acres. It lies midway between Amherst and Keene, being 20 miles from each. It is 75 miles from Portsmouth, 60 from Boston, 40 from Concord, and 510 from Washington city. Peterborough lies in a N. E. direction from the Grand Monadnock, and is bounded on the E. by a chain of hills called *Pack Monadnock*. Contoocook river runs in a N. E. and N. direction through the centre of the town, affording several good privileges for mills and factories. The N. branch, from Dublin, originating partly from waters near the Monadnock and partly from Long, or Hunt's pond, lying in Nelson and Hancock, affords a never failing supply of water, and furnishes those noble falls, on which are situated several factories, and particularly the long known mills and factories of Hon. Samuel Smith. There are extensive and valuable meadows on this branch above these falls; and the soil generally throughout the town is excellent. The forests in the vicinity of the S. branch of the Contoocook, were composed of large and lofty pines; the hills on the E. crowned with majestic oaks; and the intermediate lands principally clothed with hard wood and other valuable timber. In the centre of the town is a high hill, on which is situated the meeting-house, at an elevation of 200 feet above the river. The chain of hills on the E. is distinguished by two principal summits. Between these summits is a depression of a quarter part of the mountain's height. About 60 rods W. of the ridge, or summit of this depression, on an *embenchment* of the mountain, is a pond of about 9 acres extent, very deep and replenished with fish, at an elevation of 200 feet above the site of the meeting-house. There is another pond near the foot of the southern summit of 33 acres, from which, during the dry season, there is no visible outlet. The southern summit terminates abruptly at its southern extremity with marks of a violent disruption, forming what is termed the *Notch in the mountain.* The county road passes through this aperture. The hill rises again in Sharon; and the chain, with some depressions and variations, continues for several miles. There are rocks in several places, which afford indications of sulphur, and crumble on exposure to the sun and air. Iron ore of an excellent quality has been discovered, but, as yet, in small quantities. Besides the common medicinal plants, the Cohush, Ginseng and Buck bean are found here. The surface of this town being much varied with hills, vales, meadows, great swells of land, brooks and rivulets, while the larger streams are broken by falls and rapid in their course—the air and waters are pure; the inhabitants remarkably healthy. No sickness has ever been experienced to any considerable extent. The first settlers generally attained to more than 80 years of age—several to almost a century. The oldest persons who have died in town, were Mr. John Morrison in his 98th year, and Mrs. Cunningham in her 99th year. The former died June 14, 1776, retaining the full possession of his faculties till within a short time of his death. He, with his parents and family, was in the City, and his age 10 years, at the famous siege of Londonderry, Ireland. The principal village embraces about half a mile in extent. Here are 3 cotton factories, including Mr. Smith's extensive establishment, his cotton factory, oil mill, fulling mill and paper manufactory. His mansion on the eastern side of the main stream, commands a pleasing view of the principal buildings. Two miles S. are situated a cotton factory and a woollen factory. About the same distance N., is another cotton factory. Besides these, there are on the various streams, several grain and saw mills. The public buildings are a congregational and baptist meeting-house, and six school houses.—There is a social library containing a handsome selection of books. There is a bible society, established Oct. 2,1814. Peterborough was granted in 1738, by the government of Massachusetts to Samuel Heywood and others. The first settlement took place in 1739, by William Robbe, Alexander Scott, Hugh Gregg, William Scott, and Samuel Stinson. Some of them had brought their families into the settlement, but they were compelled to retire in 1744, on occasion of the war which then commenced, and did not terminate till 1748. On their return, a large accession of settlers from Lunenburg, Londonderry and other places joined them. In 1759, there were 45 families, and on the 17th Jan. the next year, the town was incorporated. The first settlers of Peterborough were Scotch presbyterians, from Ireland, or their immediate descendants. Wholly unused to clearing and cultivating of wild lands, they endured great hardships. Their nearest gristmill was at Townsend, 25 miles distant—their road a line of marked trees. The first child baptized was Catherine, daughter of Hugh Gregg, the now aged and venerable mother of general Miller, governor of Arkansaw. The first male child born here, was John Ritchie; he was born Feb. 22, 1751, and died in the service of his country at Cambridge, in 1776. This town has produced a large number of worthy, and several highly distinguished citizens. Men, who have adorned the bench, the bar and the pulpit, the legislature, the hall of congress and the chair of state, have been natives of this town. Of those who have been celebrated for their heroism, may be mentioned Col. Andrew Todd, distinguished in the wars of 1744 and 1755, and Capt. William Scott, noted for his military enterprize in the French war, and in the war which achieved our independence. Of these worthy men, and of Lieut. William Robbe, an account may be seen by referring to the Collections, published by the authors of this work, vol. 1, p. 134-137. The first settled minister was Rev. John Morrison, born at Pathfoot, in Scotland, May 22, 1743; graduated at Edinburgh, 1765; ordained at Peterborough, Nov. 26, 1766; resigned in March 1772; died Dec. 10, 1782. Rev. David Annan succeeded in 1778; dismissed, June 1792. He was born at Cupar of Fife in Scotland, April, 1754; died in Ireland in 1801. Both of these were presbyterians. The congregational church was embodied Oct. 23, 1799, at which time, Rev. *Elijah Dunbar*, who graduated at Harvard college in 1794, was ordained. Pop. 1500.

PHILLIP'S river, a considerable branch of the Upper Amonoosuck, rises in Dixville and Columbia, and after passing through Ervin's location, Millsfield, Dummer and Winslow's location, unites with the main stream in Piercy.

PIERCY, township, Coos county, lat. 44° 33', is situated on the Upper Amonoosuck river, about 3 miles from its mouth; bounded N. by Stratford and ungranted lands, E. and S. by Kilkenny, W. by Northumberland—comprising about 20,000 acres. In the N. E. part of the town the N. and S. branches of the Amonoosuck form a junction. Nash's stream, flowing from Stratford, falls into this river in the N. part of the town. Piercy's pond lies on the E. side the town, the waters of which fall into the Upper Amonoosuck in Paulsburg. The soil of Piercy is extremely broken and uneven, though in the valleys there are some tolerable farms. Mill mountain is in Piercy, and a part of Pilot mountain. There is also a singular ledge opposite Mill mountain, called the *Devil's Sliding-place*. On the S. it breaks abruptly into a precipice of nearly 300 feet, while on the N., cattle may be driven to the top. The settlement of this town commenced in 1788, by Caleb and Benjamin Smith; in the year following, several other families arrived, and their population is now 218. There are no settled ministers in this place. Pop. 218.

PIERMONT, a post-township, in Grafton county, in lat. 43° 58', is bounded N. by Haverhill, E. by Warren, S. by Orford, W. by Bradford, Vt. containing 23,000 acres. It is 70 miles from Concord and 132 from Boston. The soil, especially on the Connecticut, is good. The meadows or intervals, are extensive, and in some instances highly cultivated. The plains, adjoining the meadows, are composed of sandy loam, and in some places inclined to marle, and are favorable to the growth of wheat, corn and every kind of grain and of grass. Back from the river, the town is made up of swells of fine grazing and mowing land well watered with brooks and springs. The forest trees on the river are white pine; E. from the river, sugar maple, birch, elm, bass and every species of timber found in the country. In the N. E. part of the town are three considerable ponds, called

T2

Eastman's ponds. On a plain, between these ponds, and on Coos turnpike, 6 miles from Haverhill corner, is the seat of the late Col. Tarleton, formerly counsellor and sheriff of Grafton county. From these ponds, issues Eastman's brook, which passing in a S. E. direction, falls into Connecticut river, forming a number of excellent mill seats. Indian brook, on which mills are erected, is in the S. part. There is a small island in Connecticut river in the S. W. part of this town, called Barron's island. In the N. part is an extensive quarry of stones disposed in layers, convenient for mill stones and various uses in building. The charter of Piermont was granted Nov. 6, 1764, to John Temple and 59 others. The settlement commenced in 1770. The congregational church was gathered in 1771. Rev. John Richards was settled in 1776. He continued his labors till 1802, when his advanced age deprived the church and society of his usefulness. He died in Vermont in 1814. Rev. Jonathan Hovey was settled in 1810 for 5 years. Rev. *Robert Blake*, a gentleman from England, commenced his services here in 1819. There is a society of baptists; and also one of methodists, over which the Rev. Dan Young formerly presided. Pop. 1000.

PIGWACKET. See *Pequawkett*.

PILOT, a mountain. See *Kilkenny*.

PINE river, is a small stream, issuing from a pond in Wakefield, and passing N. W. into Ossipee lake.

PISCATAQUOG river is formed of two principal branches, one from Francestown, the other from Henniker and Deering, which unite and form the main stream near the W. line of Goffstown. It pursues a S. easterly course through Goffstown and the N. E. corner of Bedford, where it falls into Merrimack river.

PISCATAQUOG village, on the river of the same name and near its mouth, in the N. E. part of Bedford, contains 20 dwelling houses, a neat and handsome meeting-house, a post office, 2 attorneys' offices, 3 stores, 1 tavern and a number of mechanics' shops. A handsome bridge is constructed over the Piscataquog in this village, 60 feet in length. Since the Union Canal commenced operation, the boating business to this place has been carried on with much success. Several of the stores are so situated that by the assistance of a lock at the mouth of the river, the boats may be brought up under them, and their freight hoisted from the boats into the stores—by which the vicinity is supplied with the heavy articles of salt, lime, iron, fish, plaster, &c. at the Boston prices with the addition of a small sum for freight.—On the S. side of the river below this village, is a public landing place, extending to the Merrimack, and from this place lumber of all descriptions from the circumjacent country, is conveyed down the river to market by rafts and boats to Newburyport, and through the Middlesex canal, to Charlestown and Boston. The rise and present flourishing appearance of this village is owing, in a great measure, to the enterprize and industry of William Parker and Isaac Riddle, esquires, who were the first to commence the mercantile business in this place. William Parker, Esq. who died in July, 1819, and Hon. James Parker, a senator in the legislature, in 1819, who died in 1822, resided in this village.

PISCASSICK, a small river, rises in the N. E. part of Brentwood, and passes through New-Market into the Lamprey river at Durham.

PITTSFIELD, post-town, Rockingham county, in lat. 43° 15', contains an area of 14,921 acres, 94 of which are water. It is bounded N. E. by Barnstead, S. E. by Strafford and Northwood, S. W. by Chichester and Epsom, and N. W. by Loudon. Pittsfield has a very uneven and rocky surface, but its soil is generally fertile. Suncook river passes through this town from N. to S. furnishing numerous mill seats. Catamount mountain stretches across the S. E. part of the town, from the summit of which the ocean is visible. Berry's pond is situated on this mountain, being about half a mile in length, and 50 rods wide—supplied by springs in the mountain. A stream issuing from it furnishes four mill seats. East of this is Wild-goose pond, 1 1-2 miles long, 1 wide. West of these ponds the magnetic-needle varies materially. There are also three other ponds in Pittsfield—Shaw's, Eaton's and Bachelder's. This town was settled in 17—, by John Cram and others; and in 1789 the congr. church was formed, and Rev. Christopher Page settled. He was dismissed in 1795. Rev. Benjamin Sargent was settled over a baptist church in 1801, and died in 1818. There is a large society of free-will baptists, over which Elder *Ebenezer Knowlton* presides. There is also a society of friends. Pittsfield social library was incorporated in 1804—has about 100 volumes. The spotted fever raged here with much violence in 1813-14, during which 84 persons fell its victims. Number of deaths since the first settlement of the town, 483. Pop. 1170.

PLAINFIELD, a post-town in Cheshire county, on Connecticut river, in lat. 43° 33', is bounded N. by Lebanon, E. by Grantham, S. by Cornish, and W. by Hartland, Vt. containing 23,221 acres. It is 12 miles from Dartmouth college, 55 from Concord, and 111 from Boston. The forest trees, on the river, are pine ; on the highlands, maple, beech, birch, elm. There is considerable valuable interval, on Connecticut river, and in other parts are excellent meadows. There are two ponds. At the S. W. part of this town, in Connecticut river, is Hart's island, which contains 19 acres. Waterqueechy falls are in this town. A bridge was erected here in 1807. A small stream flowing from Croydon mountains, waters this town. Plainfield has a pleasant village, situated on a handsome plain, through the centre of which the street passes N. and S. There are two meeting houses and two congregational churches. On a pleasant eminence in Meriden parish, is located "The Union Academy," incorporated June 16, 1813. It is endowed with a permanent fund, of $40,000, the liberal bequest of the late Hon. DANIEL KIMBALL, the interest of which as directed by his last will, is to be applied as follows, viz.—$150 annually to the support of a Calvinistic preacher, and the remainder for the instruction of pious young men for the ministry. This seminary is in a flourishing condition. Plainfield was granted Aug. 14, 1761, and was settled in 1764, by L. Nash and J. Russell. The name is derived from a place in Connecticut, where the proprietors held their first meeting. A congregational church was formed in 1765 and Rev. Abraham Carpenter was ordained the same year, and was afterwards dismissed. Rev. Experience Esterbrooks was settled June 6, 1787; dismissed April 19, 1789. Rev.

Siloam Short was ordained 1799; died Sept. 1803. Rev. David Dickinson was ordained July 4, 1804; dismissed in Feb. 1819. Rev. *Micaiah Porter* was installed July 19, 1805. The second church, which is in Meriden parish, consists of members belonging to this town and Grantham. Rev. *Dana Clayes* was ordained July 4, 1821. There is a baptist society, of which the church was formed in 1792. Rev. Jonathan Cram was ordained in Aug. 1793. Pop. 1460.

PLAISTOW, a small township, Rockingham county, in lat. 42° 50', is bounded N. W. by Hampstead, N. E. by Kingston and Newtown, S. E. and S. W. by Haverhill, Ms. W. by Atkinson—contains 6,839 acres, and is 36 miles from Concord, 30 from Portsmouth, and 35 from Boston. Plaistow was originally a part of Haverhill, and included in the purchase of the Indians, Nov. 15, 1642, and its settlement commenced early, but the precise time cannot be ascertained. Among the first settlers were Capt. Charles Bartlett, Nicholas White, Esq. Dea. Benjamin Kimball and J. Harriman. Their posterity now inhabit the town. After it became annexed to New-Hampshire, a charter was granted, Feb. 28, 1749. The soil of this town is good, being a mixture of black loam, clay or gravel. The N. W. part of the town is rocky, and mineral substances have been discovered. Clay abounds near the centre—and a great number of springs water the fields and pastures. The principal stream is formed near the centre of the town by the confluence of two smaller streams, one from Kingston, the other from Hampstead. The congregational church was gathered here Dec. 2, 1730, and Rev. James Cushing settled, who died May 13, 1764. Rev. Gyles Merrill succeeded him March 6, 1765, and died April 27, 1801, aged 62. Both were graduates of Cambridge, and eminent men. The congregational society is in connexion with the N. parish in Haverhill. There are small societies of baptists and methodists, each of which have occasional preaching. Rev. Messrs. True Kimball, formerly of Newbury; Rev. Francis Welch, of Amesbury; Rev. Asa Eaton, episcopal clergyman in Boston; Rev. Samuel Gile, of Milton; Rev. Moses Welch, of Amesbury, and Rev. Johnson Chase, of New-York, were natives of this town. Deac. J. Harriman, said to have been the first man in N. H. who embraced baptist sentiments, died here in 1820, aged 97. Pop. 563.

PLYMOUTH, a post town, and the half shire of Grafton county, in lat. 43° 44', is bounded E. by Holderness, from which it is separated by Pemigewasset river, W. by Rumney and part of Hebron, N. by Campton and S. by Bridgewater. It contains 16,256 acres. It is 75 miles N. W. from Portsmouth, 31 from Haverhill, and 40 from Concord. This town is well watered. Besides numerous smaller streams, there are two rivers, Pemigewasset and Baker's, both of which are of considerable importance. They take their rise in the height of land between the Connecticut and Merrimack, called the eastern ridge. Baker's river is 30 miles in length. The soil is tolerably good, and, in general, is well cultivated. The prevailing kinds of wood are beech, maple, birch, hemlock, and white pine. The land is divided into upland and interval. The proportion of the former to the latter is about seven eighths. The upland is mountainous. There is a small, but pleasant village in this place, containing 37 dwelling houses. The church, a neat building, with a steeple, stands on a hill at the N. E. corner of the town, and commands an extensive prospect. There is a social library containing 164 volumes. There is a musical society, incorporated in 1808, and a religious tract society, formed in 1819. Plymouth was granted July 15, 1763, to Joseph Blanchard, Esq. and others. The first settlement commenced in August, 1764, by Zachariah Parker and James Hobart, who, before the succeeding winter, were joined by Jotham Cumings, Josiah Brown, Stephen Webster, Ephraim Weston, David Webster and James Blodgett, all of whom except Mr. Weston were from Hollis. The congregational church was gathered in 1765. Rev. Nathan Ward was ordained its pastor at Newburyport, July 10, 1765. He died in June, 1804, aged 83, having been dismissed April 22, 1794. Rev. Drury Fairbank was ordained Jan. 1, 1800; dismissed March 18, 1818. In August the same year, Rev. *Jonathan Ward* commenced his ministerial labors. A methodist church was formed in 1803. The intervals in this town were formerly the resort of Indians for hunting. At the mouth of Baker's river, they had a settlement, where Indian graves, bones, &c. have been found; also gun barrels, stone mortars, pestles and other utensils. Here, it is said, the Indians were attacked by Capt. Baker and a party from Haverhill, Ms. who defeated them, killed a number and destroyed a large quantity of fur. From him, Baker's river derives its name. Dea. Noah Johnson, one of Lovewell's men, died in Plymouth in the 100th year of his age. David Webster, Esq. sheriff of Grafton county, and Dr. John Rogers, an eminent physician, and somewhat distinguished for his poetical powers, resided in this town. Pop. 1000.

PONDICHERRY, name of a mountain, &c. *See Jefferson.*

POPLIN, post-township, Rockingham county, in lat. 43°, is 24 miles from Portsmouth, 33 from Concord, and 50 from Boston. It is bounded N. by Epping, E. by Brentwood, S. by a corner of Kingston, and by Hawke and Sandown, W. by Chester and Raymond; and contains 10,320 acres. There is a small pond in the N. part of the town called Loon pond; and the town is watered by Squamscot, or Exeter river, beside several small streams. The soil is generally of a good quality, and the surface of the town is not broken by high hills. Spruce swamp is in the E. part of the town. The meeting-house is situated near the centre of the town. A methodist church has existed here for several years, over which Rev. *Orlando Hinds* presides. Poplin was incorporated June 22, 1764; the date of its first settlement is not ascertained. The inhabitants are principally industrious farmers. Pop. 453.

PORTSMOUTH, a post-township, in the county of Rockingham, is the principal town in the state, and the only sea-port which it contains. It is situated in lat. 43° 5′; long. 6° 23′ E. from Washington; and bounded N. W. by Newington, N. E. by Pascataqua river, which separates it from Maine, S. E. and S. by Rye, W. by Greenland and Newington. Portsmouth is built on a beautiful peninsula, on the S. side of the river; and, as seen from the towers of the steeples, the river, harbor, points, islands, and adjacent country present a delightful assemblage of objects. In the W. and N. parts of the town are some beautiful and productive gardens. This town originally included New-Castle, Rye, Greenland and a part of Hampton (now North-Hampton.) It was settled under the auspices of Sir Ferdinando Gorges and Capt. John Mason, in 1623, and was incorporated by charter in 1633. That part of it which lies round Church hill, extending N. towards Rindge's wharf, and W. towards the academy was originally called *Strawberry-Bank*. The first house of which we have any account, erected in what is now the compact part of the town, was built by Humphrey Chadbourne, and according to tradition, stood near the corner of Court and Pond streets. It was called the "Great house," and is frequently referred to in our early histories. Within the memory of the present generation, a garrison house stood in Water street, at the head of Jacob Sheafe's wharf, another in Fore street on Moffatt's wharf, and a third at the ferry-ways. These were probably the principal houses on "the Bank." The first meeting-house stood on Pleasant street, near Doct. Goddard's house. After a short time, it was taken down; and another erected on the hill beyond the S. bridge. The S. mill was granted to John Pickering, on condition of his making a foot bridge over the mill-pond for persons to pass to and from meeting. On the erection of the present N. and S. meeting-houses, and a division of the parishes, the old meeting-house was made a school house. Except the garrison houses above mentioned, the earliest settlements were probably on the South road. The creek, which flows across Water street (under Liberty bridge) formerly extended to Pleasant street, and at high tides flowed over Rogers' field to the S. mill pond. The channel of this creek, in Pleasant street, has been filled up within fifty years. The N. mill-pond formerly extended from Nathaniel Adams', S. E. through Vaughn street, to John Melcher's house; and the S. mill-pond (or rather the marshes around it) extended through Jaffrey street to the Hay-market. From the peculiar advantages of its situation, Portsmouth appears almost wholly to have escaped the ravages of the Indians. Secured on three sides by the Pascataqua, the ocean, and an inlet, it was accessible to the savages only by the isthmus which connects it with the main; and across that a stockade fence was extended for defence. The settlements were also compact, and the number of inhabitants, at an early date considerable. There are in Portsmouth seven churches, 2 for congregationalists, 1 for independents, 1 for episcopalians, 1 for universalists. 1 for baptists, 1 for methodists; a court-house; jail; a branch of the U. S. bank; 4 other banks; a loan office; several printing-offices, and several extensive book-stores; 2 insurance offices; an academy; alms-house; 2 markets; a custom-house; 280 stores; 2 extensive rope-walks; 3 distilleries, &c. A large brick market, 2 stories high, was erected in 1800, near the centre of the town, the upper story of which, called Jefferson-Hall, makes a commodious town-house. This market is constantly supplied with good provision. Back of Merchant's Row stands the Fish-market. In 1822, the wealthy and enterprising citizens of this town connected Portsmouth with Kittery in Maine, by two bridges, one 480 feet in length, supported by 20 framed sections of piers; the other 1750

VIEW OF PORTSMOUTH FROM THE NAVY YARD.

feet, supported by 70 framed sections of piers. Under the long bridge, for 900 feet, the water varies from 45 to 53 feet in depth at low water. The length of the sections supporting the bridge in this place varies from 61 to 72 feet. The draw is 1336 feet from the island, and the water is 21 feet deep at ebb tide. This bridge greatly increases and facilitates the travel from Portland and its vicinity to this town and Boston. The public have long felt the need of it; but owing to the depth of the river and rapidity of the tide, it was thought impracticable. There have been difficulties overcome in erecting this bridge never before attempted in New-England. It was completed in less than six months from its commencement, at the expense of about $32,000 only. The town is also connected with New-Castle by a bridge built in 1821. There are in this town 63 streets, 41 lanes 13 roads, and 3 squares. The streets, though not laid out with much regularity, are pleasant. Portsmouth aqueduct company was incorporated in 1797; and commenced its operations in 1799. Water of excellent quality is brought from a fountain about 3 miles distant, and conducted into all the principal streets. Portsmouth pier, 340 feet in length, and about 60 feet wide, was incorporated in 1795. Portsmouth Athenæum was incorporated in 1817; and has a library of about 1600 volumes; and cabinets of mineralogy and natural history, &c. The institution is rapidly increasing in value. The people of this town were at an early period friendly to literature; and for seven years commencing 1669, paid £50 per annum to Harv. college. Portsmouth is the centre of a considerable trade directed by wealthy and enterprizing citizens. There belong to this port, 146 vessels, of which 36 are ships, 30 brigs, 8 sloops, 25 schooners, 53 fishing vessels. There are 58 wharves. The commerce of Portsmouth is already noticed in p. 30 of this work. The Pascataqua, as it passes this town, is from 1-2 to 3-4 of a mile wide; and although the current is so swift as to prevent the river from freezing, yet it forms one of the most secure and commodious harbors in the United States, into which ships of any size or burthen may enter with perfect safety. It is protected by nature from the ravages of the N. E. storms, and can very easily be rendered inaccessible to enemies.* The harbor is protected by four batteries—Fort Constitution, on Great Island (New-Castle;) Fort M'Clary opposite, about a mile distant, in Kittery; Fort Sullivan, on Trefethen island; and Fort Washington, on Peirce's island. The two latter were manned in the late war, but are now in a state of decay. About one mile below the town, the navigation is rendered somewhat difficult by the rapidity of the current; the main body of the river being forced through a channel only about 45 rods wide. There are in the Harbor a number of islands, the most considerable of which is Great island. The others are Continental island, on which is the Navy-Yard, one of the safest and most convenient on the coast; Badger's island,

---

* The main entrance to the harbor is on the N. between New-Castle and Kittery; the other entrance, on the S. of New-Castle, is called *Little-Harbor*, where the water is shoal, and the bottom sandy. At this place, in the spring of 1623, the first settlers of this state, made their landing, and in the same year commenced settlements here and at Dover.

on which the *North America*, (the first line of battle ship launched in the western hemisphere) was built during the revolutionary war. Portsmouth marine society was incorporated in 1808, and has a fund of $2500. The *New-Hampshire Gazette, Portsmouth Journal* and the *Christian Herald*, are published here. [A particular notice of the different papers, &c. published in this town will be given in the *Appendix*.] Few towns in New-England have suffered so much from fires as Portsmouth. In 1781, the house, stable and a large store of Hon. Woodbury Langdon were destroyed, and a large portion of the town must have been laid in ashes, but for a sudden change of wind. Dec. 26, 1802, 102 buildings were burnt. Dec. 24, 1806, 14 buildings, including St. John's church, were destroyed. But the most calamitous fire broke out Dec. 22, 1813, when 397 buildings were burnt, of which more than 100 were dwelling houses. The ravages extended over about 15 acres. In Sept. 1798, a malignant fever prevailed here, and 55 persons died. About 50 also died in this season of dysentery. This town has generally been healthy—its air is pleasant and salubrious. In Portsmouth, there exist different religious denominations, which we shall endeavor to arrange according to the time of their appearance. (1.) The first religious society in this town was a small one of *Episcopalians*, who built a church prior to 1638, and employed Rev. Richard Gibson to preach in it. He remained here till 1642. From this period to 1680, and afterwards to 1732, there exist no authentic records of this church. In 1732, a new church, called Queen's Chapel, now St. John's Church, was erected, and Rev. Arthur Browne became the first incumbent in 1736. He died in June, 1773, aged 73. Rev. John Cosens Ogden succeeded in 1786; removed in 1793; died in 1800. Rev. Joseph Willard succeeded in 1795; resigned in 1806. Rev. *Charles Burroughs* succeeded Feb. 1, 1810. Number of communicants, 90. (2.) Of *Congregationalists*, there are three societies. The 1st congregational church was under the care of Rev. Joshua Moodey, who graduated at Harvard college in 1653; was ordained 1671; died July 4, 1697, aged 65. Rev. Nathaniel Rogers, who graduated at Harvard college in 1687, was ordained May 3, 1699; died Oct. 3, 1723, aged 54. Rev. Jabez Fitch, who graduated at Harvard college in 1694, was settled in 1725; died Nov. 22, 1746, aged 73. Rev. Samuel Langdon, D. D. afterwards President of Harvard college, graduated 1740, was ordained Feb. 4, 1747; dismissed Oct. 9, 1774. Rev. Joseph Buckminster, D. D. who graduated at Yale college in 1770, was ordained Jan. 27, 1779; died June 10, 1812, aged 61. Rev. *Israel W. Putnam*, who graduated at Dartmouth college in 1809, was ordained March 15, 1815. Number of communicants, 140. The 2d congregational church (in the S. parish) was formed about 1715. Rev. John Emerson, who graduated at Harvard college in 1689, was ordained March 28, 1715; died June 21, 1732, aged 62. Rev. William Shurtleff, who graduated at Harvard college in 1707, was installed Feb. 21, 1733; died May 9, 1747. Rev. Job Strong, who graduated at Yale college in 1747, was ordained June 28, 1749; died Sept. 30, 1751, aged 27. Rev. Samuel Haven, D. D. who graduated at Harvard college in 1749, was ordained May 6, 1752; died March

3, 1806, aged 79. Rev. Timothy Alden, now President of Alleghany college in Penn. who graduated at Harvard college in 1794, was ordained colleague with Dr. Haven, Nov. 20, 1799; dismissed Aug. 11, 1805. Rev. *Nathan Parker*, who graduated at Harvard college in 1803, was ordained Sept. 14, 1808. Number of communicants, 110. The 3d congregational, or independent church has had the following pastors; viz. Rev. Samuel Drown, ordained Nov. 2, 1761; died Jan. 17, 1770, aged 49. Rev. Joseph Walton, ordained Sept. 22, 1789; died in 1822, aged 80. (3.) The *Sandemanians* are a small society formed about the year 1764, to which, for many years, *Daniel Humphreys*, Esq. has statedly ministered. (4.) There is a *Universalist society*, the doctrines of which were first preached in Portsmouth, in Nov. 1773, by Rev. John Murray of Boston. The society was incorporated in Aug. 1793; the church was constituted in July, 1805, consisting of 12 members. The ministers have been, Rev. George Richards, ordained in July, 1799; dismissed in April, 1809 – Rev. Hosea Ballou, installed in 1809; removed in 1815—and Rev. *Sebastian Streeter*, who succeeded Mr. Ballou in Aug. 1815. Communicants, 44. (5.) The *Methodists*, who have a church, organized April 27, 1809, have had regular preaching since 1808. Communicants, 100. (6.) The *Baptists* formed a society in 1802; and a church was constituted in March, 1803. Elder Elias Smith officiated here several years.

Among the citizens of Portsmouth distinguished for their talents or public services, we may mention GEORGE VAUGHAN, grandson of Maj. William Vaughan, the intrepid opposer of the arbitrary Cranfield, who was born April 13, 1676, and in 1715 was appointed lieutenant governor. This office he sustained but a short time, and died in Dec. 1725. His son, WILLIAM VAUGHAN, the original projector of the expedition against Louisbourg, was born at Portsmouth, Sept. 12, 1703; exhibited much bravery in the siege of that fortress, and died in London in Dec. 1746. JOHN WENTWORTH, the first governor of that name in N. H. was grandson of William Wentworth, who was an elder of the church at Dover in 1662. In early life, he commanded a ship, and acquired a fortune by mercantile pursuits. Without superior talents, his industry and activity in business, together with an obliging deportment, recommended him to the esteem of the people; and in 1717, he was appointed lieutenant governor, and after Shute's departure, commander in chief. He died Dec. 12, 1730, aged 59. He had sixteen children. BENNING WENTWORTH, his son, graduated at Harvard college in 1715; was a member of the assembly and council; went to London on some mercantile business, where he solicited and obtained the commission of governor. He continued in office about 20 years. He was superseded in 1767, by his nephew, John Wentworth, and died Oct. 14, 1770, aged 75. JOHN WENTWORTH, the second, was bred a merchant, possessed amiable qualities, and by his enterprize and zeal for public improvements, soon became a favorite of the people. Favoring the cause of the mother country, on the breaking out of the revolution, he was obliged to retire, and embarked for Nova-Scotia, where he was governor several years. He was honored with the degree of LL. D. from the universities of Oxford and Aberdeen, and from Dartmouth college. He was made a baronet before he left N. H. He died at Halifax, April 8, 1820, aged 84. DANIEL RINDGE, Esq. an eminent merchant, and member of the provincial council, died Jan. 12, 1799, aged 68. Hon. PEIRCE LONG, died in April, 1789: during the revolution, he commanded a regiment—was a member of the old congress, and frequently in the legislature of the state. Col. GEORGE GAINS, a patriotic revolutionary soldier, died April 25, 1809, aged 73. Dr. JOSHUA BRACKETT, a distinguished physician and founder of the Medical Society, died July 17, 1802, aged 69. Hon. SAMUEL HALE, a native of

Newbury, Ms. graduated at Harvard college in 1740; in 1745 commanded a company of provincials at the siege of Louisbourg; and afterwards for more than 30 years taught a public school in Portsmouth. "His fame in the regions of the Pascataqua was equal to that of his cotemporary Lovell, in the metropolis of New-England." He was subsequently a judge of the common pleas, and died July 10, 1807, aged 89. Rev. SAMUEL HAVEN, D. D. was born at Framingham, Ms. Aug. 4, 1727; graduated at Harvard college in 1749; settled at Portsmouth in 1752; received the degree of D. D. from the University of Edinburgh in 1772; and died March 3, 1806, aged 79. He was an eminently useful man; seven of his sermons have been printed. Dr. AMMI R. CUTTER, was born at North-Yarmouth, Me. in March, 1735; graduated at Harvard college in 1752; studied the science of medicine, and was surgeon of a regiment at the capture of Cape Breton; was appointed to the charge of the northern medical department in 1777; and was a member of the convention which formed the constitution. For 60 years he was an eminent practitioner, and during life a firm supporter of his country. He died Dec. 8, 1820, aged 36. Hon. JOHN PICKERING, LL.D. was a native of Newington; graduated at Harvard college in 1761; and having devoted some time to theological studies, was offered the rectorship of an episcopal church in England. He declined, and applied himself to the study of the law—in which he became eminent. He was a member of the convention which formed the constitution; frequently a member of the legislature; president of the senate in 1789; and governor ex-officio of the state, on the election of Gov. Langdon to the Senate of the U. S. He was appointed chief-justice of the superior court in 1790, and continued in office five years. He was afterwards district judge of the U. S.; and died April 11, 1805, aged 67. Hon. JOHN LANGDON, LL. D. was born at Portsmouth in 1740. His father, who was a respectable farmer, resided about three miles from the compact part of Portsmouth. In the early part of the revolution we find this distinguished patriot boldly asserting our rights and actively engaged in their defence. Since the attainment of our liberties, he acted equally as conspicuous a part, in vigilantly watching and protecting them. In 1775, he was a delegate from this state to the congress which met at Philadelphia. In 1785, he was chosen president of the state. He was elected to the same office in 1788, and after the adoption of the present constitution, was governor six years. He ever discharged the duties of the offices to which he was elected faithfully and acceptably. He possessed a good heart, a sound mind, and was remarkably pleasing in his manners. The object of his life was more to do good than to dazzle. Unlike many elevated to office, he remembered that the people clothed him with authority, and his only study was to serve the people honestly and faithfully. He died Sept. 18, 1819, aged 79. Hon. WOODBURY LANGDON, only brother of Gov. L. was a member of the old congress, judge of the superior court several years, and through life a firm patriot and useful citizen. He died in Jan. 1805. Hon. RICHARD EVANS was born at Portsmouth, May 13, 1777; commenced business as a merchant; afterwards studied law; was elected member of the legislature; and in 1809 was appointed judge of the superior court. He died July 18, 1816, aged 39. JONATHAN M. SEWALL Esq. counsellor at law, and a respectable poet, was born at Salem, Ms. in 1748; and died at Portsmouth March 29, 1808. Rev. JOSEPH BUCKMINSTER, D. D. a native of Rutland, Ms. was graduated at Yale college in 1770; was tutor at that institution four years; settled at Portsmouth in 1779; received the degree of D. D. from N. J. college in 1803; and died at Reedsborough, Vt. June 10, 1812, aged 61. Dr. B. was a distinguished scholar and eminent divine. Many other worthy men might be named, had we not already extended this article to a great length. Portsmouth contains an area of 9,702 acres; and is 45 miles from Concord, 55 from Boston—mail-route 64; and 58 from Portland. Pop. in 1820—7,327.

Powow river, has its principal source in Great and Country ponds in Kingston, and passes over the S. W. part of East-Kingston into South-Hampton; thence into Amesbury, where it turns E. into South Hampton again, and returns into Amesbury, falling into the Merrimack between Salisbury and Amesbury. There are several falls in this river: those in Amesbury being the most remarkable, the water falling 100 feet in the distance of 50 rods, and presenting, with the variety of machinery and dams, houses and scenery on the falls, one of the most interesting views in the country.

PUBLIC LANDS. The ungranted lands belonging to the state of New-Hampshire, are situated within the counties of Grafton and Coos. They consist of a large tract N. of lat. 45° containing about 160,000 acres; a tract of about 28,000 acres, E. of Stratford; and large tracts of mountainous territory S. and S. W. of the White Mountains, extending up their summits. Pop. 17.

Q.

QUAMPHEGAN, name of the falls on the Pascataqua, between Somersworth and Berwick.

QUONEHTIQUOT, the ancient spelling of Connecticut, a Moheakanneew word, and literally signifying *long river*.

QUOCHECHO. See *Cocheco*.

R.

RAGGED MOUNTAINS, so called from their rough appearance, lie between Andover and New-Chester, extending in a chain about 10 miles from the Pemigewasset to the vicinity of Kearsarge. It is a bleak and precipitous range, and is nearly 2000 feet high, in its N. points.

RAYMOND, post-township, Rockingham county, in lat. 43° 2′, 55 miles from Boston, 25 from Portsmouth, 25 from Concord, 13 from Exeter, is bounded N. by Deerfield and Nottingham, E. by Epping and Poplin, S. by Chester, W. and N. W. by Chester and Candia, and contains an area of 16,317 acres. Two branches of the Lamprey river, from Deerfield and Candia, unite in Raymond; and the waters of two ponds also fall into this river as it passes through town. The Patuckaway, from Nottingham, crosses the N. E. corner into Epping. The soil is various: that of the meadows bordering on the river is productive, and considerable attention has been recently paid to its cultivation. The high lands are covered with a growth of oak and forest pines. The public highways through this town are good, and constantly improving. In the N. part of the town, about 100 rods from the principal road leading to Deerfield, near the summit of a hill about 100 feet high, is a natural excavation in a ledge, called the *Oven*, from the appearance of its mouth. It is a regular arch about 5 feet high and of the same width, extending into the hill about 15 feet, and terminating in a number of fissures. Many rattlesnakes were formerly found here. Raymond was originally that part of Chester called *Charming-fare*. In 1762, it was made a distinct parish, and incorporated May 9, 1765, by its present name. The names of 24 of the inhabitants of Raymond are found enrolled among the soldiers of the revolution, beside numbers of the militia engaged for short periods. Four were killed or died in service. Over the congregational church, Rev. Jonathan Stickney was ordained 22d Oct. 1800. He was succeeded by Rev. Stephen Bailey in 1817, who continued to preach until 1822. The church is now vacant. Hon. JOHN DUDLEY, a distinguished patriot of the revolution, member of the committee of safety, speaker of the House, and judge of the superior court, died here May 21, 1805, aged 80. (For a memoir of his life, see Hist.

Coll. for 1822, p. 155.) The deaths in this town from April, 1766, to Dec. 1821, were 514—the greatest number in one year 20, the least 2—averaging about 9 per annum. Pop. 961.

RED HILL, a noted and beautiful eminence situated in Moultonborough, commanding a varied and enchanting prospect. See *Moultonborough*.

RED HILL river, originating in a pond in Sandwich, falls into the Winnepisiogee in Moultonborough.

RICHMOND, a post-township in Cheshire county, in lat. 42° 45', is bounded N. by Swanzey, E. by Fitzwilliam, S. by Royalston and Warwick, Ms. W. by Winchester, containing 23,725 acres. This town is 12 miles from Keene, 70 from Concord, and 72 from Boston. It is watered by branches of Ashuelot and Miller's rivers, which fall into the Connecticut. The ponds are three in number, one of which is one of the sources of Miller's river. The soil here is favorable for yielding rye, wheat, Indian corn, and most of the productions found in this section of New-England. The land is generally level. There are no remarkable elevations. There is a small village of 15 or 20 dwelling houses; and there are two meeting-houses, which are near the centre of the town. The Ashuelot turnpike road passes through Richmond in an E. and W. direction. Richmond was granted Feb. 28, 1752, to Joseph Blanchard and others. It was settled within 5 or 6 years afterwards, by people from Massachusetts and Rhode-Island. The first child born in town was Lemuel Scott—born in 1757. The first baptist church was formed in 1768. Rev. Maturin Ballou was ordained in 1770; died in 1804. Rev. Artemas Aldrich was settled in 1777. The second baptist church was formed in 1776, and Rev. Isaac Kenny was settled in 1792. There is a large society of friends in this town. Pop. 1400.

RINDGE, a post-township, in Cheshire county, in lat. 42° 45', is 7 miles in length and 5 in breadth, containing 23,838 acres; bounded N. by Jaffrey and Sharon, E. by New-Ipswich, S. by Massachusetts, and W. by Fitzwilliam. It is 20 miles from Keene, 56 from Concord, and 60 from Boston. The soil is very productive, lying on swells of land for the most part inclining to the S. It was originally covered with a mixture of beech, maple, birch, hemlock, &c. There are 13 ponds, the largest of which are called Manomonack, Emerson, Perley, Long, Grassy, Bullet: the others are of less note. The 3 first discharge their waters into Miller's river in Mass., thence communicating with the Connecticut; the 3 last discharge themselves into Contoocook river, and from thence into the Merrimack. These ponds abound with fish, and were much frequented by the Indians for procuring fur, &c.—There is a small elevation of land in Rindge, from which the waters that issue on one side descend into the Merrimack, and those on the other side, into the Connecticut. Iron is found here; also a species of paint nearly equal to the best quality of spanish brown. A mineral spring has been discovered, but its virtues have not been sufficiently tested to acquire celebrity. The principal village lies on the Rindge turnpike, leading from Boston to Keene, and contains about 20 dwelling houses. The street is nearly straight, and is one fourth of a mile in length. Rindge was originally granted from Massachusetts, and called *Rowley*

Canada, or *Monadnock* No. 1. It received its present name from one of the proprietors, when it was incorporated, Aug. 11, 1768. The settlement commenced in 1752, by Jonathan Stanley, George Hewitt and Abel Platts, followed by a number of other families the same year. The first native of Rindge was Samuel Russell. The date of the congregational church is not certainly known. Rev. Seth Deane was ordained over it in 1765, and was dismissed 1780. Rev. Seth Payson, D. D. was ordained Dec. 4, 1782; died Feb. 26, 1820, aged 62. Rev. *Amos Wood Burnham*, was ordained Nov. 14, 1821. There are small societies of methodists and universalists. Rev. SETH PAYSON, D. D. is deserving respectful notice. He graduated at Harvard college in 1777. He was held in high estimation not only by the people of his charge, but was universally acknowledged to be a man of quick perception and powerful talents. In 1809, he received his doctorate of divinity from Dartmouth college; in 1813, he was elected a trustee of that institution, which office he held till his death. He was several years president of the N. H. bible society and a member of the A. B. C. for foreign missions. Edward Jewett, Esq. is among the oldest and most respected inhabitants of this place. For many years, he sustained several town offices, and was a representative in the legislature. In 1785, he was appointed a justice of the peace, and afterwards a justice throughout the state. At the age of 82, he holds an office in the church, in which he is still able to officiate. Pop. 1300.

ROCHESTER, a post-township in the county of Strafford, is in lat. 43° 17', and in the E. part of the state, bounded N. E. by the middle of Salmon-fall river, S. E. by Dover and Somersworth, S. W. by Barrington and a part of Strafford, and N. W. by Farmington and Milton, which two last mentioned towns were formerly a part of Rochester. It is 10 miles from Dover, 22 from Portsmouth, 40 from Concord. Besides Salmon-fall river, which divides this town from Berwick and Lebanon, in the state of Maine, the Cocheco river runs the whole length of the town and nearly in the middle, and the Isinglass river crosses the southerly corner of the town just before its junction with Cocheco river, at a place called Blind Will's Neck. Both Salmon-fall and Cocheco rivers afford several valuable mill seats; on the latter of which, near the centre of the town, stands the principal village, called *Norway Plains*. It is a place of considerable trade, and the great thoroughfare roads, from the upper towns in the county, to Dover and Portsmouth, pass through this village. Here are several stores, 1 cotton factory, 1 trip hammer, 2 potteries, besides mills, &c. of every description necessary to the wants of the place; also one meetinghouse, court-house, and about 60 dwelling-houses. There is another village about 2 miles S. W. from this, called *Squamanagonnick*, the Indian name of the falls in the Cocheco at that place. Much of the soil in Rochester is good, affording many valuable farms, with a proportion of pine plains which are useful for raising corn and grain, and some of a cold and inferior quality. The surface is uneven, with several swells, the principal of which is Squamanagonnick hill, which constitutes a considerable part of several valuable farms. In the W. part of the town, is a large tract of oak land, which is hard and stony; has a deep rich soil, and is very productive when well cultivated. Between Norway plains and Salmon-fall river is a considerable quantity of land formerly called *Whitehall*, the soil of which was destroyed by fire in the dry years of 1761 and 1762, so as to be of little value for cultivation. Rochester was granted by Massachusetts to a number of proprietors, in 127 shares, and contained upwards of 60,000 acres of land. That part now Rochester contains 22,000 acres. The town was incorporated May 10, 1722. Capt. Timothy Roberts moved into the town with his family and made the first permanent settlement, Dec. 28, 1728; he was soon followed by Eleazar Ham, Benjamin Frost, Joseph Richards, Benjamin Tebbets and others, and in perilous times, as might be expected, the inhabitants made slow progress in settlement and wealth. Until Canada was taken by the British and American troops in 1760, it remained a frontier town; the people were poor and distressed, but not discouraged. When a war broke out with the Indians, they had to move their families into garrisons, and be on their watch night and day; nor could they improve their little farms but at the hazard of their lives, and in such companies as they could collect, with armed sentinels kept on watch. Their men were bold, hardy and industrious; and their sons were trained to the use of arms. They early became a terror to their foes. They did not suffer so much as many towns whose situation appeared less hazardous. June 27, 1746, Joseph Heard, Joseph Richards, John Wentworth and Gersham Downs were killed, and John Richards wounded, taken captive and carried to Canada; but not long after returned. He died in 1792, aged 70 years. Jonathan Door, a boy, was also carried captive, and remained with the Indians until the reduction of Canada, when he returned. May 23, 1747, Samuel Drown was wounded in the hip—the ball was never extracted; he died in 1795, aged 90 years. May 1, 1748, the wife of Jonathan Hodgdon was killed on a Sunday morning by the Indians, on refusing to be taken to Canada with the party. Her husband married again, had 21 children in all, and died in 1815, aged 90 years. In Belknap's history, mention is made of another man's being killed by the Indians, which upon enquiry appears to have been a mistake. Moses Roberts was shot by a sentinel, who supposed him to be an Indian. In less than ten years after the settlement of this town a church was gathered and Rev. Amos Main ordained; he died April 5, 1760; aged 51, Rev. Samuel Hill was ordained Nov. 5. 1760; died Nov. 19, 1764. Rev. Avery Hall was ordained Oct. 15, 1766; and dismissed April 10, 1775. The present venerable pastor, Rev. *Joseph Haven*, was ordained Jan. 10, 1776. There are societies of baptists and methodists, each of which have stated ministrations. With the former Eld. *Enoch Place* is the pastor. There are two meetings of the friends' society in the town—one consisting of about 20 families, partly from Farmington; and the other of about 15 families. They have two meeting houses, which are about 8 miles apart. There is also a universalist society. By the bills of mortality, it appears that there have died in Rochester in 46 years, 1047 persons, of whom there appear to have died 19 above 90 years old; 75 between

80 and 90; 107 between 70 and 80; 67 between 60 and 70; 53 between 50 and 60; 65 between 40 and 50. The inhabitants have sometimes been visited with the malignant throat distemper, particularly in 1780, when 28 children died of the disorder within 6 months. In the revolutionary war, many of the inhabitants bore a part. Captains David Place and John Brewster led companies to Ticonderoga, and suffered much in their retreat from that place in 1777. Of the soldiers from Rochester, 29 were killed or died in that contest. Rochester social library was incorporated Feb. 14, 1794, and contains nearly 400 volumes. JAMES KNOWLES was many years a deacon in the church, a representative to the general court from 1765 until after the revolutionary war, and a magistrate for several years; he died at an advanced age. Hon. JOHN PLUMER was appointed a judge of the court of common pleas by Gov. John Wentworth, when the county was organized; and by his judicious conduct, was continued through, and after the revolution, until his voluntary resignation, the latter part of which time, he was chief justice. He was the first magistrate appointed in the town, and by his remarkably conciliatory conduct was enabled to settle most disputes that came before him in an amicable manner, and was justly entitled to the character of peacemaker. He died Nov. 19, 1815, aged 95 years. Col. JOHN M'DUFFEE was born soon after his parents arrived from Ireland; was an officer in the French war. In 1762, he was chosen representative to the general court, being the first from Rochester. He early embarked in the cause of his country; was a colonel in the revolutionary army, and several years a member of the senate and house of representatives of the state. He was a man of strong mind and memory, and of extensive information, and a sincere friend to his country; and died Oct. 15, 1817, aged 91 years. Dr. JAMES HOW, a respectable physician, and sometime member of the general court, died Oct. 13, 1807, aged 54. JOHN P. HALE, Esq. was a distinguished lawyer. Open, generous and affable, yet strictly correct, he will long be remembered as an ornament to the profession. He died Oct. 15, 1819, aged 44 years. Josiah Main, son of the first minister, was 33 years successively town clerk, commencing in 1771. Pop. 2471.

ROXBURY, a small town in Cheshire county, in lat. 42° 57', is bounded N. by Sullivan, E. by Nelson and Dublin, S. by Marlborough and W. by Keene, containing about 6000 acres. It is 5 miles from the court house in Keene, 76 N.W. from Boston, and 50 S. W. from Concord. The N. branch of Ashuelot river forms the boundary between this town and Keene. Roaring brook, on which are several small meadows, waters the S. part, and empties into the Ashuelot at the S. W. corner. On the E. side of the township is a pond, called Roaring Brook pond, at the outlet of which stand a saw mill and grist mill. Roxbury presents a rough and uneven surface, rising into considerable swells, affording excellent grazing land, and furnishing the various productions found in the county of Cheshire. There is a post road leading from Keene to Concord. There is a meeting house in the centre of the town, and a congregational church was formed Aug. 15, 1816. Rev. Christopher Paige was installed

Nov. 21, the same year; dismissed March 11, 1819. This town was formed of a part of Nelson, Marlborough and Keene, and incorporated Dec. 9, 1812. The number of deaths from its incorporation to Jan. 1, 1822, was 44; births 108. Pop. 366.

ROYSE mountain is situated in the ungranted lands N. of Chatham.

RUMNEY, a post township in Grafton county, in lat. 43° 49′, is bounded N. E. by Ellsworth, E. by Campton and Plymouth, S. by Groton and Hebron, and N. W. by Wentworth, containing 22,475 acres. It is 8 miles from Plymouth, 47 from Concord and 110 from Boston. It is watered by Baker's river, of which a considerable branch flows from Stinson's pond, and is called Stinson's brook. The pond is in the N. part of the town, and is 400 rods long and 280 rods wide. Part of Loon pond is on the E. line of this town. The principal elevations are Stinson's and Webber's mountains in the E. part, and a small part of Carr's mountain, which here obtains the name of Rattlesnake mountain, on its N. W. border. The soil here exhibits considerable degrees of fertility. The forest trees are white pine, sugar maple, oak, beech and birch. Rumney was granted first to Samuel Olmstead, afterwards, on the 18th of March, 1767, to Daniel Brainard and others. It was first settled in Oct. 1765, by Capt. Jotham Cummings, and in 1766, by Moses Smart, Daniel Brainard, James Heath and others. The first minister was a congregationalist, Rev. Thomas Niles, who graduated at Yale college in 1758. He was settled by the proprietors, Oct. 21, 1767. A baptist church was formed in 1780, and Rev. Cotton Haines ordained the same year. Rev. Ezra Wilmarth succeeded in April, 1799; was dismissed in May, 1811. There is also a free-will baptist church in Rumney. It was in this town, on the 28th of April, 1752, that the late General STARK, while on a hunting expedition, was captured by a party of 10 Indians, commanded by Francis Titigaw. He was in company with Amos Eastman of Concord, David Stinson of Londonderry, and his brother William. Eastman was taken prisoner on the next morning. Stinson and William Stark, attempting to escape, were fired upon: Stinson fell, was killed, scalped and stripped of his wearing apparel. William made his escape. This event, and the name of Stinson as connected with it, will long be perpetuated by the name of the pond, mountain, and brook, in the town, where the unfortunate man was slain. Pop. 864.

RYE, is a township in the county of Rockingham, pleasantly situated on the sea coast, in lat. 43° 1′; 6 1-2 miles from Portsmouth, by the road, 4 1-2 on a straight line, and 51 from Concord. It is bounded N. and N. W. by Portsmouth, N. E. by Little Harbor, E. by the sea, S. by North-Hampton, W. by Greenland, comprising 7,780 acres. Its name is supposed to have originated from the circumstance of some of its first settlers emigrating from a town of the same name, in Great-Britain. It was originally taken from Portsmouth, Greenland, Hampton and New-Castle, chiefly the latter; and though it began to be settled as early as the year 1635, it was not incorporated till 1719. For about 90 years the people here had no settled minister of the gospel among them; but attended public worship in some of the neighboring towns, particularly at Portsmouth and New-Castle. The first settlers of this town were of the names of Berry, Seavey, Rand, Bracket, Wallis, Jenness and Locke; which names, except that of Bracket, are still retained here, and most of them are numerous. The soil, in this town, is in general hard and stubborn, and not naturally fertile; but, by the hand of industry, and the help of various kinds of sea-weed, which the coast affords in considerable abundance, and which is annually spread upon the farms, it is rendered very productive of corn, potatoes, hay, &c. The sea coast here, is about 6 miles in extent, being nearly one third of the coast in the state. On the shore, there are three considerable and very pleasant beaches, viz: Sandy, Jenness' and Wallis'; to which many persons resort in the summer season from neighboring towns and the country, both for health, and for pleasure. There is here, a small harbor, near Goss' mill, into which vessels of 70 or 80 tons burden may conveniently enter, at high water. This harbor, with the expense of 1 or 2000 dollars, it is thought, might be made to answer very important purposes, both public and private. The boat fishery is carried on to considerable advantage, particularly in the fall and winter seasons. There was formerly a large fresh water pond, lying contiguous to the sand bank or bounds of the sea, covering a surface of about 300 acres. Between this and the sea, a communication was opened by the inhabitants about a century since. The waters were discharged into the sea, leaving a tract of marsh, which, being watered by the regular flowing of the tide, yields annually large quantities of salt hay. Breakfast Hill, between this town and Greenland, is distinguished as the place where a party of Indians were surprised at breakfast, at the time of their incursion in 1696. There are small circular holes in the rocks of which this hill is principally composed, supposed to have been made use of by the natives. This town has suffered considerably in times of war and danger. In 1694, John Locke, living on the Neck, was ambushed and killed by the Indians, while reaping grain in his field. In 1696, at one time, 21 persons, at Sandy beach, were either killed or carried away by them. In the Canada or French war, 14 persons, belonging to this town, were killed or died, in service: and in the American or revolutionary war, 38 of its inhabitants lost their lives, by sea or land; most of them young men. A meeting-house was first erected here, about the year 1725; a church was organized July 20, 1726; and the Rev. Nathaniel Morrill, ordained 14th Sept. of the same year. He continued in the ministry about seven years, and was then dismissed. His successor, Rev. Samuel Parsons, was ordained Nov. 1736; and deceased Jan. 4, 1789, in the 78th year of his age, and the 53d of his ministry. His memory is still dear to those who survive him, and recollect his virtues. During his ministry, 206 persons were admitted into full communion with the church, and between six and seven hundreds received baptism. Rev. *Huntington Porter*, D. D. was ordained, as colleague with Mr. Parsons, Dec. 29, 1784. From that time to 1822, 84 have been received into full communion, and 811 baptized. During the same period, 31 members of the church have been dismissed, or removed from this to other towns, and a few more than that number have died. The present number of communicants is between 50 and 60. There has been a social library in this town for many years. The proprietors of the one, now existing were incorporated in 1812. The library contains at present about 220 volumes, and is annually increasing. The annual average number of deaths, in this town, for 37 years past, is between 11 and 12, or not far from one to an hundred. In the year 1803, during Feb., March and a part of April, a very unusual sickness and mortality prevailed in this town. In the course of less than 3 months, 230 persons were visited with sickness, of various kinds; while other towns in general, around, enjoyed usual health. The deaths were 35; a number remarkably large for so short a time, in proportion to the number of inhabitants; though not very great considering the number visited with sickness. According to received, and pretty authentic accounts, about 40 persons, chiefly strangers, have at different times, lost their lives, and been taken up, on, or near the coast, within the limits of the town; to whom, though strangers, a decent burial was given, attended with those solemnities, which are usual on funeral occasions. The oldest person who has died here, within present recollection, was a female, by the name of Tucker, being 99 years and 9 months old. Several other persons have exceeded 90 years. Pop. 1127.

S.

SACO, a river, one of the largest in New-England, has its source near the Notch of the White Mountains within a few feet of the sources of the Lower Amonoosuck. It thence flows in a S. course down the mountains about 12 miles; then taking an easterly direction, it enters the town of Bartlett, where it receives Ellis' river, which rises in the easterly pass of the mountain near the source of Peabody river. Within the distance of half a mile from these fountains, two large streams flow down the highest of the mountains, one of them into Ellis' river. The former of these is Cutler's river and the latter is New river. The latter made its appearance in October, 1775, during a long rain. In its course, it broke down many rocks and trees and presented a wide spectacle of ruin. At its junction with Ellis' river, there is a noble cascade of 100 feet in height. Several other branches of Saco river flow from other parts of the mountains. From Bartlett the course of the Saco is S., about 10 miles to the lower part of Conway, where it receives Swift river from Burton, thence in an easterly course, it passes into Fryeburg and Brownfield in Maine, and from thence to the sea, it has a S. E. course of about 45 miles. This river rises and overflows very suddenly in rainy seasons, and subsides very rapidly after the cessation of the rains. In the great flood of 1775, when the New river broke out, the banks of the Saco were overflowed very suddenly, and the waters were of a deep brown color for several days, probably from passing over iron ore. On the subsiding of the waters, it was observed, that the bed of the river in some places was widened, and the course of several of its branches changed. In great freshes it has risen 25 feet, but its common rise is about 10 feet.

SADDLEBACK, between Deerfield and Northwood, is a part of the chain called Blue Hills.

SALEM, post-township, Rockingham county, in lat. 42° 47′, 30 miles from Concord, 40 from Portsmouth,

34 from Boston, is bounded N. by Londonderry, N. E. by Atkinson, E. by Methuen, Ms. S. by Pelham, W. by Windham; containing 15,600 acres. Policy pond, partly in this town, and partly in Windham, is the largest collection of water; World's-End pond and Captain pond are in the S. E. and E. parts of the town; and there are other small ponds. The Spiggot river, passing from N. to S. through the town, receives in its course numerous branches, and waters the different portions of the town, furnishing also excellent mill privileges. The soil is generally fertile, and the surface uneven. The Londonderry turnpike passes over this town, from N. W. to S. E. There is a mineral spring in this town, the waters of which have been used. There is one woollen factory, besides mills and other machinery. Salem was incorporated by charter May 11, 1750. Rev. Abner Bayley, who was born at Newbury, Ms. Jan. 19, 1716, graduated at Harvard college in 1736; was ordained here over a congregational church, Jan. 30, 1740; died March 10, 1798. Rev. John Smith was settled colleague in 1797; dismissed in 1816. Rev. *William Balch* was ordained in 1819, and his church consists of about 40 members. There is also a respectable society of methodists, who have occasional preaching, and a small society of baptists. Hon. SILAS BETTON, who graduated at Dartmouth college in 1787, was elected a representative prior to 1800, was 3 years senator from district No. 3, and in 1802 was elected member of congress. He subsequently filled the office of sheriff of the county of Rockingham, and died in 1822, aged —. Pop. 1311.

SALISBURY, a post-town, in Hillsborough county, in lat. 43° 23', is pleasantly situated on the W. banks of Pemigewasset and Merrimack rivers, 15 miles N. of Concord and 78 from Boston. It is bounded N. by Andover, E. by the rivers just mentioned, separating it from Sanbornton and Northfield, S. by Boscawen, and W. by Warner, being 9 miles from E. to W. and 4 miles from N. to S., and containing 28,600 acres. The Pemigewasset waters the E. part, and unites with the Winnepisiogee, forming the Merrimack. Boat navigation terminates a short distance above the junction of these rivers. When a few obstructions are removed, and one or two locks erected on the Merrimack above Concord, communication by water, through the Middlesex canal, will be rendered safe and easy from Boston to the E. village in this town. Blackwater river passes through the W. part of Salisbury. (*See Blackwater river.*) There are 5 bridges across this stream in this town. The 4th N. H. turnpike passes from N. W. to S. E. and is incorporated for the term of 40 years. The forest trees on the rivers are pitch, Norway, and white pine, white, black and yellow oak. The most valuable trees have been cut for building and for ship timber. The hilly lands were originally covered with a heavy growth of sugar maple, white maple, beech, birch, elm, ash and red oak—the valleys were interspersed with evergreens. The soil of the upland is strong, deep and loamy; producing Indian corn oats, peas, beans, flax, rye, &c. The hilly land affords some fine tracts for tillage, but chiefly abounds in excellent pasturage. The valleys produce grass. On Blackwater river, there is some very fertile interval, which united with the adjacent hilly land, composes several very valuable farms. A short turn in the Merrimack to the E. forms a fine tract of fertile interval, of about 300 acres, which appears to be an alluvion of the river. The mineralogical productions have never been scientifically examined. The prevailing rock is granite. A fine quarry has lately been discovered on Mr. William Webster's farm, yielding readily to the wedge and hammer. A considerable portion of Kearsarge mountain ranges within the bounds of Salisbury, the N. W. corner bound of which extends nearly to the summit. (*See Kearsarge mountain*.) The summit of this mountain was formerly covered with evergreens; but its cloud-capped head has long been stripped of its primitive honors by the combined agency of fire and wind. It now presents a bald rock of granite, many parts of which appear to be in a gradual state of disintegration. In the spring of 1819, a large mass of rocks and earth of several thousand tons' weight was loosened from the southern declivity of Bald hill and precipitated with great violence to the valley below, carrying all before it, for the space of 40 rods in length and 4 in breadth. The prospect from the summit of Kearsarge is variegated and highly magnificent. There are 3 considerable villages, the South road, the Centre road, and Pemigewasset, or East village. The *first* is pleasantly situated on the S. road, running from E. to W. through the town, and also on the 4th N. H. turnpike, leading to Hanover. This is also on the northern mail route from Boston to Burlington, Vt. It contains about 30 houses, 1 congregational meeting-house, 2 stores, 1 tavern, 2 law offices, 1 post office and the academy. The *Centre Road* village is 1 1-2 miles N. W. of the preceding, on the same mail route. It contains 30 dwelling houses, a baptist meeting-house, 3 stores, 1 law office, &c. The scenery here is beautiful and picturesque in a high degree. The distant azure mountains, the fertilizing streams, the "tempest torn rocks," the expanded hills, cultivated fields, the glens, and valleys, and extensive pasture grounds, interspersed with forests, conspire to render it delightful to the eye, and to afford fine subjects for the pencil. *Pemigewasset*, or *East* village is in the N. E. corner of the town, at the great falls on Pemigewasset river. Here are an elegant meeting-house, a number of handsome dwelling houses, 2 stores, 1 tavern, 1 post office, &c. Boats laden with 20 tons have already passed up to this place. A toll bridge across the Pemigewasset leads from this village to Sanbornton and Northfield. About 3 miles below this village, on the alluvion before mentioned, is a pleasant settlement of farmers, containing 10 or 12 dwelling houses, several mechanic shops, and one law office. There is a flourishing academy in the S. Road village, incorporated Dec. 10, 1808. The late Benjamin Gale, Esq., a worthy and respectable citizen of Salisbury, made a donation of $1000 to this institution. The Literary Adelphi society, consisting of the students of the academy, has a library of 100 volumes. This town has had a considerable number of its natives liberally educated, some of whom take their rank among the first advocates not only in this state, but in the U. S. Their names are as follows, viz. at *Dartmouth college*, —1794, Moses Eastman, A. M.— 1799, Rev. Moses Sawyer, A. M.— 1801, Hon. Daniel Webster, LL. D.—

1804, Ebenezer O. Fifield, A. B.; Thomas H. Pettengill, A. M.; Ezekiel Webster, A. M.—1805, Nathaniel Sawyer, A. B.—1806, John True, A. B.—1808, Ichabod Bartlett, A. M.; 1811, Rev. Valentine Little, A. B.—1812, James Bartlett, A. M.—1813, Joseph Wardwell, A. B.— 1816, Charles B. Hadduck, A. M.—1817, Rev. Benjamin Huntoon, A. M.—1819, William T. Hadduck, A. M.—1821, Joseph B. Eastman, A. B. At *Middlebury college*, 1812, Benjamin Pettengill, A. M. There is a library of 324 volumes. There is also a musical society. Salisbury was originally granted by Massachusetts, and was known by the name of *Bakers-town*. It was afterwards granted by the Masonian proprietors, Oct. 25, 1749, and then called *Stevens-town*, from Col. Ebenezer Stevens, of Kingston. The number of grantees was 57, of whom 54 belonged to Kingston. It was incorporated by charter from the government of N. H., March 1, 1768, when it took the name of Salisbury. It was settled as early as 1750. The first settlers were Philip Call, Nathaniel Meloon, Benjamin Pettengill, John and Ebenezer Webster, Andrew Bohonnon, Edward Eastman, and many others, mostly from Kingston. The first inhabitants experienced the inroads of the Indians. On the 16th of May, 1753, Nathaniel Meloon, living in the W. part of the town, was captured, together with his wife, and three children, viz. Sarah, Rachel, and Daniel. They were carried to Canada, where he and his wife were sold to the French in Montreal. The three children were kept by the Indians. After the parents had resided in Montreal about a year and a half, they had a son born, who was baptized by a French friar by the name of Joseph Mary. Mr. Meloon returned from captivity after four years and a half, to his farm in Salisbury. Sarah died with the Indians. Rachel, who was 9 years old when captured, returned after 9 years. She had become much attached to the Indians, was about to be married to Peter Louis, son of Col. Louis, of Cognawaga. She had the habits, and acted like an Indian; understood the Indian language and could sing their songs. In August, 1753, the wife of Philip Call was killed; and on the same day, Samuel Scribner and Robert Barber, of this town, and Enos Bishop, of Boscawen, were captured by the Indians. Scribner was sold to the French at Chamblee, and Barber to a Frenchman near St. Francois. It was in Salisbury, that Sabatis and Plausawa, mentioned under *Canterbury*, were buried under a bridge now called Indian bridge. The congregational church was formed Nov. 17, 1773, consisting of 10 male members. Rev. Jonathan Searle, who graduated at Harvard college, was ordained Nov. 17, 1773; dismissed Nov. 8, 1791; died in 1818, aged 74. Rev. Thomas Worcester was ordained November 9, 1791; dismissed in April, 1823. Under his ministry, 270 were added to the church. The baptist society was established May 25, 1789. A church was constituted May 10, 1810, consisting of 9 members. Rev. *Otis Robinson* commenced preaching in 1809, and has continued the minister of the society ever since. Hon. EBENEZER WEBSTER was one of the early settlers; a patriot of the revolution; an officer of the militia; for several years a senator in the legislature, and a judge of the court of common pleas till his death in 1806. Dr. Joseph Bartlett was the first justice of the peace and the first physician in town. Capt. Matthew Pettengill was a useful and respected citizen. Pop. 2000.

SALMON FALL, a river.—See *Pascataqua*. In this river, between Rochester and Lebanon, Me. is a fall, which, from its singularity, deserves notice. The river is confined between two rocks, about 25 feet high, the breadth at the top of the bank not more than 3 rods. It is called the *flume*, and is about 4 rods in length, its breadth varying from 2 1-2 feet to less than 1 foot; but here the water has a subterraneous passage. In the rocks are many cavities from 1 to 7 feet in diameter, mostly cylindrical, and from 1 to 4 feet in depth.

SANBORNTON, post-township, co. of Strafford, in lat. 43° 31′, is situated on the peninsula formed by Great and Little bays and Winnepisiogee river on the E. and S., and the Pemigewasset on the W. These two rivers unite at the S. W. corner of the town, and form the Merrimack. Sanbornton has New-Hampton and Meredith on the N., Gilmanton E. and S. E., Northfield S., a part of Salisbury, Andover, and part of New-Chester on the W.; and is 20 miles from Concord, 60 from Portsmouth, 9 from Gilford. The bays and rivers encircling this town measure nearly 30 miles, and the bay between Sanbornton and Meredith is three miles in width. There are no rivers or ponds of magnitude in this town, though it is almost surrounded by water. Salmon brook pond, in the N. part, and a brook of the same name its outlet, are the only ones worth mentioning. This brook passes through the N. W. part of the town, and affords several mill-sites. There are also excellent mill privileges on the Winnepisiogee river. Over this river are 8 bridges. Sanbornton presents an uneven surface, but contains no considerable mountains with the exception of Salmon brook mountains in the N. part of the town. The highest hills, with one or two exceptions, admit of cultivation. The soil is almost universally good, and well rewards the labor of patient industry. There is a gulf in this town extending nearly a mile through very hard rocky ground, 38 feet in depth, the walls from 80 to 100 feet asunder, and the sides so nearly corresponding as to favor an opinion that they were once united. There is also a cavern in the declivity of a hill, which may be entered in a horizontal direction to the distance of 20 feet. This town was once the residence of a powerful tribe of Indians, or at least a place where they resorted for defence. On the Winnepisiogee, at the head of Little Bay, are found the remains of an ancient fortification. It consisted of six walls, one extending along the river, and across a point of land into the bay, and the others in right angles, connected by a circular wall in the rear. Traces of these walls are yet to be seen, though most of the stones, &c. of which they were composed have been removed to the dam thrown across the river at this place. Within the fort have been found numbers of Indian relics, implements, &c., and also on an island in the bay. When the first settlers of Sanbornton arrived, these walls were breast high, and large oaks were growing within their enclosure. This town was granted by the Masonian proprietors in 1748, to several persons of the name of Sanborn, and others; and was settled in 1765 and 1766, by John Sanborn, David Duston, Andrew Rowen and others. It was incorporated

March 1, 1770. Rev. Joseph Woodman was ordained in Nov. 1771, when there were about 50 families in town. His church then consisted of 7 members. He was dismissed in 1806, and died in 1807. Rev. *Abraham Bodwell*, was ordained Nov. 13, 1806, when the church consisted of 50 members; there are now about 150. Rev. *John Crockett* was settled here over the first baptist church in 1793, now consisting of about 230 members. Another baptist church has recently been established. In order to perpetuate preaching in the society to which they belonged, a few liberal individuals some time since formed themselves into an association, to which they gave the name of the "Congregational Fund Association." Each member gave his security to the amount of his rateable estate for that year; and the interest is appropriated annually to the increase of the funds, which now amount to about $1400. Here are two social libraries, each containing between 200 and 300 volumes. The academy, incorporated in 1820, is at present in a flourishing state. From 1790, to 1822, the deaths in this town were 977, or about 31 yearly. Mrs. Copp and Mrs. Smart are living in Sanbornton, at the age of 100 each. Pop. 3329.

SANDOWN, township, Rockingham county, in lat. 42° 57′, is bounded N. by Chester and Poplin, E. by Hawke, S. by Hampstead, W. by Chester and Londonderry. It is 31 miles from Concord, and contains 8,532 acres—200 of which are water. The surface of this town is rather uneven, but the soil in general is well adapted to the production of various kinds of grain and grass. Phillip's pond, lying in the S. part of the town, is the largest, being about 340 rods long, 200 wide. Angle pond, in the S. E. part of this town, is about 200 rods long, and 90 or 100 wide. There are several other smaller ponds. Squamscot river flows from Phillip's pond, and pursues a nearly level course for 1 1-2 miles, where another stream unites with it: from this junction, whenever the waters are raised by sudden freshes, the current passes back with considerable force towards the pond. The settlement of Sandown was commenced about the year 1736, by Moses Tucker, Israel and James Huse, and others. A congregational church was formed here in 1759, which consisted of 57 members. Rev. Josiah Cotton was ordained the same year, and died in 1780. He was succeeded by Rev. Samuel Collins, who was settled that year; but was removed in 1788. In 1795, a brother of the late President Webber, Rev. John Webber, was settled, who was removed in 1800. Since that period the church has been vacant. A methodist church was formed in 1807, consisting of about 30 members—and ministers of that denomination preach here statedly, and of others occasionally. They have but one place of public worship. The post roads from Boston to Concord, and from Exeter to Chester pass through Sandown. The town was originally a part of Kingston, and was incorporated April 6, 1756. It contains 527 inhabitants—the number having decreased since 1790.

SANDWICH, post-town, Strafford county, in lat. 43° 50′, is bounded N. by ungranted lands, E. by Burton and Tamworth, S. by Moultonborough, W. by Holderness, Campton, and Thornton. It is 70 miles from Portsmouth, and about 50 from Concord. This town was originally granted by Gov. Benning

Wentworth, Oct. 25, 1763, and comprised 6 miles square. On the 5th Sept. 1764, upon the representation of the grantees that the N. and W. sides thereof were "so loaded with inaccessible mountains and shelves of rocks as to be uninhabitable"—an additional grant was made of territory on the E. and S., called *Sandwich Addition.* The Sandwich mountains are a lofty range extending N. E. and terminating in Chocorua Peak in Burton. Squam mountain, extending from Holderness through a corner of Campton into Sandwich, is of considerable height. There are other considerable mountains. The Bearcamp river, its branches rising in the mountains N. and W., passes E. into Tamworth. The W. branch passes through Bearcamp pond. There is another pond not far distant from this, from which issues Red Hill river, passing S. into the Winnepisiogee lake. A small stream passes W. into the Pemigewasset river. About one fourth of Squam lake lies in the S. W. corner of Sandwich; and taken in connection with the surrounding mountains, affords many fine views. Here is an oil mill, several saw and grain mills, besides other machinery. A congregational church was established here some years since; but no minister was ever settled. There are respectable societies of methodists, freewill baptists and friends; and people of other denominations. Hon. DANIEL BEEDE, for a number of years, representative to the general court, a justice of the quorum and a judge of the court of common pleas, resided in this town, and was a useful and respected character. Pop. 2368.

SAWYER'S Location. *See Nash and Sawyer's Location.*

SCHOOGAWNOCK, the Indian name of Israel's river.

SEABROOK, a township, in Rockingham county, lat. 42° 53′, is situated at the S. E. corner of the state, 17 miles S. S. W. of Portsmouth, and 7 N. of Newburyport, bounded N. by Hampton-Falls, E. by the Atlantic, S. by Massachusetts, W. by South-Hampton and Kensington. It was formerly a part of Hampton-Falls, and was granted June 3, 1768 to Jonathan Weare, Richard Smith, John Moulton, Ebenezer Knowlton, Winthrop Gove, Henry Robie, Elisha Brown, Benjamin Leavitt, Isaac Brown and others. Settlements commenced here in 1638, by Christopher Hussey, Joseph Dow, and Thomas Philbrick. The place on which the latter settled, has continued in the immediate possession of his descendants unto the 6th generation, who still possess the same. The rivers are Black river, Brown's river and Walton's river. Many of the rivulets abound with bog ore of iron. The public buildings are a town house and 3 houses of public worship, one for presbyterians, one for methodists, and one for friends. This town derives its name from the number of rivers and rivulets meandering through it. A society of friends was formed here in 1701. A presbyterian society was formed in 1764; and Rev. Samuel Perley ordained in 1765; removed in 1775. Rev. Elias Hull, settled in 1799, died February, 1822, aged 44. A methodist society was formed in 1820. There is a social library, consisting of 200 volumes. There has been some remarkable instances of longevity. Mrs. Comfort Collins lived to the age of 105; Phebe Dow to 101; and several others to 90 and upwards. The average number of deaths annually, is about 14. In 1737, the *angina maligna* prevailed and destroyed many of its inhabitants. Whale-boat building is the most important manufacture, and is carried on to a greater extent than in any other town in N. England. The larger part of the male inhabitants are mechanics and seamen, the latter of which are about 120. Perhaps no town in the state is better situated for carrying on the Bay and Labrador fisheries than this. Pop. 885.

SHARON, a small township in the W. part of Hillsborough county, is bounded N. by Peterborough, E. by Temple, S. by New-Ipswich and Rindge, and W. by Jaffrey, containing about 10,000 acres. It is 18 miles from Amherst, and 48 from Concord. The streams in Sharon are small branches of Contoocook river, and rise near the S. E. corner of the town. They are sufficient to supply a grist mill with water only a part of the year. Boundary mountain lies on the line between this town and Temple, and has an elevation of 200 feet above the surrounding country. The roads here are of little notoriety and travel, except the 3d N. H. turnpike, which passes through the S. W. extremity of the town. Sharon was incorporated June 24, 1791. It has no regularly organized religious society; has no meeting-house, nor has ever had a settled minister. Pop. 400.

SHELBURNE, township, Coos county, in lat. 44° 21′, is bounded N. by Success and Maynesborough, E. by Maine, S. by unlocated lands, and W. by Durand, comprising an area of 45,140 acres. Ameriscoggin river passes through the centre of this town, into which fall the waters of Rattle river and some smaller streams. The soil on each bank of the river is very good, producing in abundance grain and grass; but as we rise from the river, the tracts are mountainous and unfit for cultivation. Mount Moriah, an elevated peak of the White Mountains, lies in the S. part of Shelburne. Moses' Rock, so called from the first man known to have ascended it (Moses Ingalls) is on the S. side of the river near the centre of the town. It is about 60 feet high and 90 long, very smooth, and rising in an angle of nearly 50°. In 1775, David and Benjamin Ingalls commenced a settlement at Shelburne, and not long after, several families were added. In August, 1781, a party of Indians visited this town, killed one man, made another prisoner, plundered the houses, and returned to Canada in savage triumph. This town was incorporated Dec. 13, 1820. There are three small societies, one of congregationalists, one of baptists and one of methodists; but no regular preacher. Pop. 205.

SHOALS. *See Isles of Shoals.*

SIMS' stream rises in the mountains in Columbia from several ponds and springs, and falls into the Connecticut river near the N. W. extremity of the town.

SMITH'S river, in Grafton county, rises from several ponds in Grafton and Orange, and after pursuing a winding, but generally an E. course, of from 12 to 18 miles, through Danbury and Alexandria, falls into the Pemigewasset between Bristol and New-Chester.

SOCIETY-LAND, a small township in Hillsborough co., is bounded N. by Deering, E. by Francestown, S. by Greenfield, and W. by Hancock and Antrim, from which it is separated by Contoocook river. It contains 3,300 acres. It is 17 miles from Amherst and 33 from Concord. The land is generally uneven. There is a small mountain on its S. line, called Crotched mountain. There are no mills or mill seats. There are three school districts and one school house. There is a small baptist society; also a meeting-house, built by Capt. Gideon Dodge, which, with a tract of land, was presented by him to the society. Society-Land formerly included Hancock, Antrim, Hillsborough, Deering, Francestown and part of Greenfield. The number of deaths for the last 20 years has been 41. Pop. 153.

SOMERSWORTH, in the S. E. part of the county of Strafford, in lat. 43° 14', was formerly a part of Dover. It was made a parish, Dec. 19,1729; and incorporated April 22, 1754. It is bounded N. W. by Rochester, N. E. by Salmon-fall river, which divides it from Berwick, Me., and S. W. by Dover. It is 11 miles from Portsmouth, and 45 from Concord. Otis' hill, the highest in this town, is situated about a mile N. from Varney's hill in Dover. The White Mountains may be seen from the summit of this hill; also the steeples of the meeting-houses in Portsmouth, and the masts of the shipping in the harbor. The soil in this town is well adapted to Indian corn, and almost all kinds of grain, grass, &c. The growth of the wood land is oak, pine, walnut, elm, &c. The tide flows on the E. side of this town four miles to Quamphegan falls. The river is of sufficient depth, till within a mile of said falls, for vessels of 250 tons. The S. part of this town is bounded on Cocheco river, from its confluence with the Pascataqua to the mouth of Fresh-creek, nearly a mile; and from thence by said creek to its head, nearly a mile and a half. There are but two ponds of note in this town, viz. Humphrey's pond on the line of Dover, 200 rods long and 120 rods wide; and Cole's pond, 150 rods long and 75 wide. There are several mineral springs in this town; but at present their waters are not much used. Red and yellow ochre, also iron ore, have been found in this town. The ochre has been used in painting houses, and has been found to make a durable paint. The post road from Boston to Portland, and the Dover turnpike pass through this town and over Quamphegan bridge. There are three bridges over Salmon-fall river between this town and Berwick; viz. at Quamphegan-falls, at Salmon-falls, and at the Great-falls. The first meeting-house in this town was erected in 1729; and taken down in 1773. The second meeting-house was erected in 1772; and consumed by lightning in a violent thunder storm, May 4, 1779. It happened about the middle of the day. Its severity was caused by the junction of two clouds directly over this town; one of which rose in the N. W. and the other in the S. W. The clouds ran low; and during the space of half an hour it rained and lightened incessantly, accompanied with tremendous peals of thunder. The steeple of the meeting-house was struck with the lightning which passed down by one of the posts of the belfry adjoining the house; and in about an hour it was in ashes. The bell was melted and fell in a state of fusion. The third meeting-house was erected in 1780, and is yet standing. Large and valuable factories have been erected at Salmon-falls. The buildings are of brick, one 84 by 44 feet, 4 stories in front and 6 in rear, for carding and spinning; another, 60 by 31 feet, 3 stories by 4, for wearing, dressing and fulling, capable of making 200 yards of superfine broad-cloth a day; a third, 60 by 30 feet, 2 stories, for dying, &c. There are grist and sawmills, an oil mill, &c. belonging to this establishment, which promises to become very extensive and profitable. There is also a nail factory in this town. This town was settled between 1650 and 1700, by William Wentworth, John Hall, Wm. Stiles and others. George Ricker and Meturin Ricker were surprised and killed by a party of Indians lying in ambush about half a mile N. E. from Varney's hill, Oct. 7, 1675. They had their arms with them, which together with their upper garments were carried away by the Indians. Ebenezer Downs, who was a quaker, was taken by the Indians at Indigo hill in 1724, and carried to Canada. He was grossly insulted and abused by them, because he refused to dance as the other prisoners did for the diversion of their savage captors. He was redeemed in 1725, by John Hanson of Dover. Jabez Garland was killed by the Indians on his return from public worship in the summer of 1710, about three quarters of a mile N. E. from Varney's hill. Gershom Downs was killed by the Indians in 1711, in the marsh between Varney's hill and Otis' hill. Rev. James Pike, the first minister of Somersworth, was born at Newbury, Ms. March 1, 1703; graduated at Harvard college in 1725; was ordained Oct. 28, 1730; and died March 19, 1792. Rev. Pearson Thurston was born at Lancaster, Ms. in Dec. 1763; graduated at Dartmouth college in 1787; was ordained Feb. 1, 1792; removed Dec. 2, 1812; and died at Leominster, Ms. Aug. 15, 1819. The house in which Mr Thurston lived was consumed by fire, Jan. 22, 1812, together with the church records, communion vessels, and a social library. The church is now vacant. NICHOLAS PIKE, son of Rev. James Pike and author of a popular system of arithmetic, was born in this town, October 6, 1743. He was graduated at Harvard college, 1766; taught a grammar school, first at York, and afterwards at Newburyport; where he died Dec. 9, 1819. JOHN WENTWORTH, son of the Hon. John Wentworth, was born in this town, July 14, 1745; and was graduated at Harvard college, 1768. He entered on the study of the law, and settled at Dover. When application was made to him to put an action in suit, it was his practice to see the parties or to write to them, stating the consequences of a legal process, and advising them to settle their differences between themselves. By this mode of procedure he was instrumental in preventing many vexatious lawsuits; and was entitled to the appellation of peace-maker. He was a member of the continental congress in the revolution, and died January 10, 1787. Col. PAUL WENTWORTH, by his will, bequeathed £500 to the parish in this town; the interest of which was to be expended for pious and charitable uses. He also gave a silver tankard and cup for the use of the church. He died June 24, 1748. Dr. MOSES CARR was born at Newbury, Ms. Nov. 1715. He came to this town in 1735; where he practised in his profession more than 60 years with reputation, and died March 30, 1800. Hon. THOMAS WALLINGFORD was born at Bradford, Mass. in 1697. He came to this town in the early part of his life; and by a diligent application to business, from a small beginning became one of the richest men in the province. He was one of the judges of the superior court, and died Aug. 4, 1771. Hon. JOHN WENTWORTH was born in this town March 30, 1719. He was one of the judges of the superior court, and died May 18, 1781. Hon. ICHABOD ROLLINS, was born in this town, 1721. He was a judge of probate for the county of Strafford, and died Jan. 31, 1800. The number of deaths in this town since the beginning of the present century will average 12 annually; or 1 in 70 of its inhabitants. During the last 20 years, 28 have died between 70 and 80, 17 between 80 and 90, and 7 between 90 and 100 years of age. Samuel Downs died April 22, 1820, aged 99. Mrs. Lydia Stiles is now living (1823) at the age of 101 years. She was born Feb. 27, 1722, is a member of the church, and travelled on foot two miles to public worship till she was 90 years of age. Pop. 841.

SOUCOOK river has its source in three ponds in the S. part of Gilmanton, lying near each other, called Loon, Rocky and Shellcamp ponds. It passes through Loudon, receiving several branches, and forms the boundary between Concord and Pembroke, falling into the Merrimack below Garven's falls.

SOUHEGAN, originally *Souhegenack*, the name of a river in Hillsborough county, and the former name of Amherst and Merrimack. The principal branch of this river originates from a pond in Ashburnham, Ms. It passes N. through Ashby, at the N. W. angle of the county of Middlesex, into New-Ipswich, and through Mason, Milford, Amherst, into Merrimack, where it unites with Merrimack river. In its course it receives several streams from Temple, Lyndeborough and Mont-Vernon, and just before it falls into the Merrimack, receives Babboosuck brook, a considerable stream issuing from Babboosuck pond. *See Amherst.*

SOUTH-HAMPTON, township, Rockingham county, in lat. 42° 53′, is bounded N. by East-Kingston and Kensington, E. by Seabrook, S. by Amesbury, Ms., W. by Newtown; and is 50 miles from Concord, 18 from Portsmouth, and 45 from Boston. The surface is generally even, and the soil of a good quality. Powow river passes through this town, affording valuable mill seats. South-Hampton was incorporated by charter, May 25, 1742. Rev. William Parsons, who graduated at Harvard college in 1735, was ordained here over a congregational church in 1743; and dismissed Oct. 6, 1762. Rev. Nathaniel Noyes, was settled Feb. 23, 1763; and dismissed Dec. 8, 1800. Since that time, there has been no stated worship. There are people of other denominations here, who have occasional preaching. Hon. PHILLIPS WHITE, who was a member of the old congress, justice of the peace throughout the state, a counsellor in 1792 and 1793, and for many years judge of probate, died June 24, 1811, aged 82. Pop. 416.

SPIGGOT river rises in Hampstead, and passes through Salem, and into the Merrimack between Methuen and Dracut, Ms. nearly opposite Shawsheen river, which comes from the S. through Andover.

SPAFFORD's lake. *See Chesterfield.*

SPRINGFIELD, a post-township, in Cheshire county, in lat. 43° 30′, is bounded N. by Grafton, E. by Wilmot, S. E. by New-London, S. by Wendell and Croydon, W. by Croydon and Grantham, containing 28,330 acres, 2300 of which are water. It is 35 miles from Concord and 90 from Boston. A branch of Sugar river has its source in this town; and also a branch of the Blackwater river. The former empties into the Connecticut, the latter into the Merrimack. There are several ponds, viz. Station pond, about 250 rods long, 140 wide; Cilley pond, 240 rods long, and about 80 wide; Star, Stony, and Morgan's ponds. The land is rough and stony, but the soil is capable of producing the various agricultural products found in the contiguous towns. In 1820, there were produced 17,500 lbs. of butter, 25,000 lbs. of cheese, 45,000 lbs. of beef, 60,000 lbs. of pork, 5,500 lbs. of flax, and 200 barrels of cider. There is, in the E. part of the town, a quarry of stone, from which can be raised stones from 20 to 30 feet in length and from 8 to 12 inches in thickness. There is a library, which was incorporated Dec. 15, 1803. This town was granted Jan. 3, 1769, by the name of *Protectworth*, to John Fisher, Daniel Warner, Esquires, and 58 others. Its first settlement commenced in 1772, by Israel Clifford, Israel Clifford, Jr. Nathaniel Clark, Samuel Stevens and others. It was incorporated by the name of Springfield, Jan. 24, 1794. The spotted fever prevailed here a few years since, of which several children died. The average number of deaths per annum, for 20 years past, has been 5. There is a congregational church, but it is destitute of a minister. Pop. about 1000.

SQUAMSCOT, or *Swamscot*, called also Great or Exeter river. See *Exeter*.

SQUAM lake, lying on the borders of Holderness, Sandwich, Moultonborough and Centre-Harbor, is "a splendid sheet of water, indented by points, arched with coves, and studded with a succession of romantic islands." It is about 6 miles in length, and where widest, not less than 3 miles in breadth. The surface has been estimated at from 6000 to 7000 acres.

The largest island is about 1 mile long, and 1-3 of a mile wide. A communication by water between this lake and Winnepisiogee might be easily effected, the distance being less than 2 miles.

SQUAM river, the outlet of Squam lake through Squam pond in Holderness, forms a junction with the Pemigewasset near the S. W. angle of that town.

SQUAMANAGONICK, the name of a village at the falls on Cocheco river in Rochester—so called from the Indian name of the falls.

STATE-HOUSE. *See p.* 41.
STATE-PRISON. *See p.* 43.

STEWARTSTOWN, township, Coos county, in lat. 44° 56', lies on the E. side of the Connecticut, which washes its W. boundary a distance of 7 miles: it is bounded S. by Colebrook, N. by the first College grant, E. by Dixville; distant 150 miles from Portland, 170 from Portsmouth, 150 from Concord—containing about 27,000 acres. The Connecticut river is about 15 rods in width at this place. Bishop's brook, a considerable stream, rises in this town, and falls into the Connecticut at the N. W. corner. Dead water and Mohawk rivers have their sources here. Hall's stream, also, unites with the Connecticut in Stewartstown. There are 2 ponds in the E. part of this town, called Little and Great Diamond ponds, the waters of which form the Diamond river, passing S. E. into Margallaway river, a branch of the Ameriscoggin. The larger of these ponds is one mile long, 3-4 mile wide; the smaller, 2-3 mile wide, 100 rods long—both well stocked with salmon trout. There is another pond in the W. part of this town, called Back pond, covering about 60 acres. There are no large mountains in Stewartstown, although there are many elevations. The soil of the interval is rich, and the uplands are not unproductive. The growth of wood is a mixture of sugar maple, birch, beech, ash, spruce, fir, &c. Stewartstown was originally granted by Gov. John Wentworth to four individuals, viz. Sir George Cockburn, Sir George Colebrook, John Stewart and John Nelson, Esqrs.—three of whom resided in England. Before the revolution, they surveyed the lands, and gave a few lots to settlers, who made some small improvements. But after the commencement of hostilities, they abandoned their settlements until peace was restored. Improvements were then made under grants from Col. David Webster, sheriff of Grafton. Stewartstown was incorporated in Dec. 1799. During the late war a block-house or fort was erected in this town for defence by a company of militia, and occupied until Aug. 1814, when it was destroyed. On the site of this fort, the American and British surveyors and astronomers, met to ascertain the 45° of north latitude between the two governments, under the treaty of Ghent. Pop. 363.

STODDARD, post-township in the E. part of Cheshire county, in lat. 43° 4′, is bounded N. by Washington, E. by Windsor and Antrim, S. by Nelson and Sullivan, and W. by Gilsum and Marlow, containing 35,925 acres, of which 1100 are water. It is 14 miles from Keene, 20 from Charlestown and 42 from Concord. This town is situated on the height of land between Merrimack and Connecticut rivers. It is mountainous and very rocky. The soil is deep, with a clay bottom. As cold and moisture are its predominant qualities, Indian corn does not thrive well, except in hot and dry seasons. Rye and wheat succeed well on lands newly cleared; and ploughed lands produce good crops of barley, oats, flax, potatoes, &c. The soil however is better adapted to grazing than tillage. The S. branch of Ashuelot river has its source near the centre of the town. The streams in the E. section, fall into the Merrimack; those on the W. into the Connecticut. There are fourteen ponds, some of which are of considerable magnitude. The agricultural products in 1820, were 32,000 lbs. of butter, 43,000 lbs. of cheese, 71,000 lbs. of beef, 85,000 lbs. of pork, 5,700 lbs. flax, and 600 bbls. of cider. This town was formerly called *Limerick*. It was incorporated Nov. 4, 1774, when it received the name of Stoddard from Col. Samson Stoddard of Chelmsford, to whom with several others it was granted. The settlement commenced in June, 1769, by John Taggard, Reuben Walton, Alexander Scott, James Mitchel, Richard Richardson, Amos Butterfield, Joseph Dodge and Oliver Parker. The first family was that of John Taggard, whose privations and hardships were very great. Their grain was procured at Peterborough, at the distance of 20 miles, which was conveyed by Mr. T. on his back through the pathless wilderness. At one time, they had nothing, for six days, on which to subsist, but the flesh of the moose. A congregational church of seven members was formed Sept. 4, 1787. Rev. Abisha Colton, was ordained Oct. 16, 1793, and was dismissed Sept. 9, 1795; died in Vermont, Jan. 12, 1823. Rev. *Isaac Robinson* was ordained Jan. 5, 1803. Pop. 1203.

STRAFFORD, a post-township, in Strafford county, in lat. 43° 16′, is bounded N. E. by Farmington, S.

E. by Barrington, S. W. by Northwood, W. by Pittsfield, N. W. by Barnstead. It is 70 miles from Boston, 15 from Dover, 25 from Concord, and is about 7 miles in length, 6 1-2 wide. Bow pond is in the S. W. part of the town, and is about 650 rods long, 400 wide; its waters form one of the principal branches of the Isinglass river. Trout pond lies W. of the Blue hills, and Wild goose pond between this town and Pittsfield. The range of Blue hills crosses the N. W. part of the town. The soil here is generally of a good quality. There are four free-will baptist churches in this town; the 1st, over which Elder *William Sanders* was ordained in May, 1822, contains 100 members; the 2d, of about 100 members, has no settled minister, but is under the pastoral care of Elder Place of Rochester. Elder Micajah Otis was ordained over this church, Oct. 16, 1799; died May 30, 1821, aged 74. The 3d church has 96, and the 4th, 37 members. Strafford was formerly a part of Barrington, and was disannexed and incorporated June 17, 1820. Pop. 2144.

STRATFORD, post-town, in the county of Coos, on the E. bank of Connecticut river, in lat. 44° 41', is 16 miles above Lancaster; bounded N. by Columbia, E. by ungranted lands, S. by Piercy and Northumberland, W. by Vermont. The town is large, extending 10 miles on the river, with a fertile interval of 1-4 to 1 mile wide. This meadow is skirted in many places by a narrow plain, succeeded by the mountainous regions, covering the whole E and N. divisions of the town. The soil, except along the river, is rocky, gravelly and cold. The back lands are therefore not settled to any extent. The Peaks, two mountains of a conical form, situated in the S. E. part of the town, are seen at a great distance. They are apparently disconnected from the great range of Bowback mountains stretching over the N. and E. parts of the town. They are discovered immediately on entering Dalton, 30 miles below, and stand as landmarks in front or to the right, till, on nearer approach, they are lost behind the intervening hills. Bog brook and several smaller streams here fall into the Connecticut; and Nash's stream crosses the S. E. part of the town into the Amonoosuck. There is a pond in the S. E. part of the town, the waters of which pass into the Amonoosuck. Stratford was incorporated Nov. 16, 1779. The first settlers were Isaac Johnston, James Curtis, James Brown, Josiah Lampkins and Archippus Blodget. There is a meeting-house here, and congregationalists and methodists; but no settled minister. Pop. 335.

STRATHAM, a township, in the county of Rockingham, in lat. 43° 1', 51 miles from Boston, 39 from Concord, 3 from Exeter, is situated on the E. side of the W. branch of the Pascataqua river; bounded N. E. by Greenland, E. by Greenland and North-Hampton, S. W. by Exeter, W. and N. W. by the river and bay, which separate it from Exeter and New-Market; and has an area of 10,120 acres. Stratham is distant about 8 miles from the sea. The land is even, and well calculated for agricultural purposes. Farming is so exclusively the employment of the people, that, although a navigable river adjoins it, there is little attention given to any other pursuit. In the E. part of the town, in a swamp, is perhaps the largest repository of peat in the state. This town was a part of the Squamscot patent, or Hilton's purchase. In 1697, there were 35 families in the place, who petitioned for an act of incorporation. It was made a distinct town by charter, March 20, 1716. The first town meeting was on the 10th of April, 1716; Deac. David Robinson was chosen town clerk, and held that office 47 years. A congregational church was formed here at an early date, and Rev. Henry Rust ordained in 1718; he died in 1749, aged 63. Rev. Joseph Adams was ordained in 1756, and died 1785, aged 66. Rev. James Miltemore, ordained in 1786, was removed in 1807. The church is now vacant. There was formerly a baptist society here, under the ministration of Rev. S. Shepard. There is a freewill baptist society, lately under the care of Eld. N. Piper.— From the year 1798 to 1812, inclusive, the number of deaths in this town was 186. The greatest number in any one year was 20, and the smallest number 5, averaging about 12 annually. Between the years 1742 and 1797, inclusive, the number of deaths was 1080, averaging about 20 annually. PHINEHAS MERRILL, Esq. was a native of this town; was eminent as a surveyor, assisted in preparing the elegant Map of N. H. published by Carrigain; was several years a representative in our state legislature, and died Dec. 31, 1814, aged 47. Pop. 892.

SUCCESS, an uninhabited township, in Coos county, in lat. 44° 27′, is bounded N. by Cambridge, E. by Maine, S. by Shelburne, W. by Shelburne, Maynesborough and Paulsburgh; comprising an area of about 30,000 acres. There are several considerable mountains in this tract; and two or three ponds.— Narmarcungawack and Live rivers rise here, and pass westerly into the Ameriscoggin. Success was granted Feb. 12, 1773, to Benjamin Mackay and others; and is 143 miles from Concord.

SUGAR river. *See Claremont.*

SULLIVAN, a township in Cheshire county, in lat. 43°, is bounded N. by Gilsum and Stoddard, E. by Stoddard and Nelson, S. by Roxbury and Keene, W. by Keene and Gilsum, containing 12,212 acres. The distance from Keene is 6 miles, from Concord 42 miles. The S. E. part of this town is watered by Ashuelot river. The soil produces rye, corn, oats, &c. There are no considerable ponds; no elevations worthy of particular notice. This town was incorporated Sept. 27, 1787, and received its name from President Sullivan, the chief magistrate of N. H. that year. There are two religious societies, congregational and baptist. Of the former, Rev. *William Muzzy*, who graduated at Harvard college in 1793, was ordained in 1798. Over the latter Rev. *Charles Cummings* was ord. Oct. 24, 1810. Pop. 600.

SUNAPEE lake, is situated in the N. W. part of Hillsborough county and the N. E. part of Cheshire, in the towns of Wendell, New-London and Fishersfield. The centre of it is in lat. 43° 22′. It is 9 miles long and about 1 1-2 miles in width. Its outlet is on the W. side through Sugar river. In 1816, Loammi Baldwin, Esq. and Professor John Farrar, were appointed a committee by the government of Massachusetts, with whom was associated Henry B. Chase, Esq. appointed by the government of this state, to explore and survey a route for a navigable canal from the Connecticut to the Merrimack. The contemplated line of communication was from the mouth of Sugar river, which empties into the Connecticut, to the mouth of the Contoocook river, which empties into the Merrimack. The survey comprehended the shores of Sunapee lake, the elevation of the lake above the waters of the rivers, the highest of the falls in either of the rivers, and of the land adjoining, so that it might serve as the basis of a calculation of the expense of such water communication. By the report of this committee, it appears that the fall, each way from the lake to these rivers, exceeded 820 feet, which shews the impracticability of a project which, before the survey was made, was thought to be feasible.

SUNCOOK river rises in a pond between Gilmanton and Gilford, near the summit of one of the Suncook mountains, elevated 900 feet above its base. The water from this pond passes through two others at the foot of the mountains, and thence through a flourishing village in the S. E. part of Gilmanton, into Barnstead, where it receives several tributaries; thence through Pittsfield and Epsom, and between Allenstown and Pembroke, into the Merrimack.

SURRY, a small township in Cheshire county, in lat. 43° 1′, is bounded N. by Alstead, E. by Gilsum, S. by Keene and W. by Westmoreland and Walpole, containing 12,212 acres. It is 54 miles from Concord. It is watered by Ashuelot river, on which there is a valuable tract of meadow land, extending almost the whole length of the own. On the E. side of Ashuelot river is a steep and high mountain, on the summit of which is a pond of about 3 acres in extent, and about 25 feet depth of water. Viewing its elevated height and situation above the river, it may be esteemed as a natural curiosity. The Cheshire turnpike from Charlesown to Keene, passes through the central part of Surry, and the 3d N. H. turnpike from Walpole to New-Ipswich passes through the S. W. part. Surry was originally part of Gilsum and Westmoreland. It was incorporated by charter, March 9, 1769, deriving its name from *Surry* in England. The first settlement was made in 1764, by Peter Hayward. He commenced clearing land and laboring on his farm in the summer preceding, making his home at the fort in Keene. He practiced going to his farm in the morning, and returning to the fort in the evening, guarded by his dog and gun, while many of the savages at that time were lurking in the woods. The congregational church was formed June 12, 1769, of 8 males and 7 females. Rev. David Darling, who graduated at Yale college in 1779, was ordained Jan. 18, 1781; dismissed Dec. 30, 1783. Rev. *Perley Howe*, who graduated at Dartmouth college in 1790, was ordained Sept. 16, 1795. There are some persons professing to be of the *Christ-ian* and methodist orders, but of such, there are no regular churches. Surry contains 80 families and 90 rateable polls. Hon. LEMUEL HOLMES, a judge of the court of common pleas and a counsellor in 1793, resided in this town. Pop. 570.

SUTTON, a post-town in Hillsborough county, in lat. 43° 19′, is 7 1-2 miles in length, and 5 in breadth, containing 24,300 acres. It is bounded N. by New-London, E. by Wilmot and Warner, S. by Warner and Bradford, and W. by Fishersfield. It is 17 miles from Hopkinton, 25 from Concord, 65 from Portsmouth and 80 from Boston. The southerly and largest branch of Warner river enters this town on the S., runs a short distance, and passes off into Warner again. The northerly branch of this river runs nearly through the centre of the town from N. to S.; affords several good mill seats, and is adorned with many pleasant and valuable meadows on its borders. Stevens' brook, another considerable branch of Warner river, has its source on the W. side of Kearsarge and runs about 4 miles in this town in a S. E. direction. There is also a large branch of Blackwater river, which has its source about the western confines of Kearsarge, and flows through this town in a N. E. course about 3 miles. On the margin of this stream, there is some rich meadow and interval land. There are several ponds, the most important of which are Kezar's pond, situated towards the N. part of the town, which is about 190 rods square; and Long pond, situated at the south part of the town, 350 rods long and 70 wide. Kearsarge mountain extends more than half the length of Sutton on its E. side. Here this mountain has a grand and lofty appearance. From its firm and everlasting base, it raises its towering summit far above the clouds. In the morning, at the rising of the sun, it throws its huge shadow over a vast extent of territory, comprising an immense number of inferior mountains, hills, plains and valleys, and eclipses the sun to hundreds and thousands of its western inhabitans. Hundreds of people visit this mountain annually, and climb to its top, where they have, in a fair day, a pleasing and picturesque view in every direction. King's Hill is situated on the W. part of Sutton. On the most elevated part of this hill, which rises within a few feet as high as Kearsarge, there is one of the most extensive landscape views in the country. On the W. is seen the Sunapee lake, the Ascutney, and highlands in Vermont to the Green mountains; on the S. the Sunapee and Monadnock; on the E. you almost overlook Kearsarge; and on the N. the Cardigan and White hills, with an innumerable host of mountains, hills and peaks, present themselves to view, of all shapes and sizes. On this hill and in the meadows at its foot, is found clay of a superior quality, in great quantities. Here are also found quarries of stone, remarkable for their dimensions, and valuable for their quality. These stones are found in extensive strata, of almost any thickness, length or width wished for. They are split and prepared for buildings at very little expense or labor, as nature seems almost to have given many of them the finishing stroke. A mineral is found in this town resembling black lead. It is frequently used for paint, on roofs and doors of buildings, and produces a handsome and durable slate color. The soil in this town presents all the varieties of productiveness and sterility; and though the surface is diversified with a succession of hills and vales, and is often rough and mountainous, it, in many places, produces fine crops of wheat, rye, oats, Indian corn, and most of the other products common to New-England. The original forest growth of this town, consisted of the white, yellow, Norway and pitch pine, white and red cedar, hemlock, spruce, juniper, fir, poplar, bass, sugar maple, white maple, white, red and black birch, beech, white and brown ash, white, red and yellow oak, elm, oil nut, or butternut, and some others. The principal road through this town is from Hopkinton to Dartmouth College, to which place it is 33 miles. Sutton was granted by the Masonian proprietors, in 1749, to inhabitants of Haverhill, Newbury and Bradford, Mass. and Kingston, N. H. It was called *Perrys-town*, from Obadiah Perry, one of its original and principal proprietors. The first settlement was made in 1767, by David Peaslee, who was soon followed by a considerable number of other settlers. "To the early inhabitants, it was not unfrequent to see the harmless moose approach their humble cottages; and the inoffensive deer was frequently seen feeding on their little improvements. The beaver, the otter, and the muskrat sported up and down the rivers and brooks almost unmolested; while the midnight howlings of the bear and wolf announced to them, their intended depredations on their fields, flocks and herds. Although the Indian was not seen, yet it seemed that he had just put out his fire and gone. His track was still plain and visible." On the W. bank of Kezar's pond, were several acres of land, which appeared to have been cleared of their original forest. Here were found several Indian hearths, laid with stone, and with much skill and ingenuity. Here was found an Indian burial place. Gun barrels and arrows have been found in this sacred repository. Near the pond, have been found stone pestles, mortars and tomahawks. A baptist church was formed in April, 1782, and in Oct. of the same year, Rev. Samuel Ambrose was ordained. He was dismissed in March, 1795. Rev. *Nathan Ames* succeeded in May, 1821. Number of communicants, 110. There is a free-will baptist society, over which Elder *Elijah Watson* was settled in 1818. There is a society of universalists. Within 10 years past, 5 persons have died more than 100 years of age, 1 at the age of 99, and 3 from 90 to 99. Jacob Davis died in April, 1819, aged 105; and in the week following, his wife, aged 99, with whom he had lived more than 70 years. After he was 100 years of age, he attended the polls, and voted. Thomas Walker, a native of Wales, who died in March, 1822, at the age of 103, was a soldier of the revolution, and took part in several important battles, such as Saratoga, White plains, Brandywine, &c. Pop. 1573.

SWANZEY, a post-township in Cheshire county, in lat. 42° 51', is bounded N. by Keene, E. by Marlborough and Troy, S. by Richmond, W. by Winchester and Chesterfield, containing 28,057 acres. It is 6 miles from Keene, 60 S. W. from Concord, and 78 from Boston. The principal streams are the Ashuelot and the S. Branch rivers. The former passes through Swanzey in a S. W. direction, and empties into the Connecticut at Hinsdale. This is a stream of much importance, and is made navigable for boats as far up as Keene, excepting a carrying place about the rapids at Winchester. The South Branch unites with the Ashuelot about one mile N. from the centre of the town. The surface here is somewhat diversified with hills, valleys, and swells of upland. Nearly one third part is almost perfectly level, consisting of nearly equal proportions of plain and interval. The level grounds are free from stone. The divisions of soil are interval, plain and upland. The principal production of the former is grass, which grows luxuriantly. The plains are easily cultivated, and produce rye, corn, &c. The uplands possess a deep and strong soil, and are divided into convenient proportions of arable, mowing, grazing, orchard, and wood land. The original growth comprises, with a few exceptions, the whole variety of perennial and deciduous forest trees. The pine affords sufficient lumber for local use, and a considerable quantity for exportation. From the maple, large quantities of sugar have been made. There is one pond in the S. W. part of the town, 1 mile in length and 3-4 of a mile wide. It is the source of the S. Branch. There is a mineral spring, the water of which is impregnated with sulphate of iron. Some iron ore has been discovered. There are about 30 houses on the street, which is level, and extends N. and S. 2 1-2 miles. Few towns, so large, are less compact. There are 2 houses for public worship. There is a social library of 200 well selected volumes, incorporated June 10, 1802. There are 2 cotton factories, 1 cotton and woollen factory, 3 carding machines, &c.— Swanzey was first granted by Massachusetts, in 1733, to 64 proprietors, whose first meeting was at Concord, Mass. June 27, 1734. After the divisional line was run, it was granted July 2, 1753, by N. H., to 62 proprietors. Until that time it had been called *Lower Ashuelot*, from the Indian name of the river, which was originally *Ashaelock*. From 1741 to 1747, this town suffered much from Indian depredations. Several of the inhabitants were killed and many were made prisoners. Massachusetts, under whose jurisdiction this town had remained for 13 years, withdrew her protection, and left the inhabitants defenceless, and exposed to the fury of the savages. It was therefore thought advisable to abandon the place. The settlers collected together their household furniture, such as chests, tables, iron and brass ware, and concealed it in the ground, covering the place of concealment with leaves, trees, &c., and left their plantation to the disposition of the Indians, who were not tardy in setting fire to their forts, which, with every house except one, they reduced to ashes. Most of the people went to their former places of residence in Mass. They returned about three years afterwards, and nothing about their former habitations was to be seen, but ruin and desolation. The congregational church was first gathered in 1741, and Rev. Timothy Harrington, a native of Waltham, Ms. was settled as pastor. He left the place in consequence of the war in 1747; was settled at Lancaster, Ms. in 1748; died Dec. 18, 1795, aged 80. He was a truly venerable and worthy divine. Rev. Ezra Carpenter was settled over this town and Keene, Oct. 4, 1753; dismissed soon after. Rev. Edward Goddard was ordained Sept. 27, 1769; dismissed July 5, 1798. Rev. Clark Brown settled Sept. 5, 1810; dismissed Aug. 16, 1815. Rev. *Joshua Chandler* was ordained Jan. 1819. The baptist church here was founded about the year 1804. The number of deaths from Jan. 1810, to June 3, 1822, was 231. Pop. 1716.

SWIFT RIVER. rises among the mountains in the ungranted lands N. W. of Burton, and passes through the town from W. to E. with great rapidity, and falls into the Saco in Conway. Its whole course is rapid, and in one place it falls about 30 feet in the distance of 6 rods, through a channel in the solid rock of about 12 feet wide—the sides being from 10 to 30 feet perpendicular height. At the upper part of these falls, are found several circular holes worn perpendicularly into the rock, several feet in depth and from 6 inches to 2 feet diameter. There is another small river in Tamworth of the same name.

T.

TAMWORTH, a post-township, Strafford county, in lat. 43° 51', is situated on the post-road from Concord to Portland, and about 68 miles from each; 30 miles from Gilford, and 120 from Boston. It is bounded N. by Burton, E. by Eaton, S. by Ossipee, W. by Sandwich, and contains 28,917 acres. There is no mountain situated wholly in this town. On the N. are the mountains of Burton, and the S. the line crosses a part of Ossipee mountain. The mountains to the N. have a romantic and picturesque appearance. The town lies in ridges and valleys, generally rocky and fertile. The principal rivers are Bearcamp, which passes through the town in an easterly direction, and discharges its waters into Ossipee lake; Swift river, which rises near the N. W. corner of the town, and passing through its centre, mingles its waters with the Bearcamp; and Corway river, proceeding from Corway pond, near Burton; and crossing the S. line of Tamworth, near the S. E. corner of the town, near which it empties into Bearcamp river. By these rivers, and other small streams, the town is uncommonly well watered. On these streams is a great number of excellent mill privileges. Tamworth was granted Oct. 14, 1766, to John Webster, Jonathan Moulton and others; and was settled in 1771, by Richard Jackman, Jonathan Choate, David Philbrick and William Eastman. The congregational church, in this town, consists of about 200 members, under the pastoral care of the Rev. *Samuel Hidden*, who was ordained Sept. 12, 1792. Here is also a large society and church of freewill baptists. Pop. 1442.

TEMPLE, post town, in Hillsborough county, in lat. 42° 49', is bounded N. by Greenfield and Lyndeborough, E. by Lyndeborough and Wilton, S. by New-Ipswich and Mason, and W. by Sharon and Peterborough. It is 6 miles in length; its medial breadth is 3 1-2 miles. Temple is 12 miles from Amherst and 40 from Concord. The several streams which empty into Souhegan river at Wilton, rise among the mountainous tracts on the W., and generally from sources within the limits of Temple.— This town is of considerable elevation. The prospect towards the E. and S. is very extensive, and presents a rich and diversified scenery. From the highest point of elevation, in a clear atmosphere, about 20 meeting houses may be seen by the naked eye. The surface is very rocky and uneven. The soil is tolerably good, and every part of it may be improved to advantage, either for tillage, mowing, pasturage, or woodland. This place is free from early frosts. For the last 35 years, there has been no general mortal sickness. In 1813, there occurred 137 cases of fever, of which only 7 died. The deaths for 15 years past, have annually averaged about 14. The congregational church was organized Oct. 2, 1771, at which time, Rev. Samuel Webster, from Salisbury, Mass., was ordained. He died in 1778, aged 35. Rev. *Noah Miles*, his successor, was ordained in 1782. There is a library in this town called the "Columbian Library," incorporated in 1797, having 237 volumes. Temple is the easterly part of what was called *Peterborough Slip*. It was incorporated Aug. 26, 1768. Hon. FRANCIS BLOOD, a representative to the general court, a senator, counsellor, judge of the court of common pleas, and brigadier general, resided in this town. Pop. 752.

TENERIFFE. *See Milton.*

THORNTON, a post township in Grafton county, in lat. 43° 54′, is bounded N. by Peeling and Lincoln, E. by ungranted land and Gillis' and Foss' grant, S. by Campton, W. by Ellsworth and Peeling, containing 28,490 acres, including Thornton Gore. It is 12 miles from Plymouth, 58 from Concord, and 120 from Boston. It is watered by Pemigewasset river, passing through the town from N. to S., by Mad river at the S. E. extremity, and by several small brooks. On Mill brook, there is a cascade, of which the water falls 7 feet in 2 rods, and then falls over a rock 42 feet perpendicular. The soil is suitable for wheat, rye, oats, flax, &c. The intervals on the Pemigewasset are very productive. There are many elevations, but none distinguished for a remarkable height. Maple sugar is made in considerable quantities, frequently from 500 to 1000 lbs. by one family. Thornton was granted July 6, 1763, to Matthew, James, and Andrew Thornton and others. It was first settled in 1770, by Benjamin Hoit, whose son Benjamin was the first child born in town. Thornton was incorporated Nov. 8, 1781. A congregational church was formed, and Rev. Experience Esterbrooks was ordained Aug. 10, 1780; afterwards dismissed. Rev. Noah Worcester, now D. D., of Brighton, Ms., was ordained in 1787; dismissed in 1810. There are 2 meeting houses, one of which is used as a town house. There are several religious denominations in this place. Number of deaths from 1810 to 1822, 75. Pop. 857.

TROY, a small township in Cheshire county, in lat. 42° 50′, is bounded N. by Marlborough, E. by Jaffrey, S. by Fitzwilliam, and W. by Richmond and Swanzey. It is about 60 miles from Concord. The soil and productions of this town are similar to those of Fitzwilliam. Possessing but few water privileges, its advantages for mills and factories are limited. The inhabitants are principally agriculturalists. This town was taken from Marlborough and Fitzwilliam, and incorporated June 23, 1815. A congregational church was organized Sept. 14, 1815. Rev. Ezekiel Rich was installed at the time the church was formed. He was dismissed July 18, 1818. Rev. *Seth E. Winslow* has since been employed. The church has about 30 communicants. Pop. 700.

TUFTONBOROUGH, post town, Strafford county, in lat. 43° 40′, is about 50 miles from Concord, situated on the N. E. shore of Winnepisiogee lake; bounded N. E. by Ossipee, S. E. by Wolfeborough, S. W. and W. by the lake, N. W. by Moultonborough. There are several ponds in this town, together with many small streams running into the lake. The soil is alternately good and indifferent; the surface, an interchange of rough and pleasant grounds. There are several arms of the lake stretching far into the town, and presenting to the spectator, from the elevated parts of the town, a succession of beautiful views. Tuftonborough was originally granted to J. Tufton Mason, and took its name from him. It was settled about 1780, and incorporated Dec. 17, 1795. Among the early settlers were Benjamin Bean, Phinehas Graves and Joseph Peavey. There are societies of congregationalists, baptists and methodists ; of the latter, Rev. *Joseph Kellum* is pastor. They have a meeting house; and there is also a commodious town house. This has generally been a healthy town. The spotted fever prevailed in 1816, and numbers fell its victims. Pop. 1232.

U.

UMBAGOG lake, is a large body of water, situated mostly in the state of Maine, and extending about 300 rods in width along the E. of the townships of Errol and Cambridge, in N. H. This lake is very imperfectly known ; is said to be about 18 miles long, and in some parts 10 wide ; being but little inferior to Winnepisiogee, in extent and beauty. Its outlet is on the W. side, in Errol, its waters flowing into the Ameriscoggin.

UNCONOONOCK, a mountain.—See *Goffstown*.

UNITY, post-township, in Cheshire county, in lat. 42° 51′, is bounded N. by Claremont and Newport, E. by Goshen, S. by Lempster and Acworth, and W. by Charlestown, containing 24,447 acres. It is 43 miles from Concord, 88 from Portsmouth and 90 from Boston.—The 2d N. H. turnpike and the post road from Goshen to Charlestown pass through this town. Little Sugar river has its source in Whortleberry pond and Beaver meadow, in the N. part of the town, passes through its centre, and empties itself into the Connecticut at Charlestown. Cold pond, the head of Cold river, is partly in this town. From Gilman's pond, in the E. part of Unity, proceeds a branch of Sugar river, flowing through Newport. Perry's mountain is in the S. W. part, and partly in Charlestown. Unity is an uneven township, and abounds in rocks. They are principally the common granite ; some are oriental granite. The soil is highly favorable for grazing. It is excellent for flax, few towns in the state producing a greater quantity. From 5 pecks of seed sowed in 1821, were raised, without any extraordinary cultivation, 25 bushels of flax seed, of the best quality, and 700lbs. of good flax. The agricultural products in 1820, were 21,000lbs. of butter, 30,000lbs. of cheese, 72,-000lbs. of beef, 85,000lbs. of pork, 5,700lbs. of flax, 600 barrels of cider. Unity was granted by charter, July 13, 1764, to Theodore Atkinson, Meshech Weare, and 45 others. It was called Unity, from the happy termination of a dispute which had long subsisted between certain of the inhabitants of Kingston and Hampstead, claiming the same tract of land under two different grants. The first settlement was made by John Ladd and Moses Thurston, in 1769. Joseph Perkins the only native graduate, proceeded A. B., at Williams' college, in 1814. There are methodist, baptist and friend societies, each of which have meeting houses. Charles Huntoon, Esq., one of the first settlers, died here in 1818, aged 93. Pop. 1280.

UPPER COOS, a name formerly applied to the tract on the Connecticut, now comprising the towns of Lancaster and Northumberland, and the towns opposite, in the state of Vermont.

W.

WAKEFIELD, a post-township, Strafford county, in lat. 43° 35′, is 100 miles from Boston, 50 from

Concord, 30 from Dover; bounded N. W. by Ossipee and Effingham, E. by Maine, S. E. by Milton, W. by Middleton and Brookfield. Lovewell's pond, in the S. part of the town, is about 700 rods long, 275 wide. Province pond lies between Wakefield and Effingham, and is 450 rods long, 400 wide. Pine river pond is the source of the river of that name flowing N. W. into Ossipee lake. The principal branch of the Pascataqua has its rise in East pond, between Wakefield and Newfield, Me. The soil of this place is generally good, but it is more favorable for mowing and grazing than for tillage. This town was formerly called *East-town*, and was incorporated Aug. 30, 1774, by its present name. A congregational church was formed in 1785, and Rev. Asa Piper ordained. He was dismissed in 1810; but has since preached without compensation. There are also societies of methodists and freewill baptists. There are 2 cotton factories, besides other mills and machinery. Lovewell's pond in this town derived its name from Capt. John Lovewell, of Dunstable, who, on the 20th Feb. 1725, surprised and destroyed a party of Indians encamped on the side of the pond. (See Hist. Coll. p. 26.) Robert Macklin, distinguished for longevity, died here in 1787, at the age of 115. He was born in Scotland, and lived several years in Portsmouth in the occupation of a baker. He frequently walked from Portsmouth to Boston in one day, and returned in another. This journey he performed the last time, at the age of 80. Pop. 1518.

WALES' LOCATION, in the co. of Coos, was granted May 4, 1773, to Nathaniel Wales, and comprised 5822 acres—now constituting a part of Columbia.

WALPOLE, a post-town in the county of Cheshire, in lat. 43° 4′, is bounded N. by Charlestown and Langdon, E. by Alstead and Surry, S. by Westmoreland and Westminster, Vt. containing 24,301 acres. It is 25 miles from the S. line of the state, 48 from Dartmouth college, 60 from Concord, and 90 from Boston, with which it has easy and frequent communication. The face of the town is beautifully diversified with hills and vales. The soil is similar to that of other towns on Connecticut river. The intervals afford excellent tillage; the uplands are inferior to none in the state. The agricultural products in 1820, were 40,000 lbs. of butter, 60,000 lbs. of cheese, 110,000 lbs. beef, 180,000 lbs. of pork, 5,500 lbs. of flax, with 1225 barrels of cider. Cold river passes through the N. part, and forms a junction with the Connecticut. There is a lofty hill, called Fall mountain, a part of the range of Mount Toby; the highest parts of which are not less than 700 or 800 feet above the surface of the river. The village of Walpole is situated at the foot of this hill on a plain; the margin of the intervals. The principal street runs N. and S. and is bordered on both sides with houses, stores and shops. A turnpike road from Boston passes through this village, and by a bridge crossing the well known cataract, Bellows' Falls, passes over the Green mountains to Rutland, and from thence through Middlebury and Burlington, by lake Champlain, to Montreal. The transportation and travelling in this channel of communication between Boston and the country on the N. W. are very great. There are 2 toll bridges across the Connecticut, one below the mouth of Cold river; the other at Bellows' Falls, which affords to the traveller, as he passes, a view most sublime and interesting. The Cheshire turnpike and the 3d N. H. turnpike pass through this town. There is a large and commodious meeting-house, built in 1787, and furnished with a good bell and organ. The first minister of Walpole was Rev. ———— Leavitt, who was settled over the congregational church in 1761; and was dismissed in 1763. He was succeeded by Rev. Thomas Fessenden, a graduate at Harvard college in 1758, who was ordained in Jan. 1767; died May 9, 1813, aged 74. Rev. Pliny Dickinson, who graduated at Dartmouth college in 1798, was ordained as colleague with Mr. Fessenden, March 6, 1805. Walpole was granted by the government of N. H., Feb. 16, 1752, to Col. Benjamin Bellows and 61 others. It was previously known by the name of *Great Fall.* Its first settlement was made in 1749, by Col. Bellows, who, for a long time was exposed, without any other defence than a small fort, with a trifling garrison, to the incursions of the Canadians and savages. In time of war he was encircled by hazard and peril. In 1755, a party of Indians, from St. Francis invaded Walpole; killed two men; and took possession of the fort. Col. Bellows was abroad. On his return with 20 men, he met 50 of the savages; fought his way through them, and recovered the fort without losing a man. The descendants of Col. Bellows are numerous and highly respectable. Pop. 2000.

WARNER, a post-township in Hillsborough county, in lat. 43° 16′, is bounded N. by Sutton and Salisbury, E. by Boscawen, S. by Hopkinton and Henniker, W. by Bradford, containing according to the survey of 1805, 27,571 acres, besides Kearsarge gore, which was annexed to this town, in June 1818. This gore is a strip of land lying between Salisbury and Sutton, extending from the former N. line of Warner to the highest part of Kearsarge mountain, and contains 4280 acres. The distance of Warner from Hopkinton is 8 miles; from Concord, 15; and from Boston, 72 miles. It is watered by Warner river, a handsome stream, which rises in the Sunapee mountain in Fishersfield. It passes through Bradford, enters Warner at the N. W. corner, and running in an E. and S. E. direction, divides the town into nearly two equal parts. It passes out at the S. E. corner, and falls into Contoocook river in Hopkinton. On this river and its tributary streams in this town, are 16 saw mills, 8 grist mills, 1 paper mill, &c. Most of the perennial and deciduous trees common to this section of the country, are found here. The lands, though broken, have, in general a good soil, and produce grass, corn, rye, &c. Mink hills lie in the W. part, and furnish fine orchards, and good pasturage. There are 4 ponds, viz. Tom, Bear, Bagley and Pleasant ponds. Pleasant pond, the waters of which are clear and cold; deep, and of a greenish cast, has no visible outlet or inlet, and overflows its banks in the driest seasons. There are 16 school districts, which average 40 scholars to each. One native of the town, John Kelly, Esq., counsellor at law in Northwood, graduated at Dartmouth college in 1804. Another is a member of the senior class at the same institution. This town was granted in 1735 by the general court of Mass. to Deac. Thomas Stevens and 62 others, inhabitants of Amesbury and Salisbury, Ms:

It was first called *Number* 1, and afterwards *New-Amesbury*. In 1737, 63 five acre house lots were laid out by the proprietors; a small log hut was built on each; and in 1739, a saw mill was erected where Gen. A. Davis' mills now stand. Soon after the divisional line between N. H. and Mass. was established, this town was re-granted by the Masonian proprietors to 63 persons belonging to Rye, between whom and the first grantees arose controversies and lawsuits, which were not finally settled till 1773. The name under the last grant was *Jennis-town*. It was incorporated Sept. 3, 1774, by the name of Warner, contrary to the petition of the proprietors, who desired the name to be Amesbury. The first settlement was made in 1762, by David Annis and his son-in-law, Reuben Kimball, whose son Daniel was the first child born in town. Mrs. Hannah Kimball, the widow of Mr. Kimball, died at Warner, Feb. 23, 1823, aged 83,—the first English female who slept in the town. In 1774, Warner contained 50 families. On the 5th of Feb. 1772, a congregational church was organized. Rev. William Kelly, a native of Newbury, Ms., was the first minister. He was born Oct. 31, 1744; graduated at Harvard college in 1767; ordained Feb. 5, 1772; dismissed March 11, 1801; and died May 18, 1813. His successor, Rev. *John Woods*, was ordained June 22, 1814. There are baptists, freewill baptists and universalists. On the 9th of Sept. 1821, this town was visited by a most violent and destructive hurricane, by which five individuals lost their lives, several were seriously injured, and considerable property was destroyed. (See *Cabinet of Curiosities, Vol.* 1, *p.* 64.) The number of deaths from Jan. 1817 to Jan. 1, 1823, was 179. The number which died of consumption was 43. Pop. 2246.

WARNER'S LOCATION, was annexed to Chatham June 23, 1817.

WARNER river. *See Warner.*

WARREN, township in Grafton county, in lat. 43° 36', is bounded N. by Coventy, E. by Peeling and Ellsworth, S. by Wentworth, W. by Piermont, containing 27,720 acres. It is 10 miles from Haverhill corner, and 63 from Concord. This town is watered by the north branch of Baker's river, which has its source on the E. side of Moosehillock mountain. It passes in a north direction to Wentworth, and, near the S. line of Warren, furnishes several valuable mill seats. Here are situated Clement's mills. The soil of Warren varies not materially from the contiguous towns. The S. E. part presents a mountainous aspect, having a large portion of Carr's mountain on its S. eastern border. There is considerable travel through the S. W. part of this town, over which the Coos turnpike passes. Warren was granted by charter, July 14, 1763. Of its history or religion we know nothing, and could obtain nothing. Pop. 544.

WASHINGTON, a post-township in Cheshire county, in lat. 43° 10', is bounded N. by Goshen, E. by Bradford, Hillsborough and Windsor, S. by Stoddard, and W. by Marlow and Lempster, containing 30,765 acres. It is 22 miles from Keene, 20 from Charlestown, 35 from Concord and 80 from Boston. This town is hilly, but not mountainous. Lovewell's mountain, so called from Capt. Lovewell's killing seven Indians near it, (See Hist. Coll. for 1822, page 25,) is of a conical shape, about 3-4 of a mile in diameter, and may be seen at a considerable distance. Washington abounds with springs, rivulets, and natural ponds, of the last of which, there are no less than 16, and some of them of considerable magnitude. Island pond, so called from its being full of islands, is 2 miles long, and 1 1-2 wide. Half moon pond is 1 1-2 miles in length. Ashuelot pond is 1 1-2 miles long, and 1 mile wide, and is the source of one of the principal branches of Ashuelot river. Brockway's pond, a beautiful sheet of water, lying on a white sand, is 1 mile long and 1-2 a mile wide. Long pond, lying in this town and Stoddard, is 5 miles in length. These ponds abound with a variety of fish. A branch of Contoocock river has its source from several small ponds in the E. part of the town. The soil is generally deep and moist. It is better for grass than tillage. The forest trees are rock and white maple, black ash, black, yellow and white birch, beech, elm, bass, red oak, pine, spruce, hemlock, fir, cedar, &c. There is a plenty of clay; and peat abounds in the swamps and low lands. Iron ore has been found in several places. Plumbago, (graphite) and antimony, it is said, have been found. Washington village is pleasantly situated, and contains a large meeting-house, with a handsome cupola; a brick school house, 25 dwelling houses, 3 stores and 2 taverns. The 2d N. H. turnpike runs from N. W. to S. E. through this village, where it is intersected by the Croydon turnpike from the N. There are several falls on the various streams, affording fine water privileges. Besides the mills, &c. under the statistical table, there is one cotton factory; also, an oil mill and a distillery. Washington was granted by the Masonian proprietors to Reuben Kidder, Esq. of New-Ipswich, under whom it was settled in 1768. It was first called *Monadnock, No. 8.* From its settlement, it was called *Camden*, till Dec. 13, 1776, when it was incorporated by its present name. The first settlers had 150 acres of land each for settling. The first year of their settlement, they erected a grain mill and a saw mill. The grants of Marlow and Lempster interfered with the grant of Monadnock, No. 8, and caused some long and vexatious lawsuits, and much trouble and expense to the claimants on both sides. There are 3 religious societies; viz. (1,) the congregational, of which a church was organized May 18, 1780. Rev. George Lesslie was installed July 12, 1780; died Sept. 11, 1800, aged 72. Rev. John Lord, ordained Nov. 9, 1803; dismissed June 12, 1806 Rev. *Broughton White*, installed Dec. 23, 1818. (2.) The baptists, who have no minister. (3.) The universalist society, over which Rev. Ebenezer Paine was formerly settled. Washington is a healthy place. No remarkable sickness has ever prevailed here. The deaths in 1819, were 13; in 1820, 14; in 1821, 8. Pop. 1000.

WEARE, a post town, and the largest township in Hillsborough county, both in extent and population, is situated in lat. 43° 4'. Its length is about 7 1-2 miles; its breadth, which does not vary, except at the S. W. angle, is 6 1-2 miles. It is bounded N. by Henniker and Hopkinton, E. by Dunbarton and Goffstown, S. by New-Boston, and W. by Francestown and Deering, containing 33,648 acres. The only river in Weare, is the N. W. branch of Piscataquog, which enters the W. boundary from Deering, and meanders through the N. and E. sections of the town, and passes the S. line about half a mile from the S. E. corner. This river affords the best mill seats in town. On this, and the several other streams, are 1 cotton and woollen factory, 1 oil mill, 11 saw mills, 9 grist mills, 3 fulling mills, and 3 carding machines.— There are three ponds of note in this town. The largest lies nearly one mile S. of the town house. It is known by the name of Mount-William pond, and contains 40 acres. Ferrin's pond, which is nearly as large, is situated in the S. E. part of the town. Duck pond, about half a mile N. of the town house, is less than either of the others.— Two of the largest hills in Weare are called mountains. Mount William lies N. E. of the pond of that name, and mount Misery is E. of Ferrin's pond. Neither of them are of very considerable magnitude, considered as mountains.— Rattlesnake hill, nearly in the centre of the N. line of the town, abounds with shelving rocks, abrupt precipices, forming dens and caves. During the summer season, the reptile from which the hill takes it name is frequently found. The soil of this town exhibits different degrees of fertility. That of the uplands is favorable for agriculture; is well supplied with springs of water, brooks and rivulets. The town, though rather broken, is not mountainous. It has small swamps, and some good meadows. It is now settled and cultivated' to its extreme limits by industrious and wealthy husbandmen. There are two libraries. "The Social Library," incorporated Dec. 7, 1798, containing 90 volumes; and the "Friends Library," established 3d mo. 30th day, 1809, and containing 68 volumes. Two natives of the town have received a collegiate education, viz. James Hadley, who graduated at Dartmouth college in 1809, and David Bailey, Esq., who graduated at Middlebury college, in 1814. There are 4 meeting houses, two belonging to the society of friends. The baptist meeting house, erected in 1789, is in the S. part; and the congregational meeting house, built in 1790, is in the N. E. part of the town. There is a town house near the centre. Weare was granted to Ichabod Robie, Esq. and others, Sept. 20, 1749, by the Masonian proprietors. It was settled by emigrants from Massachusetts and the easterly part of N. Hampshire. It contained, in 1764, probably between 20 and 30 families. It was incorporated September 21, 1764, and received its name in honor of Meshech Weare, chief justice of the province of N. H. The first church formed in Weare was of the baptist denomination. It was gathered Jan. 26, 1783. Rev. Amos Wood was ordained Nov. 19, 1788, and died Feb. 3, 1798. Rev. Ezra Wilmarth succeeded, and was installed April 29, 1813; dismissed Aug. 11, 1817. Rev. John B. Gibson was installed May 6, 1818; dismissed 1822. A congregational church was formed June 17, 1789. Rev. John Cayford was ordained Oct. 20, 1802; dismissed May 4, 1808. A freewill baptist church was formed of members who seceded from the first baptist church, Oct. 20, 1806. Eld. *Hezekiah D. Buzzell* removed to Weare, Nov. 27, 1812, and took charge of it, no installation being necessary, according to the faith and order of that connection. There is also a large, respectable and wealthy society of friends, some of whom settled here as early as 1770. Since that time, they have been annually increasing in numbers, wealth and respectability. There is a small society of universalists. Samuel Philbrick, Esq. was a worthy citizen of this town. He was a native of Seabrook, removed to Weare in 1770, and died Dec. 28, 1806, aged 72. The number of deaths from March 1, 1813, to Jan. 1, 1822, was 281. Pop. 2800.

WENDELL, a township in Cheshire county, in lat. 43° 22', is bounded N. by Springfield, E. by Sunapee lake, separating it from New-London and Fishersfield, S. by Goshen, W. by Newport and Croydon, containing 15,666 acres, 3000 of which are water. It is 35 miles from Concord and 80 from Portsmouth. A considerable part of lake Sunapee, a noble sheet of water, lies in this town. The surface of this lake is said to contain 4,095 acres, of which 2720 acres are in Wendell. Here is the principal source of Sugar river, which flows from the lake near its centre from N. to S.; passes through the centre of the town into Newport, from thence into Claremont, where it unites with the Connecticut. There are three small ponds, containing an area of about 300 acres. This town was granted by the name of *Saville*, Nov. 7, 1768, to John Sprague and others. It was settled in 1772 by emigrants from Rhode-Island. It was incorporated April 4, 1781, when it received its name from John Wendell, one of the principal proprietors. The first minister was Rev. N. Woodward, a baptist. A congregational society was incorporated June 24, 1819. The number of deaths for 4 years was about 20. Pop. 603.

WENTWORTH, a post-township in Grafton county, in lat. 43° 50', is bounded N. by Warren, E. by Rumney, S. by Dorchester, and W. by Orford, containing 23,040 acres. It is 15 miles from Plymouth, and 52 from Concord. This town is watered by Baker's river, on which is a fall of 18 or 20 feet, affording an excellent privilege for all kinds of water machinery. Over this fall is a bridge, maintained at the public expense. Near the bridge is a flourishing village, containing about 20 houses, several stores, shops for mechanics, and mills of various kinds. The S. branch of Baker's river passes through the southerly part of this town and joins the main branch near Rumney line. There are but few ponds. Baker's, situated on Orford line, is the most considerable; the outlet of which is called Pond brook, and affords water sufficient for several valuable mill seats. This stream unites with Baker's river just below the village. These streams contain all the various kinds of fish found in the state. Salmon, however, are not so plenty as formerly. In the E. part of the town, lies part of Carr's mountain, composed of a variety of valuable stone, among which is found a great supply of the best granite. This kind is also found in various other parts of the town. This mountain was covered in its natural state with a heavy growth of forest trees. A part of the elevation called Mount Cuba lies in the W. part of Wentworth. This mountain contains inexhaustible quantities of the best limestone, of which a constant supply of good lime is made, and sold at a low price. Iron ore is found in various parts. The soil is generally good; the lands in the vicinity of the rivers are of the first quality; the upland is in general of a strong rich soil, but is uneven, and in some instances, quite elevated, which renders it an excellent grazing town. Copperas is manufactured in small quantities, and might be made a source of profit. Wentworth was granted November 1, 1766, to John Page, Esq. and others. It received its name from governor Benning Wentworth. The first settlement commenced a few years before the revolutionary war by emigrants from the S. part of this state and from Massachusetts. Articles of subsistence, potatoes and seeds for the propagation of vegetables, were transported thither from the lower part of the state on pack horses, hand-sleighs and in knapsacks. The only remarkable instance of longevity in this place is Widow Jane M'Lellan a native of Ireland, who died Oct. 14, 1821, aged 101. The dysentery prevailed here about 20 years since; and in 1812 and 1815, the spotted fever carried off many persons of different ages. In this town are various denominations of christians all living harmoniously together. Pop. 807.

WENTWORTH'S LOCATION, situated N. of Errol in the county of Coos, in lat. 44° 48', was granted June 17, 1796, to George Wentworth, and comprised 10,000 acres.

WEST RIVER MOUNTAIN.— *See Chesterfield and Hinsdale.*

WESTMORELAND, a post-town on Connecticut river, in Cheshire county, is in lat. 42° 58'. It is bounded N. by Walpole, E. by Surry and Keene, S. by Chesterfield, and W. by Dummerston and Putney, Vt., containing 22,426 acres. Its distance from Concord is 65 miles; from Boston, 100. This town is watered by several small streams which empty into the Connecticut. The one issuing from Spafford's lake in Chesterfield is the largest, and affords some of the best water privileges in town. The surface here is much less variegated with hills, mountains, vales, rivers and ponds, than the circumjacent towns. There are tracts of fine intervals—and the land generally has an excellent soil, and is well suited for cultivation. A bridge connects this town with Putney, and the 3d N. H. turnpike crosses its N. E. extremity. Westmoreland was first granted by Massachusetts and was called, *Number* 2. It was afterwards known by the name of the *Great Meadow*. The present charter of the town was granted by N. H., Feb. 11, 1752. The first settlement was made in 1741, by four families. Mrs. Lydia How, who died in 1806, at the age of 91, was one of the first inhabitants, and mother of the first child born in the township. The early settlers were several times attacked by the Indians, and various mischief was done, but of no great magnitude. In one of their excursions, they killed William Phips, the first husband of Jemima How; and in another, carried Nehemiah How, the father of her second husband, a captive to Canada, where he died. (*See Belknap's Hist. N. H. Vol. II, pages* 240, 241.) There is a congregational church, over which Rev. William Goddard was ordained in 1764. He graduated at Harvard college in 1761. Rev. *Allen Pratt*, who graduated at Harvard college in 1785, is the present minister. There are two baptist churches. The 1st was formed in 1771; the 2d in 1785. There are universalists and other denominations. There are 3 meeting-houses. Major Ezra Pierce, a senator in the legislature in 1802 and 1803, resided in this town. Pop. 2000.

WHEELWRIGHT'S pond is in Lee; and is the principal source of Oyster river. It is memorable for

VIEW OF THE WHITE MOUNTAINS FROM SHELBURNE.

the battle which was fought near it in 1690, between a scouting party of Indians and two companies of rangers, under Capts. Floyd and Wiswall. The engagement lasted 2 hours. Wiswall, his lieutenant, sergeant, and 12 men were killed and several wounded. Floyd continued the fight, till his men, wearied and wounded, drew off and obliged him to follow. The enemy also retreated.

WHITEFIELD, in Coos county, lat. 44° 21', is an irregular township, lying S. of Lancaster, W. of Jefferson, N. of Bretton-Woods and Bethlehem, E. of Dalton, comprising 20,800 acres. Its soil is generally thin and light, of easy cultivation and tolerably good; though in the N. part low spruce swamps abound. No town in the county possesses an equal share of pine timber; this is now transported in great quantities down John's river to the Connecticut. In this town lie part of Blake's, Long, Round and Little River ponds, beside two other small ponds. The second of these is a beautiful pond of considerable size, abounding with fish. John's river passes through this town. Whitefield was granted July 4, 1774, to Josiah Moody and others, and soon after settled by Maj. Burns and others. It has increased in population more rapidly than any other town in the county. In 1810 there were but 51 inhabitants, and there are now upwards of 280. The new road from Lancaster to Concord passes through this town; it shortens the distance usually travelled about 30 miles. A turnpike from Peeling to the S. line of this town has been granted, which, if completed and extended to Lancaster, would turn much of the trade of Coos county through Concord, the seat of government; and being the direct route from Quebeck to Boston, would be much the nearest way to the markets for the northern parts of this state and Vermont. Whitefield is 120 miles from Concord. Pop. 281.

WHITE MOUNTAINS.—The lofty pile, designated by the name of *White Mountains*,* is situated in the N. part of New-Hampshire, and nearly in the centre of the county of Coos. These mountains extend about 20 miles from S. W. to N. E. being the more elevated parts of a range extending many miles in that direction. Their base is 8 or 10 miles broad; and situated about 25 miles S. E. from Lancaster, 70 N. of Concord, 82 N. by W. from Portsmouth; and in lat. 44° 15', long. 71° 20' W. These mountains are the loftiest in New-England, and perhaps in the United States. Although distant more than 60 miles from the nearest part

---

* The Indian name (according to Dr. Belknap) was *Agiocochook*. An ancient tradition prevailed among the savages, that a deluge once overspread the land, and destroyed every human being, except a single powaw and his wife, who sheltered themselves in these elevated regions, and thus preserved the race from extermination. The fancy of the natives peopled this mountain with beings of a superior rank, who were invisible to the human eye, but sometimes indicated their presence by tempests, which they were believed to control with absolute authority. The savages, therefore, never attempted to ascend the summit, deeming the attempt perilous, and success impossible. But they frequented the defiles and environs of the mountain, and of course propagated many extravagant descriptions of its appearance; declaring, amongst other things equally credible, that they had seen carbuncles at immense heights, which, in the darkness of night, shone with the most brilliant and dazzling splendor.

President Alden states, that the White mountains were called by one of the eastern tribes *Waumbekketmethna*. Waumbekket signifies *white*, and *methna*, *mountains*.

of the coast, their snow-white summits are distinctly visible many leagues at sea, and along the coast of Maine. Their great elevation has always rendered them interesting, both to our ancestors, and to the aboriginal inhabitants of the country. As early as 1632, they were visited by Neal, Jocelyn and Field, who gave romantic accounts of their adventures, and of the extent and grandeur of the mountains, which they called the *Crystal Hills.* Since that time, these regions have been repeatedly explored by hunters, and by men of science. The height of the mountains has been a subject of much speculation. Dr. Williams supposed the summit of Mount Washington to be 7,800 feet above the sea. Dr. Cutler fixed the height of this mountain at 10,000; and Dr. Belknap supposed it to exceed this elevation. Late computations, however, have given far different results; one making it 7,108, another 6,634, another 6234, another 6,225, and another 6,103. Capt. Partridge, from a series of barometrical observations, makes the height of Mount Washington 6,234 feet above the level of the sea, and the base of the range 1,770. In 1820, A. N. Brackett, and J. W. Weeks, Esqrs. from Lancaster, ascertained the height of all the principal peaks by means of a spirit level. In this undertaking they spent 7 days; and according to their measurement, Mount Washington is 6,428 feet above the level of the sea, 5,850 above the river at Lancaster, and 4,781 above Crawford's, the nearest dwelling to the summit. This mountain is easily known by its superior elevation, and its being the southern of the three highest peaks. The heights of the other peaks above the Connecticut at Lancaster, are as follow:

Mount Adams,	- - - - -	5,383 feet.
" Jefferson,	- - - -	5,281
" Madison,	- - - -	5,039
" Monroe,	- - - -	4,932
" Franklin,	- - - -	4,470
" Pleasant,	- - - -	4,339

The *names* here given are those generally appropriated to the different summits. Mount *Adams* is known by its sharp terminating peak, and being the second N. of Washington. *Jefferson* is situated between these two. *Madison* is the eastern peak of the range. *Monroe* is the first to the S. of Washington. *Franklin* is the second S. and is known by its level surface. *Pleasant* is known by its conical shape, and being the third S. of Washington. The ascent to the summits of these mountains, though fatiguing, is not dangerous; and the visitant is richly rewarded for his labor and curiosity. In passing from the Notch to the highest summit, the traveller crosses the summits of Mounts Pleasant, Franklin and Monroe. In accomplishing this, he must pass through a forest, and cross several ravines. These are neither wide nor deep, nor are they discovered at a great distance; for the trees fill them up exactly even with the mountain on each side, and their branches interlock with each other in such a manner, that it is very difficult to pass through them, and they are so stiff and thick as almost to support a man's weight. Mount Pleasant is easily ascended. Its top, to the extent of 5 or 6 acres, is smooth, and gradually slopes away in every direction from its centre. It even has a verdant appearance, as it is every where covered with short grass, which grows in little tufts to the height of four or five inches. Among these tufts, mountain flowers are thinly scattered, which add life and beauty to the scene. The prospect from this summit is beautiful: to the N. the eye is dazzled with the splendor of Mount Washington; N. W. are seen the settlements in Jefferson; W. the courses of the Amonoosuck, as though delineated on a map; S. W. the Moosehillock and Haystack are discovered; S. Chocorua peak; S. E. the settlements and mountains in Bartlett; E. only dark mountains and forests. On descending this mountain, a small patch of water is found at its base; from which the ascent is gradual to the summit of Mount Franklin. After crossing this mountain, you pass over the E. pinnacle of Mount Monroe, and soon find yourself on a plain of some extent, at the foot of Mount Washington. Here is a fine resting-place, on the margin of a beautiful sheet of water, of an oval form, covering about 3-4 of an acre. The waters are pleasant to the taste, and deep. Not a living creature is to be seen in the waters, at this height on the hills; nor do vegetables of any kind grow in or around them, to obscure the clear rocky or gravelly bottom on which they rest. A small spring discharges itself into this pond at its southeast angle. Another pond, of about 2-3 its size, lies N. W. of this. Directly before you, the pinnacle of Mount Washington rises with majestic grandeur, like a immense pyramid, or some vast Kremlin in this magnificent city of mountains. The pinnacle is elevated about 1500 feet above the plain, and is composed principally of huge rocks of granite and gneiss piled together, presenting a variety of colors and forms. In ascending, you must pass enormous masses of loose stones; but a walk of half an hour will generally carry you to the summit. The view from this point is wonderfully grand and picturesque. Innumerable mountains, lakes, ponds, rivers, towns and villages meet the delighted eye, and the dim Atlantic stretches its waters along the eastern horizon. To the N. is seen the lofty summits of Adams and Jefferson; and to the east a little detached from the range stands Mount Madison. Mount Washington is supported on the N. by a high ridge, which extends to Mount Jefferson; on the N. E. by a large grassy plain, terminating in a vast spur extending far away in that direction; E. by a promontory, which breaks off abruptly at St. Anthony's Nose; S. and S. E. by a grassy plain, in summer, of more than 40 acres. At the southeastern extremity of this plain, a ridge commences, which slopes gracefully away towards the vale of the Saco; upon which at short distances from each other, arise rocks, resembling, in some places, towers; in others representing the various orders of architecture. It would be vain in us to attempt a description of the varied wonders which here astonish and delight the beholder. To those who have visited these mountains, our descriptions would be tame and uninteresting; and he who has never ascended their hoary summits, cannot realize the extent and magnificence of the scene. These mountains are decidedly of primitive formation. Nothing of volcanic origin has ever yet been discovered on the most diligent research. They have for ages, probably, exhibited the same unvarying aspect. No minerals are here found of much rarity or value. The rock which most abounds, is schistus, intermixed with greenstone, mica, granite and gneiss. The three highest peaks are composed entirely of fragments of rocks heaped together in confusion, but pretty firmly fixed in their situations. These rocks are an intermediate substance between gneiss and micaceous schistus; they are excessively rough and coarse, and grey, almost black, with lichens. The mica in them is abundant, of different colors, red, black, and limpid, and though sometimes several inches in diameter, yet most often irregularly stratified. The granite contains emerald, tourmaline of which are found some beautiful specimens, and garnets, besides its proper constituents. Crystals of quartz, pyrites, actinote, jasper, porphyry, fluate of lime, and magnetic iron ore, are sometimes obtained. During nine or ten months of the year, the summits of the mountains are covered with snow and ice, giving them a bright and dazzling appearance. On every side are long and winding gullies, deepening in their descent to the plains below. Here some of the finest rivers of New-England originate. The Saco flows from the E. side of the mountains; the branches of the Ameriscoggin from the N.; the Amonoosuck and other tributaries of the Connecticut from the W.; and the Pemigewasset from the S., its fountain being near that of the Saco. The sides of the hills are in many parts covered with soil; but this is very superficial in all cases, and every spot, that can be reached by running water, is left destitute of every thing but rocks and pebbles, of which likewise the river-bottoms are exclusively composed. In these cold and elevated regions, the period for the growth of vegetables is extremely brief; the mountains must be forever sterile. Moss and lichens may be found near the summits, but of meagre and scanty growth—looking as if they had wandered from their proper zone below, into these realms of barren desolation.

The *Notch of the White Mountains*, is a phrase appropriated to a very narrow defile, extending two miles in length between two huge cliffs apparently rent asunder by some vast convulsion of nature—probably that of the deluge. The entrance of the chasm is formed by two rocks standing perpendicular at the distance of 22 feet from each other: one about 20 feet in height, the other about 12. The road from Lancaster to Portland passes through this notch, following the course of the head stream of the Saco. The scenery at this place is exceedingly beautiful and grand. The mountain, otherwise a continued range, is here cloven quite down to its base, opening a passage for the waters of the Saco. The gap is so narrow, that space has with difficulty been found for the road. About half a mile from the entrance of the chasm is seen a most beautiful cascade, issuing from a mountain on the right about 800 feet above the subjacent valley, and about 2 miles distant. The stream passes over a series of rocks almost perpendicular, with a course so little broken as to preserve the appearance of a uniform current, and yet so far disturbed as to be perfectly white. This beautiful stream, which passes down a stupendous precipice, is called by Dwight the *Silver Cascade*. It is probably one of the most beautiful in the world. At the distance of three fourths of a mile from the entrance of the chasm is a brook, called the *Flume*, which falls from a height of 240 or 250 feet over three precipices—down the two first in a single current, and over the last in three, which unite again at the bottom in a small basin formed by the

NOTCH OF THE MOUNTAINS.

hand of nature in the rocks. The water is pure and transparent, and it would be impossible for a brook of its size to be moddeled into more diversified or delightful forms. It is by no means strange that the unlettered Indian fancied these regions to be the abodes of celestial beings; while the scholar, without a stretch of fancy, in calling to mind the mythology of Greece, might find here a fit place for the assemblies and sports of the Dryads, Naiads and Oreades. For a more particular notice of these mountains, the reader is referred to Belknap's Hist. N. H.; Dwight's Travels; N. E. Journal; and N. H. Hist. Coll. for 1823.

WILMOT, a township in the N. extremity of Hillsborough county, in lat. 43° 27', is bounded N. W. by Springfield, N. E. by Danbury New-Chester and Andover, S. by Warner, S. W. by Sutton and New-London, containing 15,000 acres, of which 9000 were taken from New-London and 6000 from Kearsarge gore. It is 30 miles from Concord, and 87 from Boston. The streams forming Blackwater river have their origin in the vicinity of Wilmot. They afford a number of good mill seats. The 4th N. H. turnpike from Concord to Hanover passes through this town. It was made in 1803, through an entire forest without any inhabitants for 14 miles above, and about 6 miles below Wilmot. The land near the turnpike appears rude and barren: but the acclivities on either side are susceptible of cultivation. The town is composed of hills and valleys, presenting a rough surface. There are no large collections of water, nor any mountains, excepting Kearsarge, whose summit forms the southern boundary. Wilmot, for the last 10 years has had a more rapid growth than any other town in the county, having more than doubled its population. The greater part of Wilmot was originally included in a grant made in 1775, by the Masonian proprietors, to Jonas Minot, Matthew Thornton and others. It was incorporated June 18, 1807. It received its name in honor of Dr. Wilmot, an Englishman, who, at one time, was supposed to be the author of the celebrated letters of Junius. Pop. 670.

WILTON, a post-township, Hillsborough county, in lat. 42° 50', is bounded N. by Lyndeborough, E. by Lyndeborough and Milford, S. by Mason, and W. by Temple, containing 15,280 acres. It is 9 miles from Amherst, 37 from Concord and 58 from Boston. Souhegan is the principal river. Its main branch enters this town near the S. W. corner and proceeds in a N. E. course till it forms a junction with several branches running from Lyndeborough and Temple. These flow through the N. part, and are sufficiently large for mill streams. This town has neither mountains, ponds, nor swamps. It is, in general, pretty rocky, but of a strong and excellent soil. The principal growth of wood is oak, pine, beech, maple, birch, hemlock, and some chesnut. Good clay is found in plenty near streams of water. There are several quarries of excellent stone for splitting and hewing. No uncommon sickness has ever been known here except in 1801, when a malignant and contagious fever prevailed, which was supposed to be introduced in a parcel of old feathers brought into town and sold by pedlers. The whole number of deaths, from 1783 to July, 1820, was about 387. There is a female charitable society, a literary and moral society, and a library society. Wilton was owned by the proprietors of land purchased of John Tufton Mason, Esq., and by them was surveyed and laid out into 80 acre lots and designated by the name of *Number* 2. The first settlement was made in 1738, by three families from Danvers, Ms., two by the name of Putnam, and one by the name of Dale. Hannah, the daughter of Ephraim Putnam, was the first child born in town. She was born in March, 1741; married a Mr. Woodward of Lyndeborough, where she died in Oct. 1811, aged 70. The town was incorporated June 25, 1762, and derived its name from Wilton, an ancient borough in Wiltshire, England. A distressing accident occurred in raising the second meeting-house, Sept. 7, 1773. The frame fell, and 3 men were instantly killed; two died of their wounds soon afterward, and a number of others were badly injured. On July 20, 1804, the same meeting-house was struck by lightning and considerably shattered. A congregational church, consisting of 8 male members, was gathered Dec. 14, 1763. Rev. Jonathan Livermore was ordained the same day. He was dismissed in Feb. 1777, and died at Wilton, July 20, 1809, aged 80. Rev. Abel Fiske was ordained November 18, 1778, and died April 21, 1802, aged 50. Rev. *Thomas Beede* was ordained March 2, 1803. The number of admissions to the church, from its formation to 1820, was 472; baptisms 1197. A baptist church was formed April 7, 1817, over which Rev. *Ezra Wilmarth* was installed Nov. 11, 1818. There is a small society of universalists. Pop. 1070.

WINCHESTER, a post-township, in the S. W. part of Cheshire county, in lat. 42° 46′, is bounded N. by Chesterfield and Swanzey, E. by Richmond, S. by Warwick and Northfield, in Mass., W. by Hinsdale, containing 33,534 acres, 600 of which are water. It is 15 miles from Keene, 70 from Concord, 83 from Boston, 80 from Hartford and 85 from Albany. Ashuelot river enters this town at its N. E. angle, and runs in a S. W. and W. course to Hinsdale. It receives on the E., Muddy brook, and on the N., Broad brook and several other small streams. Humphrey's pond is in the N. E. part of the town. It is 300 rods long and 80 rods wide. From the centre to the S. E., the land is very level. In other parts, the surface is more uneven. The soil is generally good. The principal forest trees are white and yellow pine, chesnut, white and red oak, rock maple, &c. In 1822, there were sent to Connecticut market, from this town, 200 thousand white oak staves, from 8 to 10 hundred thousand feet of pine lumber, and large quantities of shingles, casks, &c. Winchester has two villages, both pleasantly situated on Ashuelot river, one in the centre, containing 27 dwelling houses, 1 meeting-house, with a clock, bell and well toned organ, a school house, the most elegant in the county of Cheshire, 3 taverns, 4 stores, and several mechanic shops, &c.; the other, in the W. part, containing 21 dwelling houses, 1 cotton factory, 1 small woollen factory, 1 nail factory, 1 scythe factory, 1 large oil mill, 1 furnace, 1 tavern, 1 store, &c. The 6th N. H. turnpike passes through Winchester. There is a respectable library in this town. Only one native has received a collegiate education. It is a singular fact, recollected by the early inhabitants, that Josiah Willard, one of the principal grantees of this town.

refused to have Dartmouth college located in Winchester, on account of his belief that it would have a tendency to depreciate the value of his possessions. This town was probably first granted by Massachusetts. Its first name was *Arlington*. It was chartered by N. H., July 2, 1753, to Josiah Willard and others, who had, about the year 1732, effected a settlement. In the Indian war, which commenced a number of years afterwards, the inhabitants had all their private buildings and their meeting-house burnt by the enemy. On the 7th of June, 1756, Josiah Foster and his family were taken captives by the Indians. A congregational church, consisting of 12 members, was formed November 12, 1736. Rev. Joseph Ashley, who graduated at Yale college in 1730, was ordained Nov. 12, 1736; removed in 1747, on account of the Indian war. Rev. Micah Lawrence, who graduated at Harvard college, was ordained Nov. 14, 1764; dismissed Feb. 19, 1777. Rev. Ezra Conant, who graduated at Harvard college in 1784, was ordained Feb. 19, 1788; dismissed Oct. 13, 1806. Rev. Experience Porter, a graduate of Dartmouth college in 1803, was ordained Nov. 12, 1807; dismissed Feb. 20, 1810. Rev. Salmon Bennet was ordained Sept. 10, 1817; dismissed 1822. Communicants about 100. There is a methodist society, and some universalists. Pop. 1849.

WINDHAM, post-township, in Rockingham county, lat. 42° 48′, is bounded N. by Londonderry, E. by Salem, S. by Pelham, W. by Nottingham-West and Londonderry. It is 35 miles from Boston, 34 from Concord, 30 from Exeter, 45 from Portsmouth, 22 from Amherst; and contains 15,744 acres. Policy pond lies in this town and Salem—about one half in each. Cabot's pond lies E. of the centre of the town. Golden pond is in the S., and Mitchell's in the N. E. part of the town. There is another small pond between Windham and Salem, N. E. of Policy pond. Beaver river or brook forms the W. boundary, upon which are some meadow lands. The town is also well supplied with small streams. The Londonderry turnpike passes over this town. Windham was originally a part of Londonderry; and was detached and incorporated Feb. 25, 1739. The inhabitants, principally derived from the first settlers of Londonderry, have firmly adhered to the religious principles of their fathers—to the doctrines and forms of the presbyterian church as originally established in Scotland, and administered in this country. A presbyterian church was organized, and Rev. William Johnston installed in 1747: he was dismissed in July, 1752. In 1753, a meeting-house was erected on the S. side of Cabot's pond. Rev. John Kinkead was ordained in Oct. 1760; and dismissed in April, 1765. Rev. Simon Williams was ordained in Dec. 1766; continued to preach 27 years, and died Nov. 10, 1793, aged 64. A new meeting-house was erected in 1798. Rev. *Samuel Harris* was ordained by the Londonderry presbytery in Oct. 1805. The spotted fever appeared at Windham in 1812. From March 30, to April 18, there died 16—3 adults, and 13 children. 13 died in 8 days. Pop. 889.

WINDSOR, a small township of a triangular form, in Hillsborough county, in lat. 43° 6′, is bounded N. by Washington, E. by Hillsborough, S. by Antrim and W. by

Stoddard, containing 5,335 acres. It is diversified with hills; its soil is strong, good for grazing, and for bread stuffs, of which quantities sufficient for use at home, and some for the markets are raised. Black pond, near the centre, is said to be 160 rods long and 80 broad; and one near the S. E. corner of the town, is about 80 rods long and 40 wide. This town has 3 school districts, 2 school houses, 1 tavern, 1 grain mill, 2 saw mills and 1 fulling mill. The 2d N. H. turnpike passes through the N. part. Windsor was formerly called *Campbell's Gore*. It was incorporated with town privileges in Nov. 1798. Among its early settlers was Capt. Swett, whose posterity still reside here. Pop. 240.

WINSLOW'S LOCATION, in Coos county, lat. 44° 34', is bounded N. by ungranted lands, E. by Dummer, S. E. by Paulsburgh and Kilkenny, W. by Piercy; and contains 5,060 acres. It was granted Oct. 21, 1773, to John Winslow, of Marshfield, Ms. who served as Maj. Gen. Com. of the Prov. forces of New-England, New-York and New-Jersey. There were only 6 inhabitants, in 1820.

WINNEPISIOGEE LAKE, is situated between lat. 43° 29', and 43° 44'; and between long. 71° 5', and 71° 25', W. from Greenwich; and a little E. of the centre of New-Hampshire. Its form is very irregular. At the W. end, it is divided into three large bays; on the N. is a fourth; and at the E. end there are three others. Its general course is from N. W. to S. E ; its length about 22 miles, varying in width from 1 to 10 miles. The townships on its borders may be seen by referring to the map. The waters of the Winnepisiogee are remarkably pure; and when taken from a sufficient depth to give them a proper temperature, are perfectly sweet and palatable. This lake has a great number of islands. Like those in Lake George, and in Casco Bay, they are here declared to be three hundred and sixty-five. Without supposing the days of the year to have been consulted, on the subject, we may naturally conclude that the number is considerable. Several of these islands are sufficiently large for farms—one containing 500 acres. The prospect of this lake from the mountains surrounding it, is enchanting, and in no degree inferior to that of Lake George, long celebrated, and visited by thousands. A variety of excellent fish are found in this lake. The waters are frozen during the winter, presenting a beautiful icy expansion. This lake might be connected by canals with the Pascataqua; and open an immense field of business between Portsmouth and the interior. *See p.* 14, *Gen. View.*

WINNEPISIOGEE RIVER is the great outlet to the lake of that name; and issues from the S. W. arm of the lake. It thence passes through two bays between Meredith and Gilford, entering the Great Bay in the N. E. part of Sanbornton. From thence it passes through two other bays, forming the boundary between Sanbornton on the N. W. and Gilmanton and Northfield S. E.; and unites with the Pemigewasset a short distance below Webster's falls. The stream is rapid in its course, and has a fall of 232 feet from the lake to its junction with the other branch of the Merrimack: this name being given to the confluent stream. There are numerous bridges over the Winnepisiogee; which also furnishes many excellent privileges for factories or other machinery. *See Merrimack river.*

WINNICUT or WINNICONETT, a tributary of the Pascataqua, rises in a swamp between Hampton and North-Hampton, and passes N. into the Great Bay at Greenland.

WOLFEBOROUGH, post-township, Strafford county, in lat. 43° 36′, is about 105 miles from Boston, 45 from Portsmouth, 45 from Concord. It is bounded S. E. by Brookfield and New-Durham, S. W. by Winnepisiogee lake and Alton, N. E. by Ossipee, N. W. by Tuftonborough, and contains 28,600 acres. The soil is rocky, but productive, and the face of the country level. The wood is principally oak and other hard timber. The only river is Smith's, so called from a hunter of that name; it issues from a large pond of the same name in the S. E. part of the town, and discharges its waters into the lake. There are four other ponds of considerable magnitude, called Crooked, Rust's, Barton's and Sargent's ponds. There is a bridge over Smith's river about 60 feet long, near its entrance into the lake. Near this bridge is a pleasant village. This town is divided into ten school districts, in which are kept good schools during a portion of the year. The academy in this town has funds to the amount of $5000; and is in a flourishing condition. Here are two meeting-houses, a social library, several mills, &c. The charter of Wolfeborough was granted in 1770, to Gov. John Wentworth, Mark H. Wentworth and others. In the course of the year there were 30 families settled in the town. Gov. Wentworth, distinguished for his enterprize and taste, and a fondness for agricultural improvements, erected a splendid mansion about 5 miles east of the bridge, and made it his summer residence. After Gov. Wentworth left the country, the house fell into other hands, and was accidentally consumed by fire a few years since. Among the first settlers of this town were Benjamin Blake, James Lucas, Joseph Lary, Ithamar Fullerton and others, from Pembroke. Rev. Ebenezer Allen, who graduated at Harvard college in 1771, was settled over a congregational church here Oct. 25, 1792. At the same time, Elder Isaac Townsend was settled over a freewill baptist society. Rev. Mr. Allen died in 1806, at the age of 60; since which time his church has been vacant. The freewill baptist church is also vacant. At the foot of a hill, near one of the ponds in this town, is a mineral spring, the waters of which are of a quality similar to those of Saratoga. Pop. 1794.

ADDITIONS AND CORRECTIONS.

IN THE GENERAL VIEW.

Page 11. James Atwood, who died in 1812, belonged to *Hampstead.*
" 12. For Mrs. Cilley, who is said to have died in 1820, read *Patience Sibley.*
" " For Tryphena Stiles, read *Lydia Stiles.*

Page 12. Mrs. Bailey, [*Widow Hannah Bayley*] of Chesterfield, died in Nov. 1822, aged 104 years and 3 months, as mentioned under Chesterfield, page 101.
" " The venerable Samuel Welch, of Bow, died April 5, 1823, aged 112 years, 6 months and 23 days.
" " To the living instances of longevity may he added *Mrs. Copp* and *Mrs. Smart*, of Sanbornton, each over 100 yrs.
" 20. In the 2d line, for excel, read *exceed*.
" 50. Northwood has 8 school-houses and 2 bark mills.

IN THE GENERAL DESCRIPTION OF TOWNS.

BATH. For Edinburg, read *Edinburgh*.

BOW. This town was settled in 1727 by some of the proprietors, while most of the surrounding country, except Concord, remained uncultivated for several years.

CANTERBURY. [Richard] Blanchard was killed, according to a memorandum of Rev. Mr. Walker, of Concord, June 11, 1746.

CHESTERFIELD. Rev. *John Walker* was installed as colleague with Rev. *Abraham Wood*, April 30, 1823.

DUBLIN is in lat. 43° 54'.

DUNSTABLE. On page 122, 2d col. line 14, for were, read *was*.

DURHAM. Hon. EBENEZER THOMPSON was not a lawyer, but a physician; and at different periods of his life, a judge of the court of common pleas, and of the superior court.

EPPING. In the 5th line 2d col. of page 129, erase the words "and representative." On the next page, read Rev. Samuel Shepard, who received the title of *Dr.* on account of his being a physician.

EPSOM. Hon. JOHN M'CLARY of this town deserves respectful notice. He was a native of Ireland, and, at an early period of his life, came to this country. He was a useful and worthy man;—a member of the committee of safety during the revolution, a justice of the peace throughout the state, one of the first senators chosen by the people under the new government, and from the senate was elected the first counsellor for the county of Rockingham under the new constitution. He died June 16, 1801, aged 82.

EXETER. Where mention is made of Hon. NATHANIEL PEABODY as being a "senator in 1792," it ought to be understood that he was a *senator* of the *N. H. legislature*, of which, in the house of representatives, he was speaker in 1793.

FRANCONIA. The altitude of the peak mentioned under this town is put as we received it. Dr. George, who has visited it, estimates the height at 600 feet.

GILMANTON. "The Gilmanton Museum" was published in this town about 6 months in 1800, by Elijah Russell. It was followed about Sept. 1, the same year by the "Gilmanton Gazette & Farmers' Weekly Magazine," published by Leavitt & Clough. We have also seen a number of "The Miscellaneous Repository and Farmers' and Tradesman's Magazine," containing 104 pages, published in Gilmanton in 1805, by Dudley Leavitt, one of the editors of the last named paper.

HAMPSTEAD. Hon. John Calfe was an *inhabitant* of this place, instead of a "native." He was born in Newbury, Ms., June 13, 1741. Rev. John Kelly was *ordained* Dec. 5, 1792.

HAMPTON-FALLS. Hon. MESHECH WEARE was one of the most worthy and distinguished citizens of N. H. He was descended from ancestors who had been in public stations, from the first establishment of the province. He himself had been employed in public business about forty-five years. He was chosen speaker of the house in 1752; commissioner to the congress at Albany in 1754; afterwards one of the justices of the superior court, and in 1777, chief justice. From the declaration of independence to the conclusion of the war, he was invested at the same time, with the highest offices, legislative, judicial and executive. Under the new constitution, adopted in 1784, he was elected the first president; but he resigned before the close of the year. He died, worn out with public services, Jan. 15, 1786, in the 73d year of his age. President Weare received a liberal education, and graduated at Harvard college in 1735. He was elected a fellow of the American academy of arts and sciences on the 30th of Jan. 1782, and his election was announced to him, by a letter from Rev. Dr. Willard, president of Harvard college. Rev. SAMUEL LANGDON, D. D. passed the last 16 years of his life in this town. He was a native of Boston, graduated at Harvard college in 1740. He was a chaplain of the N. H. regiment in the expedition against Louisbourg, and in consequence of his services, his "fatigues and dangers," received a grant of 1000 acres of land in this then province. He was afterwards minister of the first church in Portsmouth, from Feb. 4, 1747. In 1774, he was invited to the presidency of Harvard college, and was inducted into office, Oct. 14, 1774. He resigned Aug. 30, 1780, and on the 18th Jan. 1781, was installed at Hampton-Falls, where he died Nov. 29, 1797, aged 75.

HANOVER. A newspaper, besides those mentioned, called "The American," was published in this town by David Watson, jun. It commenced Feb. 7, 1816; and was discontinued April 2, 1817.

HILLSBOROUGH. For Lyon pond, read *Loon* pond. In Hillsborough, there is an academy in operation, which was incorporated June 29, 1821. Rev. Stephen Chapin was dismissed May 10, 1808.

HOPKINTON. This town was granted Jan. 16, 1736. Rev. Elijah Fletcher was ordained Jan. 27, 1773.

JEFFERSON. In the 10th line from the bottom, 1st col. read *Mark* H. Wentworth.

KEENE. The "Rising Sun" commenced in Aug. 1795, instead of 1799.

KENSINGTON. Rev. *Joseph A. E. Long*, a CONGREGATIONALIST, was ordained June 5, 1822.

LANCASTER. Rev. Joseph Willard was dismissed in 1822.

LITCHFIELD. We are informed by an obliging friend, that Rev. Samuel Cotton was ordained Jan. 2, 1765.

LONDONDERRY. Rev. *Thomas* Thompson [Dr. Belknap says *Alexander:* We follow Rev. Mr. Parker's century sermon.] died Sept. 22, 1738.

NELSON. Rev. *Gad Newell* was ordained June 11, 1794.

NEWINGTON. The age of Rev.

Mr. Adams is stated, on the authority of our correspondent, to be 95. Dr. Belknap says 93.

NEW-IPSWICH. Hon. EBENEZER CHAMPNEY died Sept. 1810, aged 67. The late Jesse Appleton, D. D., President of Bowdoin college, was a native of this town. He was son of Mr. Francis Appleton, a descendant of John Appleton, Esq. of Waldingfield, in Suffolk, England, who died in 1436. Dr. A. was born Nov. 17, 1772; died at Brunswick, Nov. 12, 1819. He was one of the greatest theologians which N. H. has produced.

NEW-LONDON. There have been some alterations of the limits of this town since the survey was made. We are informed by Mr. Colby, that the superficial content is but 14,000 acres.

NEW-MARKET. WINTHROP HILTON, of this town, an active and useful officer of the militia, was killed by the fall of a tree in Northwood, Jan. 11, 1775. Mr. Hilton was descended from the first Edward Hilton, who came from London to N. H., in 1623, and settled at Dover; afterwards removed to Exeter, where he died in 1671. Four of his sons, Edward, William, Samuel and Charles, were his administrators. Edward, probably his oldest son, married into the family of Gov. Thomas Dudley. He died in 1699, leaving three sons, Winthrop, Dudley and Joseph, and four daughters. Winthrop was born about 1671; was a man of great worth and respectability. [See a memoir of him in Hist. Coll. for 1822, page 241—251.] He was killed by the Indians, June 23, 1710. Winthrop, a posthumous, and his only son, was born Dec. 21, 1710. He was father to Winthrop at the head of this article. Another son was Ichabod, who died in March, 1822, aged 82.

NORTHWOOD. Rev. Eliphalet Merrill was ordained Oct. 31, 1804.

PEMBROKE. For "and on the Soucook," read *and on it*, [the Suncook.] RICHARD BARTLETT, Esq. was an eminent physician in this town and several years its representative in the N. H. legislature. He was a descendant from John Bartlett, the great ancestor of the respectable name of Bartlett in N. H. and Mass., and was of the same lineage with Gov. Bartlett. He was born March 23, 1743; died Aug. 5, 1805, aged 62.

PLAINFIELD. The ministers, though arranged as furnished us by the late Mr. Read, are not placed correctly. Of the 2d church, (Meriden parish) there have been three pastors, viz. Rev. Siloam Short, Rev. David Dickinson, and Rev. *Dana Clayes*, who were settled at the times mentioned.

RAYMOND. This town was originally that part of Chester called *Freetown;* "Charmingfare" being the former name of Candia.

RINDGE. Rev. SETH PAYSON, was Vice-President, not President, of the N. H. bible society. He was a senator in the legislature of N. H. in 1802 and 1803.

SANDWICH. This township, granted originally to Nicholas Gilman, J. T. Gilman, and others of Exeter, was settled in 1768, by Daniel Beede, John Prescott, David Bean, Jeremiah Page, Richard Sinclair and others. Rev. Jacob Jewett was settled about 1780 over a baptist society here; left the town in 1806; returned again in 1812; and died a few years since.

WALPOLE. The congregational church was formed June 10, 1761, at which time Rev. Jonathan Leavitt, who graduated at Yale college in 1758, was ordained He was dismissed in June, 1763.

Appendix.

POPULATION of the several towns in the state of New-Hampshire, in 1775, 1790, 1800, 1810, and 1820.

[Those having a º annexed, are post-towns; and their number denotes the number of post-offices.]

TOWNS.		Population.				
Present Name.	Former Name.	1775	1790	1800	1810	1820
Acworth º			704	1376	1523	1479
Adams				180	244	363
Alexandria		137	298	303	409	707
Allenstown		149	254	315	346	433
Alstead º	Newtown	317	1111	1666	1694	1611
Alton º	New-Durham Gore	100	445	721	1279	2058
Amherst º	Souhegan-West	1428	2369	1470	1554	1622
Andover º	New-Breton	179	645	1133	1259	1642
Antrim º	Society Land		528	1059	1277	1330
Atkinson	Part of Haverhill	575	479	474	556	563
Barnstead º		252	807	1161	1477	1805
Barrington º		1655	2470	2773	3564	1610
Bartlett º			248	548	436	511
Bath º		144	498	825	1316	1498
Bedford º º	Souhegan-East	495	898	1182	1296	1375
Bethlehem				171	422	467
Boscawen º	Contoocook	585	1108	1414	1829	3
Bow		350	568	719	729	935
Bradford º	New-Bradford		217	740	1034	1318
Brentwood	Part of Exeter	1100	976	899	905	892
Bretton-Woods				18	12	19
Bridgewater			281	664	1104	727
Bristol º	Part of Bridgewater					675
Brookfield				504	657	690
Brookline	Raby		338	454	538	592
Burton			141	264	194	209
Cambridge						
Campton º		190	395	635	873	1047
Canaan º		67	483	835	1094	1198
Candia º	Charmingfare	744	1040	1186	1290	1273
Canterbury º		723	1038	1114	1526	1696
Centre-Harbor º				263	349	486
Chatham			58	183	201	298
Charlestown º	Number 4	594	1093	1364	1501	1702
Chester º	Cheshire	1599	1902	2046	2030	2262
Chesterfield º	Number 1	874	1905	2161	1839	2110
Chichester º		418	491	775	951	1010
Claremont º		523	1435	1889	2094	2290

APPENDIX.

TOWNS.		Population.				
Present Name.	Former Name.	1775	1790	1800	1810	1820
Colebrook o	Colburne	4	29	160	325	469
Columbia o	Cockburne	14	26	109	142	249
Concord o	Penacook. Rumford	1052	1747	2052	2393	2838
Concord o	Gunthwaite	47	313	663	1126	1126
Conway o	Pequawkett	273	574	705	1080	1365
Cornish o		309	982	1268	1606	1701
Coventry			88	69	162	315
Croydon		143	537	984	864	1060
Dalton o	Apthorp	50	14	62	235	347
Danbury			111	165	345	467
Deerfield oo		929	1619	1878	1851	2133
Deering o o	Society Land		928	1244	1363	1415
Dixville					12	2
Dorchester	Part of Nottingham		175	349	537	584
Dover o	Cocheco. Northam	1666	1998	2062	2228	2871
Dublin o	Monadnock, No. 2	305	901	1188	1184	1620
Dummer					7	27
Dunbarton o	Starks-Town	497	917	1222	1256	1450
Durham o	Oyster River	1214	1247	1126	1449	1538
Dunstable o		705	632	862	1049	1142
Durand					62	78
East Kingston	Part of Kingston	428	358	392	442	443
Eaton o			253	381	535	1071
Effingham o	Leavitt's Town	83	154	451	876	1368
Ellsworth	Treeothick			47	142	213
Enfield o	Relhan	50	724	1121	1291	1370
Epping o	Part of Exeter	1569	1233	1121	1182	1158
Epsom o		387	799	1034	1156	1336
Errol					38	26
Exeter o	Swamscot-Falls	1741	1722	1727	1759	2114
Farmington o	Part of Rochester			1029	1272	1716
Fishersfield o		180	331	526	563	874
Fitzwilliam o	Monadnock, No. 4		1038	1240	1301	1167
Francestown o		200	982	1355	1451	1479
Franconia o	Morristown	29	72	129	358	373
Gilford o	Part of Gilmanton					1816
Gilmanton o o o o		775	2613	3752	4338	3752
Gilsum	Boyle	178	298	484	513	601
Goffstown o		831	1275	1612	2000	2173
Goshen o				383	563	687
Gosport	Appledore	44	93	85	72	66
Grafton			403	682	931	1094
Grantham	New-Grantham	74	338	713	864	1032
Greenfield o				934	980	974
Greenland o	Part of Portsmouth	759	634	548	592	634
Groton	Cockermouth	118	373	391	549	686

APPENDIX.

TOWNS.		Population.				
Present Name.	Former Name.	1775	1790	1800	1810	1820
Hampstead ○	Timber-Lane, &c.	768	724	790	738	751
Hampton ○	Winicumet	862	853	875	990	1098
Hampton-Falls ○	Part of Hampton	645	541	519	570	572
Hanover ○		434	1380	1912	2135	2222
Hancock ○			634	1120	1184	1178
Haverhill ○	Lower Cohos	365	552	805	1105	1609
Hawke	Part of Kingston	504	420	389	412	421
Hebron	Cockermouth			281	563	572
Henniker ○	Number 6	367	1127	1476	1608	1900
Hillsborough ○	Number 7		798	1311	1592	1982
Hinsdale ○	Fort Dummer		522	634	740	890
Holderness ○	New-Holderness	172	329	531	835	1160
Hollis ○	Nissitissit	1255	1441	1557	1529	1543
Hooksett ○	Isle of Hookset					
Hopkinton ○	New-Hopkinton	1085	1715	2015	2216	2437
Jaffrey ○	Monadnock, No. 3	351	1235	1341	1336	1339
Jefferson ○	Dartmouth			112	197	252
Keene ○	Upper Ashuelot	756	1314	1645	1646	1895
Kensington	Part of Hampton	797	800	776	781	709
Kilkenny				18	28	24
Kingston ○		961	906	785	746	847
Lancaster ○	Upper Cohos	61	161	440	717	844
Landaff		40	292	461	650	769
Langdon ○			244	484	632	654
Lebanon ○		347	1180	1574	1808	1710
Lee ○		954	1029	978	1329	1224
Lempster ○	Dupplin	128	415	729	854	950
Lime ○		252	816	1318	1670	1824
Lincoln			22	41	100	32
Litchfield	Brenton's Farm	284	357	372	382	465
Littleton ○○	Chiswick, &c.		96	381	873	1096
Londonderry ○	Nutfield	2590	2622	2650	2766	3127
Loudon ○	Part of Canterbury	349	1084	1279	1472	1694
Lyman			202	534	948	1270
Lyndeborough ○	Salem Canada	713	1280	976	1074	1168
Madbury	Part of Dover	677	592	544	582	559
Manchester	Harry-Town	285	362	557	615	761
Marlborough ○	Monadnock, No. 5	322	786	1185	1142	766
Marlow ○		207	313	543	566	597
Mason	Number 1	501	922	1179	1077	1313
Maynesborough						
Meredith ○○	New-Salem	259	881	1609	1940	2416
Merrimack ○○	Souhegan-East	606	819	926	1048	1162
Middleton		233	617	431	439	482
Milford ○	Mile Slip, &c.			939	1117	1243
Milton	Part of Rochester				1005	1232
Millsfield						

APPENDIX.

Present Name.	Former Name.	1775	1790	1800	1810	1820
Mont-Vernon	Part of Amherst			680	762	729
Moultonborough o		272	565	857	994	1279
Nelson o	Packersfield	186	721	977	1076	907
New-Boston o	Lane's New-Boston	569	1202	1491	1619	1686
New-Castle	Great Island	449	534	524	592	932
New-Chester o		196	312	615	895	971
New-Durham o		286	554	742	888	1168
New-Hampton o o	Moultonborough Add.		652	1095	1293	1500
Newington		332	542	481	508	541
New-Ipswich o	Ipswich-Canada	960	1241	1266	1395	1278
New-London o	Dantzick		311	617	692	924
New-Market o	Part of Exeter	1289	1137	1027	1061	1033
Newport o		157	780	1266	1427	1679
Newtown		540	530	450	454	477
Northfield	Part of Canterbury		606	925	1057	1304
North-Hampton o	Part of Hampton	652	657	653	651	764
Northumberland		57	117	205	281	205
Northwood o	Part of Nottingham	313	744	950	1095	1260
Nottingham o		999	1068	964	1063	1126
Nottingham-West o	Part of Dunstable	649	1064	1267	1376	1227
Orange	Cardigan		131	203	229	298
Orford o		222	540	988	1265	1568
Ossipee o	New-Garden	26	339	1143	1330	1988
Paulsburgh					14	57
Peeling	Fairfield			83	203	224
Pelham o		749	791	918	998	1040
Pembroke o	Suncook	744	956	982	1153	1256
Peterborough o		546	861	1333	1537	1500
Piercy			48	140	211	218
Piermont o		168	426	670	877	1016
Pittsfield o	Part of Chichester		888	987	1050	1178
Plainfield o		308	1024	1435	1463	1460
Plaistow	Part of Haverhill	575	521	459	424	492
Plymouth o		382	625	743	937	983
Poplin o	Part of Exeter	552	493	408	462	453
Portsmouth o	Pascataquack	4590	4720	5339	6934	7327
Raymond o	Freetown	683	727	808	898	961
Richmond o		864	1380	1390	1290	1391
Rindge o	Rowley-Canada	542	1143	1196	1226	1298
Rochester o		1548	2857	2646	2118	2471
Roxbury						366
Rumney o		237	411	624	765	864
Rye	Sandy Beach	870	865	890	1020	1127
Salem o	Part of Methuen, Ms.	1084	1218	1077	1179	1311
Salisbury o o	Stevens' Town	498	1372	1767	1913	2016
Sanbornton o o		459	1587	2695	2834	3329
Sandown	Part of Kingston	459	561	501	504	527

APPENDIX. 275

TOWNS.		Population.				
Present Name.	Former Name.	1775	1790	1800	1810	1820
Sandwich º		243	905	1413	2232	2368
Seabrook	Part of Hampton	607	715	628	774	885
Sharon			259	428	446	391
Shelburne			31	45	176	205
Society-Land		177	319	146	199	153
Somersworth	Part of Dover	965	943	932	878	841
South Hampton	Part of Hampton	498	448	387	427	416
Springfield º	Protectworth		210	570	614	967
Stewartstown	Stewart			99	186	363
Stoddard º	Limerick	224	701	1148	1132	1203
Strafford º	Part of Barrington					2144
Stratford º		41	146	281	339	335
Stratham º	Winnicot	1137	882	890	874	892
Success						
Sullivan			220	488	516	582
Surry º		215	448	569	564	570
Sutton º	Perry's-Town		520	878	1328	1573
Swanzey º	Lower Ashuelot	647	1157	1271	1400	1716
Tamworth º º		151	266	757	1134	1442
Temple º	Peterborough Slip	491	747	867	941	752
Thornton º			385	535	794	857
Tuftonborough			109	357	709	1232
Troy						676
Unity º		146	538	902	1044	1277
Wakefield º	East-town	320	646	835	1166	1518
Walpole º º	Bellows' Town	658	1245	1743	1894	2020
Warren º			206	336	506	544
Warner º	New-Amesbury	262	863	1569	1838	2246
Washington º	Camden	163	545	819	820	992
Weare º º	Hale's Town	837	1924	2517	2634	2781
Wendell	Saville	65	267	355	447	603
Wentworth º			241	488	645	807
Westmoreland º	Great Meadow	758	2018	2066	1937	2029
Whitefield	Whitefields				51	281
Wilmot	Kearsarge				298	670
Wilton º		632	1105	1010	1017	1070
Winchester º	Arlington	238	1209	1413	1478	1849
Windham º	Part of Londonderry	529	663	751	742	889
Windsor	Campbell's Gore		120	249	238	237
Wolfeborough º		211	447	941	1376	1794

RECAPITULATION BY COUNTIES.

	1775	1790	1800	1810	1820
Rockingham	37,463	43,169	45,427	50,175	55,246
Strafford	12,513	23,742	32,878	41,595	51,117
Hillsborough	15,986	32,871	43,899	49,249	53,884
Cheshire	10,252	28,772	38,825	40,988	45,376
Grafton	3,597	12,429	20,171	28,462	32,989
Coos	227	882	2,658	3,991	5,549
Total	80,038*	141,885	183,858	214,460	244,161

* To this number ought to be added 2162, for Locations and Gores, not included in the above aggregate, making the total in 1775, 82,200. See p. 27.

Newspapers and other periodical journals, published in Portsmouth, N. H.

NEWSPAPERS.

New-Hampshire Gazette and Historical Chronicle, commenced Oct. 7, 1756, by Daniel Fowle, who continued to publish it until 1784, with the exception of one year commencing May 25, 1776. On the 25th May, 1776, it assumed the title of "The Freeman's Journal, or N. H. Gazette," and retained this title about a year; after which it was called the "New-Hampshire Gazette, or State Journal and General Advertiser." Its publishers were successively, John Melcher; N. S. and W. Peirce; Peirce, Hill and Peirce; Peirce and Gardner; William Weeks. Since Dec. 14, 1813, it has been published by Beck and Foster, and is called *New-Hampshire Gazette*.

The New-Hampshire Mercury and Weekly Advertiser, was commenced in 1765, by Furber and Russell, and continued 2 years.

The N. H. Mercury and General Advertiser, by Robert Gerrish, commenced 1784, and continued 4 or 5 years.

The New-Hampshire Spy was commenced about 1787, by George Jerry Osborne, and published most of the time semi-weekly until 1793.

Portsmouth Oracle, commenced June 4, 1793, and was published twice a week by Charles Peirce until Jan. 1796. Its subsequent proprietors were William and Daniel Treadwell; William Treadwell to Sept. 1813; Charles Turell, from Sept. 25, 1813, to July 1821. Its title was then changed to *Portsmouth Journal of Literature and Politics*.

The Federal Observer was commenced Nov. 22, 1798, by William Treadwell and Samuel Hart; discontinued June 12, 1800.

Republican Ledger, established Aug. 31, 1799, by George J. Osborne, and afterwards published by Nutting and Whitelock; discontinued Dec. 27, 1803.

Political Star, by M. J. de Rochemont, from June to Oct. 31, 1804.

The Intelligencer, by Samuel Whidden, from Dec. 1806, to May, 1817.

The Literary Mirror, by Stephen Sewall, commenced Feb. 10, 1808, and discontinued Feb. 11, 1809.

War Journal, by Beck and Foster, from March 13, to Dec. 10, 1813.

People's Advocate, by Weeks and Drown, from Nov. 19, 1816, to May 17, 1817.

Novator and Independent Expositor, by Samuel Whidden, (first called Paraclete and Tickler) commenced in 1822.

RELIGIOUS PUBLICATIONS.

The Piscataqua Evangelical Magazine, published by Wm. and Daniel Treadwell, commenced Jan. 1, 1805, and was issued once in 2 months for about 1 year. Was afterwards published at Amherst by Joseph Cushing.

Herald of Gospel Liberty, by Elias Smith, commenced May 12, 1815, and continued until Sept. of that year.

Christian Herald, by Robert Foster, commenced May, 1818; and is published in 8mo. size, 8 Nos. in a year.

Name and Place Index

ABBOT, Benjamin 132 Dorcas 106
  Edward 106 Ephraim 146
  George 146 Jacob 150 Reuben
  12
ACWORTH, Nh 16 58 65 67 94-95
  104 172-173 183 251 271
ADAMS, 124 Benjamin 198 Daniel
  190 Ephraim 198 Hugh 125
  John 71 125 Jonathan 141
  Joseph 76 196 244 Moses 120
  Mrs 75 Nathaniel 218 Nh 61-63
  66 77 93 97-98 126 271 Pres 75
  Rev Mr 269-270 Thomas 96
  Winborn 125
AIKEN, Dea 74 James 74 142 John
  79 Thomas 115 William 115
AINSWORTH, Laban 164
ALBANY, Ny 94 157 264 269
ALDEN, Pres 259 Timothy 221
ALDRICH, Artemas 224
ALEXANDER, John 120 158
ALEXANDRIA, Nh 60 66 86 113 155
  194 205 237 271
ALLEN, 21 Amos 120 Ebenezer 267
  Rev Mr 267 William 146
ALLENS-TOWN, Nh 66
ALLENSTOWN, Nh 11 16 50 66-67
  93 113 130 160 186 209-210 245
  271
ALLINE, Henry 202
ALSTEAD, Nh 16 21 58 65 67-68 141
  172 183 245 252 271
ALTON, England 68 Nh 52 68 75-76
  139-140 188 195 267 271
AMBROSE, Samuel 247
AMES, James 139 Nathan 247

AMESBURY, Ma 147 216 222-223
  240 253 Nh 254
AMHERST, Lord Jeffrey 70 Nh 6 11-
  12 15 19 21-22 40 47 54-56 69-
  71 73 78 85 87 98 102 115 121-
  122 135-136 141 145 150 155-
  156 159 161 166 175 180 184
  186-188 190 192-193 200 204
  211 237 240 249 263 265 271
  274 Nh? 115
AMOSKEAG, Falls Nh 45-46 71-72
  182 186
ANDOVER, Ma 75 210 Nh 15-16 18
  21 54-55 72-73 81 144 194 211
  223 231 234 240 263 271
ANDROS, 48
ANGLESEA, Wales 20
ANNAN, David 213
ANNIS, David 254
ANTRIM, Ireland 74 Nh 15 54-55 73-
  74 110 115 150 156 192 237-238
  242 265 271
APLIN, Joanna 12
APPLEBEE, Zebedee 139
APPLEDORE, Nh 143 272
APPLETON, Dr 270 Francis 270
  Jesse 149 270 John Esq 270
  Samuel Esq 197
APTHORP, Nh 176 272
ARCHIBALD, Thomas 65
ARLINGTON, Nh 265 275
ARNOLD, 204 Joel R 100 Seth S 67
ASHBURNHAM, Ma 69 197 240
ASHBY, Ma 15 184 240
ASHLEY, 102 Joseph 265 Samuel
  102-103

ASPEY, John 151
ATHERTON, Joshua 71
ATKINSON, Nh 12 45 50 74-75 113 115 121 147 154 176 216 231 271 Theodore 75 130 174 194 251
ATWOOD, James 11 267
AUSTIN, Nicholas 87
AVERY, James 171 175
BACHELDER, Abraham 180 Increase 203 Jethro 180 John 203
BACHELOR, Stephen 149
BACON, Jacob 167 Margaret 11
BADCOCK, Josiah 72
BADGER, Joseph 141
BADGER'S, Island Nh 219
BAILEY, David Esq 256 Jacob 148 Mrs 12 268 Stephen 223
BAKER, Capt 217
BAKERS-TOWN, Nh 233
BALCH, Benjamin 76 William 231
BALDWIN, Loammi Esq 244 Thomas 90
BALLOU, Hosea 221 Maturin 224
BANNISTER, 152
BARBADOES, (brit W Indies) 185
BARBER, Daniel 103-104 Robert 233
BARKER, Joshua 75 William 183
BARKER'S, Location Nh 75
BARNARD, Jeremiah 70 Mary 12 Silas 72
BARNES, Isaac O 79
BARNET, Vt 115 180
BARNETT, Lemuel 139
BARNEY, Jacob 144
BARNS, Jona 115 Jonathan 157
BARNSTABLE, ?? 168 Ma 103
BARNSTEAD, Nh 11 52 68 75-76 140 215 243 245 271
BARRETT, Charles 198
BARRINGTON, Nh 11 15 45 52 76-77 80 116 159 163 173 181 204 225 243 271 275
BARRON, 208 Moses 79 Silas 79
BARRON'S, Island Nh 77 214
BARSTOW, Zedekiah S 167
BARTLETT, 270 Charles 216 Gov 77 270 Ichabod 233 James 233 John 270 Joseph 201 233 Josiah 169 Nh 16 62 66 77 97 110-111

BARTLETT (cont.) 126 211 230 261 271 Richard Esq 270 Robert 172 Thos 204
BATCHELDER, Benjamin 114 Breed 193 Mr 114
BATH, Nh 22 40 60 77-78 108 141 153 171 180 268 271
BATTEN, Richard 138
BAUM, Col 183
BAVARIA, Germany 108
BAYLEY, Abner 231 Hannah 101 268 Josiah 101 150
BAYNE, Elisha 206
BEALS, Mrs 12
BEAN, Benjamin 251 David 270 Hill Nh 78 201 John 107 Mary 11
BEAN'S, Hill Nh 91
BEARD, 124-125 Mr 204
BECK, 276
BECKWITH, Eleazar 184
BEDFORD, Nh 19 22 46 54-55 69 78-80 141-142 186-187 193 214 271
BEDFORDSHIRE, England 122
BEEDE, Daniel 236 270 Thomas 264
BEEMAN, John 158
BELKNAP, 10 12 125 158 211 226 258 263 Dr 13 47 75 119 135 199 259-260 269-270 Jeremy 118 Mrs 12 Rev Dr 48
BELL, Joseph 79 Samuel 179
BELLOWS, Benjamin 253 Col 253 Falls Nh 45 57 80 109 172 197
BELLOWS', Falls Nh 252 Town Nh 275
BENNET, Phinehas 147 Salmon 265
BENNINGTON, Vt 70 80 179 183
BERRY, 229
BERWICK, Me 16 125 181 223 225 238
BETHLEHEM, Nh 59-60 80-81 86 108 113 138 175 259 271
BETTON, Silas 231
BICKFORD, 209 Solomon 203 William 158
BICKNELL, Nathaniel 128
BIGELOW, Benjamin 136 Dr 13
BILLERICA, Ma 79 122 160 175
BINGHAM, Elias 128 Elisha 128
BIRD, Simon 122
BISHOP, Enos 83 233 Job 92 127 Of London 103

BLAISDELL, William 139
BLAKE, Benjamin 267 Henry 166
    Israel 127 John L 203 Moses
    113 Nathan 11 166-167 Robert
    214 William 72
BLANCHARD, 91 122 Abel 210
    Benjamin 201 John 122
    Jonathan 123 Joseph 224
    Joseph Esq 217 Richard 268
BLIND, Will's Neck Nh 81 225
BLISS, Lemuel 85
BLODGET, 205 Archippus 243
    Samuel Esq 182
BLODGETT, James 217
BLOOD, Caleb 184 Francis 250
    Mighill 160
BLOODY, Point Nh 81
BLOSS, Walter 113
BLUNT, John 194
BOAR'S, Head Nh 81 148
BODWELL, Abraham 235
BOHONNON, Andrew 82 233
    Tabitha 11
BOLTON, Ma 72
BOODY, Joseph 195
BOSCAWEN, Edward 82 Nh 15 17-
    19 54-55 81-83 90-91 105 110
    115 161-162 201 231 233 253
    271
BOSTON, Ma 14-15 18-19 21 30 65-
    66 69 73-74 76-78 81 85-87 90
    93-94 97-100 102-104 106 108
    110-113 115-116 119-121 127
    129 135-138 140-141 144-146
    148 150-151 153 155-157 159-
    161 164 166-167 172-173 175-
    176 180 182-184 186-188 190
    192-194 197-200 204 206 209
    211 213-217 219 221-224 227-
    228 231-232 235 238 240 243
    245 247 249-254 258-259 263-
    265 267 269
BOW, Nh 12 14 16-17 19 50 83-84
    105-106 120 160-162 210 268
    271
BOYD, George Nh 189
BOYLE, Nh 141 272
BRACKET, 229
BRACKETT, A N Esq 260 George
    Esq 146 Joshua 221

BRADFORD, Andrew 188 Ephraim P
    194 Ma 85 239 247 Moses 137
    Nh 55 85 135 155-156 245 253-
    254 271 Vt 213
BRADLEY, Jonathan 107 Samuel
    107
BRADSTREET, Nathan 100
BRAINARD, Daniel 228
BRAINTREE, Ma 47 130
BRANDYWINE, Pa 247
BRATTLEBOROUGH, Village Vt
    157 Vt 15 17 99-100 157
BRAY, Ebenezer 111
BREAKFAST, Hill Nh 85 229
BREED, Nathaniel 193
BRENTON'S, Farm Nh 175 273
BRENTWOOD, Nh 22 50 85-86 128
    130-131 168 214 217 271
BRETTON, Woods Nh 165 192
BRETTON-WOODS, Nh 16 62 80 86
    165 259 271
BREWSTER, John 227
BRIDGEWATER, Nh 60 86-87 155
    158 196 211 216 271
BRIDGMAN, Abel 153
BRIDGMAN'S, Fort Nh 158
BRIGHAM, Benjamin 136
BRIGHTON, Ma 71 250
BRISTOL, Nh 16 18 20 60 66 86-87
    194-196 211 237 271 Village Nh
    66
BRODHEAD, John 199
BROOKE, Lord 118
BROOKFIELD, Nh 52 87 188 190
    195 252 267 271
BROOKLINE, Nh 54-55 87 122 159
    184 188 271
BROWN, Amos P 89 Benjamin 80
    Clark 248 Edmund 72 Elisha
    236 Francis 32 152 Isaac 236
    James 243 Jonathan 178
    Joseph 133 Josiah 217 Pres 33
    Thomas 201
BROWNE, Arthur 220
BROWNFIELD, Me 110 156 230
BRUCE, John 190
BRUNSWICK, Me 68 270
BUCKMINSTER, Dr 222 Joseph 220
    222
BUCKNAM, Edward 171

BUEL, Horatio 200
BULLARD, Asa 120 Ebenezer 198
 John 167 Joseph 198
BUNKER, Mrs 11
BUNTIN, Andrew 67 Robert 67
BURBANK, Caleb 162 Ebenezer 111
 Jonathan 162 Moses 82 Samuel
 162
BURDET, George 118
BURGE, Benjamin 160 Josiah 160
BURGESS, Archibald 151
BURGOYNE, 204
BURLINGTON, Vt 232 252
BURNAP, Jacob 187
BURNAPS, Miss 187
BURNHAM, Abraham 210 Amos
 Wood 225
BURNS, John 188 Maj 259 Robert 79
BURNSIDE, Thos 203
BURROUGHS, Charles 220 Eden
 153 Rev Dr 153
BURT, Federal 125 Gideon 126
 Joseph 109
BURTON, Nh 21 52-53 88 110 112
 126 139 147 230 235-236 248-
 249 271
BUSS, John 10 125
BUTLER, Benjamin 204 Henry 204
 John 209 Rev Mr 204
BUTTERFIELD, Amos 242 Joseph
 Jr 66
BUZZELL, Hezekiah D 256 William
 188
CALDWELL, 193
CALFE, John 148 269
CALKINS, Charles 90
CALL, Philip 233
CAMBRIDGE, Ma 19 212 Nh 62 88
 120 131 168 208 244 251 271
CAMDEN, Nh 255 275
CAMPBELL, James 99
CAMPBELL'S, Gore Nh 266 275
CAMPTON, Nh 60 88-89 127 139 158
 181 186 211 216 228 235-236
 250 271
CANAAN, Ct 90 Nh 16 60 89-90 116
 127-128 151 184 205 271
CANDIA, Nh 16 50 90-91 98 100 113
 160 170 223 270-271
CANTERBURY, Nh 17 38 50 81 91-
 92 105 128 131 140 179-180 201

CANTERBURY (cont.)
 233 268 271 273-274
CAPE, Breton (island) Canada 95
 103 222
CAPE-ANN, Ma 148
CAPE-BRETON, (island) Canada 72
CARDIGAN, Nh 206 274
CARLETON'S, Falls Nh 180
CARPENTER, Abraham 215 Ezra
 167 248 Josiah 102
CARR, James 67 210 John 99 Moses
 239
CARRIGAIN, 244 Philip 108
CARSON, John 137
CARTER, Ezra 107
CASWELL, Apthorp 176 Mr 207
 Nathan 176
CAYFORD, John 256
CEDAR, Isle Me 163
CENTRE, Harbor Nh 159 Road
 Village Nh 232
CENTRE-HARBOR, Nh 53 93 158
 185 190 195-196 241 271
CHADBOURNE, & Hart's Location
 Nh 93-94 192 Humphrey 218
 Thomas 93
CHAMBERLAIN, 181 Ebenezer 93
 Jacob 68
CHAMBLEE, ?? 233
CHAMPNEY, Ebenezer 198 270
CHANDLER, John 129 Joshua 248
CHAPIN, Seth 157 Stephen 157 190
 269 William 200
CHAPMAN, Eliphaz 181
CHARLES, II King Of England 48
CHARLESTN, Nh 6
CHARLESTOWN, Ma 78 129 214 Nh
 16-17 21-22 58-59 61 65 67 78
 94-97 102 111 139 172-173 182
 242 245 251-252 254 271
CHARMING-FARE, Nh 223
CHARMINGFARE, Nh 100 270-271
CHASE, Ebenezer 128 Henry B Esq
 244 Johnson 216 Samuel 67 113
 Stephen 194
CHATHAM, Nh 61-62 66 77 93 97-98
 110 211 228 254 271
CHEEVER, Ebenezer 190
CHELMSFORD, Ma 14 19 175 186
 209 242
CHESHIRE, England 59 Nh 99 271

281

CHESLEY, Capt 125
CHESMORE, Martha 11
CHESTER, Nh 10-11 16 22 45 49-50 90 98-100 111 115 131 160-161 176 182 184 194 217 223 235 270-271
CHESTERFIELD, Nh 12 20-21 57-58 100-101 157 166 240 247 258 264 268 271
CHESWELL, Thomas 199
CHICHESTER, Nh 15 21 50 101-102 105 130 179 209 215 271 274
CHISWICK, Nh 176 273
CHOATE, Jonathan 249 Rev Mr 169
CHURCH, John H 209 Selden 89
CILLEY, Col 114 Joseph 204 Mrs 12 267
CLAGETT, Wyseman 175
CLAREMONT, Nh 15 40 57-58 94 102-104 111 175 199-200 244 251 257 271
CLARK, Matthew 178 Nathaniel 241 Peter 140 Samuel 193 Ward 169 Zephaniah Esq 135
CLARKE, John 133 Jonathan Esq 203 Timothy 146
CLARY, Joseph W 118
CLAYES, Dana 145 216 270
CLEAVELAND, 22
CLEMENT, 254
CLIFFORD, Israel 241 Israel Jr 241
CLIVE, Lord 103
CLOUGH, 268 Thomas 91
COCHECO, Falls Nh 117 Nh 272
COCHRAN, 193 Peter 193 Robert 193 Thomas 193
COCKBURN, Sir George 242
COCKBURNE, Nh 105 272 Sir James 105
COCKERMOUTH, Nh 147 155 272-273
COE, Curtis 125
COFFIN, Peter 126
COLBURN, 122 205 Andrew 183
COLBURNE, Nh 272
COLBY, B 99 E 99 Jonathan 158 Mr 270 Zaccheus 100 210
COLCHESTER, Ct 103
COLE, Samuel Esq 103
COLEBROOK, Nh 62-63 78 104 115 189 241 272 Sir George 104 242

COLEFAX, Sampson 96
COLERAIN, Ireland 65
COLLEGE, Grant Nh 62 241 Lands Nh 104 115
COLLINS, Mrs Comfort 236 Samuel 153 235
COLMAN, Jabez 169
COLTON, Abisha 242 Chester 86
COLUMBIA, Nh 13 61-62 104-105 115 131 213 237 243 252 272
CONANT, Ezra 265 William 174
CONCORD, Ma 210 248 Nh 6 12 14-19 22-23 38-43 46 49-51 60 65-69 73-78 80-81 83-89 91 93-94 98-102 105-113 115-116 119-121 126-128 130 134-138 140-141 143-146 148 150-151 153 155-162 164 166-168 170-176 179-180 183-186 188 190 192-194 197-199 201-206 208-209 211 213 215-217 222-225 227-228 230-231 234-235 237-238 240-245 247 249-254 257-259 263-265 267-268 272 Vt 175
CONNER, Benjamin 11
CONTINENTAL, Island Nh 219
CONTOOCOOK, Nh 82 271
CONWAY, Nh 11 53 77 88 97 110-111 126 139 147 211 230 248 272
COOK, Thomas 83 Timothy 83
COOKE, Phinehas 65
COOS, Nh 63 171
COPP, Benjamin 66 Mrs 235 268
CORLISS, John M 66 Jonathan 66 William 66
CORNISH, Nh 17 58 102 111-112 215 272 Vt 112
CORSER, Enoch 180
COSSIT, Ranna 103
COTTON, John 149 Josiah 235 Roland 136 Samuel 137 175 269 Seaborn 149 Theophilus 150 Ward 149
COVENTRY, Ct 153 Nh 6 59-60 75 112 153 171 190 205 208 272
COVENTY, Nh 254
COVERLY, Nathaniel 70 154
CRAIG, Abigail 11
CRAIGE, Mrs 10 William 10
CRAM, 181 Jacob 162 John 215

CRAM (cont.)
　Jonathan 216 Rev Mr 121
CRANE, Mr 201
CRANFIELD, 221
CRAWFORD, 260 Jona 86 Thomas Esq 86
CREIGHTON, Dorothy 11
CROCKER, John 11
CROCKET, Ephraim 144
CROCKETT, John 235
CROMWELL, John 187 Oliver 133
CROSBY, Jaazaniah 97 Josiah 188
CROSS, 205 Mr 207
CROWN, Point Ny 91
CROYDON, Nh 16 22 57-58 111-113 144 199 240 257 272
CUMINGS, 122 205 Dr 160 Henry 160 John 122 Jotham 217
CUMMINGS, Charles 244 Joseph 183 Jotham 228
CUNNINGHAM, Mr 133 Mrs 212
CUPAR, Of Fife Scotland 213
CURRIER, Joseph 142
CURTIS, James 243 Jonathan 130
CUSHING, James 216 Jonathan 118 Joseph 276
CUSHING'S, Gore Nh 113 143
CUTLER, Dr 260 Robert 129
CUTTER, Ammi R 222 Chas W 117
DALE, 264
DALTON, Nh 62 80 113 165 170 175-176 243 259 272 Timothy 149 Tristram 113
DAME, Sarah 197
DAME'S, Gore Nh 89 116 184 205
DANA, Daniel 33 178 Dr 13 87 Jedediah 128 Prof 128 130 189 Rev Dr 33 Samuel 71 Sylvester 207 William 173
DANBURY, Nh 16 60 66 81 113 143 194 237 263 272
DANFORTH, Abigail 82 Nathaniel 82
DANTZICK, Nh 135 199 274
DANVERS, Ma 70 264
DARLING, David 245 Elizabeth 11 Timothy 155
DARTMOUTH, Nh 165 273
DAVIDSON, Mary 11 William 178
DAVIS, A 254 Benjamin 153 Daniel 11 Jacob 11 247 Moses 107

DAVIS (cont.)
　152 Simon 101 Widow 11
DAVISON, John 164
DEAN, John 124
DEANE, Seth 225
DEARBORN, Ebenezer 99 Henry 129 202
DEBELINE, Mons 97
DEER, Islands Nh 115 Isle Me 154
DEER-FIELD, Nh 114
DEERFIELD, Ma 95 110 Nh 12 49-50 66 113-114 130 160 170 203-204 223 230 272
DEERING, Frances 115 Nh 15 55 73 110 115 136 155-156 214 237-238 255 272
DEMERITT, Eli 208
DENNIS, John 97
DEOLPH, Ezra 11
DERING, Frances 115
DEROCHEMONT, M J 276
DERRYFIELD, Nh 100 182
DEVIL'S, Den Nh 76 Sliding-place Nh 213
DEWEY, Ebenezer 141
DICKINSON, David 216 270 Pliny 253
DIX, Timothy Jr 115
DIXVILLE, Nh 61-62 104 115 131 189 213 241 272
DOCK, Nh 135
DODGE, Gideon 238 Joseph 242
DOLLOFF, John 111
DOOR, Jonathan 226
DORCHESTER, Nh 60 89 115-116 122 127 146 174 184 257 272
DORMAN, Ephraim 167
DOUGLASS, 8 142
DOVER, Neck Nh 80 Nh 6 10 14 16 27 29 37 40 46-48 51 53 68 75-76 104 108 116-119 124-125 157 178 181 196 208 219 221 225 238-239 243 252 270 272-273 275
DOW, John 75 Joseph 236 Moses 154 Phebe 11 236
DOWN, Ireland 57
DOWNER, William 173
DOWNING, Richard Esq 197
DOWNS, Ebenezer 239 Gersham 226 Gershom 239 Samuel 11 240

DRACUT, Ma 78 142 209 240
DREW, 124 John 125
DREWSVILLE, Nh 119
DROWN, 276 Samuel 221 226
DUBLIN, Ireland 120 Nh 6 57-58 110 119-120 150 164 183 189 192 211 227 268 272
DUCK, Isle Me 163
DUDLEY, John 223 Samuel 133 Thomas 270
DUKE, Of Bavaria 108 Of Grafton 61 Of New-castle 160
DUMBARTON, Scotland 121
DUMMER, Nh 62 71 88 120 131 189 208 213 266 272
DUMMERSTON, Vt 100 258
DUNBAR, Charles I 87 Elijah 213
DUNBARTON, Nh 11 55 84 120-121 141 161 210 255 272
DUNHAM, Josiah 152 Mosely 154
DUNSTABLE, ?? 87 England 122 Ma 121-122 Nh 8 12 19 54-56 121-123 159-160 164 175 186-187 192 204-205 252 268 272 274
DUPPLIN, Nh 273
DURAND, John 123 Nh 62 123 163 165 168 185 190 237 272
DURHAM, Nh 10-11 15 18 45 53 117 123-125 145 159 170 173 181 195-196 199 203 207-208 215 268 272
DUSTIN, Caleb 103 Paul 184
DUSTON, David 234 Hannah 83 90 Jonathan 90 Mrs 105 110
DUSTON'S, Island Nh 83 110
DWIGHT, 10 262-263 Pres 9 157 166 Timothy Esq 183
DYER, Samuel B 204
DYKE, Mr 112
EAMES, David 206 Jeremiah 203 Jona 201
EARL, Of Dartmouth 31 Of Fitzwilliam 136 Of Hillsborough 57 Of Strafford 54
EAST, Haddam Ct 89 Kingston Nh 50 272 Village Nh 232
EAST-KINGSTON, Nh 126 131 167-169 222 240
EAST-TOWN, Nh 252 275
EASTMAN, Amos 228 Ebenezer 106 Edward 233 Jonathan 160

EASTMAN (cont.)
Joseph B 233 Luke 160 Moses 232 Richard 111 William 249
EASTON, Nicholas 148
EATON, Asa 216 Nh 52-53 88 110 126 211 249 272
EDGERLY, 124 Thomas 125
EDINBURG, Scotland 78 268
EDINBURGH, Scotland 210 213 268
EFFINGHAM, Nh 53 126 207 252 272
ELIOT, William 185
ELKINS, Daniel 66
ELLIOT, Daniel 120 Me 116
ELLIS, Caleb 104 Ferdinand 133
ELLSWORTH, Nh 6 59-60 127 208 228 250 254 272
EMERSON, Daniel 160 John 194 220 Joseph 160 Mr 147 194 Ralph 160 Samuel 160
EMERY, Edward 82 Jacob 210 Stephen 204
EMMONS, Abel 101 Benj 87
ENDICOTT, Gov 106
ENFIELD, Falls Ct 109 Nh 15 38 60-61 89 127-128 143-144 172 184 272
EPPING, Nh 11 50 85 128-131 142 170 173 199 202 204 217 223 268 272
EPSOM, England 130 Nh 11 15 49-50 66 101 113-114 130-131 203 209 215 245 268 272
ERROL, Nh 88 104 120 131 183 189 251 258 272
ERROLL, Nh 62
ERVIN, William 131
ERVIN'S, Location Nh 104 115 131 189 213
ESTERBROOKS, Experience 215 250 Mr 107
EVANS, Daniel 67 Edward 25 128 Israel 107 Richard 222
EWER, Nathaniel 199
EXETER, Nh 6 11 22 27 37 40 45 47-48 50-51 85 98-99 126 128 131-134 147-148 150 167-169 178 199 203 223 235 241 243 265 268 270-272 274
FAIRBANK, Drury 217
FAIRFIELD, Nh 208 274 Walter 174

FAIRLEE, Vt 17 206
FARLEY, Abel 160 Benjamin M 160 George F 160 Samuel 147 Stephen 103 160
FARMER, Jacob 141
FARMINGTON, Ct 103 Nh 53 76 81 104 134-135 189 195 225-226 242 272
FARNSWORTH, 95 David 96 Ebenezer 96 James D 207 Stephen 95
FARRAR, John 244 Joseph 120 Stephen 198
FARWELL, 103 122
FASSETT, John 136
FAVOR, Cutting 195
FELLOWS, Isaac 206 Joseph 72
FERNALD, Mary 11
FERSON, 193 William 193
FESSENDEN, Thomas 253
FFROST, George 125
FIELD, 260
FIFIELD, Ebenezer O 233
FIFTEEN, Mile Falls Nh 109
FIFTEEN-MILE, Falls Nh 113 165 175 180
FISH, Elisha 141 Holloway 183
FISHER, David 144 Elias 174 Jabez P 115 Jabez Pond 205 John 135 John Esq 241 Josiah 166-167
FISHERSFIELD, Nh 6 54-55 85 135 143 198 244-245 253 257 272
FISKE, Abel 264
FITCH, Jabez 220 Theophilus 112
FITZROY, Augustus Henry 61
FITZWILLIAM, Nh 15-16 58 74 135-136 164 224 250 272
FITZWILLIAM-VILLAGE, Nh 16
FLAGG, Ebenezer 99 Rev Mr 100
FLETCHER, Elijah 162 269 Simeon 146
FLINT, Ebenezer 86
FLOYD, Capt 259
FOGG, Jeremiah 168 Parker 186
FOLLANSBEE, William 195
FOLSOM, Benjamin 130 Joshua 130 Mrs 204 Nathaniel 134
FORD, Mr 147
FORSAITH, William 115
FORT, Dummer Nh 158 273
FOSS, Hannah 11 Joshua 11

FOSS (cont.)
Moses Jr 139-140
FOSTER, 276 Abiel 92 Dan 97 Daniel 111 Jacob 193 Jonathan 12 185 Josiah 265 Obadiah 121 Robert 276
FOWLE, Daniel 276 Robert 159
FOX, 89 Point Nh 136 196-197
FRAMINGHAM, Ma 222
FRANCESTOWN, Nh 15 19 21-22 54-56 115 136-138 145 180 193 214 237-238 255 272
FRANCONIA, Nh 20-22 45 60 80 108 138-139 141 171 174 186 211 268 272
FRANKLIN, Jonathan 174
FREEMAN, 153 Edmund 153
FREETOWN, Nh 100 270 274
FRENCH, 122 Jonathan 202 Nathan 158 Samuel 122
FRISBIE, Levi 32
FROST, Benjamin 226 John 158
FRYEBURG, Me 211 230
FRYEBURGH, Me 110
FULLER, Daniel 137
FULLERTON, Ithamar 267 Walter 74
FURBER, 276
GAFFIELD, Benjamin 158
GAINS, George 221
GALE, Benjamin Esq 232
GARDNER, 276 Andrew 78
GARLAND, Jabez 239 Jacob 119
GARVEN'S, Falls Nh 84 105 186 240
GAY, Bunker 158
GEE, Solomon 184
GEESE, Islands Nh 139
GEORGE, Dr 268 Enos 76 II King Of England 83 III King Of England 57
GEORGETOWN, Me 72
GERRISH, Robert 276 Stephen 82
GHENT, ?? 242
GIBBONS, Mr 163
GIBBS, 22
GIBSON, 156 John B 142 256 Richard 38 220 Samuel 156
GILBERT, Mr 141
GILE, Samuel 216
GILES, Mark 119
GILFORD, Nh 6 11 52-53 68 88 126

GILFORD (cont.)
139-141 179 185 234 245 249
266 272
GILLET, Rev Mr 115
GILLIS, & Foss' Grant Nh 139-140
Josiah 139
GILLIS', & Foss' Grant Nh 250
GILMAN, 140 J T 270 Jacob 169
Jeremy 133 John Taylor 134 N
147 Nicholas 125 134 270 S S
139 Stephen 169
GILMANTON, Nh 11 21-22 53 68 75
91 113 115 139-141 179 201 234
240 245 266 268-269 272
GILSON, M 158
GILSUM, Nh 58 67 74 141 166 183
242 244-245 272
GLASGOW, Scotland 194
GLIDDEN, Abel 140
GLINES, Israel 163 165 John 165
GLYNVILLE, Nh 141 176
GOAT, Island Nh 124 196
GODDARD, Dr 218 Edward 248
William 258
GODFREY, Moses 203 Mrs 12 Sarah
114
GOFFE, John 79 142 165 Joseph 79
GOFFE'S, Falls Nh 79
GOFFSTOWN, Nh 11 54-55 78 120
141-143 160-161 193 214 251
255 272
GOODENOUGH, Daniel 183
GOODHUE, Jonathan 99 Josiah 160
GOODRICH, Sewall 181
GOOKIN, Daniel 202 Mr 202
Nathaniel 101 149 202
GORDON, Adam 79 William 71 79
GORGES, 47 Sir Ferdinando 218
GOSHEN, Nh 58 135 143 173 199
251 254 257 272
GOSPORT, Isle Nh 163 Nh 143 272
GOSS, 229 James C 155 Sylvester T
154
GOTHAM, Mr 165
GOULD, James 147
GOVE, Charles F 142 Jonathan 143
Winthrop 236
GRAFTON, Nh 15-16 21 60 113 127
143-144 205 237 240 242 272
GRANT, Benjamin 145
GRANT'S, Island Nh 145
GRANTHAM, Nh 16 57-58 112 127
144-145 215-216 240 272
GRAVES, Phinehas 251
GRAY, Robert 118 Samuel 32
GREAT, Fall Nh 80 253 Island Nh
194 219 274 Meadow Nh 258
275
GREAT-FALLS, Nh 238
GREAT-ISLAND, Nh 145
GREELEY, 205
GREEN, Jacob 11
GREENFIELD, Nh 55 136 145-146
150 180 211 237-238 249 272
GREENLAND, Nh 50 111 130 145-
146 196 202 208 217-218 228-
229 243 267 272
GREENWICH, ?? 266 England 5
GREGG, Catherine 212 Hugh 212
GRIFFITH, James D 166
GRIMES, Francis 115 John 151
GRINDLE, Daniel 143
GROTON, Ma 71 95 192 Nh 60 116
121-122 146-147 151 155 205
228 272
GROUT, 164 Hilkiah 158
GUILDHALL, Vt 17 171 202-203
GUNTHWAITE, Nh 109 272
GUSTIN, John 184 Samuel 184
HADDUCK, Charles B 233 William
T 233
HADLEY, James 256 Ma 95
HAINES, Cotton 228
HALE, Enoch 80 John 147 John P
Esq 227 Moses 99 Samuel 147
221
HALE'S, Location Nh 62 110 147
Town Nh 275
HALEY'S, Isle Me 163
HALIFAX, Nova Scotia (canada) 221
HALL, 21-22 Aaron 167 Avery 226
Jeremiah 166 John 239 Nathan
185 Richard 198
HAM, Eleazar 226 Joseph 119
HAM'S, Island Nh 18
HAMPSTEAD, Nh 49-50 74 147-148
154 168 176 216 235 240 251
267 269 273
HAMPTON, Falls Nh 50 Nh 11 16 27
45 47-48 50-51 81 99 131 133
148-150 168-169 178 191 196
202 209 218 228 267 273-275

HAMPTON-FALLS, Nh 22 131 148 150 167 236 269 273
HANCOCK, Gov 151 Nh 54-55 73 119 145 150-151 192-193 211 237-238 273
HANOVER, Nh 11 16-17 19-22 25 31-32 40 59-60 87 89 101 109 113 116 136 144 146 151-153 172 174 190 194 206-207 232 263 269 273
HANSON, John 239 Richard 87
HARDICLAY, John 158
HARDWICK, Ma 151
HARDY, N 160 Noah 160 Solomon 160 Thomas 120
HARPER, Samuel 65
HARRIMAN, J 216 John 149
HARRINGTON, Timothy 248
HARRIS, George 90 Joshua 90 Samuel 265 Silas 206 Walter 121
HARRY-TOWN, Nh 273
HARRYTOWN, Nh 182
HART, George 93 Samuel 165 276
HART'S, Island Nh 153 215 Location Nh 16 62
HARTFORD, Ct 30 94 101 109 157 264 Vt 172
HARTLAND, Vt 17 215
HARVARD, Ma 192
HASSELL, Mr 187
HASTINGS, 95 Joseph S 202
HATCH, John 81 Roger C 162 Thomas 80-81
HATFIELD, Ma 95
HAVEN, Dr 221 Jacob 113 Joseph 226 Nathaniel A 120 Samuel 220 222
HAVERHILL, Corner Nh 153 171 175 214 254 District Nh 147 Ma 74-75 78 83 90 147 154 176 216-217 247 Nh 6 16-17 40 60-61 71 77 89 98 108 112 116 121 138-139 147 153-154 171 180 194 201 205-206 213 216 271 273-274
HAWKE, Nh 50 147 154-155 168-169 217 235 273
HAYLEY, Mrs 11
HAYWARD, Peter 245
HAZELTINE, Ebenezer 130

HAZEN, John 154
HAZZEN, Richard Esq 148
HEARD, Joseph 226
HEATH, James 228 Mr 147
HEATON, Seth 166
HEBRON, Ct 103 141 Nh 16 60 66 86 146 155 216 228 273
HEIDLEBURG, Nh 199
HENDERSON, Howard 10
HENNIKER, John Esq 156 Nh 55 85 110 115 155-156 161 214 253 255 273
HERRIMAN, John 78
HEWITT, George 225
HEYWOOD, Samuel 212 William 97
HIBBARD, Augustine 103 Jedidiah 173 Salmon 196
HIDDEN, Samuel 249
HIGBEE, Jeremiah 68
HIGHT, Elizabeth 10 197
HILL, 205 276 Charles 173 Ebenezer 185 Isaac 107 John 157 Samuel 226
HILLIARD, Timothy 168
HILLS, Wills 57
HILLSBOROUGH, Nh 15 18 55-56 73 85 110 115 155-157 238 254 265 269 273
HILTON, 124 243 Charles 270 Dudley 270 Edward 47 53 117 157 270 Ichabod 270 Joseph 270 Samuel 270 William 47 53 117 157 270 Winthrop 133 270
HILTON'S, Point Nh 157 208
HINDS, Orlando 217
HINGHAM, Ma 75
HINSDALE, Col 158 Ebenezer 158 Nh 5 15 17 21 57-59 74 100-101 157-158 166 247 258 264 273
HIXON, Joanna 11 Mrs 11
HOBART, James 217 Jonas 147
HOBBS, James 209
HODGDON, Jonathan 226
HOG, Isle Me 163
HOIT, 107 Benjamin 250
HOLDEN, Ma? 192
HOLDERNESS, Nh 11 60 86 88 93 158-159 186 195-196 211 216 235-236 241 273
HOLLIS, Duke Of New-castle 160 Nh 11 19 55 69-70 87 121-122

HOLLIS (cont.)
    151 154 159-160 187-188 192
    217 273 Thomas 160
HOLMES, Lemuel 245
HOLT, Fifield 160 Peter 129
HOLYOKE, Dr 8
HOOK, Jacob 155
HOOKSETT, Nh 16-18 55 66 71 84
    98 100 120 141 160-161 186 273
HOOPER, Lisa M 13 William 181
HOPK'N, Nh 6
HOPKINS, Benjamin 188
HOPKINTON, Ma 162 Nh 11 17-18
    22 40 55-56 69 81 84 105 107
    110 120 135 155-156 160-162
    245-247 253 255 269 273
HOUGH, George 107
HOUSTON, John 80
HOVEY, Jonathan 214
HOW, Daniel 158 James 227
    Jemima 258 Lydia 258
    Nehemiah 258
HOWE, Caleb 158 James B 103
    Perley 245 Solomon 201 Tilly
    155
HOYT, Joseph 144
HUBBARD, John 152
HUBBARD'S, Island Nh 102
HULL, Elias 236
HUMPHREYS, Daniel Esq 221
HUNT, Samuel 97
HUNTING, Ebenezer 199
HUNTLEY, Nathan 184
HUNTOON, Benjamin 233 Charles
    Esq 251
HURD, Carlton 200 Isaac 133 John
    115 Samuel 200
HUSE, Carr Esq 195 Israel 235
    James 235
HUSSEY, Christopher 236
HUSTON, Caleb 180
HUTCHINS, Samuel 173
HUTCHINSON, Anne 133 Elisha
    201 Nathan 188 Samuel 67
HYDE, Levi 173 Samuel 181
INDIAN, Blind Will 81 Camp Nh 114
    Chocorua 88 Christi 91 Col
    Louis 233 Francis Titigaw 228
    Hoophood 136 197 King Philip
    56 81 Passaconaway 46 74
    Passaquo 74 Peter Louis 233

INDIAN (cont.)
    Plausawa 91 233 Rowls 46
    Sabatis 91 233 Saggahew 74
    Wahangnonawitt 45
    Wonalanset 46 Wonolanset 72
INDIAN?, Dye 11
INGALLS, Benjamin 237 David 237
    Moses 237 Samuel 99-100
IPSWICH, ?? 169 Ma 84
IPSWICH-CANADA, Nh 274
IRON, Works' Village Nh 140
ISLE, Of Hooksett Falls Nh 161 Of
    Hooksett Nh 273
ISLES, Of Shoals Nh 143 148 163
    237
JACKMAN, 91 George Esq 83
    Richard 249
JACKSON, Levi 101
JAFFREY, George 85 George Esq
    164 Nh 15 20 22-23 57-58 74
    110 119 164-165 183 189 197
    211 224 237 250 273
JAMES, II King Of England 178
JARVIS, Leonard 102
JEFFERSON, 165 Nh 16 61-62 86
    163 165 168 170 217 259 261
    269 273 Pres 183
JENNESS, 229 Richard 114
JENNIS-TOWN, Nh 254
JEWETT, David 90 160 Edward Esq
    225 Jacob 270 Leonard 160
JILLSON, Stephen 123
JOCELYN, 260
JOHNSON, Captive 96 James 96
    Jesse 128 Jesse Esq 128
    Kilburn 142 Mrs 96 Noah 217
JOHNSTON, Charles 154 Isaac 243
    William 265
JONES, Caleb 188 Elisha 83 Isaac
    90 John 162 Samuel 90
KEADRICK, Daniel 160
KEARSARGE, Gore Nh 253 263 Nh
    275
KEENE, Nh 6 11-12 15-16 40 57-59
    67 69 74 95 100 108 119 135-
    136 141 150 161 166-167 172
    183 197 211 224 227-228 242
    244-245 247-248 254 258 264
    269 273 Sir Benjamin 167
KELLEY, Samuel 196 Sarah 12 196
KELLUM, Joseph 251

KELLY, John 147 269 John Esq 253 William 254
KELSEY, Jesse 200
KENDRICK, Ariel 112 William P 160
KENNEDY, Nathaniel 168 175
KENNEY, Jonathan 195 Joseph 206
KENNY, Isaac 224
KENSINGTON, Nh 50 126 131 148 150 167-168 236 240 269 273
KEYES, William 65
KIDDER, Joseph 122 Reuben 198 Reuben Esq 198 255
KILBURN, Josiah 141
KILKENNY, Nh 61-62 120 123 165 168 170 185 208 213-214 266 273
KIMBALL, 162 Abraham 162 Benjamin 216 Captive 96 Daniel 215 254 David 254 George 96 Hannah 254 John 65 108 True 216
KING, Of England 106 159 Samuel 181
KINGSTON, Nh 8 10 49-50 84-85 126 147 154 168-170 201 216-217 222 233 235 247 251 272-274
KINKEAD, John 265
KIRK, Of Scotland 99
KITTERY, Me 18 218-219
KNEELAND, Abner 172
KNIGHT, Artemas 139
KNOLLYS, Hanserd 118
KNOWLES, James 227 John 140-141 Sir Charles 97
KNOWLTON, David 76 Ebenezer 215 236
LABARREE, Peter 96
LADD, Ezekiel 154 John 251
LAFAYETTE, Marquis De 183
LAKIN, William 151
LAMB, James 199 John 199
LAMBERT, Nathl 174
LAMPKINS, Josiah 243
LAMPSON, Jonathan 190 Samuel 70
LANCASTER, Ma 239 248 Nh 6-7 13 16-17 22 63 75 77 104 108 113 141 163 165 168 170-171 175 192 202 208 243 251 259-260 262 269 273
LANDAFF, Nh 60 77 108 112 138

LANDAFF (cont.) 171-172 174 208 273
LANE'S, New-boston Nh 274
LANG, William 143
LANGDON, Gov 172 222 John 222 Joseph 196-197 Nh 16 58 65 67 94 172 252 273 Rev Dr 123 Samuel 86 150 220 269 Woodbury 220 222
LANKTON, Levi 68
LARKHAM, Thos 118
LARY, Joseph 267
LAWRENCE, Enoch 185 Micah 265
LAWTON, John 157
LEAR, Mrs 10
LEATHERS, Abednego 11 Ezekiel 11
LEAVITT, 268 Anna 11 Benjamin 236 Dudley 269 Jonathan 270 Rev 253
LEAVITT'S, Town Nh 126 272
LEBANON, Ct 173 Me 225 234 Nh 14-17 20 22-23 60-61 127 151 172-173 184 200 207 215 273
LEDOYT, Biel 201
LEE, Ann 92 Nh 15 53 76 117 123 128 170 173 181 188 199 202 204 258 273
LEECHMAN, Prof 194
LEGGE, William 31
LEMPSTER, Nh 15-16 58 65 95 143 173-174 183 251 254-255 273
LEOMINSTER, Ma 239
LEONARD, George 112 Levi W 120
LESSLIE, George 255
LEVERICH, Mr 118
LEWIS, 137 Eber 184
LEXINGTON, Ma 131
LIMAVADY, Ireland 194
LIME, Ct 184 Nh 16 21 60 116 145 151 174 180 184 206 273
LIMERICK, Nh 242 275
LINCOLN, Ma 198 Nh 60 138 171 174-175 186 208 250 273
LINDSEY, 208
LITCHFIELD, Ma 175 Nh 56 78 122 137 175-176 182 186 204 269 273
LITTLE, Daniel Esq 148 Harbor Nh 228 Valentine 233 Walter 74
LITTLE-HARBOR, Nh 175 219
LITTLETON, Nh 22 60 80 108 113

LITTLETON (cont.)
    141 175-176 180 273 Village Nh
    141
LIVERMORE, Arthur 179 Jonathan
    264 Samuel 159
LIVERPOOL, England 92
LIVIUS, Peter 98
LOCKE, 229 John 229
LONDON, England 103 105 117 123
    147 156 221 270
LONDONDERRY, ?? 212 Ireland
    177-178 212 Nh 10 16 38 50 74
    78 84 98-100 115 121-122 147
    151 156 175-179 182 204-205
    228 231 235 265 269 273 275
LONDONNER'S, Isle Nh 163
LONG, D 115 Joseph A E 269 Peirce
    221
LONG-MEADOWS, Nh 100
LORD, John 255 Nathan 70
LOUDON, Nh 50 91 101 105 140
    179-180 215 240 273
LOUISBOURG, ?? 221-222 269
LOUISBURGH, ?? 198
LOVEJOY, Abiel 111 Hannah 11
LOVELL, 222
LOVEWELL, 122 205 217 Capt 122
    254 John 122 210 252 Mr 12
    Zaccheus 12
LOWER, Ashuelot Nh 248 275 Cohos
    Nh 154 273
LUCAS, James 267
LUFKIN, John 107
LUND, 122
LUNENBURG, ?? 212 Ma 95 101 Vt
    171
LUNENBURGH, Vt 113
LYMAN, Daniel 180 Nh 22 59-60 77
    87 108 113 115 175-176 180 273
LYME, Ct 174 Nh 180
LYNDE, Benjamin Esq 181 David
    103
LYNDEBOROUGH, Nh 15 54-55
    136-137 145 180-181 188 190
    193 240 249 263-264 273
LYON, Eliphalet 199 James 156
M'CALLEY, James 156 John 156
M'CLARY, Andrew 131 David 179
    John 131 268 Michael 131
M'CLENCH, Mrs 11
M'CLINTOCK, Dr 146 Samuel 146

M'CLOUD, George 151
M'CLURE, David 202 Robert 156
M'DUFFEE, John 227
M'FARLAND, Asa 107
M'INTIRE, Mrs 11
M'KEEN, Joseph 179
M'KENNEY, Mrs 167
M'LELLAN, Jane 12 258
M'NEIL, 193 John 179
MACK, Solomon 184
MACKAY, Benjamin 244
MACKLIN, Robert 10 252
MADBURY, Nh 53 76 80 116-117
    123 173 181 273
MAGOON, John 133
MAIDSTONE, Vt 17 171 202
MAIN, Amos 226 Josiah 227
MALAGA, Isle Me 163
MANCHESTER, Nh 54 56 72 78 98
    121 141 160 176 181-183 186
    273
MANN, Jacob 67 John Esq 207
MANSFIELD, Ct 32 153 173 Isaac
    133
MARCH, Clement 88 126
MARLBOROUGH, Ma 156 Nh 15 58
    119 164 166 183 197 227-228
    247 250 273
MARLOW, Nh 58 65 67 74 141 173
    183-184 242 254-255 273
MARQUIS, De La Fayette 183 Of
    Rockingham 51
MARSH, 205
MARSHFIELD, Ma 266
MARTIN, 170 Aaron 139 Richard
    139 173
MARY, Joseph 233
MASON, 67 164 209 Benjamin 120 J
    Tufton 250 John 47 218 John
    Tufton Esq 264 Nh 12 22 30 56
    87 184-185 188 197 240 249 263
    273
MAST, Camp Nh 112
MAUD, Daniel 118
MAYNE, Bart 185 Edward 185
    Robert 185 Sir William 185 208
    Thomas 185
MAYNESBOROUGH, Nh 63 123 168
    185 208 237 244 273
MAYO, Mrs 10
MC'KEAN, William 115

MCALISTER, 183
MCCLINTOCK, Samuel 111
MCCOY, Mrs 131
MCGAW, Thornton 79
MCGREGORE, David 80 178 James 177 Mr 178
MCNEE, William 120
MCQUADE, James 79
MEACHAM, Samuel 90
MEAD, Samuel 67
MEADER, 124-125
MEANS, Robert 71 Roswell 111
MEDFORD, Ma 146
MELCHER, John 218 276
MELLEN, Henry 162
MELOON, Daniel 233 Nathaniel 233 Rachel 233 Sarah 233
MELVIN, Ebenezer 147
MEREDITH, Nh 11 19 22 53 93 139 145 179 185-186 195-196 234 266 273
MERIDEN, Parish Nh 215-216 270
MERRILL, 205 Daniel 205 Eliphalet 203 270 Gyles 216 Nathaniel 83 181 199 205 Phinehas Esq 244 Thomas 111
MERRIMACK, Nh 11 19 54 56 69 78 121-122 141 186-188 240 273
MERRIT, Ebenezer 200
METCALF, Alfred 146
METHUEN, Ma 130 231 240 274
MIDDLE, Monadnock Nh 164
MIDDLEBURY, Vt 252
MIDDLETON, Nh 52-53 87 188-190 195 252 273
MIDDLETOWN, Ct 109
MILE, Slip & Duxbury Nh 188 Slip Nh 273
MILES, Noah 249
MILFORD, Nh 22 56 69-70 87 122 159 180 184 188-190 240 263 273
MILLER, Gen 212 James 179 N 184
MILLS, Joseph 114 Sir Thomas 189
MILLSFIELD, Nh 63 104 115 120 131 189 213 273
MILTEMORE, James 244
MILTON, ?? 216 Ma 72 Nh 53 81 134 188-189 225 250 252 273
MINER, Thomas 90
MINOT, Jonas 263

MITCHEL, James 242
MITCHELL, Daniel 210 Dr 87
MOFFATT, 218
MONADNOCK, No 1 Nh 225 No 2 Nh 272 No 3 Nh 120 273 No 4 Nh 136 272 No 5 Nh 273 No 6 Nh 193 No 8 Nh 255
MONSON, Nh? 70
MONT-VERNON, Nh 15 56 69-70 78 180-181 188 190 240 274
MONTAGUE, Ma 109-110
MONTPELIER, Vt 115
MONTREAL, Canada 36 67 115 233 252
MOODEY, Joshua 220
MOODY, Amos 209 Betty 163 John 199 Josiah 259 Samuel 194 William 133
MOOR, Joshua 32 Solomon 193
MOORE, Adams 79 Coffin 113 Ephraim 210 Ferris 167 198 Humphrey 189 J B 107 Jacob B 72 107 Solomon 115
MOREY, Israel 207
MORRIL, David L 142
MORRILL, Elisha 155 Nathaniel 229 Paul 102 Robie 83
MORRISON, Dr 178 John 212-213 John Esq 178 Moses 151 Uriah 139 William 178
MORRISTOWN, Nh 139 272
MORSE, Abel 100 Ebenezer 120 Eli 120 John 120 Samuel 120 Sarah 11 Thomas 120
MOULTON, Ezekiel 191 John 236 Jonathan 149 191 196 207 249
MOULTONBOROUGH, Add Nh 274 Nh 22 52-53 93 158-159 185 190-192 196 207 224 235 241 250 274
MUDGETT, Benjamin 140 John 140
MURCH, Stephen 116
MURRAY, John 221
MUSSEY, Widow 149
MUZZY, William 244
N, Boston Nh 180 Castle Nh 145 Hampton Nh 86
NARRAGANSET, No 3 Nh 70 No 5 Nh 79 Townships Nh 187
NASH, & Sawyer's Loc Nh 63 & Sawyer's Location Nh 86 192

NASH (cont.)
    236 L 215 Nh 16 Timothy 192
NASHUA, Village Nh 121 192
NATTICOTT, Nh 175
NEAL, 260 James Armstrong 146
NEGRO, Corydon 11 Zene 11
NELSON, John Esq 242 Nh 58 73
    110 119 150 192-193 211 227-
    228 242 244 269 274
NEW, Boston Nh 136 Bradford Nh
    85 Chester Nh 60 Market Nh
    128
NEW-AMESBURY, Nh 254 275
NEW-BOSTON, Nh 15 22 56 69 74
    78 141 190 193-194 255 274
NEW-BOSTON-ADDITION, Nh 137
NEW-BRADFORD, Nh 271
NEW-BRETON, Nh 72 271
NEW-CASTLE, Nh 18 50 130 194
    218-219 228-229 274
NEW-CHESTER, Nh 16 18 66 72 86-
    87 113 194-195 211 223 234 237
    263 274
NEW-DURHAM, Gore Nh 68 271 Nh
    38 52-53 68 87 104 134 188 195
    267 274
NEW-GARDEN, Nh 274
NEW-GRANTHAM, Nh 145 272
NEW-HAMPTON, Nh 12 17-18 53 86
    93 158 185 194-196 211 234 274
NEW-HOLDERNESS, Nh 273
NEW-HOPKINTON, Nh 162 273
NEW-IPSWICH, Nh 15-16 21-22 56
    151 184 197-198 224 237 240
    245 249 255 270 274
NEW-LONDON, Nh 54 56 81 135
    198-199 240 244-245 257 263
    270 274
NEW-MARKET, Nh 10 18 49-50 123
    131 145 173 199 215 243 270
    274
NEW-SALEM, Nh 185 273
NEW-YORK, Ny? 87 92 216
NEWBURY, Ma 82 115 149 209 216
    222 231 239 247 254 269 Vt 17
    148 153-154
NEWBURYPORT, Ma 30 33 163 175
    182 186 188 209 214 217 236
    239
NEWELL, Gad 193 269

NEWFIELD, Me 252
NEWINGTON, Nh 10-11 18 49-50 81
    136 145-146 196-197 217 222
    269-270 274
NEWMARCH, Sarah 11
NEWPORT, Nh 16 57-58 102 112
    143 161 199-201 251 257 274 Ri
    142
NEWTON, ?? 175 Hubbard 200 Nh
    67
NEWTOWN, Ireland 193-194 Nh 38
    50 168 201 210 216 240 271 274
NICHOLS, Daniel Esq 73 John 73
    Moses 70
NIFF, Mary 83
NILES, Thomas 228
NISITISSIT, Nh 160
NISSITISSIT, Nh 273
NO, 1 Nh 185 2 Nh 164
NOBLE, Oliver 194 207
NORFOLK, England 148
NORRIS, Jonathan 130
NORTH, Killingworth Ct 200
NORTH-HAMPTON, Nh 22 50 146
    148 202-203 218 228 243 267
    274
NORTH-HILL, Nh 202
NORTH-YARMOUTH, ?? 32 Me 222
NORTHAM, Nh 117 272
NORTHAMPTON, Ma 95
NORTHFIELD, Ma 95 97 157-158
    264 Nh 49-51 59 78 81 91 140
    201 231-232 234 266 274
NORTHUMBERLAND, Nh 13 17 61
    63 71 93 170-171 202-203 213
    243 251 274
NORTHWOOD, Nh 15 22 49-50 76
    113-114 130 170 202-204 215
    230 243 253 268 270 274
NORWAY, Plains Nh 225-226
NORWICH, Ct 173 Vt 17 151-152
NOTCH, In The Mountains Nh 212
    Of The White Mountains Nh
    203 230 260 262-263
NOTTINGHAM, Nh 11 13 15 50 76
    81 113-114 128 131 173 202-204
    223 272 274 Square Nh 204
NOTTINGHAM-WEST, Nh 56 121-
    122 175-176 204-205 209 265
    274

NOVA-SCOTIA, Canada 202 221
NOYES, Joseph 72 Nathaniel 240
    William 184
NUMBER, 1 Nh 254 271 273 2 Nh
    258 264 4 Nh 95 271 5 Nh 162
    187 6 Nh 156 273 7 Nh 156 273
NUTFIELD, Nh 177 273
NUTTER, Elder 118
NUTTING, 276
NYE, Jonathan 103
ODLIN, John 133 Woodbridge 133
OGDEN, John C 112 John Cosens
    220
OLCOTT, Bulkley 97 Simeon 97
OLIPHANT, David 167
OLMSTEAD, Samuel 228
ONCANOUIT, Nh 142
ORANGE, Nh 16 59-60 66 75 89 93
    113 143 146 155 205-206 237
    274
ORDWAY, Moses 180 Nehemiah 188
ORFORD, Nh 16-17 19-22 60 152 174
    206-207 213 257 274
ORR, Benj 79 Isaac 79 John 80
    Robert 79 William 79
OSBORNE, George Jerry 276 John
    173
OSGOOD, 208 Benjamin 111 James
    111 Joseph 141
OSSIPEE, Gore Nh 207 Nh 45 53
    126 190 207 249-250 252 267
    274
OTIS, Micajah 243
OYSTER, River Nh 124 272
PACKER, Thomas 193
PACKERSFIELD, Nh 193 274
PADDLEFORD, Jonathan 128
PAGE, C 115 Caleb 121 Christopher
    215 David 171 Edmund 75
    Jeremiah 270 John 68 155 John
    Esq 258 Jonathan 75 Thomas
    147
PAIGE, Christopher 227 Reed 151
    Robert 85
PAINE, Capt 96 Ebenezer 255
PARKER, 95 Alexander 146 Asa 153
    Clement 100 Edward L 178
    Elizabeth 96 Frederick 92 Isaac
    95-96 James 158 214 Jeremy
    158 Mrs 12 Nathan 221 Oliver
    242 Rev Mr 269 Thomas 142

PARKER (cont.)
    William Esq 214 Zachariah 217
PARKER'S, Island Nh 151 207
PARKHURST, John 198
PARMELE, James H 200
PARSONS, Samuel 229 William 240
PARSONSFIELD, Me 126
PARTRIDGE, Capt 13 190 260
PASCATAQUACK, Nh 274
PATHFOOT, Scotland 213
PATRICK, William 92
PATTEN, Matthew 80 Matthew Esq
    79 Samuel 79
PAULSBURG, Nh 88 213
PAULSBURGH, Nh 63 120 168 185
    192 208 244 266 274
PAYSON, Seth 225 270
PEABODY, Mr 201 Nathaniel 134
    193 268 Rev Mr 75 Richard 164
    Stephen 75 William 188
PEACHAM, Vt 162
PEAK, John 201
PEAKE, John 103
PEARL, William 119
PEASE, Pelatiah 141
PEASLEE, David 247
PEAVEY, Joseph 251
PECKENS, John 103
PEELING, Nh 59-60 112 127 174 186
    208-209 211 250 254 259 274
PEIRCE, 276 Charles 276 John 85 N
    S 276 W 276
PEIRCE'S, Island Nh 219
PELHAM, Nh 11 49-50 78 204 209
    231 265 274
PEMBROKE, Nh 16 19 29 49-51 79
    84 101 105 130 186 209-210 240
    245 267 270 274
PEMIGEWASSET, Village Nh 232
PENACOOK, ?? 79 Nh 106 272
PENTUCKETT, Ma 74
PEPPERELL, Ma 87 122 185 192 Sir
    William 163 William 163
PEQUAWKETT, Nh 210-211 214 272
PERKINS, Joseph 251 William 10
PERLEY, Samuel 147 191 236
PERRY, Baxter 174 Obadiah 122 247
PERRY'S-TOWN, Nh 275
PERRYS-TOWN, Nh 247
PERSONS, Ira 201
PETERBOROUGH, Nh 8 29 56 74

PETERBOROUGH (cont.)
  110 119 134 145 150-151 164
  211-213 237 242 249 274 Slip
  Nh 250 275
PETERS, James 156 Obadiah 107
PETTENGILL, Benjamin 233
  Matthew 234 Thomas H 233
PHILADELPHIA, Pa 134 222
PHILBRICK, David 249 Samuel Esq
  257 Thomas 236
PHILLIPS, 96 John 132
PHIPS, William 258
PICK-POCKET, Falls Nh 85
PICKERING, John 218 222
PICKWOCKET, Nh 211
PIERCE, Ezra 258
PIERCY, Nh 61 63 71 168 192 202
  213 243 266 274
PIERMONT, Nh 16 60 77 153 206
  213-214 254 274
PIGWACKET, Nh 211 214
PIKE, Eleanor 11 James 239 John
  118 Moses 78 Nicholas 239
PILLSBURY, Edmund 203
PILSBURY, Enoch 175
PINKERTON, John 177-178
PIPER, Asa 252 N 244 William 159
PISCATAQUOG, Village Nh 78 142
  214
PITMAN, Benjamin H 142 Elizabeth
  11
PITTSFIELD, Nh 49 51 75 84 93 101
  130 179 203 215 243 245 274
PIXLEY, Alexander 144
PLACE, David 227 Elder 243 Enoch
  226
PLAINFIELD, Nh 14 16 58-59 111
  144-145 153 172 215-216 270
  274
PLAISTOW, Nh 51 74 147 168 201
  216 274
PLATTS, Abel 225
PLUM-ISLAND, Nh 90
PLUMER, John 227 William 129
PLYMO, Nh 6
PLYMOUTH, Ma 84 104 209 Nh 14
  16 22 60-61 75 86 86 89 118 141
  146 153-155 158-159 175 186
  208 211 216-217 228 250 257
  274 Nh? 167 Village Nh 75

POLLARD, 205
POOR, Col 75
POPLIN, Nh 12 51 85 98 128 144
  154 217 223 235 274
PORTER, Experience 265
  Huntington 229 Martha 11
  Micaiah 216 Nathaniel 111 173
  195
PORTLAND, Me 77 110 116 165 170
  219 222 238 241 249 262
PORTSMOUTH, Harbor Nh 194 Nh
  9-11 14-15 18-20 22 27 30 38 40
  47-49 51 53 65-66 74-77 81 88-
  89 92-93 98-99 102 108 110 112
  115-116 123 126-128 134 140
  146-148 150-151 158-159 161
  163-164 166 168 170 172-173
  175-176 178-179 181 185 194
  196-198 201-204 208-209 211
  216-223 225 228-230 234-236
  238 240-241 245 251-252 257
  259 265-267 269 272 274 276
POTTER, Isaiah 173
POWERS, Grant 154 160 Peter 154
  160 Walter 140 201
PRATT, Allen 258
PRENTICE, John 179 Josiah 203
  Nathaniel 122
PRENTISS, John 166
PRESBURY, William 85
PRESCOTT, James 169 John 270
  William 11
PRESTON, John 198
PRICE, Ebenezer 83
PRIEST, Nathan Esq 194
PRINCE, Joseph 76 90
PROCTOR, David C 155 John 160
PROTECTWORTH, Nh 241 275
PUBLIC, Lands Nh 63 77 131 223
PUSLEY, 163
PUTNAM, 181 264 Daniel 112
  Ephraim 264 Hannah 264
  Israel W 220 Seth 96
PUTNEY, 162 Joseph 121 Samuel
  162 Vt 17 258 William 121
QUAMPHEGAN, Falls Nh 223 238
QUEBEC, Canada 138
QUEBECK, Canada 259
QUIMBY, Joshua 109
RABY, Nh 87 271

RAMSAY, Hugh 179
RAND, 229 Benjamin 143 Capt 143
 John 181 Mrs 143
RANDALL, Benjamin 38 195
RANDOLPH, Edward 48 Ma 130
RAY, Patrick 158
RAYMOND, Nh 51 98 100 113 128
 170 204 217 223-224 270 274
READ, 175 Mr 270
READING, Ma 160 187
RED, Hill Nh 224
REED, James 136
REEDSBOROUGH, Vt 222
REID, George 179
RELHAM, Nh 128
RELHAN, Nh 272
REMELEE, John 201
REMINGTON, Jesse 90
REYNER, John 118 John Jr 118
RIANT, John 208
RICE, Benjamin 116 153 Jacob 156
 Nathaniel 172
RICH, Ezekiel 250
RICHARDS, Benjamin 75 Elizabeth
 11 George 221 John 214 226
 Joseph 226
RICHARDSON, Hon Judge 209
 Joseph 158 Phineas 140
 Richard 242 William 209
RICHMOND, Nh 11 16 58 135 224
 247 250 264 274
RICKER, George 239 Meturin 239
RIDDLE, Dr 79 Freeman 79 Isaac
 Esq 187 214 James 46 Robert
 79
RINDGE, 218 Daniel Esq 221 Nh 16
 22 58 110 135-136 164 197 224-
 225 237 270 274
RIPLEY, Rev Mr 153 Sylvanus 32
RITCHIE, John 212
ROBBE, William 212-213
ROBBINS, William 158
ROBERTS, Moses 226 Timothy 226
ROBERTSON, John 114
ROBESON, James Esq 136
ROBIE, Henry 236 Ichabod Esq 256
 John 99 S 99
ROBINSON, Alexander 115 David
 194 244 Isaac 242 Otis 233
ROBY, Luther 107
ROCHESTER, Nh 13 53 75-76 81

ROCHESTER (cont.)
 104 116 134 163 188-189 225-
 227 234 238 241 243 272-274
ROCKINGHAM, Vt 17 80
ROCKWOOD, Nathaniel 166
ROGERS, 103 218 Daniel 133 James
 121 John 65 133 217 Nathaniel
 88 220 Robert 121
ROLFE, Benjamin Esq 107 William
 147
ROLLINS, Ichabod 240
ROOT, Elisha 166
ROWE, Dorcas 11 James 85
ROWELL, Joseph 112
ROWEN, Andrew 234
ROWLAND, William F 133
ROWLEY, ?? 167 Canada Nh 224-
 225 Ma 137
ROWLEY-CANADA, Nh 274
ROXBURY, Nh 58 119 166 183 192
 227-228 244 274
ROYALSTON, Ma 135 224
ROYCE, N 184
ROYSE, Mr 93
RUGGLES, Timothy 131
RUMFORD, Count 108 Nh 106 272
RUMNEY, Nh 11-12 60 75 89 127
 146 155 182 216 228 257 274
RUSSELL, 209 276 Elijah 107 268 J
 215 Samuel 225 Thomas 111
RUST, Henry 244
RUTLAND, Ma 95-96 222 Vt 252
RYE, Great Britain 228 Nh 12 51 85
 99 130 146 202 217-218 228-230
 254 274
RYEGATE, Vt 77
SABIN, John 136
SAINT, Francis Canada 253
 Francois Canada 233
SALEM, ?? 8 115 138 Canada Nh 273
 Ma 70 77 222 Nh 11-12 16 51 74
 176 181 209 230-231 240 265
 274
SALEM-CANADA, Nh 181
SALISBURY, Ma 249 253 Nh 11 15
 17 22 56 72 81 92 133 165 201
 211 222 231-234 253 274
SALMON-FALLS, Nh 238
SANBORN, 234 Catharine 11 John
 234 Jonathan 155
SANBORNTON, Nh 11 17-18 45 53

SANBORNTON (cont.)
72 145 185 194-195 201 211
231-232 234-235 266 268 274
SANDBORNTON, Nh 140
SANDEMAN, Robert 38
SANDERS, William 243
SANDOWN, Nh 51 98 147 154-155
169 176 217 235 274
SANDWICH, Addition Nh 236 Nh 53
88 139 158-159 181 190-191 207
224 235-236 241 249 270 275
SANDY, Beach Nh 274
SARATOGA, Ny 176 183 247 267
SARGENT, Benjamin 84 215 Jacob
99 John 90 100
SARTWELL, 95 Obadiah 96
SARTWELL'S, Island Nh 94
SAVAGE, Ozias 109
SAVILLE, Nh 257 275
SAWTELL, Eli 160 Jonathan 158
SAWYER, Benjamin 192 200 John
78 207 Moses 156 232
Nathaniel 233
SAWYER'S, Location Nh 16 236
SAY, Lord 118
SCALES, James 162
SCOBY, William 10 179
SCOFIELD, John 90
SCOTT, Alexander 212 242 Lemuel
224 William 120 212-213
SCRIBNER, Samuel 233
SEABROOK, Nh 6 11 38 51 148 150
236-237 240 257 275
SEABURY, Bishop 159
SEAMANS, Job 199
SEARLE, Isaac 139 Jonathan 185
233
SEAVEY, 229
SECOMBE, Joseph 169
SENTER, Joseph 88 93
SEVER, Nicholas 118
SEWALL, Jonathan M Esq 222
Judge 106 Stephen 276
SEWALL'S, Falls Nh 105 Island Nh
105
SHAKERS', Village Nh 92-93
SHARON, Nh 56 110 164 197 211-
212 224 237 249 275
SHAW, Benjamin 206 Jeremiah 191
John 11 Napthali 168
SHEAFE, Jacob 218

SHELBURNE, Nh 61 63 123 185 190
237 244 275
SHEPARD, Amos 68 Gen 67 Isaac
114 John 159 John W 107 Mrs
67 S 244 Samuel 86 130 268
SHEPHERD, 91
SHERBURNE, Catherine 11
SHERMAN, Caleb H 118 Ephraim
144
SHIRLEY, Gov 95 97 James 10-11
142 L B 142 Ma 192
SHOALS, Nh 237
SHORT, Siloam 215-216 270
SHURTLEFF, Rev Mr 153 William
194 220
SHUTE, 221 Fanny 199 Gov 177
SIBLEY, Patience 267
SILLIMAN, 21
SIMMONS, Samuel 111
SIMPSON, Andrew 204 Mrs 204
SINCLAIR, Richard 270
SLACK, John H 199
SLEEPER, Nehemiah 72 Peter 87
SLEIGH, William 115
SLOAN, John 174 William 174
SMART, Moses 228 Mrs 235 268
SMITH, 193 Abraham 126 Andrew
67 Benjamin 213 Caleb 213
David 93 185 Ebenezer 186 195
Eli 160 Elias 173 221 276
Eliphalet 114 Ethan 154 162
Gideon 153 Isaac 140 190 Jacob
114 Jeremiah 134 179 John 47
152 154 163 231 Luther 160
Mary 12 Moses 101 Mr 207 212
Rev Mr 153 Richard 236
Richard R 111 Robert 99
Samuel 211 Thomas 99 Uriah
144 William 126
SMITH'S, Isles Nh 163
SNOW, Nathl 81
SOCIETY, Land Nh 115 137 271-272
SOCIETY-LAND, Nh 54 56 136 145
150 237-238 275
SOMERSWORTH, Nh 11-12 16 53
116-117 223 225 238-240 275
SOUCOOK, Village Nh 179
SOUHEGAN, East Nh 79 187 Nh
240 Village Nh 184
SOUHEGAN-EAST, Nh 271 273
SOUHEGAN-WEST, Nh 70 271

SOUTH, Hadley Ma 109 Hampton Nh 275 Road Village Nh 232
SOUTH-HAMPTON, Nh 51 126 167 201 222 236 240
SOUTHAMPTONSHIRE, England 68
SOUTHBURY, Ct 33
SPAFFORD, Elijah 103 John 95 Moses 103
SPARROW, Richard 174
SPAULDING, Daniel 203
SPENCER, Jabez 89
SPERRY, Ebenezer P 122
SPOFFORD, Luke A 140
SPOONER, Alden 152
SPRAGUE, Edward 119-120 John 257
SPRINGFIELD, Ma 109 Nh 15 58 112 143-144 198 240-241 257 263 275 Vt 17 94
SQUAMANAGONICK, Falls Nh 241 Nh 241
SQUAMANAGONNICK, Nh 225
STANLEY, Jonathan 225
STAR-ISLAND, Nh 143 163
STARBUCK, Elder 118
STARK, 138 204 Archibald 121 Gen 70 75 80 183 228 John 179 182 Maj 210 William 121 228
STARKS-TOWN, Nh 121 272
STEARNS, Josiah 129
STEBBINS, Asahel 96
STEELE, Jonathan 179
STEVENS, 95 180 Benjamin 106 Capt 95-97 Col 102 Ebenezer 169 233 Enos 96 Joseph 198 Phinehas 83 95-96 Samuel 95 133 241 Samuel Esq 97 Thomas 253
STEVENS', Town Nh 274
STEVENS-TOWN, Nh 233
STEWART, John Esq 242 Nh 275
STEWARTSTOWN, Ireland 71 Nh 63 78 81 104 115 147 189 241-242 275
STICKNEY, Jonathan 223 Moses 164
STILES, Lydia 240 267 Tryphena 12 267 Wm 239
STINSON, David 228 Samuel 212 William 121 228

STOCKBRIDGE, Ma 31-32
STOCKWELL, Capt 171 Emmons 171
STODDARD, Col 95 Nh 58 73-74 110 141 183 192 242 244 254-255 266 275 Sampson 120 Samson 65 242 Samuel 136
STONE, Isaiah 194 Silas 120
STRAFFORD, Nh 53 75-77 81 117 125 134-135 163 203 215 225 242-243 275
STRATFORD, Nh 13 61 63 85 104 171 192 202 208 213 223 243 275
STRATHAM, Nh 18 51 130-131 145-146 202 243-244 275
STRAWBERRY, Bank Nh 194
STRAWBERRY-BANK, Nh 218
STREETER, Sebastian 221
STRICKLAND, John 205
STRONG, Job 220
STRONGMAN, Henry 120
STURTEVANT, C Jr 166
SUCCESS, Nh 63 88 185 192 208 237 244 275
SUDBURY, Ma 96
SUFFOLK, England 270
SULLIVAN, 211 Gen 107 John 125 Nh 58 141 166 192 227 242 244 275 Pres 244
SUMNER, 102 Benjamin 103 Clement 167 Mr 141 William 103
SUNCOOK, Nh 210 274
SUNDERLAND, Ma 95
SURRY, England 245 Nh 15-16 58 67 141 166 245 252 258 275
SUTHERLAND, David 78
SUTTON, Ma 112-113 Nh 11-12 21 56 85 135 165 198 245-247 253 263 275
SWAMSCOT-FALLS, Nh 272
SWAN, Josiah 122
SWANZEY, Ma 199 Nh 15 57-58 74 100 166-167 183 224 247-248 250 264 275
SWEAT, John 128
SWETT, Capt 266
SYMMES, William 145
SYMS, Capt 167
TAGGARD, John 242

TAMWORTH, Nh 21 53 88 126 190 207 235-236 249 275
TAPPAN, Amos 169 John 103
TARLETON, Col 214
TASH, Thomas 195
TAYLOR, 89 Joseph 103 William 107
TEBBETS, Benjamin 226
TEMPLE, John 214 Nh 56 145 180 184 197-198 211 237 240 249-250 263 275
TEMPLETON, ?? 136
TENNEY, Caleb J 160 David 76 Samuel 133 William 160
TEWKSBURY, David 201
THAYER, Ebenezer 149 Elihu 169
THETFORD, Vt 174
THOMAS, Joshua 104 Mary 101 William 101
THOMPSON, Alexander 269 Benjamin 108 David 47 Ebenezer 125 268 Thomas 178 269 Thomas W 108 142
THORNTON, 175 187 Andrew 250 Gore Nh 250 James 250 Matthew 120 179 188 250 263 Nh 60 88 127 139 174 181 186 208 211 235 250 275
THURSTON, 152 Benjamin 202 James 199 Moses 251 Pearson 239
TIBBETS, Nathaniel 119
TICONDEROGA, Ny 227
TIMBER-LANE, Nh 147 273
TODD, Andrew 213
TOLFORD, John 99
TOMBS, S 199
TOPPAN, Christopher 148-149 Edmund 149 Sarah 149
TOPSHAM, England 163
TOWNE, Josiah 153
TOWNSEND, Charles Esq 123 Isaac 267 Ma 87 122 184 197 212
TRASK, Nathaniel 86
TREADWELL, Daniel 276 William 276
TRECOTHICK, Barlow 127 Nh 127 272
TREFETHEN, Island Nh 219
TRENTON, Nj 183
TROWBRIDGE, Judge 159

TROY, Nh 58 135-136 164 183 247 250 275
TRUE, Henry 147 John 233
TUBBS, Joseph 184
TUCKE, John 130 143 163
TUCKER, 230 Benj 183 Jedidiah 180 Moses 235 Mrs 12
TUFTONBOROUGH, Nh 53 190-191 207 250-251 267 275
TUFTS, Joshua 175
TURELL, Charles 276
TURKEY, Falls Nh 84
TURNER, James 80 John 169 William 90
TUTTLE, 107 Mr 119
TWITCHELL, Amos 120 Samuel 120
TYLER, Bennet 33
TYNG, Edward 122 Jonathan 122 Mrs 122
TYNGSBOROUGH, Ma 19 121-122 204
TYRONE, Ireland 71
ULRICK, Mrs 11 160
ULSTER, Ireland 71 100
UN-CAN-NU-NUC, Nh 142
UNCONOONOCK, Nh 142
UNITY, Nh 15 22 58 65 78 94 102 143 147 173 199 251 275
UPHAM, Timothy 114
UPPER, Ashuelot Nh 167 273 Cohos Nh 273
USHER, Lt Gov 169
VAUGHAN, George 221 William 221
VEAZEY, Henry 84
VERNON, Vt 157-158
VOSE, John 79
WADSWORTH, Lemuel 87
WAITE, Joseph 103
WAKEFIELD, Nh 10 52-53 87 126 180 188-189 207 214 251-252 275
WALDINGFIELD, England 270
WALDO, 122 Cornelius 122
WALDRON, Maj 81 118 Richard 91
WALES, Nathaniel 252
WALES', Location Nh 105 252
WALKER, James 79 134 John 79 146 268 Rev Mr 268 Robert 79 Seth 172 Thomas 12 247 Timothy 107 111

WALLACE, James 156 Judge 156
   Mary 155 Robert 156 179
   William 188
WALLINGFORD, Thomas 239
WALLIS, 229
WALPOLE, Ma 104 Nh 14-17 21 57-
   58 67 80 94 109 119 143 172
   197 245 252-253 258 270 275
WALTHAM, Ma 19 159 248
WALTON, Joseph 221 Reuben 242
   Samuel 70
WARD, Jeremiah 196 Jonathan 217
   Nathan 217 Solomon 155
WARDWELL, Joseph 233
WARNER, Daniel Esq 241 Jonathan
   Esq 168 Nh 6 56 81 85 155 161
   166 231 245 253-254 263 275
   Samuel 122
WARNER'S, Location Nh 98 254
   Patent Nh 63
WARREN, Jonas 80 Nh 6 16 59-60
   75 112 127 208 213 254 257 275
WARWICK, Ma 15 224 264
WASHINGTON, City (dc) 81 108 140
   151 185 197 211 Dc 33 69 Gen
   183 Gore Nh 85 Nh 15-16 57-58
   74 85 110 143 156 166 173 183
   217 242 254-255 260 265 275
   Village Nh 255
WASON, Thomas 11
WATERFORD, Vt 175
WATERMAN, Silas 173 Thomas 84
   Thomas Esq 173
WATERQUEECHY, Falls Nh 215
WATERS, Cornelius 142 Rev Mr 121
WATSON, David Jr 269 Elijah 247
WEARE, Jonathan 236 Jonathan
   Esq 72 Meshech 251 256 269
   Mesheck 48 Nh 56 115 120 136
   155 161 193 255-257 275 Pres
   269
WEATHERSFIELD, Vt 102
WEBBER, John 89 235 Pres 235
WEBSTER, Daniel 232 David 217
   242 David Esq 217 Ebenezer
   169 233 Ezekiel 233 John 233
   249 Josiah 149 Samuel 249
   Stephen 217 William 232
WEBSTER'S, Falls Nh 201 266
WEDGEWOOD, John 133
WEED, Dorothy 140 Orlando 140

WEEKS, 276 J W Esq 260 Samuel 73
   William 276
WELCH, Francis 216 Moses 216 Mrs
   12 Samuel 12 84 268
WELD, 122 Thomas 122
WELLS, Joseph 95 Me 19 133
   Nathaniel 114
WELMAN, James 112
WENDELL, John 257 Nh 57-58 102
   112 135 143 198-199 240 244
   257 275
WENTWORTH, B 167 Benning 48 90
   95 147 221 235-236 258 Charles
   Watson 51 Elder 118 Frances
   115 137 George 104 258 Gov 51
   54 79 114 137 156 196 267 John
   32 48 115 159 221 226-227 239-
   240 242 267 John II 221 March
   H 165 Mark H 120 267 269 Nh
   12 14 60 75 116 201 206 228
   254 257-258 275 Paul 239 Sir
   Thomas 86 William 54 221 239
WENTWORTH'S, Location Nh 115
   131 258
WESCOTT, Stephen K 144
WEST, Benjamin 97 Samuel 97
   Thomas 97
WEST-CAMBRIDGE, Ma 19
WEST-POINT, ?? 204
WESTFORD, ?? 162
WESTMINSTER, Vt 17 252
WESTMORELAND, Nh 15 17 22 58
   100 166 245 252 258 275
WESTON, Ephraim 217
WHEAT, Joseph 90 144
WHEATON, George 103
WHEELER, Abraham 90 Amos 81
   Hosea 200 Nathan 81
WHEELOCK, Dr 32 153 Eleazar 31
   152 James R 201 John 32 152
   Pres 32 Rev Mr 153
WHEELWRIGHT, 209 John 47 132-
   133 149 177
WHIDDEN, Samuel 276
WHIPPLE, Col 165 Enoch 66 Joseph
   150 165 Thomas 209
WHITE, Archibald 198 Broughton
   255 Isle Nh 163 Nicholas Esq
   216 Phillips 240 Plains Ny 247
WHITE-PLAINS, Ny 67
WHITEFIELD, 114 Nh 63 80 86 113

WHITEFIELD (cont.)
    165 170 259 275
WHITEFIELDS, Nh 275
WHITEHALL, Nh 226
WHITELOCK, 276
WHITING, Benjamin 139 Leonard
    109
WHITON, John M 74
WHITTEMORE, A 146 Aaron 210
    Maj 145-146
WIGGIN, Jonathan 83
WILCOX, Jesse 200-201 John 200
    Obadiah 141 Uriah 200
WILDER, Joseph 123
WILKINS, Daniel 70
WILLARD, 101 168 Col 158 Elijah
    120 Jonathan 172 Joseph 96
    171 220 269 Josiah 102 264-265
    Moses 96 Rev Dr 269 Rev Mr 96
WILLIAM, King Of England 178
WILLIAMS, 251 Dr 260 Oliver 144
    Simon 265 Stephen 136
WILMARTH, Ezra 228 256 264
WILMOT, Dr 263 Nh 15 18 56 72
    113 166 194 198 240 245 263
    275
WILSON, 193 James 10-11 John 99
    Nathaniel 76 Rev Mr 100
    William 193
WILTON, England 264 Nh 56 180
    184 188 249 263-264 275
WILTSHIRE, England 264
WINCHENDEN, Ma 136
WINCHENDON, Ma 135
WINCHESTER, Nh 15-16 57-58 74
    100 136 157 224 247 264-265
    275
WINDHAM, Nh 16 51 176 204 209
    231 265 275 Vt 157
WINDSOR, Nh 15 56 69 73 137 156
    166 242 254 265-266 275 Vt 94
    111 200

WINES, Abijah 200-201
WINGATE, Aaron 135 Col 149 Paine
    150
WINICHAHANAT, Nh 117
WINICUMET, Nh 273
WINN, 205
WINNICOT, Nh 275
WINNICUMET, Nh 148
WINSLOW, John 266 Seth E 250
WINSLOW'S, Location 208 Location
    Nh 63 213 266
WINTER-HILL, ?? 75
WINTHROP, Judge 189
WISWALL, Capt 259
WOBURN, Ma 107-108
WOLCUTT, John 67
WOLFBOROUGH, Nh 22 52-53
WOLFE, Gen 138
WOLFEBOROUGH, Nh 68 87 159
    195 207 250 267 275
WOOD, Abraham 101 268 Amos 256
    Rev Dr 82 Samuel 83
WOODBURY, 22 Benjamin 199 Dr
    79 James 138 Lot 81
WOODMAN, Joseph 235
WOODS, John 254
WOODSTOCK, Ct 136
WOODWARD, Abel 183 Bezaleel 152
    Hannah 264 James 154 Mr 264
    N 257
WOODWELL, Mr 162
WORCESTER, Joseph E 160 Ma 83
    136 Noah 160 250 Noah Esq
    160 Samuel 160 Taylor G 160
    Thomas 160 233
WRENTHAM, Ma 167
WYMAN, Isaac 167
YORK, ?? 239
YOUNG, Dan 214 Peter 72 Winthrop
    92